# ROAD ATLAS FRANCE & SPAIN

# CONTENTS


- II Driving regulations
- III Sights of France, Portugal and Spain
- IV Ski resorts

- **1 Key to map pages**
- **2 Route planning maps**
- **6 Road maps**

- **63 City plans and approach maps**
  - 63 **Alicante** city plan
    - **Granada** city plan
  - 64 **Barcelona** city plan
    - **Barcelona** urban area map
    - **Bordeaux** city plan
    - **Bordeaux** urban area map
  - 65 **Lisboa** city plan
    - **Lisboa** urban area map
    - **Lyon** city plan
    - **Lyon** urban area map
  - 66 **Madrid** city plan
    - **Madrid** urban area map
    - **Marseille** city plan
  - 67 **Paris** urban area map
  - 68 **Paris** city plan
    - **Sevilla** city plan
    - **Strasbourg** city plan

- **69 Index to road maps**



**www.philips-maps.co.uk**

First published in 2014 by Philip's,
a division of Octopus Publishing Group Ltd
www.octopusbooks.co.uk
Carmelite House
50 Victoria Embankment
London EC4Y 0DZ
An Hachette UK Company • www.hachette.co.uk

Fourth edition 2023, first impression 2023

ISBN 978-1-84907-630-2

*The UK's best-selling European Atlases.
Data from Nielsen Total Consumer Market 2022.


Printed in China


## Legend to route planning maps pages 2–5

- **Motorway with selected junctions**
  - tunnel, under construction
- **Toll motorway, pre-pay motorway**
- **Main through route, other major road, other road**
- 25 56 **European road number, motorway number**
- 55 **National road number**
- 56 **Distances** – in kilometres
- **International boundary, national boundary**
- LE HAVRE **Car ferry and destination**
- 1089 **Mountain pass, international airport, height** (metres)

**Town** – population

| | | | |
|---|---|---|---|
| 5 million + | 500k–1 million | 50k–100k | 5k–10k |
| 2–5 million | 200k–500k | 20k–50k | 0–5k |
| 1–2 million | 100k–200k | 10k–20k | |

The green version of the symbol indicates towns with Low Emission Zones

**Scale** · pages 2–5

**1:3 200 000**
1 cm = 32km
1 in – 50.51 miles

0 20 40 60 80 100 120 140 160 180 km
0 10 20 30 40 50 60 70 80 90 100 110 miles

## Legend to road maps pages 6–62

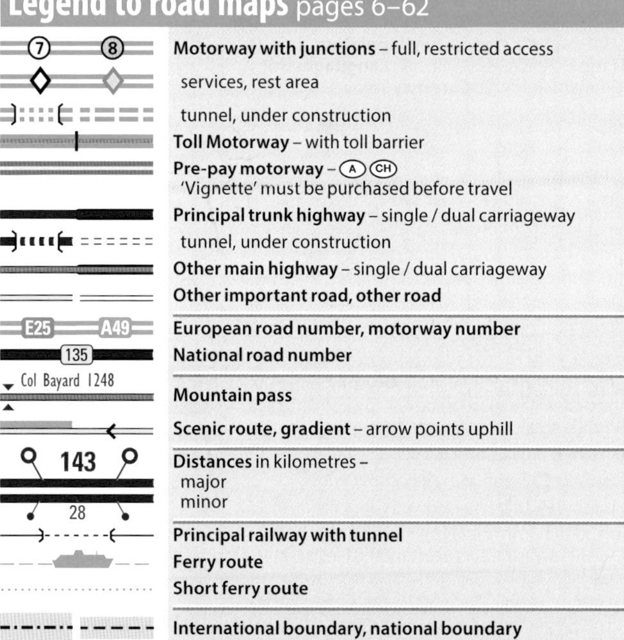


- **National park, natural park**
- **Sevilla** **Poitiers** **World Heritage town, town of tourist interest**

| | | |
|---|---|---|
| **Airport** | **Other place of interest** | **World Heritage site** |
| **Ancient monument** | **Park or garden** | 94 **Spot height** |
| **Beach** | **Religious building** | **City or town with Low Emission Zone** |
| **Castle or house** | **Ski resort** | |
| **Cave** | **Theme park** | |

**Scale** · pages 6–62

**1:753 800**
1 cm = 7.5km
1 inch = 12 miles

0 4 8 12 16 20 24 28 32 36 40km
0 2 4 6 8 10 12 14 16 18 20 22 24 26 miles

# Driving regulations

- Motorway
- Dual carriageway
- Single carriageway
- Surfaced road
- Unsurfaced / gravel road
- Urban area
- Speed limit (kilometres per hour)
- Seat belts
- Children
- Blood alcohol level
- △ Warning triangle
- First aid kit
- Spare bulb kit
- Fire extinguisher
- Minimum driving age
- Additional documents required
- Mobile phones
- LEZ Low Emission Zone
- Dipped headlights
- Winter driving
- ★ Other information

## Andorra Principat d'Andorra (AND)

**Population** 77,500 **Capital** Andorra la Vella (22,000) **Languages** Catalan (official), French, Castilian and Portuguese **Currency** Euro = 100 cents

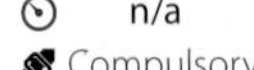

| | Motorway | Dual carriageway | Single carriageway | Urban area |
|---|---|---|---|---|
| Speed limit | n/a | 90 | 60/90 | 50 |

- Compulsory
- Under 10 and below 150 cm must travel in an EU-approved restraint system adapted to their size in the rear. Airbag must be deactivated if a child is in the front passenger seat.
- 0.05% △ 2 compulsory Recommended
- Compulsory Recommended 18
- Only allowed with hands-free kit
- Compulsory for motorcycles during day and for other vehicles during poor daytime visibility.
- Snow chains must be carried or winter tyres fitted 1 Nov–15 May
- ★ On-the-spot fines • Visibility vests compulsory

## Belgium Belgique (B)

**Area** 30,528 sq km (11,786 sq miles) **Population** 11,779,000 **Capital** Brussels/Bruxelles (2,081,000) **Languages** Dutch, French, German (all official) **Currency** Euro = 100 cents

| | Motorway | Dual carriageway | Single carriageway | Urban area |
|---|---|---|---|---|
| Speed limit | 120[1] | 120[1] | 90[2] | 50[3] |
| Over 3.5 tonnes | | | | |
| Speed limit | 90 | 90 | 70[2]–90 | 50 |

[1]Minimum speed of 70 kph may be applied in certain conditions on motorways and some dual carriageways. [2]70 kph in Flanders. [3]20 kph in residential areas, 30 kph near some schools, hospitals and churches, and in designated cycle zones.

- Compulsory
- All under 18s under 135 cm must wear an appropriate child restraint. Airbags must be deactivated if a rear-facing child seat is used in the front
- 0.05% • 0.02% professional drivers.
- △ Compulsory Compulsory Recommended
- Compulsory 18 Only allowed with a hands-free kit
- LEZ LEZs in operation in Antwerp, Brussels and areas of Flanders. Preregistration necessary and fees payable for most vehicles.
- Mandatory at all times for motorcycles and during the day in poor conditions for other vehicles
- Winter tyres permitted 1 Oct to 31 Apr. Snow chains only permitted if road is fully covered by snow or ice. Vehicles with spiked tyres restricted to 90 kph on motorways/dual carriageways and 60 kph on other roads.
- ★ Cruise control must be deactivated on motorways where indicated • If a tram or bus stops to allow passengers on or off, you must not overtake. • Motorcyclists must wear fully protective clothing • On-the-spot fines imposed • Radar detectors prohibited • Sticker indicating maximum recommended speed for winter tyres must be displayed on dashboard if using them • Visibility vest compulsory • When a traffic jam occurs on a road with two or more lanes in the direction of travel, motorists should move aside to create a path for emergency vehicles between the lanes.

## France (F)

**Population** 62,800,000 **Capital** Paris **Languages** French (official), Breton, Occitan **Currency** Euro = 100 cents

| | Motorway | Dual carriageway | Single carriageway | Urban area |
|---|---|---|---|---|
| Speed limit | 130 | 110 | 80/90* | 50 |
| On wet roads or if full driving licence held for less than 3 years | | | | |
| Speed limit | 110 | 100 | 80 | 50 |
| above 3.5 tonnes gross | | | | |
| Speed limit | 90 | 80 | 80 | 50 |

50kph on all roads if fog reduces visibility to less than 50m • *2-lane road / 4-lane road

- Compulsory in front seats and, if fitted, in rear
- Children up to age 10 must use suitable child seat or restraint.and may only travel in the front if: • the vehicle has no rear seats • no rear seatbelts • the rear seats are already occupied by children up to age 10 • the child is a baby in a rear facing child seat and the airbag is deactivated.
- 0.05% • If towing or with less than 2 years with full driving licence, 0.00% • Less than 0.02% for 2-3 years with a full driving licence • All drivers/motorcyclists are required to carry an unused breathalyser though this rule is not currently enforced.
- △ Compulsory Recommended Recommended
- 18 (16 for motorbikes up to 80cc)
- Passport,UK driving licence, insurance, registration, ownership and roadworthiness documents.
- Use permitted only with hands-free kit. Must not be used with headphones or earpieces
- LEZ An LEZ operates in the Mont Blanc tunnel and such zones are being progressively introduced across French cities. Non-compliant vehicles are banned during operating hours. Crit'Air stickers must be displayed by compliant vehicles. See http://certificat-air.gouv.fr/en
- Compulsory in poor daytime visibility and at all times for motorcycles
- Snow chains are mandatory on snow covered roads when indicated by local signs.Max speed 50 kph
- ★ GPS must have fixed speed camera function deactivated; radar-detection equipment is prohibited • Headphones or earpieces must not be used for listening to music or making phone calls while driving. • Motorcyclists and passengers must have four reflective stickers on their helmets (front, back and both sides) and wear CE-certified gloves. • On-the-spot fines imposed • Tolls on motorways. Electronic tag needed if using automatic tolls. • Visibility vests, to be worn on the roadside in case of emergency or breakdown, must be carried for all vehicle occupants and riders. • Wearers of contact lenses or spectacles should carry a spare pair

## Luxembourg (L)

**Population** 640,000 **Capital** Luxembourg **Languages** Luxembourgian / Letzeburgish (official), French, German **Currency** Euro = 100 cents

| | Motorway | Dual carriageway | Single carriageway | Urban area |
|---|---|---|---|---|
| Speed limit | 130/110* | 90 | 90 | 50* |
| If towing | | | | |
| Speed limit | 90 | 75 | 75 | 50* |

If full driving licence held for less than two years, must not exceed 75 kph • *110 in wet weather • **30 kph zones are progressively being introduced. 20 kph in zones where pedestrians have priority.

- Compulsory
- Children under 3 must use an appropriate restraint system. Airbags must be disabled if a rear-facing child seat is used in the front. Children 3–18 and/or under 150 cm must use a restraint system appropriate to their size. If over 36kg a seatbelt may be used in the back only
- 0.05%, 0.02% for young drivers, drivers with less than 2 years experience and drivers of taxis and commercial vehicles
- △ Compulsory Recommended, compulsory for buses
- Recommended
- Compulsory (buses, transport of dangerous goods)
- 18 Use permitted only with hands-free kit
- Compulsory for motorcyclists and for other vehicles in poor visibility and in tunnels. Outside urban areas, full-beam headlights are compulsory at night and in poor visibility.
- Winter tyres compulsory in winter weather
- ★ On-the-spot fines imposed • Visibility vest compulsory

## Portugal (P)

**Population** 10,264,000 **Capital** Lisbon / Lisboa **Languages** Portuguese (official) **Currency** Euro = 100 c

| | Motorway | Dual carriageway | Single carriageway | Urban area |
|---|---|---|---|---|
| Speed limit | 120* | 90/100 | 90 | 50/20 |
| If towing | | | | |
| Speed limit | 100* | 80 | 70 | 50/20 |

*50kph minimum; 90kph max if licence less than 1 year

- Compulsory in front seats and, if fitted, in rear
- Under 12 and below 135cm must travel in the rear in an appropriate child restraint; rear-facing child seats permitted in front for under 3s only if airbags deactivated
- 0.05% • 0.02% if full licence held less than 3 years
- △ Compulsory Recommended Recommended
- Recommended 18
- MOT certificate for vehicles over 3 years old, photographic proof of identity must be carried at all times. IDP required if you have old-style paper licence, vehicle registrations document, evidence of valid insurance
- Only allowed with hands-free kit
- LEZ Lisbon's LEZ has a minimum entry requirement of Euro 3 for the central zone and Euro 2 for the outer zone between 0700 and 2000.
- Compulsory for motorcycles, compulsory for other vehicles in poor visibility and tunnels
- ★ On-the-spot fines imposed • Radar detectors and dash-cams prohibited • Some motorways use traditional toll booths (green lanes are reserved for auto-payment users) but others may only be used by vehicles registered with an automated billing system. www.portugaltolls.com/en • Visibility vest compulsory • Wearers of spectacles or contact lenses should carry a spare pair

## Spain España (E)

**Population** 47,327,000 **Capital** Madrid **Languages** Castilian Spanish (official), Catalan, Galician, Basque **Currency** Euro = 100 cents

| | Motorway | Dual carriageway | Single carriageway | Urban area |
|---|---|---|---|---|
| Speed limit | 120* | 100* | 90 | 50* |
| If towing up to 750kg | | | | |
| Speed limit | 80 | 80 | 70 | 50* |

*Urban motorways and dual carriageways 80 kph. 20 kph zones are being introduced in many cities

- Compulsory
- Under 135cm and below 12 must use appropriate child restraint and sit in rear.
- 0.05% • 0.03% if less than 2 years full licence or if vehicle is over 3.5 tonnes or carries more than 9 passengers
- △ Two compulsory (one for in front, one for behind)
- Recommended Compulsory
- Recommended. Compulsory for buses and LGVs
- 18 (21 for heavy vehicles; 16 for motorbikes up to 125cc)
- Only allowed with a hands-free kit. Headphones and earpieces not permitted
- Compulsory for motorcycles and in poor daytime visibility and in tunnels for other vehicles.
- Snow chains compulsory in areas indicated by signs
- ★ Drivers who wear spectacles or contact lenses must carry a spare pair. • On-the-spot fines imposed • Radar-detection equipment is prohibited • Spare wheel compulsory • Tolls on motorways • Visibility vest compulsory

Where compulsory, visibility vests should be kept in the passenger compartment and put on before exiting the vehicle in breakdowns or emergencies.

# Sights of France, Portugal and Spain

## France

https://uk.france.fr/en

**Albi** Old town with rosy brick architecture. The vast Cathédrale Ste-Cécile (begun 13c) holds some good art. The Berbie Palace houses the Toulouse-Lautrec Museum. www.albi-tourisme.fr/en 30 B1

**Alps** Grenoble capital of the French Alps, has a good 20c collection in the Museum of Grenoble. The Vanoise Massif has the greatest number of resorts (Val d'Isère, Courchevel). Chamonix has spectacular views of Mont Blanc, France's and Europe's highest peak. www.grenoble-tourisme.com/en 26 B2

**Amiens** France's largest Gothic cathedral has beautiful decoration. The Museum of Picardy has unique 16c panel paintings. Also: Jules Verne House. www.visit-amiens.com 10 B2

**Arles** Ancient, picturesque town with Roman relics (1c amphitheatre), 11c St Trophime church, Archaeological Museum (Roman art), Van Gogh centre. www.arlestourisme.com/en/ 31 B3

**Avignon** Medieval papal capital (1309–77) with 14c walls and many ecclesiastical buildings. Vast Palace of the Popes has stunning frescoes. The Little Palace has fine Italian Renaissance painting. The 12–13c Bridge of St Bénézet is famous. https://avignon-tourisme.com/en/ 31 B3

**Bourges** The Gothic Cathedral of St Etienne, one of the finest in France, has a superb sculptured choir. Also notable is the House of Jacques Coeur. www.bourgesberrytourisme.com 17 B4

**Brittany** ***Bretagne*** Brittany is famous for cliffs, sandy beaches and wild landscape. It is also renowned for megalithic monuments (Carnac) and Celtic culture. Its capital, Rennes, has the Parlement de Bretagne and good collections in the Museum of Brittany (history) and Museum of Fine Arts. Also: Nantes; St-Malo. www.brittanytourism.com 14–15

**Burgundy** ***Bourgogne*** Rural wine region with a rich Romanesque, Gothic and Renaissance heritage. The 12c cathedral in Autun and 12c basilica in Vézelay have fine Romanesque sculpture. Monasteries include 11c Abbaye de Cluny (ruins) and Abbaye de Fontenay. Beaune has beautiful Gothic Hôtel-Dieu and 15c Nicolas Rolin hospices. www.burgundy-tourism.com 18 B3

**Caen** City with two beautiful Romanesque buildings: Abbaye aux Hommes; Abbaye aux Dames. The château has two museums (16–20c painting; history). The *Bayeux Tapestry* is displayed in nearby Bayeux. www.caenlamer-tourisme.com 9 A3

**Carcassonne** Unusual double-walled fortified town of narrow streets with an inner fortress. The fine Romanesque Church of St Nazaire has superb stained glass. www.tourisme-carcassonne.fr/en 30 B1

**Chartres** The 12–13c cathedral is an exceptionally fine example of Gothic architecture (Royal Doorway, stained glass, choir screen). The Fine Arts Museum has a good collection. www.chartres.com 10 C1

**Clermont-Ferrand** The old centre contains the cathedral built out of lava and Romanesque basilica. The Puy de Dôme and Puy de Sancy give spectacular views over some 60 extinct volcanic peaks (*puys*). www.clermontauvergnetourisme.com/en/ 24 B3

**Colmar** Town characterised by Alsatian half-timbered houses. The Unterlinden Museum has excellent German religious art including the famous Isenheim Altarpiece. Also: Espace André Malraux (contemporary arts). www.tourisme-colmar.com/en/ 20 A2

**Corsica** ***Corse*** Corsica has a beautiful rocky coast and mountainous interior. Napoleon's birthplace of Ajaccio has: Fesch Museum with Imperial Chapel and a large collection of Italian art; Maison Bonaparte; cathedral. Bonifacio, a medieval town, is spectacularly set on a rock over the sea. www.visit-corsica.com/en 62

**Côte d'Azur** The French Riviera is best known for its coastline and glamorous resorts. There are many relics of artists who worked here: St-Tropez has Musée de l'Annonciade; Antibes has 12c Château Grimaldi with the Picasso Museum; Cagnes has the Renoir Museum; Le Cannet has the Bonnard Museum; St-Paul-de-Vence; St-Paul-de-Vence has the excellent Maeght Foundation; and nearby Vence has Matisse's Chapelle du Rosaire. Cannes is famous for its film festival. Also: Marseille, Monaco, Nice. www.provence-alpes-cotedazur.com 33 B3

**Dijon** Great 15c cultural centre. The Palais des Ducs et des Etats is the most notable monument and contains the Museum of Fine Arts. Also: the Charterhouse of Champmol. https://en.destinationdijon.com 19 B4

**Disneyland Paris** Europe's largest theme park follows in the footsteps of its famous predecessors in the United States. www.disneylandparis.com 10 C2

**Le Puy-en-Velay** Medieval town bizarrely set on the peaks of dead volcanoes. It is dominated by the Romanesque cathedral (cloisters). The Romanesque chapel of St-Michel is dramatically situated on the highest rock. www.lepuyenvelay-tourisme.co.uk 25 B3

**Loire Valley** The Loire Valley has many 15–16c châteaux built amid beautiful scenery by French monarchs and members of their courts. Among the most splendid are Azay-le-Rideau, Chambord, Chenonceau and Loches. Also: Abbaye de Fontévraud. www.loirevalley-france.co.uk 16 B2

**Lyon** France's third largest city has an old centre and many museums including the Museum of Fine Arts (old masters) and the modern Musée des Confluences. https://en.lyon-france.com/ 25 B4

**Marseilles** ***Marseille*** Second largest city in France. Spectacular views from the 19c Notre-Dame de la Garde. The Old Port has 11–12c Basilique St Victor (crypt, catacombs). Cantini Museum has major collection of 20c French art, and the Mucem tells the history of Mediterranean civilizations. Château d'If was the setting of Dumas' *The Count of Monte Cristo*. www.marseille-tourisme.com/en/ 31 B4

**Mont-St-Michel** Gothic pilgrim abbey (11–12c) set dramatically on a steep rock island rising from mud flats and connected to the land by a road covered by the tide. The abbey is made up of a complex of buildings. www.ot-montsaintmichel.com/en/ 15 A4

**Nancy** A centre of Art Nouveau. The 18c Place Stanislas was constructed by dethroned Polish king Stanislas. Museums: School of Nancy Museum (Art Nouveau furniture); Fine Arts Museum. www.nancy-tourisme.fr/en/ 12 C2

**Nantes** Former capital of Brittany, with the 15c Château des ducs de Bretagne. The cathedral has a striking interior. www.nantes-tourisme.com/en 15 B4

**Nice** Capital of the Côte d'Azur, the old town is centred on the old castle on the hill. The seafront includes the famous 19c Promenade des Anglais. The aristocratic quarter of the Cimiez Hill has the Marc Chagall Museum and the Matisse Museum. Also: Museum of Modern and Contemporary Art (especially neo-Realism and Pop Art). http://en.nicetourisme.com/ 33 B3

**Paris** Capital of France, one of Europe's most interesting cities. The Île de la Cité area, an island in the River Seine, has the 12–13c Notre Dame, devastated by fire in 2019 and closed for major restoration, and La Sainte Chapelle (1240–48), one of the jewels of Gothic art. The Left Bank area: Latin Quarter with the famous Sorbonne university; Museum of Cluny housing medieval art; the Panthéon; Luxembourg Palace and Gardens; Montparnasse, interwar artistic and literary centre; Eiffel Tower; Hôtel des Invalides with Napoleon's tomb. Right Bank: the great boulevards (Avenue des Champs-Élysées joining the Arc de Triomphe and Place de la Concorde); 19c Opéra Quarter; Marais, former aristocratic quarter of elegant mansions (Place des Vosges); Bois de Boulogne, the largest park in Paris; Montmartre, centre of 19c bohemianism, with the Basilique Sacré-Coeur. The Church of St Denis is the first Gothic church and the mausoleum of the French monarchy. Paris has three of the world's greatest art collections: The Louvre (to 19c, *Mona Lisa*), Musée d'Orsay (19–20c) and National Modern Art Museum in the Pompidou Centre. Other major museums include: Orangery Museum; Paris Museum of Modern Art; Rodin Museum; Picasso Museum; Atelier des Lumières. Notable cemeteries with graves of the famous: Père-Lachaise, Montmartre, Montparnasse. Near Paris are the royal residences of Fontainebleau and Versailles. https://en.parisinfo.com 10 C2

**Pyrenees** Beautiful unspoiled mountain range. Towns include: delightful sea resorts of St-Jean-de-Luz and Biarritz; Pau, with access to the Pyrenees National Park; pilgrimage centre Lourdes. 38–39

**Reims** Together with nearby Épernay, the centre of champagne production. The 13c Gothic cathedral is one of the greatest architectural achievements in France (stained glass by Chagall). Other sights: Palais du Tau with cathedral sculpture, 11c Basilica of St Rémi; cellars on Place St-Niçaise and Place des Droits de l'Homme. https://en.reims-tourisme.com 11 B4

**Rouen** Old centre with many half-timbered houses and 12–13c Gothic cathedral and the Gothic Church of St Maclou with its fascinating remains of a danse macabre on the former cemetery of Aître St-Maclou. The Fine Arts Museum has a good collection. https://en.rouentourisme.com/ 9 A5

**St-Malo** Fortified town (much rebuilt) in a fine coastal setting. There is a magnificent boat trip along the river Rance to Dinan, a splendid well-preserved medieval town. www.saint-malo-tourisme.co.uk 15 A3

**Strasbourg** Town whose historic centre includes a well-preserved quarter of medieval half-timbered Alsatian houses, many of them set on the canal. The cathedral is one of the best in France. The Palais Rohan contains several museums. www.visitstrasbourg.fr/en/ 13 C3

**Toulouse** Medieval university town characterised by flat pink brick (Hôtel Assézat). The Basilique St Sernin, the largest Romanesque church in France, has many art treasures. Marvellous Church of the Jacobins holds relics of St Thomas Aquinas. www.toulouse-visit.com 29 C4

**Tours** Historic town centred on Place Plumereau. Good collections in the Guilds Museum and Fine Arts Museum. Also: cathedral (predominantly Gothic). www.tours-tourism.co.uk/en/ 16 B2

**Versailles** Vast royal palace built for Louis XIV, primarily by Mansart, set in large formal gardens with magnificent fountains. The extensive and much-imitated state apartments include the famous Hall of Mirrors and the exceptional Baroque chapel. http://en.chateauversailles.fr/ 10 C2

**Vézère Valley Caves** A number of prehistoric sites, most notably the cave paintings of Lascaux (some 17,000 years old), now only seen in a duplicate cave, and the cave of Font de Gaume. The National Museum of Prehistory is in Les Eyzies. www.lascaux-dordogne.com/en 29 B4

## Portugal

www.visitportugal.com/en

**Alcobaça** Monastery of Santa Maria, one of the best examples of a Cistercian abbey, founded in 1147 (exterior 17–18c). The church is Portugal's largest (14c tombs). www.mosteiroalcobaca.gov.pt/en 48 A1

**Algarve** Modern seaside resorts among picturesque sandy beaches and rocky coves (Praia da Rocha). Old towns: Lagos; Faro. www.visitalgarve.pt/en/Default.aspx 54 B1

**Batalha** Abbey is one of the masterpieces of French Gothic and Manueline architecture (tombs, English Perpendicular chapel, unfinished pantheon). www.mosteirobatalha.gov.pt/en 48 A2

**Braga** Historic town with cathedral and Baroque staircase of Bom Jesus do Monte. 42 A1

**Coimbra** Old town with narrow streets set on a hill. The Romanesque Old Cathedral is particularly fine (portal). The university (founded 1290) has a fascinating Baroque library. Also: Museum of Machado de Castro; many monasteries and convents. www.coimbraportugaltourism.com 42 B1

**Évora** Centre of the town, surrounded by walls, has narrow streets of Moorish character and medieval and Renaissance architecture. Churches: 12–13c Gothic cathedral; São Francisco with a chapel decorated with bones of some 5000 monks; 15c Convent of Dos Lóis. The Jesuit university was founded in 1559. Museum of Évora holds fine art (particularly Flemish and Portuguese). Also: well-preserved remains of Roman temple. www.evora-portugal.com 48 C3

**Guimarães** Old town with a castle with seven towers on a vast keep. Churches: Romanesque chapel of São Miguel; São Francisco. Alberto Sampaio Museum and Martins Sarmento Museum are excellent. www.visitportugal.com/en/content/guimaraes 42 A1

**Lisbon** ***Lisboa*** Capital of Portugal. Baixa is the Neoclassical heart of Lisbon with the Praça do Comércio and Rossío squares. São Jorge castle (Visigothic, Moorish, Romanesque) is surrounded by the medieval quarters. Bairro Alto is famous for *fado* (songs). Monastery of Jerónimos is exceptional. Churches: 12c cathedral; São Vicente de Fora; São Roque (tiled chapels); Torre de Belém. Museums: Gulbenkian Museum (ancient, oriental, European, Modern Art Centre); National Museum of Ancient Art; Design Museum; National Tile Museum (housed in Convento da Madre de Deus). Nearby: palatial monastic complex Mafra; royal resort Sintra. www.visitlisboa.com 48 B1

**Porto** Historic centre with narrow streets. Views from Clérigos Tower. Churches: São Francisco; cathedral. Soares dos Reis Museum holds fine and decorative arts (18–19c). The suburb of Vila Nova de Gaia is the centre for port wine. https://visitporto.travel/en-GB/home#/ 42 A1

**Tomar** Attractive town with the Convento de Cristo, founded in 1162 as the headquarters of the Knights Templar (Charola temple, chapter house, Renaissance cloisters). 48 A2

## Spain España

www.spain.info/en_GB/

**Ávila** Medieval town with 2km-long 11c walls and 12c cathedral. Pilgrimage site to shrines to St Teresa of Ávila (Convent of Santa Teresa, Convent of the Incarnation). www.avilaturismo.com/en/ 44 B3

**Barcelona** Showcase of Gothic ('Barri Gòtic': cathedral; Santa María del Mar; mansions on Carrer de Montcada) and *modernista* architecture ('Eixample' area with Manzana de la Discòrdia; Sagrada Familia, Güell Park, La Pedrera). Many elegant boulevards (La Rambla, Passeig de Gràcia). Museums: National Art Museum of Catalonia, Catalan Archaeology, Picasso Museum, Miró Museum, Tàpies Museum. Nearby: monastery of Montserrat (Madonna); Figueres (Dali Museum). www.barcelonaturisme.com/wv3/en **41 C3**

**Burgos** Medieval town with Gothic cathedral, Moorish-Gothic Royal Monastery and Charterhouse of Miraflores. **37 B3**

**Cáceres** Medieval town with originally Moorish walls and several aristocratic palaces with solar chambers. **49 A4**

**Córdoba** Capital of Moorish Spain with a labyrinth of streets and houses with tile-decorated patios. The 8–10c Mezquita is the finest mosque in Spain. A 16c cathedral was added at the centre of the building and a 17c tower replaced the minaret. The old Jewish quarter has 14c synagogue. www.turismodecordoba.org **50 C3**

**El Escorial** Immense Renaissance complex of palatial and monastic buildings and mausoleum of the Spanish monarchs. www.patrimonionacional.es/en/ **45 B3**

**Granada** The Alhambra was hill-top palace-fortress of the rulers of the last Moorish kingdom and is the most splendid example of Moorish art and architecture in Spain. The complex has three principal parts: Alcazaba fortress (11c); Casa Real palace (14c, with later Palace of Carlos V); Generalife gardens. Also: Moorish quarter; gypsy quarter; Royal Chapel with good art in the sacristy. www.turgranada.es/en/ **57 A4**

**León** Gothic cathedral has notable stained glass. Royal Pantheon commemorates early kings of Castile and León. **36 B1**

**Madrid** Capital of Spain, a mainly modern city with 17–19c architecture at its centre around Plaza Mayor. Sights: Royal Palace with lavish apartments and Royal Armoury museum; Descalzas Reales Convent (tapestries and other works). Spain's three leading galleries: Prado (15–18c); Queen Sofia Centre (20c Spanish, Picasso's *Guernica*); Thyssen-Bornemisza Museum (medieval to modern). http://turismomadrid.es/en/ **45 B4**

**Oviedo** Gothic cathedral with 12c sanctuary. Three Visigothic (9c) churches: San Julián de los Prados, Santa María del Naranco, San Miguel de Lillo. **35 A5**

**Palma** Situated on Mallorca, the largest and most beautiful of the Balearic islands, with an impressive Gothic cathedral and the Sert Studios with works by Miró. www.palma.com **60 B2**

**Picos de Europa** Mountain range with river gorges and peaks topped by Visigothic and Romanesque churches. **36 A2**

**Pyrenees** Unspoiled mountain range with beautiful landscape and villages full of Romanesque architecture. Ordesa National Park has many waterfalls and canyons. **38–39**

**Salamanca** Delightful old city with some uniquely Spanish architecture: Renaissance Plateresque is famously seen on 16c portal of the university (founded 1218); Baroque Churrigueresque on 18c Plaza Mayor; both styles at the Convent of San Esteban. Also: Romanesque Old Cathedral; Gothic-Plateresque New Cathedral; House of Shells. www.salamanca.es/en **44 B2**

**Santiago di Compostela** Medieval city with many churches and religious institutions. The famous pilgrimage to the shrine of St James the Apostle ends here in the magnificent cathedral, originally Romanesque with many later elements (18c Baroque façade). www.santiagoturismo.com **34 B2**

**Segovia** Old town set on a rock with a 1c Roman aqueduct. Also: 16c Gothic cathedral; Alcázar (13–15c, rebuilt 19c); 12-sided 13c Templar Church of Vera Cruz. **45 B3**

**Seville** *Sevilla* City noted for festivals and flamenco. The world's largest Gothic cathedral (15c) retains the Orange Court and minaret of a mosque, now its bell tower. The Alcazár is a fine example of Moorish architecture. The 18c tobacco factory, now part of the university, was the setting for Bizet's *Carmen*. Barrio de Santa Cruz is the old Jewish quarter with narrow streets and white houses. Casa de Pilatos (15–16c) has a fine domestic patio. The Museum of Fine Arts is in a former convent. Nearby: Roman Italica with amphitheatre. www.visitasevilla.es/en **56 A2**

**Tarragona** The city and its surroundings have some of Spain's best-preserved Roman heritage, including amphitheatre and Praetorium tower. Also: Gothic cathedral (cloister). www.tarragonaturisme.cat/en **41 C2**

**Toledo** Historic city with Moorish, Jewish and Christian sights. The small 11c mosque of El Cristo de la Luz is one of the earliest in Spain. Two synagogues have been preserved: Santa María la Blanca; El Tránsito. Churches: San Juan de los Reyes; Gothic cathedral. El Greco's *Burial of the Count of Orgaz* is in the church of Santo Tomé. More of his works are in the El Greco house and in Hospital de Santa Cruz. **45 C3**

**Valencia** The old town has houses and palaces with elaborate façades. Also: Gothic cathedral and Lonja de la Seda (Silk Exchange). www.visitvalencia.com/en **53 B3**

**Zaragoza** Town notable for Moorish architecture (11c Aljafería Palace). The Basilica de Nuestra Señora del Pilar is highly venerated. www.zaragoza.es/turismo **47 A3**

# Ski resorts

The resorts listed are popular ski centres, therefore road access to most is normally good and supported by road clearing during snow falls. However, mountain driving is never predictable and drivers should make sure they take suitable snow chains as well as emergency provisions and clothing. Listed for each resort are: the atlas page and grid square; the resort/minimum piste altitude (where only one figure is shown, they are at the same height) and maximum altitude of its own lifts; the number of lifts and gondolas (the total for lift-linked resorts); the season start and end dates (snow cover allowing); whether snow is augmented by cannon; the nearest town (with its distance in km) and, where available, the website and/or telephone number of the local tourist information centre or ski centre ('00' prefix required for calls from the UK). **❄ indicates resorts with snow cannon**

## Andorra

### Pyrenees

**Pas de la Casa / Grau Roig 40 B2** ❄ 2050–2640m • 31 lifts • Dec–Apr • Andorra La Vella (30km) www.pasdelacasa.com • *Access via Envalira Pass (2407m), highest in Pyrenees, snow chains essential.*

## France

### Alps

**Alpe d'Huez 26 B3** ❄ 1860–3330m • 85 lifts • Dec–Apr •Grenoble (63km) ℹ +33 4 76 11 44 44 www.alpedhuez.com/en • *Snow chains may be required on access road to resort.*

**Avoriaz 26 A3** ❄ 1800/1100–2280m • 36 lifts • Dec–Apr • Morzine (14km) ℹ +33 4 50 74 02 11 www.avoriaz.com/en • *Chains may be required for access road from Morzine. Car-free resort, park on edge of village.*

**Chamonix-Mont-Blanc 27 B3** ❄ 1035–3840m • 49 lifts • Dec–Apr • Martigny (38km) ℹ +33 4 50 53 00 24 https://en.chamonix.com/

**Chamrousse 26 B2** ❄ 1700/1420–2250m • 15 lifts • Dec–Apr • Grenoble (30km) ℹ +33 4 76 89 92 65 https://en.chamrousse.com/ • *Roads normally cleared, keep chains accessible because of altitude.*

**Châtel 27 A3** ❄ 1200/1110–2200m • 41 lifts • Dec–Apr • Thonon-Les-Bains (35km) ℹ +33 4 50 73 22 44 https://en.chatel.com/ete

**Courchevel 26 B3** ❄ 1300–2470m • 67 lifts • Dec–Apr • Moûtiers (23km) ℹ +33 4 79 08 00 29 https://courchevel.com/en/ • *Roads normally cleared but keep chains accessible. Traffic 'discouraged' within the four resort bases.*

**Flaine 26 A3** ❄ 1600–2500m • 24 lifts • Dec–Apr • Cluses (25km) ℹ +33 4 50 90 80 01 https://en.flaine.com/ • *Keep chains accessible for D6 from Cluses to Flaine. Car access for depositing luggage and passengers only. 1500-space car park outside resort. Near Sixt-Fer-á-Cheval.*

**La Clusaz 26 B3** ❄ 1100–2600m • 49 lifts • Dec–Apr • Annecy (32km) https://en.laclusaz.com/ • *Roads normally clear but keep chains accessible for final road from Annecy.*

**La Plagne 26 B3** ❄ 2500/1250–3250m • 75 lifts • Dec–Apr • Moûtiers (32km) ℹ +33 4 79 09 02 01 https://en.la-plagne.com/ • *Ten different centres up to 2100m altitude. Road access via Bozel, Landry or Aime normally cleared. Linked to Les Arcs by cable car.*

**Les Arcs 27 B3** ❄ 1600/1200–3230m • 77 lifts • Dec–Apr • Bourg-St-Maurice (15km) ℹ +33 4 79 07 12 57 https://en.lesarcs.com • *Four base areas up to 2000 metres; keep chains accessible. Pay parking at edge of each base resort. Linked to La Plagne by cable car.*

**Les Carroz d'Araches 26 A3** ❄ 1140–2500m • 80 lifts • Dec–Apr • Cluses (13km) www.lescarroz.com/en/

**Les Deux-Alpes 26 C3** ❄ 1650/1300–3600m • 49 lifts • Dec–Apr & Jun–Aug • Grenoble (75km) ℹ +33 4 76 79 22 00 www.les2alpes.com/en • *Roads normally cleared, however snow chains recommended for D213 up from valley road (D1091).*

**Les Gets 26 A3** ❄ 1170/1000–2000m • 47 lifts • Dec–Apr • Cluses (18km) ℹ +33 4 50 74 74 74 www.lesgets.com/en

**Les Ménuires 26 B3** ❄ 1815/1850–3200m • 39 lifts • Dec–Apr • Moûtiers (27km) ℹ +33 4 79 00 73 00 www.lesmenuires.com • *Keep chains accessible for D117 from Moûtiers.*

**Les Sept Laux Prapoutel 26 B3** ❄ 1350–2400m, • 24 lifts • Dec–Apr • Grenoble (38km) www.les7laux.com/winter • *Roads normally cleared, however keep chains accessible for mountain road up from the A41 motorway. Near St Sorlin d'Arves.*

**Megève 26 B3** ❄ 1100/1050–2350m • 79 lifts • Dec–Apr • Sallanches (12km) ℹ +33 4 50 21 27 28 www.megeve.com/en

**Méribel 26 B3** ❄ 1400/1100–2950m • 61 lifts • Dec–Apr • Moûtiers (18km) ℹ +33 4 79 08 60 01 www.meribel.net/en • *Keep chains accessible for 18km to resort on D90 from Moûtiers.*

**Morzine 26 A3** ❄ 1000–2460m • 46 lifts • Dec–Apr • Thonon-Les-Bains (30km) ℹ +33 4 50 74 72 72 http://en.morzine-avoriaz.com

**Pra Loup 32 A2** ❄ 1500–2600m • 20 lifts • Dec–Apr • Barcelonnette (10km) ℹ +33 4 92 84 10 04 www.praloup.com • *Roads normally cleared but chains accessibility recommended.*

**Risoul 26 C3** ❄ 1850/1650–2750m • 59 lifts • Dec–Apr • Briançon (40km) ℹ +33 4 92 46 02 60 https://en.risoul.com • *Keep chains accessible. Near Guillestre. Linked with Vars Les Claux.*

**St-Gervais Mont-Blanc 26 B3** ❄ 850/1150–2350m • 27 lifts • Dec–Apr • Sallanches (10km) ℹ +33 4 50 93 23 23 www.ski-saintgervais.com/en/

**Serre Chevalier 26 C3** ❄ 1350/1200–2800m • 68 lifts • Dec–Apr • Briançon (10km) www.serre-chevalier.com/en • *Made up of 13 small villages along the valley road, which is normally cleared.*

**Tignes 27 B3** ❄ 2100/1550–3450m • 78 lifts • Jan–Dec • Bourg-St-Maurice (26km) ℹ +33 4 79 40 04 40 https://en.tignes.net/ • *Keep chains accessible because of altitude. Linked to Val d'Isère.*

**Val d'Isère 27 B3** ❄ 1850/1550–3450m • 78 lifts • Dec–May, possibly until Jul • Bourg-St-Maurice (30km) ℹ +33 4 79 06 06 60 www.valdisere.com/en/ • *Roads normally cleared but keep chains accessible.*

**Val Thorens 26 B3** ❄ 2300/1850–3200m • 31 lifts • Nov–May • Moûtiers (37km) ℹ +33 4 79 00 08 08 www.les3vallees.com/en/ski-resort/val-thorens • *Chains mandatory – highest ski resort in Europe. Obligatory paid parking on edge of resort.*

**Valloire 26 B3** ❄ 1430–2750m • 35 lifts • Dec–Apr • Modane (20km) ℹ +33 4 79 59 03 96 https://tourism.valloire.net • *Road normally clear up to the Col du Galibier, to the south of the resort, which is closed from 1st November to 1st June. Linked to Valmeinier.*

**Valmeinier 26 B3** ❄ 1500–2750m • 35 lifts • Dec–Apr • St Michel de Maurienne (47km) ℹ +33 4 79 59 53 69 www.valmeinier.com/en • *Access from north on D1006 / D902. Col du Galibier, to the south of the resort closed from 1st November to 1st June. Linked to Valloire.*

**Valmorel 26 B3** ❄ 1400–2550m • 50 lifts • Dec–Apr • Moûtiers (15km) ℹ +33 4 79 09 85 55 /www.valmorel.com/en/ • *Near St Jean-de-Belleville. Linked with ski areas of Celliers, Doucy and St François-Longchamp.*

**Vars Les Claux 26 C3** ❄ 1850/1650–2750m • 59 lifts • Dec–Apr • Briançon (40km) ℹ +33 4 92 46 51 31 www.vars.com • *Four base resorts up to 1850 metres. Keep chains accessible. Linked with Risoul.*

**Villard de Lans 26 B2** ❄ 1050/1160–2170m • 21 lifts • Dec–Apr • Grenoble (32km) ℹ +33 4 76 95 10 38 https://uk.villarddelans-correnconenvercors.com

### Pyrenees

**Font-Romeu 40 B3** ❄ 1800/1600–2200m • 23 lifts • Nov–Mar • Perpignan (87km) ℹ +33 4 68 30 68 30 https://font-romeu.fr/en/ • *Roads normally cleared but keep chains accessible.*

**Saint-Lary Soulan 39 B4** ❄ 830/1650/1700–2515m • 31 lifts • Dec–Apr • Tarbes (75km) ℹ +33 5 62 39 50 81 www.saintlary.com • *Access roads constantly cleared of snow.*

### Vosges

**La Bresse-Hohneck 20 A1** ❄ 600–1370m • 33 lifts • Dec–Mar • Cornimont (6km) ℹ +33 3 29 25 68 78 www.labresse.net

## Spain

### Pyrenees

**Baqueira-Beret/Bonaigua 39 B4** ❄ 1500–2500m • 36 lifts • Dec–Apr • Vielha (15km) ℹ +34 973 639 000 www.baqueira.es • *Roads normally clear but keep chains accessible. Near Salardú.*

### Sistema Penlbetico

**Sierra Nevada 57 A4** ❄ 2100–3300m • 21 lifts • Dec–May • Granada (32km) ℹ +34 958 70 80 90 http://sierranevada.es • *Access road designed to be avalanche safe and is snow cleared.*

# Key to map pages

- **3** Map pages at 3 200 000
- **44** Map pages at 1: 750 000
- **Alicante** ● City plan
- **Lyon** ■ City plan and approach map
  See pages 63–68 for city plans and approach maps

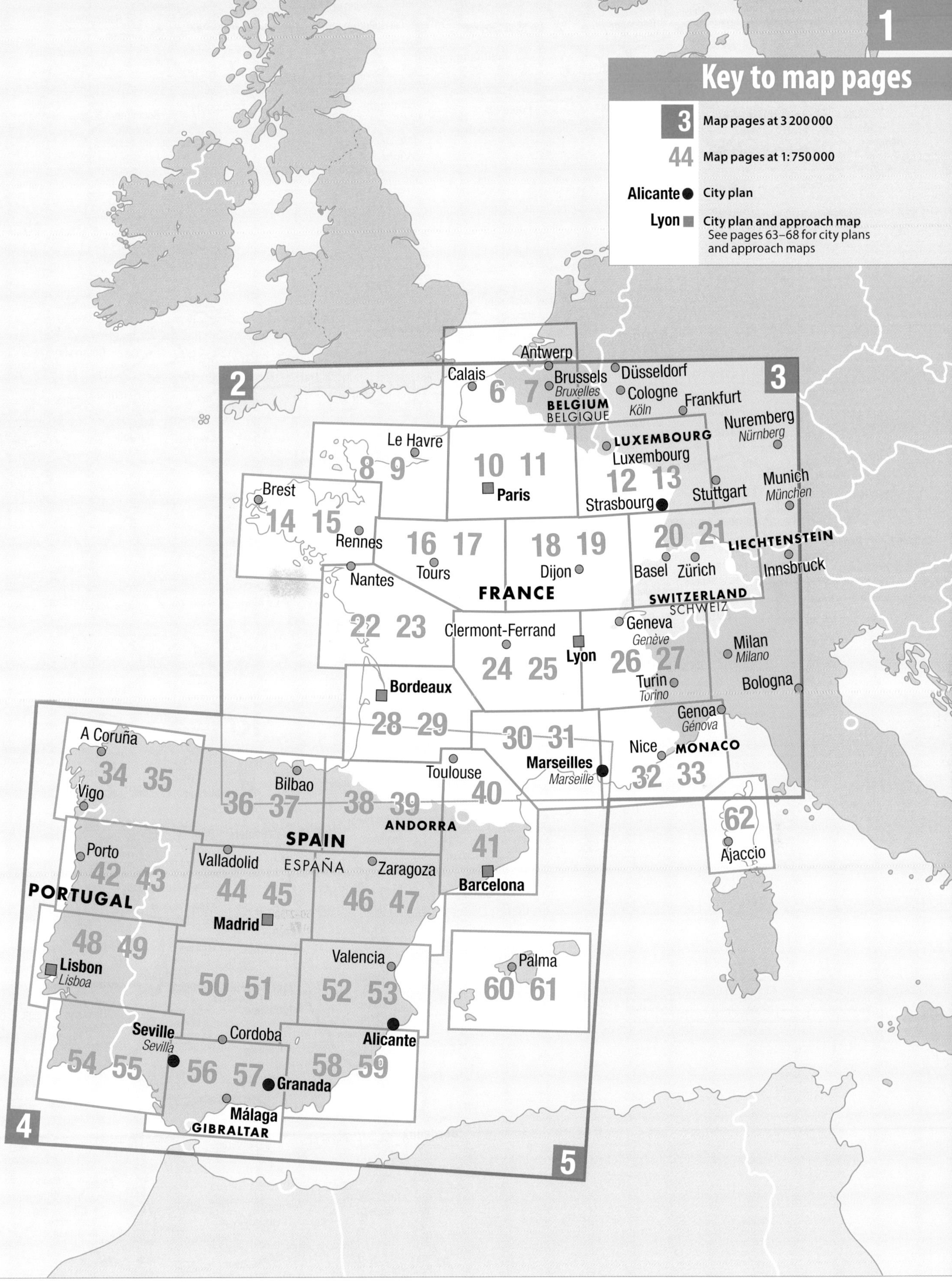

Barnstaple
Minehead
Bideford
Bridgwater
Taunton
Glastonbury
Shaftesbury
Frome
Salisbury
Andover
Basingstoke
Woking
Dorking
Guildford
Reigate
Crawley
Horsham
Royal Tunbridge Wells
Maidstone
Tonbridge
Ashford
Canterbury
Margate
North Foreland
Ramsgate
Dover
Folkestone
Bude
Okehampton
Exeter
Launceston
Newton Abbot
Torquay
Torbay
Exmouth
Sidmouth
Bridport
Dorchester
Yeovil
Southampton
Winchester
Gosport
Havant
Portsmouth
Bournemouth
Poole
Swanage
Weymouth
Portland Bill
Newport
Isle of Wight
Worthing
Brighton
Bexhill
Hastings
Eastbourne
Newhaven
Newquay
Bodmin
Redruth
Truro
St. Austell
Plymouth
Dartmouth
Start Pt.
Penzance
Land's End
Falmouth
Lizard Pt.
English Channel
La Manche
Dunkerque
Calais
Tunnel
St.-Omer
Boulogne-sur-Mer
Le Touquet-Paris-Plage
Hazebrouck
Béthune
Montreuil
Hesdin
Berck
Bruay-la-Buissière
St.-Pol-sur-Ternoise
Arras
Lens
Doullens
Albert
Abbeville
Amiens
Le Tréport
Blangy-sur-Bresle
Flixecourt
St.-Valery-en-Caux
Dieppe
Neufchâtel-en-Bray
St.-Saëns
Poix-de-Picardie
Forges-les-Eaux
Gournay-en-Bray
Breteuil
Fécamp
Le Havre
Yvetot
Rouen
Bolbec
Honfleur
Deauville
Beauvais
Clermont
Creil
Méru
Senlis
Gisors
Vernon
Pontoise
St.-Denis
St.-Germain
PARIS
Versailles
Créteil
Évry
Étampes
Melun
Mantes-la-Jolie
Évreux
Louviers
Elbeuf
Bernay
Lisieux
Caen
Bayeux
Baie de la Seine
CÔTE DE NACRE
Pte. de Barfleur
Valognes
Ste.-Mère-Église
Carentan
Cherbourg-Octeville
Auderville
C. de la Hague
Alderney
Guernsey
St. Peter Port
Sark
Jersey
St. Helier
Channel Is. (U.K.)
Barneville-Carteret
La Haye-du-Puits
Coutances
St.-Lô
Vire
Flers
Falaise
Argentan
Gacé
L'Aigle
Sées
Nonant-le-Pin
Verneuil-sur-Avre
Nonancourt
Dreux
Rambouillet
Chartres
Nogent-le-Rotrou
Mortagne-au-Perche
Alençon
Pré-en-Pail
Mayenne
Domfront
Mortain
St.-Hilaire-du-Harcouët
Fougères
Avranches
Le Mont-St.-Michel
Granville
Villedieu-les-Poêles
G. de St.-Malo
CÔTE D'ÉMERAUDE
St.-Malo
Dinard
Dinan
Pléneuf-Val-André
Lamballe
St.-Brieuc
Paimpol
Binic
Lannion
Guingamp
Perros-Guirec
Roscoff
Morlaix
Landivisiau
Ile d' Ouessant
Brest
Le Conquet
Pte. St.-Mathieu
Crozon
Châteaulin
Carhaix-Plouguer
Mur-de-Bretagne
St.-Méen-le-Grand
Loudéac
Pontivy
Douarnenez
Audierne
Pte. du Raz
Quimper
Pont-l'Abbé
Pte. de Penmarch
Concarneau
Quimperlé
Bannalec
Hennebont
Lorient
Ploërmel
Locminé
Auray
Vannes
Carnac
Quiberon
Belle-Île
Le Palais
CÔTE DE CORNOUAILLE
Rennes
Vitré
Laval
Châteaubriant
Redon
La Roche-Bernard
Nozay
La Baule
Le Croisic
St.-Nazaire
Savenay
CÔTE D'AMOUR
Pornic
Nantes
Ancenis
Angers
Clisson
Cholet
Montaigu
Î. de Noirmoutier
Challans
St.-Gilles-Croix-de-Vie
CÔTE DE JADE
Î. d' Yeu
La Roche-sur-Yon
Les Sables-d'Olonne
Luçon
Chantonnay
Fontenay-le-Comte
Parthenay
Bressuire
Thouars
Saumur
Chinon
Loudun
Le Mans
Sablé-sur-Sarthe
La Flèche
Durtal
Château-la-Vallière
Château-du-Loir
St.-Calais
Mamers
Bonnétable
La Ferté-Bernard
Conlie
Châteaudun
Cloyes
Vendôme
Blois
Amboise
Tours
Langeais
Loches
Selles-sur-Cher
Romorantin-Lanthenay
Valençay
Issoudun
Vierzon
Bourges
Orléans
Olivet
Pithiviers
Artenay
Nemours
Gien
Briare
Cosne-Cours-sur-Loire
La Charité-sur-Loire
La Ferté-St.-Aubin
Châteauneuf-sur-Loire
Châtellerault
Poitiers
Chauvigny
Montmorillon
Lussac-les-Châteaux
Le Blanc
Argenton-sur-Creuse
Châteauroux
La Châtre
Montluçon
La Souterraine
Guéret
Bellac
Civray
Ruffec
Confolens
St.-Maixent-l'École
Niort
Mauzé-sur-le-Mignon
La Rochelle
Î. de Ré
Rochefort
Î. d' Oléron
Saintes
Royan
Le Verdon-sur-Mer
Cognac
Pons
Angoulême
Chasseneuil-sur-Bonnieure
Bessines-sur-Gartempe
St.-Junien
Limoges
St.-Léonard-de-Noblat
Bourganeuf
Aubusson
Eymoutiers
Ussel
St.-Yrieix-la-Perche
Uzerche
Tulle
Brive-la-Gaillarde
Thiviers
Brantôme
Périgueux
Barbezieux
Mirambeau
Lesparre-Médoc
Blaye
St.-André-de-Cubzac
Lacanau
Bordeaux
Libourne
Mussidan
Bergerac
Terrasson-Lavilledieu
Souillac
Arcachon
C. Ferret
Langon
La Réole
Marmande
Tonneins
Bazas
Casteljaloux
Aiguillon
Villeneuve-sur-Lot
Fumel
Cahors
Figeac
Rocamadour
Aurillac
Decazeville
Villefranche-de-Rouergue
Rodez
Mimizan
Labouheyre
Mont-de-Marsan
Agen
Moissac
Montauban
Caussade
Gaillac
Albi
Carmaux
Castelsarrasin
Condom
Lectoure
Fleurance
Auch
Toulouse
L'Isle-Jourdain
Grisolles
Rabastens
Graulhet
Lavaur
Castres
Mazamet
St.-Affrique
Castelnaudary
Carcassonne
Limoux
Pamiers
Auterive
St.-Gaudens
Lannemezan
Tarbes
Lourdes
Bagnères-de-Bigorre
Pau
Oloron-Ste.-Marie
Mauléon-Licharre
Orthez
Salies-de-Béarn
Hasparren
Bayonne
Biarritz
Irún
Donostia-San Sebastián
Castets
Tartas
Dax
St.-Sever
Aire-sur-l'Adour
Mirande
CÔTE D'ARGENT
CÔTE DES LANDES
CÔTE BASQUE
Bay of Biscay
Golfe de Gascogne
COSTA VASCA
COSTA MONTAÑESA
Santander
Santoña
C. de Ajo
Castro Urdiales
Laredo
Llanes
San Vicente de la Barquera
Picos de Europa
Torrelavega
Potes
Reinosa
Getxo
Gernika-Lumo
Bilbao
Barakaldo
Eibar
Durango
Amurrio
Tolosa
Beasain
Alsasua
Pamplona
Vitoria-Gasteiz
SANTANDER
ROSSLARE
BILBAO SANTANDER
CORK ROSSLARE
PLYMOUTH PORTSMOUTH
PORTSMOUTH
F R A N C E
0 20 40 60 80 100 miles
0 40 80 120 160 km

3
BELGIQUE
BELGIUM
LUX.
G E R M A N Y
SWITZERLAND
SCHWEIZ
LIECHTENSTEIN
Antwerpen
Gent
BRUXELLES
BRUSSELS
Liège
Namur
Charleroi
Düsseldorf
Köln
Bonn
Aachen
Koblenz
Wiesbaden
Mainz
Frankfurt
Offenbach
Darmstadt
Würzburg
Mannheim
Heidelberg
Ludwigshafen
Karlsruhe
Stuttgart
Nürnberg
Augsburg
Ulm
Reutlingen
Freiburg
Saarbrücken
Metz
Nancy
Strasbourg
Reims
Luxembourg
Thionville
Mulhouse
Basel
Zürich
Bern
Luzern
St. Gallen
Winterthur
Lausanne
Genève
Geneva
Dijon
Besançon
LYON
Grenoble
St.-Étienne
Clermont-Ferrand
Valence
Avignon
Nîmes
Montpellier
Aix-en-Provence
MARSEILLE
Toulon
Nice
Cannes
MONACO
TORINO
TURIN
MILANO
MILAN
Génova
Genoa
Verona
Bérgamo
Bréscia
Livorno
La Spézia
Golfo di Génova
CÔTE D'AZUR
CÔTE D'AMÉTHYSTE
5
6
7
8
9

1 2 3 4

8° 6° 4°

C. Ortegal
COSTA VERDE
C. de Peñas
Go
Ga
PORTSMOUTH
Ortigueira
Ferrol
Vivero
Ribadeo
Luarca
Avilés
Gijón
Xixón
Villaviciosa
COSTA MONTAÑESA
C. de Ajo
Pontedeume
A Coruña
Villalba
Mondoñedo
Tineo
Salas
Oviedo
Pola de Siero
Llanes
San Vicente de la Barquera
Santander
Santoña
Castro Urdiales
Getxo
Vimianzo
C. Touriñán
Betanzos
Carballo
Ordes
Cangas de Narcea
Grado
Langreo
Picos de Europa
2648
Torrelavega
Laredo
Barakaldo
Bilbao
Corcubión
Santiago de Compostela
Baamonde
Lugo
Fonsagrada
Pola de Lena
Mieres
Puerto de Pajares
Potes
Amurrio
C. Fisterra
Melide
Becerreá
Villablino
Riaño
Reinosa
Orduña
Muros
Noia
Padrón
Lalín
Sarria
2214
Villafranca del Bierzo
La Pola de Gordón
La Robla
Vilagarcía de Arousa
A Estrada
Pontevedra
Chantada
Ponferrada
León
Saldaña
Oña
Marín
O Carballino
Monforte de Lemos
Astorga
Brivieska
Miranda
Redondela
Vigo
Ponteareas
Celanova
Ourense
Pobra de Trives
2185
2124
La Bañeza
Valencia de Don Juan
Sahagún
Osorno
Burgos
Santo Domingo de la Calzada
42°
Baiona
Tui
Valença
Xinzo de Limia
A Gudiña
Verín
Benavente
Villalón de Campos
Palencia
Salas de los Infantes
Caminha
1330
Medina de Rioseco
Villalpando
2228
Picos de Urbión
Viana do Castelo
Bragança
Alcañices
Chaves
Vila Pouca de Aguiar
Mirandela
Miranda do Douro
Valladolid
Aranda de Duero
Póvoa de Varzim
Braga
Guimarães
Zamora
Toro
Burgo de Osma
Vila do Conde
Matosinhos
Amarante
Murça
Tordesillas
Medina del Campo
San Esteban de Gormaz
Porto
Vila Real
Cuéllar
Boceguillas
Vila Nova de Gaia
Penafiel
Peso da Régua
Torre de Moncorvo
Fermoselle
Olmedo
Ovar
São João da Madeira
Lamego
Vila Nova de Foz Côa
Ledesma
Cañizal
Puerto de Somosierra
Medinaceli
Salamanca
Arévalo
Vitigudino
Peñaranda de Bracamonte
Segovia
Sigüenza
Oliveira de Azemeis
Aveiro
Albergaria-a-Velha
Celorico da Beira
Viseu
Pinhel
La Fuente de San Esteban
Villacastín
2430
Águeda
Vilar Formosa
Fuentes de Oñoro
Ciudad Rodrigo
Alba de Tormes
Ávila
El Molar
Guadalajara
Brihuega
Mira
Tondela
Mangualde
Guarda
El Escorial
Alcobendas
Mealhada
1723
Béjar
MADRID
Leganés
Alcalá de Henares
Coimbra
Belmonte
Covilhã
1367
El Barco de Ávila
2592
Pico Almanzor
San Martín de Valdeiglesias
Arenas de San Pedro
Navalcarnero
Getafe
Arganda
Figueira da Foz
1993
Fundão
40°
Penamacôr
Hoyos
Plasencia
Parla
Miranda do Corvo
Coria
Talavera de la Reina
Illescas
Aranjuez
Tarancón
Pombal
Navalmoral de la Mata
Maqueda
Ocaña
Leiria
Proença-a-Nova
Castelo Branco
Embalse de Alcántara
Toledo
Tomar
Alcántara
Belvís de la Jara
Caldas da Rainha
Peniche
Abrantes
Nisa
Quintanar de la Orden
C. Carvoeiro
Torres Novas
Gavião
Trujillo
1443
Guadalupe
Navahermosa
1419
Orgaz
Pedro Muñoz
Torres Vedras
Santarém
Portalegre
Valencia de Alcántara
Cáceres
Madridejos
Almeirim
Ponte de Sor
Zorita
Logrosán
Embalse de Cijara
Alcázar de San Juan
Cartaxo
Azambuja
Arronches
Miajadas
Fuente el Fresno
Mafra
Coruche
Monforte
Malagón
Tomelloso
Villarrobledo
Sintra
Vila Franca de Xira
LISBOA
LISBON
Estremoz
Campo Maior
Villanueva de la Serena
Manzanares
C. da Roca
Estoril
Oeiras
Vendas Novas
Montijo
Elvas
Badajoz
Mérida
Don Benito
Ciudad Real
Daimiel
Almagro
COSTA DO SOL
Almada
Barreiro
Montemor-o-Novo
Évora
Olivenza
La Albuera
Almendralejo
Almadén
Almodóvar del Campo
Valdepeñas
Villahermosa
Setúbal
Alcácer do Sal
Reguengos de Monsaraz
Villafranca de los Barros
Castuera
Puertollano
Villanueva de los Infantes
C. Espichel
Viana do Alentejo
Jerez de los Caballeros
Zafra
Los Santos de Maimona
Hinojosa del Duque
B. de Setúbal
Grândola
Peñarroya-Pueblonuevo
Pozoblanco
1300
Paso Despeñaperros
Santiago do Cacém
Ferreira do Alentejo
Barragem de Alqueva
Llerena
Azuaga
38°
Barrancos
Fregenal de la Sierra
Fuente Obejuna
Espiel
La Carolina
C. de Sines
Sines
Cercal
Beja
Aljustrel
Moura
Aracena
Montoro
Andújar
Bailén
Linares
Villacarrillo
Cortegana
Córdoba
Úbeda
Odemira
Mértola
Valverde del Camino
Posadas
Castro del Río
Baeza
Martos
Nerva
Lora del Río
La Carlota
Jaén
Huelma
Palma del Río
Montilla
Baena
902
Monchique
La Palma del Condado
Sanlúcar la Mayor
Sevilla
Seville
Carmona
Écija
Cabra
Alcalá la Real
Cúllar de Baza
Vila do Bispo
Portimão
Lagoa
Loulé
Vila Real de Santo António
Marchena
Lucena
Priego de Córdoba
C. de São Vicente
Sagres
Lagos
Albufeira
Faro
Olhão
Tavira
Ayamonte
Huelva
Almonte
Dos Hermanas
Estepa
Osuna
Loja
Santa Fe
Guadix
Baza
Utrera
Morón de la Frontera
Archidona
Granada
Mulhacén
3478
COSTA DE LA LUZ
G. de Cádiz
Lebrija
Antequera
Alhama de Granada
Orjiva
Berja
Campillos
Arcos de la Frontera
Vélez Málaga
Almería
LAS PALMAS DE GRAN CANARIA
SANTA CRUZ DE TENERIFE
Sanlúcar de Barrameda
El Puerto de Santa María
Ronda
Málaga
Albuñol
Jerez de la Frontera
Motril
Adra
Coín
Torremolinos
Cádiz
Puerto Real
Medina Sidonia
Marbella
Fuengirola
COSTA DEL SOL
San Fernando
Chiclana de la Frontera
Vejer de la Frontera
Estepona
San Roque
ISLAS CANARIAS
36°
C. Trafalgar
Algeciras
La Línea de la Concepción
MELILLA
AL HOCEIMA
NADOR
TANGER
Gibraltar (U.K.)
Pta. de Europa
MELILLA
Str. of Gibraltar
Tarifa
Ceuta (Esp.)
(Spain)
SÈTE
BARCELONA
GÉNOVA
Alborán
C. Spartel
Tanger
Tangier

PORTUGAL
ESPAÑA
SPAIN
Cordillera Cantábrica
Castilla y León
Castilla-La Mancha
Sierra Morena
Andalucía

0 40 80 120 160 km

Mont-de-Marsan
Condom
Castelsarrasin
Lectoure
Montauban
Albi
Gaillac
Rabastens
St.-Affrique
Nîmes
Castets
Tartas
Fleurance
Graulhet
Lavaur
Castres
Lodève
Montpellier
Lunel
Arles
Aigues-Mortes
Salon-de-Provence
Martigues
Dax
Aire-sur-l'Adour
Auch
Grisolles
L'Isle-Jourdain
Toulouse
Mazamet
Pézenas
Clermont-l'Hérault
Sète
Stes.-Maries-de-la-Mer
MARSEILLE
MARSEILLES
Bayonne
Biarritz
Orthez
Mirande
St.-Pons
Béziers
Agde
CÔTE BASQUE
CÔTE D'AMETHYSTE
Castelnaudary
Lézignan-Corbières
Donostia-San Sebastián
Irún
Salies-de-Béarn
Pau
Canal du Midi
Hasparren
Oloron-Ste.-Marie
Mauléon-Licharre
Tarbes
Auterive
Carcassonne
Narbonne
Tolosa
Beasain
Lannemezan
Pamiers
Limoux
Golfe du Lion
Lourdes
Bagnères-de-Bigorre
St.-Gaudens
Foix
Pamplona
Cauterets
St.-Béat
St.-Girons
Quillan
TANGER
NADOR
Alsásua
Lavelanet
Ax-les-Thermes
Perpignan
Bagnères-de-Luchon
Pico de Aneto
Argelès-sur-Mer
Port-Vendres
Cerbère
Portbou
CÔTE VERMEILLE
Jaca
Mte. Perdido
ANDORRA
Andorra La Vella
Le Perthus
Mt. Canigou
Logroño
Tafalla
Puigcerdà
Ribes de Freser
C. de Creus
La Seu d'Urgell
Figueras
Calahorra
Ayerbe
Banyoles
Olot
Ripoll
G. de Roses
Alfaro
Berga
Solsona
Girona
Tudela
Huesca
Tremp
Gironella
Palafrugell
Palamós
San Felíu de Guíxols
COSTA BRAVA
Barbastro
ORAN
Tarazona
Monzón
Sallent
Vic
Manresa
Granollers
Tossa
Lloret de Mar
Blanes
Balaguer
Cervera
Terrassa
Sabadell
Zaragoza
Fraga
Lleida
Tàrrega
Igualada
Mataró
Badalona
La Almunia de Doña Godina
Vilafranca del Penedès
Almazán
Cariñena
Montblanc
BARCELONA
Calatayud
Valls
Sitges
El Prat de Llobregat
Alhama de Aragón
Belchite
Reus
Vilanova i la Geltrú
Arcos de Jalón
Daroca
Hijar
Caspe
Falset
Tarragona
GÈNOVA
CIVITAVÈCCHIA
TANGER
LIVORNA
SAVONA
Alcañiz
Gandesa
Calamocha
COSTA DORADA
G. de Sant Jordi
Montalbán
Tortosa
C. Tortosa
Monreal del Campo
Morella
Sant Mateu
Vinarós
Benicarló
Teruel
Albocácer
Alcalá de Xivert
COSTA DEL AZAHAR
Islas Baleares
Menorca
Minorca
Fornells
Cuenca
Cañete
C. de Formentor
Ciudadela de Menorca
Maó
Onda
Castelló de la Plana
Vila-real de los Infantes
Is. Columbretes
Sóller
Alcúdia
Chelva
La Vall de Uxió
Palma de Mallorca
Inca
Manacor
Calvià
Llucmajor
Mallorca
Majorca
Olivares
Liria
Sagunt
Golfo de Valencia
Utiel
Chiva
Valencia
Requena
Torrent
Motilla del Palancar
Minglanilla
Casas Ibáñez
L'Albufera
B. de Palma
Sueca
Algemesí
Cullera
Eivissa
Ibiza
Cabrera
La Roda
Alberic
Alcira
Gandía
Sant Antoni de Portmany
Albacete
Chinchilla de Monte Aragón
Xátiva
Denia
Formentera
C. de la Nao
Alcoy
Almansa
Villena
Robledo
Tobarra
Yecla
Altea
Elda
Benidorm
Villajoyosa
Balearic Islands
Hellín
Jumilla
Novelda
Yeste
Elche de la Sierra
Alicante
COSTA BLANCA
Caravaca de la Cruz
Cieza
Elche
ALGER
Mula
Orihuela
Alcantarilla
Murcia
Torrevieja
San Pedro del Pinatar
MARSEILLE
ALICANTE
Totana
San Javier
Mar Menor
Huéscar
Vélez Rubio
Cartagena
C. de Palos
La Unión
Lorca
Huércal Overa
Aguilas
Cuevas del Almanzora
Vera
Sorbas
Níjar
MAR MEDITERRANEO
Dellys
Azeffoun
Bordj el Kiffan
C. Matifou
Bordj Menaiel
Azazga
Aïn Benian
Koléa
ALGER
ALGIERS
Thenia
Tizi-Ouzou
Bou Ismael
Cherchell
Blida
Boufarik
El Arba
C. Ténès
Ténès
Damous
C. de Gata
MARSEILLE
C. Kramis
Beni-Haoua
Gouraya
Bouïra
Miliana
Médéa
Sour el Ghozlane
Ech Cheliff
Djendel
Khemis Miliana
Berrouaghia
Aïn Tédelès
O. Chéliff
Mostaganem
Arzew
Oued Rhiou
Theniet el Had
Ksar el Boukhari
Sidi-Aïssa
Oran
Relizane
Tissemsilt
Chabounia
Mohammadia
Aïn el Hadjel

Woodbridge
Heaths
Orford Ness
Bawdsey
Felixstowe
Harwich
Hoek van Holland
The Naze
Walton-on-the-Naze
Frinton-on-Sea
Clacton-on-Sea
0 10 20 miles
0 10 20 30 km
52°
2°
3°
1
2
3
A
B
Westkap
Margate
North Foreland
Broadstairs
Ramsgate
RICHBOROUGH CASTLE
Sandwich
Deal
Walmer
St. Margaret's at Cliffe
South Foreland
Hawkinge
Dover
Folkestone
Strait of Dover
51°
Knokke-Heist
Zeebrugge
Blankenberge
De Haan
Oostende
Brugge
Middelkerke
Oudenburg
Nieuwpoort
Koksijde
Gistel
De Panne
PLOPSALAND
Ichtegem
Koekelare
Torhout
Ruddervoorde
Oostkamp
Beernem
Wingene
Veurne
Diksmuide
Lichtervelde
Tielt
Adinkerke
Woumen
Zarren
Staden
Ardooie
Ingelmunster
Dunkerque
Dunkirk
Bray-Dunes
Gravelines
Loone-Plage
Calais
Marck
Sangatte
Wissant
Cap Gris-Nez
EUROTUNNEL TERMINAL
Guînes
Ardres
Bourbourg
Bergues
Hondschoote
Vleteren
Roesbrugge
Langemark-Poelkapelle
Roeselare
Izegem
Audruicq
Watten
Wormhout
Poperinge
Moorslede
Kortrijk
CATHÉDRALE ST. MARTIN
Ieper
Ypres
BELLEWAERDE
Menen
Ambleteuse
Marquise
Licques
Nordausques
Steenvoorde
Cassel
Comines
Halluin
Mouscron
Avelgem
Wimereux
NAUSICAA
Caps et Marais d'Opale
Boulogne-sur-Mer
Le Portel
Outreau
Escoeuilles
Lumbres
St. Omer
Arques
Bailleul
Tourcoing
Armentières
LA COUPOLE
Hazebrouck
Roubaix
Hardelot Plage
Desvres
Aire-sur-la-Lys
Merville
Estaires
Villeneuve-d'Ascq
Samer
Fauquembergues
Thérouanne
Norrent-Fontes
St. Venant
Lille
Estrée-Blanche
Lillers
Béthune
Tournai
Étaples
Hucqueliers
Auchy-au-Bois
Seclin
Le Touquet-Paris-Plage
Fruges
La Bassée
Carvin
Pont-à-Marcq
Orchies
St. Amand-les-Eaux
Merlimont Plage
Montreuil
Heuchin
Bruay-la-Buissière
Divion
Noeux-les-Mines
BAGATELLE
Anvin
Houdain
Berck
Maresquel
Canche
St. Pol-sur-Ternoise
Liévin
Lens
Vimy
Hénin-Beaumont
Flines-lèz-Raches
Scarpe
Hesdin
Le Parcq
Cambligneul
Fort-Mahon-Plage
Tincques
Aubigny-en-Artois
Douai
Somain
Vitry-en-Artois
Aniche
Rue
Vron
Authie
Avesnes-le-Comte
Arras
Baie de la Somme
Crécy-en-Ponthieu
Auxi-le-Château
Frévent
Beaumetz-lès-Loges
Aubigny-au-Bac
Bouchain
Le Crotoy
Noyelles-sur-Mer
Nouvion
Bouquemaison
CITADELLE D'ARRAS
Iwuy
St. Valéry-sur-Somme
La Herlière
Marquion
Cayeux-sur-Mer
Ayette
Cambrai
St. Riquier
Doullens
Bernaville
Ault
Abbeville
Vaulx Vraucourt
Marieux
Puisieux
Bapaume
Bertincourt
Fressenville
Beauval
Acheux-en-Amiénois
Caudry
Wallers
Denain

7
3
4
5
's-Gravenhage
The Hague
Scheveningen
Voorschoten
Boskoop
Woerden
Utrecht
Zeist
Scherpenzeel
Zoetermeer
Gouda
Nieuwegein
Veenendaal
Wageningen
Monster
's-Gravenzande
Hoek van Holland
Rijnacker
Delft
Oudewater
Wijk bij Duurstede
Amerongen
Rhenen
Naaldwijk
Europoort
Oostvoorne
Krimpen a.d. IJssel
Schoonhoven
Culemborg
Schiedam
Rotterdam
Harwich
Hull
Ridderkerk
Leerdam
Geldermalsen
Tiel
Spijkenisse
Oud-Beijerland
Hellevoetsluis
Dordrecht
Gorinchem
Slot Loevestein
Oss
Goeree
Ouddorp
Stellendam
Haringvliet
Werkendam
Zaltbommel
Middelharnis
's-Gravendeel
Strijen
Biesbos
Het Land van Ooit
Dirksland
Grevelingen
Numansdorp
Raamsdonksveer
's-Hertogenbosch
Brouwershaven
Haamstede
Schouwen
Over-flakkee
Oude-Tonge
Made
Waalwijk
Efteling
Kaatsheuvel
Drunen
Klundert
Bruinisse
Zierikzee
Ooster-hout
Loon op Zand
Vught
Zevenbergen
Breda
Rijen
St. Oedenrode
Veghel
Steenbergen
St. Annaland
Nord-Beveland
Stavenisse
Oud Gastel
Oudenbosch
Etten
Tilburg
Oisterwijk
Boxtel
Roosendaal
Kasteel van Breda
Gilze
Best
Son en Breugel
Serooskerke
Walcheren
Goes
Yerseke
Oosterschelde
Tholen
Bergen op Zoom
Chaam
Goirle
Hilvarenbeek
Eindhoven
Geldrop
Middelburg
Zuid-Beveland
Zundert
Meerle
Baarle-Nassau
Poppel
Vlissingen
Hoedekenskerke
Hoogerheide
Essen
Hoogstraten
Westerschelde
Breskens
Wuustwezel
Merksplas
Ravels
Reusel
Eersel
Kalmthout
Brecht
Rijkevorsel
Turnhout
Arendonk
Valkenswaard
Kloosterzande
Stabroek
Schoondijke
IJzendijke
Terneuzen
Zaamslag
Kapellen
Oostmalle
Bergeyk
Zeeuws Vlaanderen
Aardenburg
Hulst
Axel
Brasschaat
Retie
Hamont
Museum Plantin Moretus
Antwerpen
Antwerp
Lille
Kasterlee
Lommel
Neerpelt
Overpelt
Assenede
Sas-van Gent
Stekene
Beveren
Zandhoven
Bobbejaanland
Mol
Maldegem
Zelzate
St. Niklaas
Herentals
Balen
Eekloo
Waarschoot
Moerbeke
Mortsel
Nijlen
Geel
Hechtel
Bree
Lokeren
Temse
Lier
Olen
Abdij van Tongerlo
Peer
Evergem
Kontich
Leopoldsburg
Aalter
Gent
Ghent
Hamme
Boom
Duffel
Heist-op-den-Berg
Westerlo
Beringen
Meeuwen
Helchteren
Zele
Dender-monde
Familiepark
Willebroek
Putte
Herselt
Abdij van Averbode
Houthalen
Deinze
Mechelen
Keerbergen
Begijnendijk
Wetteren
Lede
Londerzeel
Zemst
Haacht
Aarschot
Diest
Zonhoven
Melle
Lebbeke
Abdij van Grimbergen
Lummen
Genk
Eke
Merchtem
Vilvoorde
Herk-de-Stad
Hasselt
Oosterzele
Kruishoutem
Aalst
Grimbergen
St. Joris Winge
Geetbets
Diepenbeck
Waregem
Asse
Bruparck
Herent
Leuven
Alken
Bilzen
Zottegem
Ninove
Bruxelles
Brussels
Boutersem
Bunsbeek
St. Truiden
Nieuwerkerken
Maastricht
Oudenaarde
Tienen
Borgloon
Berchem
Kluisbergen
Brakel
Gooik
St. Pieters-Leeuw
Château des Trois-Fontaines
Tervuren
Overijse
Hoegaarden
Gingelom
Tongeren
Ronse
Flobecq
Geraards-bergen
Halle
La Hulpe
Grez-Doiceau
Landen
Ellezelles
Lessines
Enghien
Waterloo
Walibi Belgium
Wavre
Chaument Gistoux
Jodoigne
Walshoutem
Waremme
Juprelle
Frasnes-lez-Anvaing
Tubize
Ottignies
Hannut
Awans
Liège
Ath
Park Paradisio
Braine-le-Comte
Genappe
Perwez
Éghezée
Braives
St. Georges-sur-Meuse
Seraing
Leuze-en-Hainaut
Soignies
Nivelles
Gembloux
Amay
Ivoz Ramet
Beloeil
Basècles
Château de Beloeil
Lens
Sombreffe
Bierwart
Péruwelz
L'Escaut
Château de Roeulx
Le Roeulx
Seneffe
Pont-à-Celles
Fleurus
Seilles
Huy
Andenne
Comblain-au-Pont
Baudour
Hautrage
Condé-sur-l'Escaut
Mons
La Louvière
Courcelles
Namur
Auvelais
Tinlot
Ohey
Hamoir
Péronnes
Binche
Châtelet
Floreffe
Fosse-la-Ville
Havelange
Quiévrain
Valenciennes
Dour
Givry
Anderlues
Minières des Spiennes
Thuin
Charleroi
Profondeville
Assesse
Méan
Durbuy
Barvaux
Gozee
Gerpinnes
Abbaye de Maredsous
Annevoie-Rouillon
Yvoir
Ciney
Baillonville
Maubeuge
Quevy
Erquelinnes
Mettet
Anhée
Grotte de Mont-Fat
Dinant
Achene
Hotton
Bavay
Jeumont
Morialmé
Onhaye
Leignon
Le Quesnoy
Hautmont
Ferrière-la-Grande
Beaumont
Fraire
Florennes
Celles
Marche-en-Famenne
Dochamps
Aulnoye-Aymeries
Solre-le-Château
Philippeville
Hastière-Lavaux
Houyet
Rochefort
Famenne
Solesmes
Avesnois
Grandrieu
Rance
Villers-le-Gambon
Cerfontaine
Gouffre
Grotte de Lorette-Rochefort
Grotte de Han-s-Lesse
Bande
Le Cateau Cambrésis
Avesnes-sur-Helpe
Doische
Givet
Treignes
Mariembourg
Vireux
Beaurains
Landrecies

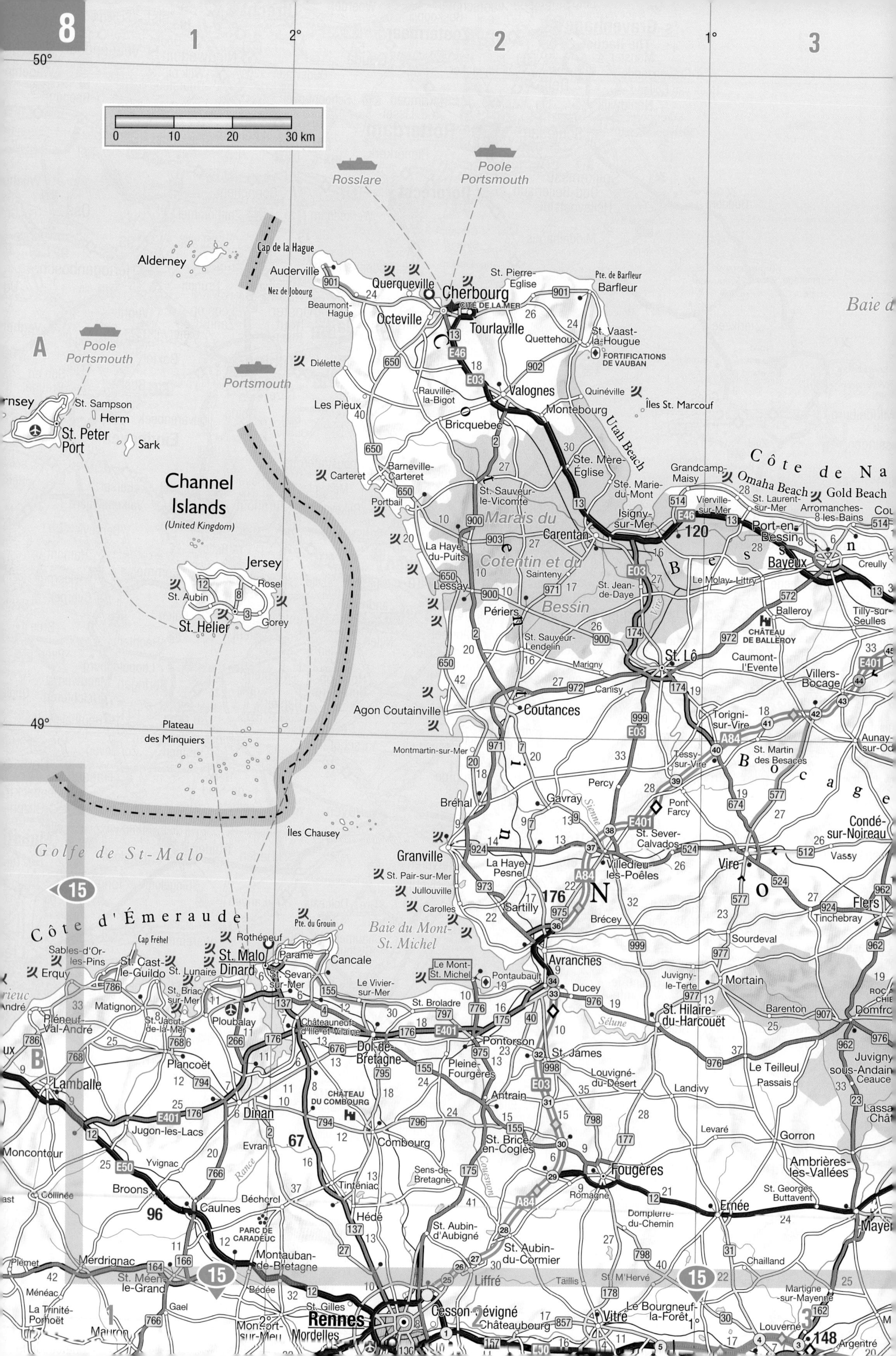
Channel Islands
(United Kingdom)
Alderney
Jersey
St. Helier
St. Peter Port
Sark
Herm
Cherbourg
Valognes
Carentan
St. Lô
Coutances
Granville
Avranches
St. Malo
Dinard
Dinan
Rennes
Fougères
Vire
Bayeux
Golfe de St-Malo
Côte d'Émeraude
Baie du Mont-St. Michel
Marais du Cotentin et du Bessin
Omaha Beach
Gold Beach
Utah Beach
Poole Portsmouth
Rosslare
Portsmouth
0 10 20 30 km

9
3
0°
4
1°
5
Newhaven
Portsmouth
Portsmouth
Mers-les-Bains
Le Tréport
Eu
Criel-sur-Mer
Biville-sur-Mer
Gamaches
Bouttencourt
Blangy-sur-Bresle
Dieppe
Varengeville-sur-Mer
Quiberville
CHÂTEAU DE DIEPPE
St. Valery-en-Caux
Veulettes-sur-Mer
St. Pierre-en-Port
Veules-les-Roses
Offranville
Bacqueville-en-Caux
Envermeu
Arques-la-Bataille
Fresnoy-Folny
Londinières
Les Grandes-Ventes
Torcy-le-Petit
Fontaine-le-Dun
Pays de Caux
Fécamp
Yport
Cany-Barville
Valmont
ST. JOSEPH
PALAIS BÉNÉDICTINE
St. Laurent-en-Caux
Neufchâtel-en-Bray
Étretat
Cap d'Antifer
Héricourt-en-Caux
Doudeville
Yerville
Tôtes
St. Saëns
Fauville-en-Caux
St-Martin-Osmonville
Gaillefontaine
Criquetot-l'Esneval
Goderville
Yvetot
Limésy
Pavilly
Clères
Buchy
Forges-les-Eaux
Heuqueville
Alvimare
Barentin
Quincampoix
Montivilliers
Bolbec
Caudebec-en-Caux
ABBAYE ST. WANDRILLE
Malaunay
Argueil
Ste. Adresse
Harfleur
St. Romain-de-Colbosc
Tancarville
Lillebonne
Duclair
Le Havre
ST. JOSEPH
CHÂTEAU DE TANCARVILLE
Quillebeuf
Boucles de Seine Normande
La Mailleraye-sur-Seine
Maromme
Mont-St. Aignan
Rouen
La Feuillie
Lyons-la-Forêt
ABBAYE DE JUMIÈGES
Jumièges
Le Grand-Quevilly
Boos
Honfleur
Berville-sur-Mer
Bourneville
Villerville
Côte Fleurie
Trouville-sur-Mer
Deauville
St. Maclou
Grand Couronne
St. Étienne-du-Rouvray
Fleury-sur-Andelle
Sword Beach
Juno Beach
Blonville-sur-Mer
Beuzeville
Pont-Audemer
Bourg-Achard
St. Aubin-sur-Mer
Luc-sur-Mer
Lion-sur-Mer
Houlgate
Villers-sur-Mer
Bourgtheroulde
Pont-de-l'Arche
Ecouis
CHÂTEAU GAILLARD
Cabourg
Douvres-la-Délivrande
Dives-sur-Mer
Pont-l'Évêque
Montfort-sur-Risle
Elbeuf
Les Andelys
Ouistreham
Cormeilles
Le Breuil-en-Auge
Lieurey
ABBAYE DE NOTRE DAME DU BEC
Dozule
Louviers
Gaillon
Caen
Troarn
Lisieux
Brionne
Le Neubourg
Acquigny
Fleury-sur-Orne
La Boissière
Thiberville
La Rivière-Thibouville
Autheuil-Authouillet
Vernon
Moult
Mézidon-Canon
Bernay
Beaumont-le-Roger
Évreux
Pacy-sur-Eure
Bonnières-sur-Seine
CHÂTEAU ST. GERMAIN-DE-LIVET
Évrecy
Bretteville-sur-Laize
St. Pierre-sur-Dives
Orbec
CHÂTEAU BEAUMESNIL
Beaumesnil
Livarot
Broglie
Thury-Harcourt
Potigny
La Barre-en-Ouche
Conches-en-Ouche
Vimoutiers
La Neuve-Lyre
Falaise
Ivry-la-Bataille
ST. MARTIN
St. André-de-l'Eure
CHÂTEAU D'ANET
Anet
Pont d'Ouilly
Trun
Damville
Nècy
Rugles
Breteuil
La Ferté-Frênel
Chambois
Gacé
Exmes
Nonancourt
Putanges-Pont-Ecrepin
Écouché
Argentan
L'Aigle
Verneuil-sur-Avre
Dreux
Ste. Gauburge-Ste. Colombe
Messei
Nonant-le-Pin
Le Merlerault
Brezolles
Laons
Le Boullay-Mivoye
Briouze
Moulins-la-Marche
Tremblay-le-Vicomte
Maintenon
La Ferté-Macé
Rânes
Mortrée
Courtomer
Tourouvre
Ste. Anne
Châteauneuf-en-Thymerais
La Ferté-Vidame
Carrouges
CHÂTEAU DE CARROUGES
Sées
Essay
Senonches
Bagnoles-de-l'Orne
Normandie Maine
Bazoches-sur-Hoëne
Mortagne-au-Perche
Longny-au-Perche
Digny
Dangers
Couterne
CATHÉDRALE DE CHARTRES
Couptrain
Le Mêle-sur-Sarthe
La Loupe
Mainvilliers
Pré-en-Pail
Perche
Rémalard
Courville
Luce
Alençon
Champrond-en-Gâtine
Javron
Thivars
St. Rémy-du-Val
Bellême
Villaines-la-Juhel
Mamers
Thiron-Gardais
Illiers-Combray
Nogent-le-Rotrou
La Hutte
St. Cosme-en-Vairais
Montainville
Fresnay-sur-Sarthe
Dangeul
Le Theil
Bais
Marolles-les-Braults
Brou
Beaumont-sur-Sarthe
Bonnétable
La Ferté-Bernard
Bonneval
Évron
Ballon
Authon-du-Perche
Sillé-le-Guillaume
Chapelle Royale
La Bazoche-Gouet
Ste. Suzanne
Conlie
Domfront-en-Champagne
Tuffé
Arrou
Parennes
Montmirail
CHÂTEAU DE CHÂTEAUDUN
Châteaudun
Normandie
Pays de Bray
Perche
Orne
Dives
Seine
Eure
Risle
Béthune

Abbeville
Doullens
Bapaume
Le Tréport
Mers-les-Bains
Eu
Gamaches
Le Translay
Oisemont
Blangy-sur-Bresle
Bouttencourt
Flixecourt
Airaines
Picquigny
Ailly-sur-Somme
Amiens
CATHÉDRALE DE AMIENS
Villers-Bocage
Albert
Corbie
Bray-sur-Somme
Villers-Bretonneux
Péronne
Hargicourt
Roisel
Longueau
Boves
St. Saufflieu
Moreuil
Rosières-en-Santerre
Chaulnes
Athies
Villers-Carbonnel
Vermand
Envermeu
Fresnoy-Folny
Senarpont
Hornoy-le-Bourg
Londinières
Les Grandes-Ventes
Aumale
Quevauvillers
Poix-de-Picardie
Conty
Essertaux
Ailly-sur-Noye
Bouchoir
Nesle
Ham
Neufchâtel-en-Bray
St-Martin-Osmonville
Gaillefontaine
Formerie
Feuquières
Grandvilliers
Crèvecœur-le-Grand
Bonneuil-les-Eaux
Breteuil
Montdidier
Roye
Flavy-le-Martel
Jussy
Guiscard
Tergnier
Chauny
Noyon
Lassigny
Buchy
Forges-les-Eaux
St. Samson-la-Poterie
Marseille en Beauvaisis
Songeons
Argueil
Crillon
Froissy
St. Just-en-Chaussée
Wavignies
Ferrières
Maignelay Montigny
Cuvilly
Ressons-sur-Matz
Ribécourt-Dreslincourt
Cuts
Carlepont
Blérancourt
La Feuille
Gournay-en-Bray
CATHÉDRALE ST. ÉTIENNE
Tillé
Beauvais
Lyons-la-Forêt
PARC SAINT PAUL
Bresles
Clermont
Estrées-St. Denis
CHÂTEAU DE COMPIÈGNE
Compiègne
Attichy
Vic-sur-Aisne
Épagny
Trosly-Breuil
Soissons
Pierrefonds
Lacroix-St. Ouen
Boos
Fleury-sur-Andelle
Ecouis
Sérifontaine
Auneuil
Étrépagny
Gisors
Chaumont-en-Vexin
Noailles
Mouy
Liancourt
Creil
Pont Ste. Maxence
Verberie
Gilocourt
Crépy-en-Valois
Villers-Cotterêts
CHÂTEAU GAILLARD
Les Andelys
Les Thilliers-en-Vexin
Méru
Ste. Geneviève
Neuilly-en-Thelle
Senlis
Chantilly
Boran-sur-Oise
CATHÉDRALE NOTRE-DAME SENLIS
PARC ASTERIX
MER DE SABLE
Ermenonville
Baron
Lévignen
La Ferté-Milon
Neuilly-St. Front
Gaillon
St. Clair-sur-Epte
Magny-en-Vexin
Marines
Chambly
Persan
Beaumont-sur-Oise
L'Isle-Adam
Luzarches
Nanteuil-le-Haudouin
Acy-en-Multien
Betz
Mareuil-sur-Ourcq
Belleau
Gasny
Vernon
GIVERNY
La Roche-Guyon
Vexin Français
Bonnières-sur-Seine
Mantes-la-Jolie
Meulan
Les Mureaux
Pontoise
Cergy
Taverny
Montmorency
Sarcelles
Dammartin-en-Goële
CHARLES DE GAULLE
St. Soupplets
Lizy-sur-Ourcq
Château-Thierry
Montreuil-aux-Lions
Charly
Pacy-sur-Eure
Mantes-la-Ville
Argenteuil
St. Denis
Claye-Souilly
Meaux
Trilport
Varreddes
MUSÉE DE LA GRANDE GUERRE
La Ferté-sous-Jouarre
Jouarre
St. André-de-l'Eure
Ivry-la-Bataille
ST. MARTIN
CHÂTEAU D'ANET
Anet
Septeuil
Maule
Poissy
St. Germain-en-Laye
Nanterre
Bobigny
Chelles
Montreuil
Lagny-sur-Marne
Esbly
Ponts-aux-Dames
Crécy-la-Chapelle
Viels Maisons
VERSAILLES
PARIS
DISNEYLAND PARIS & WALT DISNEY STUDIOS
Villeneuve-le-Comte
Rebais
Coulommiers
Houdan
Élancourt
Versailles
Vitry-sur-Seine
Créteil
Tournan-en-Brie
Pézarches
La Ferté-Gaucher
Dreux
Montfort-l'Amaury
Trappes
CHÂTEAU DE BRETEUIL
Palaiseau
Orsay
Villeneuve-St. Georges
ORLY
Fontenay-Trésigny
Vaudoy-en-Brie
Beton-Bazoches
Le Boullay-Mivoye
Nogent-le-Roi
Rambouillet
La Haute Vallée de Chevreuse
Montlhéry
Évry
Brie-Comte-Robert
Rozay-en-Brie
Jouy-le-Châtel
Tremblay-le-Vicomte
Maintenon
Épernon
St. Arnoult
Limours
Arpajon
Brétigny-sur-Orge
Corbeil-Essonnes
Guignes
Mormant
Nangis
Provins
Dangers
Gallardon
Ballancourt-sur-Essonne
Melun
Le Châtelet-en-Brie
Maison-Rouge
Donnemarie-Dontilly
CATHÉDRALE DE CHARTRES
Jouy
Ablis
Dourdan
Étréchy
La-Ferté-Alais
Dammarie-les-Lys
Forêt de Fontainbleau
Nogent
Mainvilliers
Chartres
Auneau
Étampes
CHÂTEAU DE COURANCES
Gâtinais
FONTAINBLEAU
Les Ormes-sur-Voulzie
Lucé
Voisé
Sours
Thivars
Milly-la-Forêt
Fontainebleau
Moret-sur-Loing
Montereau-Faut-Yonne
Bray-sur-Seine
Plaine
Allonnes
Ouarville
Maisse
Gâtinais Français
Avon
Monnerville
Méréville
Bourron-Marlotte
Villeneuve-la-Guyard
Montainville
Angerville
Sermaises
Malesherbes
La Chapelle-la-Reine
Villecerf
Voulx
Aqueduc de la Vanne
Voves
Charmont-en-Beauce
Nemours
Lorrez-le-Bocage
Pont-sur-Yonne
Janville
Puiseaux
Dollot
Picardie
Pays de Bray
Pays de France
Seine
Oise
Aisne
Somme
0 10 20 30 km

Solesmes
Aymeries
Avesnois
Le Cateau-Cambrésis
Landrecies
Avesnes-sur-Helpe
Solre-le-Château
Grandrieu
Rance
Philippeville
Cerfontaine
Villers-le-Gambon
Mariembourg
Doische
Givet
Beauraing
Houyet
Rochefort
Gouffre
Han-sur-Lesse
Wellin
Trélon
Chimay
Couvin
Macon
Baileux
Treignes
Vireux
Hargnies
Haut-Fays
Eurospace Center
Libin
St. Hubert
Freux
Catillon
Le Nouvion-en-Thiérache
Fourmies
Prémont
Bohain-en-Vermandois
La Capelle
Hirson
Signy-le-Petit
Rocroi
Revin
Fumay
Rienne
Gedinne
Bièvre
Paliseul
Recogne
Libramont
Bertrix
Neufchâteau
Herbeumont
Guise
Oise
Etréaupont
St. Michel
Maubert-Fontaine
Les Mazures
Monthermé
Ardennes
Thiérache
Origny-Ste Benoite
Vervins
Landouzy-le-Ville
Aubenton
Rimogne
Nouzonville
Gespunsart
Sugny
Corbion
Bouillon
Semois
Ribemont
Sains Richaumont
Rumigny
Rouvroy-sur-Audry
Liart
Vrigne-aux-Bois
St. Menges
Rossignol
Jamoigne
Marle
Brunehamel
Rozoy-sur-Serre
Signy-l'Abbaye
Charleville-Mézières
Sedan
Florenville
Crécy-sur-Serre
l'Espérance
Montcornet
Chaumont-Porcien
Flize
Douzy
Carignan
Meix-devant-Virton
Fère
Pierrepont
Dizy-le-Gros
Launois-sur-Vence
Poix-Terron
Mouzon
Chiers
Margut
Notre-Dame d'Avioth
Virton
Avioth
Crépy
St. Gobain
Laon
Athies-sous-Laon
Bucy-lès-Pierrepont
Serancourt
Novion-Porcien
Saulces Monclin
Chemery-sur-Bar
Raucourt-et-Flaba
Montmédy
Anizy-le-Château
Cathédrale Notre-Dame de Laon
Festieux
Sissonne
Sévigny
Château-Porcien
Novy-Chevrières
Tourteron
Beaumont-en-Argonne
Stenay
Lor
Rethel
Le Chesne
Tannay
Lanneuville-sur-Meuse
Chavignon
Corbeny
Asfeld
Attigny
Quatre-Champs
Marville
Vailly-sur-Aisne
Craonne
Tagnon
Neuflize
Neufchâtel-sur-Aisne
Juniville
Vouziers
Buzancy
Dun-sur-Meuse
Damvillers
Bourg-et-Comin
Braine
Bourgogne
Machault
Semide
Grandpré
Aisne
Bantheville
Hermonville
Fismes
Vesle
Jonchery-sur-Vesle
Witry-lès-Reims
Béthenville
Monthois
Consenvoye
Samogneux
Pontfaverger-Moronvillers
Courville
Reims
Beine-Nauroy
Séchault
Sommepy-Tahure
Varennes-en-Argonne
Montfaucon-d'Argonne
Côtes
Fère-en-Tardenois
Mourmelon-le-Grand
Souain
Ville-sur-Tourbe
Argonne
Verdun
Oulchy-le-Château
Pourcy
Montagne de Reims
Verzy
Livry-Louvercy
Suippes
Clermont-en-Argonne
Haudainville
Verneuil
Châtillon-sur-Marne
Louvois
Ste. Ménehould
Dugny-sur-Meuse
Trélou-sur-Marne
Dormans
Port-à-Binson
Marne
Ay
Condé-sur-Marne
La Cheppe
Somme-Tourbe
Épernay
Châlons-en-Champagne
Tilloy Bellay
Dommartin
Souilly
Condé-en-Brie
Igny-Comblizy
St. Martin-d'Ablois
Chouilly
Jâlons
Fagnières
Cathédrale St. Etienne
Givry-en-Argonne
Triaucourt-en-Argonne
Issoncourt
Mareuil-en-Brie
Avize
Le Mesnil-sur-Oger
Rembercourt-aux-Pots
Chaumont-sur-Aire
Orbais
Montmort-Lucy
Vertus
Thibie
Marson
Coupéville
Sommeilles
Pierrefitte-sur-Aire
Vauchamps
Montmirail
Champaubert
Etoges
Bergères-lès-Vertus
Villeseneux
Soudron
Pogny
Vanault-les-Dames
Possesse
Nettancourt
Laheycourt
Rumont
Sampigny
La Chaussée-sur-Marne
Revigny-sur-Ornain
Le Gault-Soigny
Bannes
Vatry
Fontaine
Parany-sur-Saulx
Fains-V4el
Bar-le-Duc
Fère-Champenoise
Sézanne
Connantre
Sommesous
Gourgançon
Coole
Blacy
Vitry-le-François
Sermaize-les-Bains
St. Aubin-sur-Aire
Esternay
Barbonne-Fayel
Sompuis
Thiéblemont-Farémont
Brillon-en-Barrois
Ligny-en-Barrois
Villiers-St. Georges
Pleurs
Mailly-le-Camp
Ancerville
Stainville
St. Dizier
St. Remy-en-Bouzemont
Villenauxe-la-Grande
Herbisse
Éclaron
Lac du Der Chantecoq
Morley
Houdelaincourt
Anglure
Plancy-l'Abbaye
Lhuître
Margerie-Hancourt
Giffaumont-Champaubert
Marcilly-sur-Seine
Aube
Vinets
Rachecourt-sur-Marne
Chevillon
Romilly-sur-Seine
Arcis-sur-Aube
Ramerupt
Wassy
Thonnance-les-Joinville
Méry-sur-Seine
Chaudrey
Chavanges
Montier-en-Der
Pancey
Châtres
Voué
Joinville
Poissons
Germay
St. Martin-de-Bossenay
Lesmont
Brienne-le-Château
Doulevant-le-Château
Dommartin-le-Franc
Savières
Marigny-le-Châtel
Feuges
Piney
Lac du Temple
Soulaines-Dhuys
Doulaincourt-Saucourt
Bercenay-le-Hayer
Marcilly-le-Hayer
La Chapelle-St. Luc
Creney
Forêt d'Orient
Thorigny-sur-Oreuse
Ste. Savine
Géraudot
Lac d'Orient
Nigloland
Dolancourt
Vignory
St. Blin
Estissac
Troyes
Lusigny-sur-Barse
Andelot Blanchville
Villemaur-sur-Vanne
Bar-sur-Aube
Colombey-les-deux-Églises
Briaucourt
Villeneuve-l'Archevêque
Aix-en-Othe
Vauchassis
Bouchères
Vendeuvre-sur-Barse
Bayel
Bologne
Burdons

La Roche-en-Ardenne
Houffalize
Troisvierges
Prüm
Daun
Cochem
Tenneville
Bertogne
St. Hubert
Bastogne
Clervaux
Hosingen
Wiltz
Deutsch-Luxemburg (Südeifel)
Neuerburg
Bitburg
Kyllburg
Wittlich
Manderscheid
Hontheim
Libin
Libramont
Recogne
Paliseul
Bertrix
Neufchâteau
Bouillon
Herbeumont
Vaux-sur-Sure
Fauvillers
Martelange
Léglise
Esch-sur-Sûre
Vianden
Diekirch
Ettelbruck
Mettendorf
Speicher
Irrel
Echternach
Schweich
Ehrang
Trier
Bernkastel-Kues
Traben-Trarbach
Neumagen
Thalfang
Morbach
LUXEMBOURG
Redange
Mersch
Larochette
Rossignol
Rulles
Habay
Jamoigne
Florenville
Tintigny
Etalle
Arlon
Hobscheid
Saeul
Useldange
Junglingster
Biwer
Grevenmacher
Konz
Carignan
Meix-devant-Virton
St. Leger
Notre-Dame de Avioth
Virton
Aubange
Messancy
Mamer
Luxembourg
Saarburg
Schillingen
Zerf
Hermeskeil
Birkenfeld
Nohfelden
Montmédy
Avioth
Musson
Pétange
Differdange
Longwy
Dalheim
Bettembourg
Remich
Mondorf-les-Bains
Esch-sur-Alzette
Audun-le-Tiche
Villerupt
Longuyon
Orscholz
Mettlach
Losheim
Wadern
Saar-Hunsrück
Primstal
Tholey
Marville
Pierrepont
Aumetz
Hettange-Grande
Sierck-les-Bains
Merzig
Lebach
Schmelz
Dun-sur-Meuse
Damvillers
Mangiennes
Spincourt
Audun-le-Roman
Fontoy
Thionville
Waldwisse
Dillingen
Neunkirchen
Saarlouis
Sulzbach
Consenvoye
Azannes-et-Soumazannes
Samogneux
Bouligny
Hayange
Metzervisse
Bouzonville
Püttlingen
Völklingen
Saarbrücken
Montfaucon-d'Argonne
Côtes de Meuse
Etain
Briey
Rombas
Walygator Parc
Hagondange
Avril
Teterchen
Völkinger Hütte
Ludweiler Warndt
Forbach
Verdun
Jarny
Jœuf
Woippy
Boulay-Moselle
Creutzwald
Freyming-Merlebach
Haudainville
Dugny-sur-Meuse
Fresnes-en-Woevre
Dieue-sur-Meuse
Mars-la-Tours
Cathédrale St. Etienne
Metz
Ars-sur-Moselle
Montigny-lès-Metz
Courcelles-Chaussy
Longeville-lès-St. Avold
St. Avold
Diebling
Sarreguemines
Souilly
Chambley
St. Benoit-en-Woevre
Faulquemont
Rémilly
Puttelange-aux-Lacs
Hambach
Herbitzheim
Vigneulles-lès-Hattonchâtel
Lacroix-sur-Meuse
Lac de Madine
Heudicourt-sous-les-Côtes
Pagny-sur-Moselle
Regniéville
Grostenquin
Sarralbe
Issoncourt
Chaumont-sur-Aire
St. Mihiel
Lorraine
Pont-à-Mousson
Solgne
Morhange
Bénestroff
Sarre-Union
Pierrefitte-sur-Aire
Flirey
Nomeny
Delme
Mittersheim
Fénétrange
Rumont
Sampigny
Apremont-la-Forêt
Rambucourt
Dieulouard
Berthelming
Gironville-sous-les-Côtes
Marbach
Château-Salins
Dieuze
Bar-le-Duc
Lérouville
Commercy
Pompey
Custines
Moncel-sur-Seille
Moyenvic
Lixheim
St. Aubin-sur-Aire
Frouard
Sarrebourg
Arrancourt
Ligny-en-Barrois
Stainville
Void-Vacon
Foug
St. Etienne
Toul
Nancy
Canal de la Marne au Rhin
Maizières-lès-Vic
Héming
Neuves-Maisons
St. Nicolas-de-Port
Einville-au-Jard
Moussey
Abreschviller
Vaucouleurs
Pont-St. Vincent
Dombasle-sur-Meurthe
Lunéville
Morley
Houdelaincourt
Maxey-sur-Vaise
Colombey-les-Belles
Crépey
Flavigny-sur-Moselle
Blainville-sur-l'Eau
Blâmont
Cirey-sur-Vezouze
Gondrecourt-le-Château
Autreville
Vezelise
Haroué
Bayon
Gerbéviller
Badonviller
Pancey
Poissons
Domrémy-la-Pucelle
Magnieres
Schirmeck
Germay
Vennezey
Baccarat
Raon-l'Etape
Senones
Trampot
Neufchâteau
Charmes
Rambervillers
Moyenmoutier
Doulaincourt-Saucourt
Liffol-le-Grand
Gironcourt-sur-Vraine
Châtel-sur-Moselle
Nomexy
Saales
St. Blin
Châtenois
St. Dié
Andelot Blanchville
Mirecourt
Thaon-les-Vosges
Dompaire
Brouvelieures
Anould
Fraize
Ste. Marie-aux-Mines
Bulgnéville
Bruyères
Deutsch-Luxemburg
Lorraine
0 10 20 30 km

Frankfurt
Offenbach
Wiesbaden
Mainz
Darmstadt
Aschaffenburg
Worms
Ludwigshafen
Mannheim
Heidelberg
Kaiserslautern
Neustadt
Speyer
Heilbronn
Karlsruhe
Pforzheim
Stuttgart
Strasbourg
Offenburg
Baden-Baden
Rastatt
Tübingen
Reutlingen
Freudenstadt
Königstein
Bad Soden
Hofheim
Kelsterbach
Flörsheim
Rüsselsheim
Neu-Isenburg
Dietzenbach
Dreieich
Langen
Rödermark
Mörfelden
Gross Gerau
Dieburg
Babenhausen
Grosse Gerau
Griesheim
Riedstadt
Pfungstadt
Seeheim-Jugenheim
Bensheim
Heppenheim
Lampertheim
Viernheim
Weinheim
Hanau
Maintal
Alzenau
Seligenstadt
Mombris
Laufach
Schöllkrippen
Goldbach
Hösbach
Sulzbach
Grossostheim
Gross Umstadt
Obernburg
Elsenfeld
Eschau
Klingenberg
Wörth
Höchst i. Odenw.
Reinheim
Brensbach
Bad König
Michelstadt
Erbach
Reichelsheim
Fürth
Wald-Michelbach
Beerfelden
Miltenberg
Amorbach
Walldürn
Mudau
Eberbach
Hirschhorn
Neckargemünd
Mosbach
Möckmühl
Obrigheim
Meckesheim
Sinsheim
Bad Rappenau
Gundelsheim
Bad Friedrichshall
Neckarsulm
Eppingen
Schwaigern
Brackenheim
Lauffen
Bönnigheim
Besigheim
Bietigheim-Bissingen
Ludwigsburg
Markgröningen
Ditzingen
Waiblingen
Leonberg
Weil der Stadt
Sindelfingen
Böblingen
Filderstadt
Metzingen
Pfullingen
Gomaringen
Mössingen
Hechingen
Haigerloch
Rottenburg
Herrenberg
Nagold
Wildberg
Calw
Bad Liebenzell
Wildbad
Bad Herrenalb
Neuenbürg
Ettlingen
Durlach
Bretten
Bruchsal
Weingarten
Mühlacker
Vaihingen
Maulbronn
Bad Schönborn
Wiesloch
Leimen
Hockenheim
Schwetzingen
Waghäusel
Germersheim
Linkenheim
Philippsburg
Wörth
Kandel
Hagenbach
Landau
Bellheim
Rülzheim
Herxheim
Edenkoben
Edesheim
Hassloch
Bad Dürkheim
Grünstadt
Frankenthal
Eisenberg
Alzey
Osthofen
Gernsheim
Biblis
Bürstadt
Kirchheimbolanden
Rockenhausen
Otterberg
Enkenbach
Landstuhl
Ramstein-Meisenbach
Homburg
Zweibrücken
Pirmasens
Rodalben
Waldfischbach-Burgalben
Annweiler
Dahn
Bad Bergzabern
Wissembourg
Bitche
Haguenau
Bischwiller
Brumath
Hochfelden
Saverne
Schiltigheim
Bischheim
Kehl
Illkirch-Graffenstaden
Molsheim
Obernai
Erstein
Barr
Benfeld
Sélestat
Lahr
Ettenheim
Herbolzheim
Elzach
Haslach
Hausach
Hornberg
Wolfach
Alpirsbach
Schramberg
Oberndorf
Dornhan
Sulz
Horb am Neckar
Balingen
Albstadt
Schömberg
Rosenfeld
Burladingen
Tailfingen
Oberkirch
Achern
Bühl
Sinzheim
Bühlertal
Gaggenau
Gernsbach
Forbach
Baiersbronn
Oppenau
Gengenbach
Zell
Friesenheim
Renchen
Rheinau
Bingen
Rüdesheim
Geisenheim
Eltville
Ingelheim
Nieder-Olm
Nierstein
Oppenheim
Bad Kreuznach
Sobernheim
Kirn
Simmern
Kirchberg
Bacharach
Oberwesel
St. Goar
St. Goarshausen
Nastätten
Bad Schwalbach
Taunusstein
Kastellaun
Meisenheim
Lauterecken
Kusel
Baumholder
Wolfstein
Pfälzer Wald
Vosges du Nord
Schwarzwald
Odenwald
Bergstrasse
Neckartal-Odenwald
Stromberg-Heuchelberg
Schönbuch
Baden - Württemberg
Nahe
Rhein
Main
Neckar

1
2
3
4°
3°
A
B
48°
47°
Cork
Rosslare
Plymouth
Côte de Granit Rose
Sillon de Talbert
Île de Bréhat
Pte. de l'Arcouest
Ploubazlanec
Plougrescant
Ploumanach
Perros-Guirec
Trégastel-Plage
Trébeurden
Pleumeur-Bodou
Tréguier
Lézardrieux
Paimpol
Pleubian
Lannion
La Roche Derrien
LA ROCHE JAGU
Plouézec
Île de Batz
Roscoff
St. Pol-de-Léon
Primel-Trégastel
Plougasnou
Locquirec
St. Efflam
St. Michel-en-Grève
Plestin-les-Grèves
Pontrieux
Plouha
Brignogan-Plage
Kerlouan
Cléder
Plouescat
Carantec
Lanmeur
Plouaret
Bégard
Lanvollon
Plouguerneau
NOTRE DAME
Lesneven
Lannilis
Portsall
Porspoder
Le Folgoet
Plouzévédé
CHÂTEAU DE KERJEAN
St. Thégonnec
Taulé
Morlaix
Plouigneau
Louargat
Guingamp
Binic
Châtelaudren
Ploudalmézeau
Plabennec
Landivisiau
Plougonven
Belle-Isle-en-Terre
Plouagat
St. Brieuc
Lanildut
St. Renan
Plouarzel
Brest
Guipavas
Landerneau
Ploudiry
Pleyber-Christ
Lannéanou
Plougonver
Mousteru
Bourbriac
Le Conquet
Pte. de St. Mathieu
Plougastel-Daoulas
Daoulas
Sizun
St. Sauveur
Mts. d'Arrée
Callac
Quintin
Kérien
Camaret-sur-Mer
TOUR VAUBAN
Pte. de Penhir
Landévennec
Le Faou
Armorique
Huelgoat
Poullaouen
St. Nicolas-du-Pélem
Corlay
Uzel
Morgat
Crozon
Brasparts
Pont-de-Buis-lès-Quimerch
Pleyben
Carhaix-Plouguer
Maël-Carhaix
Plounévez-Quintin
Rostrenen
Mer d'Iroise
Châteaulin
Spézet
Glomel
Gouarec
Mur-de-Bretagne
Baie de Douarnenez
Douarnenez
Châteauneuf-du-Faou
Aulne
Mts. Noires
ST. RONAN
Locronan
Gourin
Roudouallec
Plouray
Cléguérec
Plogoff
Pte. du Raz
Pont-Croix
Audierne
Briec
Coray
Guiscriff
Le Faouët
Guémené-sur-Scorff
Pontivy
Noyal-Pontivy
Plouhinec
Landudec
Quimper
Oder
Scaër
Kernascléden
Plozévet
Plogastel St. Germain
Rosporden
Bannalec
Bubry
Pluméliau
Scorff
Blavet
Plonéour-Lanvern
Fouesnant
CHÂTEAU DE KRIOLET
Concarneau
Arzano
Quimperlé
Plouay
Pont-l'Abbé
Bénodet
Trégunc
Pont-Aven
Pont Scorff
Baud
Locminé
St. Guénolé
Penmarch
Loctudy
Névez
Riec-sur-Bélon
Moëlan-sur-Mer
Languidic
Camors
Pte. de Penmarch
Lesconil
Guilvinec
Port Manech
Clohars-Carnoët
Hennebont
Lanester
Landévant
Pluvigner
Le Pouldu
Lorient
Îles de Glénan
Ploemeur
Ste. Anne-d'Auray
Larmor-Plage
Port Louis
Auray
Vannes
Groix
Île de Groix
Belz
Carnac
La Trinité
Locmariaquer
Port-Navalo
Presqu'île de Quiberon
Baie de Quiberon
St. Pierre-Quiberon
St. Gildas-de-Rhuys
Côte Sauvage
Quiberon
Île de Houat
Sauzon
Le Palais
Bangor
Locmaria
Belle-Île
Île de Hoëdic
Trieux
0
10
20
30 km
E50
E60
138
129

Golfe de St-Malo
Îles Chausey
Portsmouth
Côte d'Émeraude
Pte. du Grouin
Baie du Mont-St. Michel
Cap Fréhel
Rothéneuf
St. Malo
Paramé
Cancale
Dinard
St. Servan-sur-Mer
Sables-d'Or-les-Pins
St. Cast-le-Guildo
St. Lunaire
Erquy
St. Briac-sur-Mer
Le Vivier-sur-Mer
Le Mont-St. Michel
Pontaubault
Granville
St. Pair-sur-Mer
Jullouville
Carolles
Bréhal
Gavray
Percy
La Haye-Pesnel
Sartilly
Villedieu-les-Poêles
St. Sever-Calvados
Pont Farcy
Vire
Brécey
Avranches
Ducey
Juvigny-le-Tertre
Mortain
Sourdeval
St. Hilaire-du-Harcouët
Barenton
Le Teilleul
Passais
Gorron
Ambrières-les-Vallées
St. Broladre
Pontorson
St. James
Louvigné-du-Désert
Landivy
Levaré
Matignon
Le Val-André
Les Rosaires
Pléneuf-Val-André
St. Jacut-de-la-Mer
Ploubalay
Châteauneuf-d'Ille-et-Vilaine
Dol-de-Bretagne
Pleine-Fougères
Antrain
Plérin
Langueux
Lamballe
Plancoët
Dinan
Château du Combourg
Combourg
St. Brice-en-Coglès
Fougères
Romagné
Jugon-les-Lacs
Evran
Moncontour
Yvignac
Broons
Tinténiac
Sens-de-Bretagne
Ernée
St. Georges-Buttavent
Plouguenast
Collinée
Caulnes
Bécherel
Parc de Caradeuc
Hédé
St. Aubin-d'Aubigné
St. Aubin-du-Cormier
Dompierre-du-Chemin
Chailland
Loudéac
Plémet
Merdrignac
St. Méen-le-Grand
Montauban-de-Bretagne
Liffré
Taillis
St. M'Hervé
Martigné-sur-Mayenne
Ménéac
La Trinité-Porhoët
La Chèze
Gael
Bédée
St. Gilles
Rennes
Cesson-Sévigné
Châteaubourg
Vitré
Le Bourgneuf-la-Forêt
Louverné
Rohan
Mauron
Montfort-sur-Meu
Mordelles
Châteaugiron
Argentré-du-Plessis
La Gravelle
St. Berthevin
Paimpont
St. Jacques-de-la-Lande
Bruz
Piré-sur-Seiche
St. Poix
Cossé-le-Vivien
Josselin
Plélan-le-Grand
Maxent
Guichen
Corps Nuds
Janzé
Retiers
La Guerche-de-Bretagne
Quelaines-St-Gault
Ploërmel
Guer
Le Sel-de-Bretagne
Craon
St. Jean-Brévelay
Monteneuf
Maure-de-Bretagne
Messac
Bain-de-Bretagne
Martigné-Ferchaud
St. Aignan-sur-Roë
Sérent
Malestroit
Carentoir
Pipriac
Teillay
Rougé
Renazé
Elven
La Gacilly
Grand-Fougeray
Châteaubriant
Pouancé
St. Quentin-les-Anges
Rochefort-en-Terre
Questembert
Redon
Besle
Derval
Segré
St. Julien-de-Vouvantes
La Chapelle-Glain
Vern-d'Anjou
Allaire
St. Nicolas-de-Redon
Guémené-Penfao
Moisdon-la-Rivière
Noyalo
Muzillac
Nozay
La Meilleraye-de-Bretagne
St. Mars-la-Jaille
Candé
Sarzeau
Damgan
La Roche-Bernard
Pénestin
Plessé
Riallé
Le Louroux-Béconnais
Bécon-les-Granits
Château de Serrant
Herbignac
Missillac
St. Gildas-des-Bois
Blain
Nort-sur-Erdre
Joué-sur-Erdre
Les Touches
Pontchâteau
Bouvron
Héric
Ligné
Ingrandes
Brière
St. Lyphard
St. Joachim
Piriac-sur-Mer
Ancenis
Varades
Montjean-sur-Loire
Hœdic
La Turballe
Montoir-de-Bretagne
Trignac
Donges
Savenay
Le Temple-de-Bretagne
La Chapelle-sur-Erdre
Oudon
Liré
St. Florent-le-Vieil
Guérande
La Baule-Escoublac
Le Croisic
Pte. du Croisic
St. Nazaire
Paimboeuf
Orvault
Carquefou
Champtoceaux
St. Laurent-des-Autels
St. Pierre Montlimart
Montrevault
Le Pouliguen
Pornichet
St. Etienne-de-Montluc
Couëron
St. Herblain
Bouguenais
Nantes
Le Loroux-Bottereau
Beaupréau
Gesté
Jallais
St. Brévin-les-Pins
St. Père-en-Retz
Le Pellerin
Rezé
Vertou
Vallet
Le May-sur-Èvre
St. Michel-Chef-Chef
Côte d'Amour
Bouaye
Pont St. Martin
Aigrefeuille-sur-Maine
Clisson
Château de Clisson
Montfaucon
Cholet
Pte. de St. Gildas
Préfailles
Pornic
Arthon-en-Retz
La Bernerie-en-Retz
Lac de Grand-Lieu
St. Philbert-de-Grand-Lieu
Torfou
Baie de Bourgneuf
Bourgneuf-en-Retz
Machecoul
Bruffière
Mortagne-sur-Sèvre
St. Laurent-sur-Sèvre
Noirmoutier-en-l'Ile
La Guérinière
Barbâtre
Île de
Bouin
Beauvoir-
Rocheservière
Vieillevigne
Montaigu
La Gaubretière
Loire
Vilaine
Rance
Erdre
Sélune
Couesnon
Oust
Arz
Claie
Canal de Nantes à Brest
E401
E50
E03
E60
E62
A84
A11
A83
A87
8
16
22

St. Georges Buttavent
Mayenne
Bais
Fresnay-sur-Sarthe
Mamers
St. Cosme-en-Vairais
Nogent-le-Rotrou
Chailland
Dangeul
Marolles-les-Braults
Le Theil
Martigné-sur-Mayenne
Évron
Sillé-le-Guillaume
Beaumont-sur-Sarthe
Ballon
Bonnétable
La Ferté-Bernard
Authon-du-Perche
La Bazoche-Gouet
Louverné
Montsûrs
Conlie
Domfront-en-Champagne
Tuffé
Argentré
Ste. Suzanne
Parennes
La Gravelle
St. Berthevin
Laval
Vaiges
St. Denis d'Orques
Montmirail
Le Mans
Connerré
Montfort-le-Gesnois
Vibraye
Meslay-du-Maine
Brûlon
Loué
Allonnes
Arnage
Circuit Automobile
Parigné-l'Évêque
Bouloire
Mondoubleau
Cossé-le-Vivien
Quelaines-St-Gault
Grez-en-Bouère
Sablé-sur-Sarthe
Noyen-sur-Sarthe
La Suze-sur-Sarthe
Le Grand-Lucé
St. Calais
Savigny-sur-Braye
Craon
Château-Gontier
Bierné
Malicorne-sur-Sarthe
Cérans Foulletourte
Écommoy
Bessé-sur-Braye
Renazé
St. Quentin-les-Anges
Miré
Pontvallain
Mayet
Ruillé-sur-le-Loir
Trôo
Habitations Troglodytiques
Segré
Châteauneuf-sur-Sarthe
Daumeray
La Flèche
Château du Lude
Château-du-Loir
La Chartre-sur-le-Loir
Montoire-sur-le-Loir
St. Gilles
Champigné
Durtal
Le Lude
Vaas
Le Lion-d'Angers
Vern-d'Anjou
Tiercé
Feneu
Seiches-sur-le-Loir
Baugé
Neuvy-le-Roi
La Ferrière
Candé
La Pouëze
Jarzé
Château-la-Vallière
Beaumont-la-Ronce
Avrillé
Angers
Bécon-les-Granits
Château de Serrant
Château de Pignerolles
Noyant
Neuillé-Pont-Pierre
Monnaie
Trélazé
Beaufort-en-Vallée
Mouliherne
Les Ponts-de-Cé
St. Georges-sur-Loire
Varades
Ingrandes
La Ménitré
Rillé
Cléré-les-Pins
St. Cyr-sur-Loire
Tours
Vouvray
Montjean-sur-Loire
Les Rosiers
Château de Brissac
Brissac-Quincé
Longué-Jumelles
Vernantes
Gizeux
Cinq-Mars-la-Pile
Montlouis-sur-Loire
St. Florent-le-Vieil
Chalonnes-sur-Loire
Gennes
Amphithéâtre
Vivy
Allonnes
Langeais
Bourgueil
Joué-lès-Tours
Montbazon
St. Pierre Montlimart
Thouarcé
Saumur
Azay-le-Rideau
Esvres
Cormery
Bléré
Martigné-Briand
Doué-la-Fontaine
Souzay-Champigny
Montsoreau
Ussé
Chemillé
Jallais
Le May-sur-Èvre
Fontevrault-l'Abbaye
Chinon
Loire Anjou Touraine
Vihiers
Vezins
Montreuil-Bellay
L'Abbaye Royal de Fontevraud
L'Île-Bouchard
Ste. Maure-de-Touraine
Château de Loches
Manthelan
Cholet
Nuaillé
Champigny-sur-Veude
Les Trois Moûtiers
Maulévrier
Loudun
Richelieu
Argenton-Château
Thouars
La Celle-St. Avant
Ligueil
St. Laurent-sur-Sèvre
Les Aubiers
Monts-sur-Guesnes
Descartes
Château du Grand Pressigny
Dangé-St. Romain
Le Grand-Pressigny
Mauléon
Puy du Fou
St. Jouin-de-Marnes
Orches
St. Varent
Ingrandes
Preuilly-sur-Claise
St. Michel-Mont-Mercure
Cerizay
Bressuire
Airvault
Châtellerault
Pouzauges
Chiché
Lencloître
La Roche-Posay
Mirebeau
Pleumartin
Chapelle-St. Laurent
Naintré
Thénezay
Mouilleron en-Pareds
Moncoutant
Futuroscope
Bonneuil-Matours
Angles sur l'Anglin
La Châtaigneraie
Neuville-de-Poitou
St. Georges-lès-Baillargeaux
L'Absie
Parthenay
Ayron
La Ferrière-en-Parthenay
Vouillé
La Caillère
Secondigny
Poitiers
Église de Saint-Savin
Hermine
Chauvigny
St. Savin
St. Julien-l'Ars
Vausseroux
Mazières-en-Gâtine
Fontenay-le-Comte
Coulonges-sur-l'Autize
St. Hilaire-des-Loges
Champdeniers-St. Denis
Fleuré
La Trimo
Chaillé-les-Marais
St. Maixent-l'École
Rouillé
Lusignan
Vivonne
Lhommaizé
Oulmes
Maillezais
Benet
Échiré
La Crèche
La Mothe-St. Héray
Gençay
Verrières
Lussac-les-Châteaux
Marais Poitevin
Niort
Bouressé
Montmo
Mayenne
Maine
Anjou
Touraine
Hauteurs de Gâtine
Sarthe
Loir
Loire
Vègre
Thouet
Layon
Vendée
Clain
Indre
Creuse
Braye
Huisne
E402
E50
A81
E501
A11
A28
E502
A85
E60
A87
E62
E05
A10
A83
E5
15
9
22
23

Gardais
Illiers-Combray
Allonnes
Ouarville
Monnerville
Méréville
Bourron-Marlotte
Ury
Angerville
Sermaises
Malesherbes
La Chapelle-la-Reine
Nemours
Lorrez-le-Bocage
Montainville
Voves
Ymonville
Charmont-en-Beauce
Puiseaux
Brou
Bonneval
Allaines
Janville
Toury
Souppes-sur-Loing
Chéroy
St. Valérien
Orgères-en-Beauce
Pithiviers
Bazoches-les-Gallerandes
Beaumont-du-Gâtinais
Château-Landon
Chapelle Royale
Cormainville
Ascoux
Ferrières
Arrou
CHÂTEAU DE CHÂTEAUDUN
Châteaudun
Artenay
Chilleurs-aux-Bois
Beaune-la-Rolande
Châlette-sur-Loing
Courtalain
Droué
Cloyes-sur-le-Loir
Patay
Neuville-aux-Bois
Chevilly
Pannes
Montargis
Courtenay
St. Péravy-la-Colombe
Fleury-les-Aubrais
Loury
Bellegarde
Ladon
Douchy
La Ferté Villeneuil
Orléans
St. Jean-de-Braye
Fay-aux-Loges
Canal d'Orléans
Châteaurenard
Morée
Fréteval
Ouzouer-le-Marché
Olivet
Lorris
Nogent-sur-Vernisson
ARBORETUM NATIONAL
Loir
Oucques
Marchenoir
CHÂTEAU DE BEAUGENCY
Meung-sur-Loire
Cléry-St. André
Sandillon
Jargeau
Châteauneuf-sur-Loire
Les Bordes
Les Bézards
Châtillon-Coligny
St. Martin-sur-Ouanne
Champignelles
Vendôme
Villetrun
Villeromain
Beaugency
Jouy-le-Potier
Tigy
Sully-sur-Loire
Ouzouer-sur-Loire
Rogny-les-7-Écluses
Pontijou
La Ferté-St. Aubin
CHÂTEAU DE SULLY-SUR-LOIRE
La Bussière
Bléneau
St. Amand-Longpré
Mer
La Ferté-St.Cyr
Isdes
Gien
St. Fargeau
Blois
MUSÉE ADRIEN THIBAULT
Chambord
CHÂTEAU DE CHAMBORD
Cosson
Lamotte-Beuvron
Cerdon
CHÂTEAU DE GIEN
Briare
Lavau
Herbault
Vineuil
Neung-sur-Beuvron
Brinon-sur-Sauldre
Auty-le-Châtel
Châtillon-sur-Loire
Bonny-sur-Loire
Chouzy-sur-Cisse
Chailles
CHÂTEAU DE BEAUREGARD
Bracieux
Nouan-le-Fuzelier
Argent-sur-Sauldre
Aubigny-sur-Nère
Beaulieu
Beuvron
Onzain
Cour-Cheverny
CHÂTEAU DE TROUSSAY
Chaumont-sur-Loire
CHÂTEAU FOUGÈRES-SUR-BIÈVRE
Souesmes
Léré
Myennes
Cosne-Cours-sur-Loire
CHÂTEAU D'AMBOISE
Amboise
Contres
Mur-de-Sologne
Millançay
Villegenon
Vailly-sur Sauldre
Salbris
Selles-St.-Denis
Pontlevoy
Chenonceaux
Montrichard
Chémery
Romorantin-Lanthenay
La Ferté-Imbault
Presly
Nançay
La Chapelle-d'Angillon
Sancerre
Neuvy-sur-Barangeon
Henrichemont
Pouilly-sur-Loire
Selles-sur-Cher
Noyers-sur-Cher
Villefranche-sur-Cher
St. Aignan
Chabris
Vierzon
Vinon
Orbigny
Allogny
Menetou-Salon
Vignoux-sur-Barangeon
St. Martin-d'Auxigny
Les Aix-d'Angillon
Sancergues
La Charité-sur-Loire
CHÂTEAU DE VALENÇAY
Valençay
Genillé
Montrésor
Luçay-le-Mâle
Graçay
Massay
Quincy
Mehun-sur-Yèvre
St. Germain-du Puy
Brécy
Nouans-les-Fontaines
Écueillé
Lury-sur-Arnon
Reuilly
Bourges
CATHÉDRALE DE BOURGES
Baugy
Avord
Vatan
Mornay-Berry
Villedômain
Fourchambault
Châtillon-sur-Indre
Pellevoisin
Levroux
Issoudun
Chârost
St. Florent-sur-Cher
Nérondes
St. Flovier
Levet
Canal de Berry
La Guerche-sur-l'Aubois
Indre
Buzançais
Villedieu-sur-Indre
Châteauneuf-sur-Cher
Dun-sur-Auron
Blet
CHÂTEAU D'AZAY-LE-FERRON
Mézières-en-Brenne
Déols
Mareuil-sur-Arnon
Sancoins
Châteauroux
Vendœuvres
Pruniers
Bruère-Allichamps
St. Amand-Montrond
Lurcy-Lévis
Claise
Ardentes
St. Août
Lignières
Charenton-du-Cher
Bessais-le-Fromental
Méobecq
Mignè
Velles
Couleuvre
Brenne
Le Châtelet
Cérilly
Urçay
Meaulne
St. Gaultier
Bouesse
Neuvy-St. Sépulchre
Bourbon-l'Archambault
La Châtre
Saulzais-le-Potier
Châteaumeillant
Argenton-sur-Creuse
Cluis
Culan
Ygrande
Bélâbre
Creuse
Gargilesse-Dampierre
Orsennes
Hérisson
Anglin
St. Benoît-du-Sault
Ste. Sévère-sur-Indre
Cosne-d'Allier
Éguzon-Chantôme
Aigurande
Préveranges
Villefranche-d'Allier
La Chapelaude
Le Montet
Tilly
Lussac-les-Églises
St. Sulpice-les-Feuilles
Dun-le-Palestel
CHÂTEAU DE CROZANT
Boussac
Treignat
Domérat
Quinssaines
Montluçon
Doyet
Bezenet
Beauce
Orléanais
Sologne
Berry
Bourbonnais
Loire
Cher
Arnon
0 10 20 30 km

Villeneuve-la-Guyard
169
Bercenay-le-Hayer
Marcilly-le-Hayer
La Chapelle-St. Luc
Ste. Savine
Troyes
Forêt d'Orient
Géraudot
Lusigny-sur-Barse
Dolancourt
Bar-sur-Aube
Villecerf
Voulx
Aqueduc de la Vanne
Thorigny-sur-Oreuse
Estissac
Villemaur-sur-Vanne
Lorrez-le-Bocage
Pont-sur-Yonne
Soucy
Villeneuve-l'Archevêque
Aix-en-Othe
Vauchassis
Vendeuvre-sur-Barse
Chéroy
Dollot
Sens
St. Valérien
Rosoy
Cerisiers
St. Mards-en-Othe
Bouilly
Fouchères
Bar-sur-Seine
Eguilly-sous-Bois
Ferrières
Villeneuve-sur-Yonne
Dixmont
Arces-Dilo
Forêt d'Othe
Chailley
Auxon
Landreville
Châlette-sur-Loing
Montargis
Courtenay
St. Julien-du-Sault
Joigny
Brienon-sur-Armançon
Migennes
Neuvy-Sautour
St. Florentin
Ervy-le-Châtel
Chessy-lès-Pres
Chaource
Essoyes
Gyé-sur-Seine
Douchy
Châteaurenard
Sépeaux
Bassou
Pontigny
Seignelay
Flogny-la-Chapelle
Ligny-le-Châtel
Armançon
Les Riceys
Mussy-sur-Seine
Channes
Charny
Arboretum National
Appoigny
Moneteau
Auxerre
Aillant-sur-Tholon
Fleury
Tonnerre
Villon
Châtillon-sur-Seine
Châtillon-Coligny
St. Martin-sur-Ouanne
Villiers-St. Benoit
Champignelles
Chablis
Lézinnes
Ancy-le-Franc
Château Ancy-le-Franc
Laignes
Pourrain
St. Bris-le-Vineux
Lichères-près-Aigremont
Rogny-les-7-Ecluses
Champs-sur-Yonne
Coulmier-le-Sec
Aisey-sur-Seine
La Bussière
Bléneau
Mézilles
Toucy
219
Nuits
Aisy-sur-Armançon
Briare
St. Fargeau
Collines de la Puisaye
Coulanges-la-Vineuse
Vermenton
Nitry
Noyers
Ouanne
Courson-les-Carrières
Joux-la-Ville
Abbaye de Fontenay
Montbard
Baigneux-les-Juifs
Lavau
St. Sauveur-en-Puisaye
Arcy-sur-Cure
L'Isle-sur-Serein
Bonny-sur-Loire
Beaulieu
Mailly-le-Château
St. Amand-en-Puisaye
Coulanges-sur-Yonne
Châtel-Censoir
Venarey-les-Laumes
Château de Bussy-Rabutin
Epoisses
Bouhy
Avallon
Semur-en-Auxois
Leré
Myennes
Cosne-Cours-sur-Loire
Entrains-sur-Nohain
Clamecy
Vézelay
Cussy-les-Forges
Verrey-sous-Salmaise
Dornecy
Basilique de Vézelay
Nuars
Vitteaux
Donzy
Sancerre
Menou
Tannay
Quarré-les-Tombes
La Roche-en-Brénil
Précy-sous-Thil
Varzy
Pouilly-sur-Loire
Châteauneuf
Vinon
Brinon-sur-Beuvron
Corbigny
Lormes
Dun-les-Places
Saulieu
Pouilly-en-Auxois
Sombernon
Vandenesse-en-Auxois
Montsauche-les-Settons
Cervon
Les Settons
Liernais
Sancergues
La Charité-sur-Loire
Prémery
St. Révérien
Ouroux-en-Morvan
Arnay-le-Duc
Planchez
Chissey-en-Morvan
Lucenay-l'Evêque
Baugy
Pougues-les-Eaux
Guérigny
St. Saulge
Aunay-en-Bazois
Morvan
Château Chinon
Bligny-sur-Ouche
Lacanche
Mornay-Berry
Fourchambault
Bona
Châtillon-en-Bazois
Rouy
Ivry-en-Montagne
Nérondes
Cathédrale St. Cyr
Nevers
St. Benin-d'Azy
Moulins-Engilbert
La Celle-en-Moravan
Épinac
La Guerche-sur-l'Aubois
Imphy
Anlezy
Autun
Auxy
Nolay
Magny-Cours
La Machine
Vandenesse
St. Honoré-les-Bains
St. Léger-sous-Beuvray
St. Emiland
Blet
Allier
St. Léger-des-Vignes
Cercy-la-Tour
Couches
Sancoins
319
Les Brunettes
Etang-sur-Arroux
Mesvres
Marmagne
Le Creusot
St. Pierre-le-Moûtier
Decize
St. Germain-Chassenay
Charrin
Fours
Luzy
Montcenis
Givry
Bessais-le-Fromental
Lurcy-Lévis
Chantenay-St. Imbert
Cossaye
La Nocle-Maulaix
Charbonnat
Gannay-sur-Loire
Cronat
Montchanin
Dornes
Issy-l'Evêque
Toulon-sur-Arroux
Blanzy
Buxy
Couleuvre
Limoise
Couzon
Villeneuve-sur-Allier
Lucenay-les-Aix
Canal latéral à la Loire
Maltat
Montceau-les-Mines
Cérilly
Garnat-sur-Engièvre
Chevagnes
Bourbon-Lancy
Perrecy-les-Forges
St. Gengoux-le-National
Bourbon-l'Archambault
Montilly
St. Vallier
Mont-St. Vincent
Moulins
Beaulon
Chalmoux
Gueugnon
Ciry-le-Noble
Ygrande
Yzeure
Genelard
Souvigny
Montbeugny
Diou
Gilley-sur-Loire
Hérisson
L'Eglise de l'Abbaye de St. Pierre et St. Paul
Toulon-sur-Allier
Le Pal
Dompierre-sur-Besbre
St. Agnan
Digoin
Paray-le-Monial
Sacré-Coeur
Calornay-sur-Guye
St. Hilaire
Buxières-les-Mines
Neuilly-le-Réal
Coulanges
Cosne-d'Allier
Villefranche-d'Allier
Tronget
Saligney-sur-Roudon
Vaumas
Molinet
St. Bonnet-de-Joux
Le Montet
Châtel-de-Neuvre
St. Gérand-de-Vaux
St. Yan
Charolles
Beaubery
Cluny
St. Loup
Varennes-sur-Allier
Trézelles
Poisson
Pari-Gagné
Doyet
Bezenet
Voussac
0
10
20
30 km
Forêt d'Othe
Bourgogne
Nivernais
Morvan
Gâtinais

Doulaincourt
-Saucourt
Liffol-le-Grand
Vignory
St. Blin
Andelot
Blanchville
Colombey-
les-deux-Églises
Briaucourt
Juzennecourt
Bologne
Longchamp-
sur-Aujon
Chaumont
Burdons-
sur-Rognon
St. Thiébault
Bourmont
Châtenois
Bulgnéville
Contrexéville
Vittel
Gironcourt-
sur-Vraine
Mirecourt
Nomexy
Châtel-sur-
Moselle
Thaon-
les-Vosges
Épinal
Ville-
sur-Illon
Dompaire
Le Ménil
Bruyères
Chenimenil
Granges-
sur-Vologne
Éloyes
Gérardmer
St. Amé
Vagney
Remiremont
Clefmont
Lamarche
Martigny-
les-Bains
Darney
Heunezel
Monthureux-
sur-Saône
Xertigny
Bains-
les-Bains
Plombières-
les-Bains
Le Val-d'Ajol
Nogent
Richebourg
Foulain
Rolampont
Arc-en-
Barrois
Montigny-
le-Roi
Bourbonne-
les-Bains
Neuilly-
l'Évêque
Varennes-
sur-Amance
Voisey
Vauvillers
Polaincourt-
et-Clairefontaine
St. Loup-
sur-Semouse
Fougerolles
Le Thillot
Faucogney-
et-la-Mer
Servance
Boudreville
CATHÉDRALE
DE ST. MAMMÈS
DE LANGRES
Bassigny
Langres
Chalindrey
Longeau
Fayl-Billot
Vitrey-
sur-Mance
Jussey
Amance
Conflans-
sur-Lanterne
Luxeuil-les-Bains
St. Sauveur
Melisey
Faverney
St. Germain
Champagney
Plateau de Langres
Leuglay
Auberive
Recey-
sur-Ource
Vaillant
Grancey-
le-Château
Prauthoy
Chassigny
Coublanc
Genevrières
Combeaufontaine
Port-sur-Saône
Saulx
Lure
Ronchamp
Vy-lès-Lure
Belfort
Bavilliers
Barjon
Selongey
Pierrecourt
Champlitte-
et-le-Prelot
Scey-sur-Saône
et St. Albin
Vesoul
Lavoncourt
Vaite
Villersexel
Saulnot
Héricourt
Moloy
Lamargelle
Is-sur-Tille
Til-Châtel
Gemeaux
Fontaine-
Française
Dampierre-
sur-Salon
Fresne-
St. Mamès
Montbozon
Rougemont
Montbéliard
Valentigney
L'Isle-
sur-le Doubs
St. Seine-
l'Abbaye
Val-Suzon
Bèze
CHÂTEAU
DE ROSIRES
Autrey-
lès-Gray
Arc-lès-
Gray
Gray
Fretigney
Rioz
Oiselay-
et-Grachaux
Avilley
Pont-
de-Roide
Mirebeau-
sur-Bèze
Gy
Etuz
Clerval
Baume-les-Dames
Sancey-
le-Long
Talant
Dijon
Arc-
sur-Tille
Talmay
Pontailler-
sur-Saône
Marnay
Marchaux
Roulans
Roche-
lez-Beaupré
Aïssey
Chenôve
Longvic
Lamarche-
sur-Saône
Pesmes
Besançon
Gevrey-
Chambertin
Genlis
Longecourt-
en-Plaine
Auxonne
Montmirey-
le-Château
St. Vit
Mamirolle
Pierrefontaine-
les-Varans
Maîche
Champdôtre
Dampierre
Étalans
Vercel-
Villedieu-le-Camp
Valdahon
Bonnétage
Côte d'Or
Nuits-St. Georges
Brazey-
en-Plaine
St. Jean
de Losne
Losne
Rochefort-
sur-Nenon
Dole
Quingey
Ornans
Vuillafans
Orchamps-
Vennes
Nods
Villers-
le-Lac
Morteau
Arc-et-
Senans
SALINE
ROYALE
Amancey
Mouthier-
Haute-Pierre
Gilley
SAUT DE DOUBS
Beaune
St.
Aubin
Chemin
Tavaux
Parcey
Montbarrey
Villers-Farlay
Mouchard
St. Gorgon
-Main
Montbenoît
Seurre
Chaussin
Mont-sous-
Vaudrey
Salins-
les-Bains
Levier
Pontarlier
Les
Verrières
Couvet
St. Aubin
Fleurier
St. Loup-
de-la-Salle
Navilly
Le Deschaux
Demigny
Verdun-
sur-le-Doubs
Pierre-de-
Bresse
Arbois
Gergy
Andelot-
en-Montagne
Frasne
Bellevesvre
Chaumergy
Poligny
Censeau
Malbuisson
Ste. Croix
Les Hôpitaux-
Neufs
Grandson
Yverdon-
les-Bains
Chalon-sur-Saône
Mervans
St. Martin-
en-Bresse
St. Germain-
du-Bois
Sellières
St. Marcel
Thurey
St. Germain-
du-Plain
Simard
Bletterans
Voiteur
Pont-du-Navoy
Champagnole
Mouthe
Orbe
Vallorbe
Thierrens
Lons-
le-Saunier
Marigny
Le Pont
La
Sarraz
Beaurepaire-
en-Bresse
Montret
Simandre
Sennecey-
le-Grand
Conliège
Doucier
Foncine-
le-Bas
L' Isle
Cossonay
Echallens
Lac
de Joux
Le Sentier
Louhans
Sagy
Le Brassus
Épalinges
Tournus
Montpont-
en-Bresse
Le
Miroir
Cressia
Clairvaux-
les-Lacs
St. Laurent-
en-Grandvaux
Morbier
Bois-
d'Amont
CHÂTEAU
D'AUBONNE
Aubonne
Morges
Renens
Lausanne
Lutry
Cuisery
ABBAYE DE
ST. PHILIBERT
Romenay
Varennes-
St. Sauveur
Orgelet
Morez
Les Rousses
St.
Cergue
Rolle
MORGES
Cully
St. Trivier-
de-Courtes
Cuiseaux
Lac de
Vouglans
Moirans-en-
Montagne
Longchaumois
Gland
PRANGINS
Évian-
les-Bains
Lac Léman
Pont-
de-Vaux
St. Amour
Domsure
St. Julien
Arinthod
St. Lupicin
St. Claude
Divonne
les Bains
Nyon
Thonon-
les-Bains
St. Julien-
sur-Reyssouze
Coligny
Manziat
Marboz
Montrevel-
Haut-
Jura
Col de
la Faucille
Saône
Doubs
Loue
Ain
Aube
Ognon
Vingeanne
Seille
Bresse
Franche-Comté
Jura
Montagne
Vosges

St. Dié
Saales
Villé
Tunnel Maurice Lemaire
Lahr
Biberach
Zell
Alpirsbach
Steinach
Wolfach
Schiltach
Thaon-les-Vosges
Brouvelieures
Ste. Marie-aux-Mines
Château de Haut-Koenigsbourg
Sélestat
Kappel
Europapark
Ettenheim
Haslach
Hausach
Bruyères
Anould
Fraize
Ribeauvillé
Lapoutroie
Herbolzheim
Schweighausen
Hornberg
Cheniménil
Granges-sur-Vologne
Kaysersberg
Ostheim
Marckolsheim
Kenzingen
Elzach
Hardt
Ballons des Vosges
Éloyes
Turckheim
Endingen
Emmendingen
Triberger Wasserfälle
Triberg
St. Georgen
Gérardmer
Wintzenheim
Colmar
Andolsheim
Bötzingen
Waldkirch
Villingen
St. Amé
Munster
Hattstadt
Neuf-Brisach
St. Stephansmünster
Ihringen
Gundelfingen
Furtwangen
Schwenningen
Vagney
La Bresse Hohneck
La Bresse
Breisach
St. Peter
Vöhrenbach
Bad Dürrheim
Remiremont
Cornimont
Rouffach
Freiburg
Kirchzarten
Donaueschingen
Saulxures-sur-Moselotte
Le Val-d'Ajol
Guebwiller
Rhein
Titisee-Neustadt
Hüfingen
Plombières
Le Thillot
Bussang
St. Amarin
Soultz-Haut-Rhin
Ensisheim
Bad Krozingen
Staufen
Faucogney-et-la-Mer
St. Maurice-sur-Moselle
Bitschwiller
Cernay
Bantzenheim
Luxeuil-les-Bains
Oberbruck
Wittenheim
Todtnau
Bernau
Schluchsee
St. Sauveur
Servance
Collégiale St. Thiebaut
Thann
Wittelsheim
Ottmarsheim
Müllheim
Blumberg
Melisey
Masevaux
Mulhouse
Badenweiler
Klosterkirche St. Blasien
Schönau
St. Blasien
Bonndorf
Giromagny
Rixheim
Schliengen
Lure
Champagney
Rougemont-le-Château
Habsheim
Kandern
Todtmoos
Ronchamp
Belfort
Illfurth
Zell
Steinen
Schopfheim
Wehr
Waldshut
Tiengen
Vy-lès-Lure
Bavilliers
Dannemarie
Sierentz
Lörrach
Danjoutin
Altkirch
Hirsingue
St. Louis
Weil am Rhein
Rheinfelden
Bad Säckingen
Albbruck
Koblenz
Zurzach
Hohentengen
Saulnot
Héricourt
Villersexel
Châtenois-les-Forges
Arcey
Grandvillars
Seppois
Möhlin
Döttingen
Montbéliard
Delle
Pfetterhouse
Basel
Frick
Brugg
Baden
L'Isle-le-Doubs
Valentigney
Audincourt
Hérimoncourt
Ferrette
Aesch
Angenstein
Liestal
Sissach
Gelterkinden
Schloss Habsburg
Küttingen
Wildegg
Clerval
Pont-de-Roide
Mathay
Porrentruy
Laufen
Oberdorf
Aarau
Dietikon
Courgenay
Delémont
Breitenbach
Lenzburg
Wohlen
Baume-les-Dames
Sancey-le-Long
Doubs
Ramiswil
Langenbruck
Olten
Aarburg
Seon
Bremgarten
St. Hippolyte
Bassecourt
Balsthal
Zofingen
Brunegg
Kloster Muri
Adliswil
Moutier
Welschenrohr
Saignelégier
Beflelay
Tavannes
Niederbipp
Jesuitischkirche
Reiden
Reinach
Muri
Beinwil
Affoltern
Fontaine-les-Varans
Maîche
Charquemont
Solothurn
Dagmersellen
Beromünster
Tramelan
Grenchen
Cham
Reuss
Le Bélieu-le-Camp
Bonnétage
Les Bois
St. Imier
Sonceboz
Langenthal
Herzogenbuchsee
Sursee
Le Russey
Büren an der Aare
Hochdorf
La Chaux-de-Fonds
Biel/Bienne
Bätterkinden
Huttwil
Willisau
Zell
Villers-le-Lac
Le Locle
Bielersee
Lyss
Kirchberg
Schloss Burgdorf
Erlswil
Neunkirch
Morteau
Saut de Doubs
Château de Neuchâtel
La Neuveville
Aarberg
Burgdorf
Wolhusen
Emmen
Montbenoit
Les Ponts-de-Martel
Ins
Hindelbank
Sumiswald
Luzern
Neuchâtel
Kerzers
Bern
Mettlen
Entlebuch
Kriens
Vierwaldstätter See
Boudry
Couvet
Salavaux
Murtensee
Mühleberg
Flamatt
Worb
Langnau
Schüpfheim
Stans
St. Aubin
Murten
Fleurier
Lac de Neuchâtel
Estavayer-le-Lac
Avenches
Köniz
Belp
Münsingen
Grosshöchstetten
Wiggen
Flühli
Sarnen
Kerns
Grandson
Yvonand
Schwarzenburg
Oberdiessbach
Schangnau
Sarnersee
Giswil
Ste. Croix
Payerne
Fribourg
Riggisberg
Bad Kemmeriboden
Sörenberg
Engelberg
Yverdon-les-Bains
Plaffeien
Steffisburg
Stöckalp
Orbe
Lucens
Château de Romont
Uetendorf
Thun
St. Beatus Hohlen
Brienz
Lungern
Brünigpass
Gadmen
Thierrens
Romont
Le Bry
La Roche
Spiez
Interlaken
Brienzersee
Meiringen
Innertkirchen
Sustenpass
Moudon
Gypsera
Lac de Gruyères
Wimmis
Latterbach
Iseltwald
Bönigen
Echallens
Vaulruz
Bulle
Charmey
Boltigen
Simme
Schloss Spiez
Thunersee
Grindelwald
Guttannen
St. Gotthard
Carrouge
Oron-la-Ville
Jaun
Jaunpass
Frutigen
Lauterbrunnen
Wengen
Furkapass
Epalinges
Renens
Châtel-St. Denis
St. Laurent
Gruyères
Zweisimmen
Grimmialp
Mürren
Eiger
Grimselpass
Gletsch
Château de Gruyères
Stechelberg
Trummelbackfälle
Jungfrau
Finsteraarhorn
Lausanne
Lutry
Château de Vevey
Saanen
Adelboden
Kandersteg
Münster
Furka Tunnel
Cully
Vevey
La Tour-de-Peilz
Gstaad
Château-d'Oex
Gstaad-Saanenland
Lenk
Aletsch
Rhône
Montreux
Chillon
Villeneuve
Col des Mosses
Col Gstaig du Pillon
Lötschberg Tunnel
Blatten
Fiesch
St. Gingolph
Leysin
Sépey
Crans Montana
Montana-Vermala
Leukerbad
Goppenstein
Formazza
0 10 20 30 km

Hechingen
Jungingen
Freilichtmuseum Hechingen
Burladingen
Trochtelfingen
Erbach
Senden
Pfaffenhofen
Weissenhorn
Rosenfeld
Bisingen
Balingen
Gammertingen
Münsterkirche
Ehingen
Vöhringen
Thannhausen
Tailfingen
Friedrichshöhle Wimsen
Zwiefalten
Burg Hohwart
Munderkingen
Laupheim
Dietenheim
Planetarium & Volkssternwarte
Illertissen
Buch
Krumbach
Albstadt
Messtetten
Winterlingen
Veringenstadt
Uttenweiler
Schomberg
Rottweil
Nusplingen
Riedlingen
Hürbel
Kirchheim
Babenhausen
Pfaffenhausen
Obere Donau
Sigmaringen
Ertingen
Biberach
Kloster Ochsenhausen
Ochsenhausen
Erolzheim
Egg
Trossingen
Spaichingen
Dürbheim
Münsteralhöhle
Schloss Sigmaringen
Schloss Wildenstein
Mühleim
Mengen
Saulgau
Bad Buchau
Abtei Rot an der Rot
Berkheim
Steinheim
Mindelheim
Türkheim
Tuttlingen
Neuhausen ob Eck
Messkirch
Klosterkirche
Bad Schussenried
Memmingen
Dirlewang
Markt Rettenbach
Ostrach
Aulendorf
Aitrach
Benediktinerabtei Ottobeuren
Ottobeuren
Geisingen
Pfullendorf
Altshausen
Bad Waldsee
Bad Wurzach
Grönenbach
Kaufbeuren
Stockach
Engen
Wilhelmsdorf
Legau
Schloss Salem
Münsterkirche
Salem
Klosterkirche
Kloster Weingarten
Wolfegg
Leutkirch
Altusried
Obergünzburg
Weingarten
Ravensburg
Kisslegg
Kimratshofen
Thayngen
Singen
Radolfzell
Überlingen
Dettingen
Schaffhausen
Moos
Burg Hohenklingen
Stein an Rhein
Klosterinsel Reichenau
Konstanz
Markdorf
Ravensburger Spieleland
Meersburg
Meckenbeuren
Eschach
Amtzell
Wangen im Allgäu
Isny
Buchenberg
Kempten
Leuterschach
Durach
Rheinfall
Steckborn
Eschenz
Conny-Land
Allmannsdorf
Kreuzlingen
Friedrichshafen
Tettnang
Eglofs
Weitnau
Waltenhofen
Martinszell
Nesselwang
Wertach
Allgäu
Neuravensburg
Andelfingen
Pfyn
Schloss Girsberg
Weinfelden
Güttingen
Kressbronn
Lindenberg im Allgäu
Simmerberg
Oberstaufen
Immenstadt
Pfronten
Eglisau
Klostermuseum St. Georgen
Frauenfeld
Bodensee
Scheidegg
Oberjoch Pass
Amriswil
Romanshorn
Lindau
Bregenz
Lochau
Aach
Thalkirchdorf
Bühl
Blaichach
Sonthofen
Hindelang
Bülach
Winterthur
Verein Museum Schloss Kyburgs
Wängi
Wil
Sulgen
Bischofszell
Arbon
Goldach
Rorschach
Pfändertunnel
Hittisau
Ofterschwang
Fischen
Kloten
Kemptthal
Turbenthal
Flawil
St. Gallen
Gossau
St. Margrethen
Kloster St. Gallen
Lauterach
Lustenau
Wolfurt
Dornbirn
Egg
Oberstdorf
Dübendorf
Pfäffikon
Herisau
Altstätten
Hohenems
Bezau
Mittelberg
Allgäuer Alpen
Zürich
Uster
Bauma
Wetzikon
Bütschwil
Lichtensteig
Waldstatt
Appenzell
Oberriet
Götzis
Au
Baad
Hinterhornbach
Häselgehr
Thalwil
Meilen
Hinwil
Wald
Wattwil
Ebnat-Kappel
Urnäsch
Wasserauen
Sennwald
Rankweil
Damüls
Bad Inner-Laterns
Warth
Lech
Horgen
Männedorf
Stäfa
Rüti
Uznach
Kaltbrunn
Nesslau
Feldkirch
Ambergtunnel
Satteins
Schröcken
Buchboden
Steeg
Grama
Wädenswil
Richterswil
Rapperswil
Zürichsee
Gams
Frastanz
Thüringen
Oberlech
Zürs
St. Anton am Arlberg
Strenger Tunnel
Flirsch
Baar
Lachen
Amden
Grabs
Buchs
Nenzing
Bludenz
Arlberg Tunnel
Stuben
Zug
Ägeri
Niederurnen
Walensee
Walenstadt
Vaduz
Bürs
Brand
Dalaas
Klösterle
Arlbergpass
Hoher Riffler
Einsiedeln
Inerthal
Näfels
Murg
Flums
Liechtenstein
Tschagguns
Rätikon
Schruns
Kappl
Arth
Unteriberg
Netstal
Sargans
Mels
Heidihaus
Maienfeld
St. Gallenkirch
Gaschurn
Ischgl
Schwyz
Richisau
Glarus
Bad Ragaz
Schiers
Gargellen
Galtür
Muotathal
Hölloch Höhlen
Schwanden
Weisstannen
Landquart
St. Antönien
Samnaun
Dürrenboden
Brunnen
Linthal
Elm
Jenaz
Küblis
Klosters
Silvrettahorn
Martina
Altdorf
Klausenpass
Vättis
Unterschächen
Chur
Vereina Tunnel
Flims
Domat-Ems
Langwies
Erstfeld
Tödi
Bonaduz
Churwalden
Davos
Ardez
Scuol
Castel Romano
Trun
Ilanz
Versam
Arosa
Susch
Cazis
Lenzerheide
Sertig Dörfli
Dürrboden
Zernez
Disentis
Kloster Disentis
Vorderrhein
Thusis
Wiesen
Engadin
Glorenza
Filisur
Tiefencastel
Bergün Bravuogn
Benediktinerkloster
Sta. Maria
Andermatt
St. Gotthard Tunnel
Thalkirch
Viamala Schlucht
Savognin
La Punt
Livigno
Vals
Andeer
Albula Tunnel
Samedan
Passo dello Stelvio
Airolo
Olivone
Splügen
Mulegns
Pontresina
Rheinwaldhorn
S. Bernardino Tunnel
Splügenpass
Pso. del S. Bernardino
St. Moritz
Alpen
Bórmio
Faido
Fusio
Cresta
Julierpass
Silvaplana
Malvaglia
San Carlo
Bodio
Maloja
Piz Bernina
Biasca
Mesocco
Rossa
Campodolcino
Sonogno
Castasegna
Vicosoprano
Ticino
Le Prese

Nantes
St. Herblain
Rezé
Vertou
Clisson
Cholet
Pornic
Machecoul
Noirmoutier-en-l'Ile
Île de Noirmoutier
Challans
St. Jean-de-Monts
St. Gilles-Croix-de-Vie
Île d'Yeu
Aizenay
La Roche-sur-Yon
Montaigu
Les Herbiers
Chantonnay
Les Sables-d'Olonne
Château-d'Olonne
Luçon
Fontenay-le-Comte
Niort
Marais Poitevin
Île de Ré
La Rochelle
Rochefort
Île d'Oléron
Marennes
Saintes
Royan
Le Verdon-sur-Mer
Soulac-sur-Mer
Pons
Mirambeau
Côte de Jade
Pertuis Breton
Pertuis d'Antioche
Hauteurs de la Gâtine
0 10 20 30 km

Touraine
Anjou
Loire
Chinon
Montsoreau
Fontevrault-l'Abbaye
Souzay-Champigny
Ussé
Montreuil-Bellay
L'Île-Bouchard
Ste. Maure-de-Touraine
Manthelan
Loches
Château de Loches
Genillé
Montrésor
Orbigny
Château de Valençay
Luçay-le-Mâle
Écueillé
Les Trois Moûtiers
Champigny-sur-Veude
Loudun
Richelieu
Thouars
La Celle-St. Avant
Ligueil
Château du Grand Pressigny
Villedômain
Châtillon-sur-Indre
Levroux
Descartes
Le Grand-Pressigny
St. Flovier
Pellevoisin
Indre
Monts-sur-Guesnes
Dangé-St. Romain
St. Jouin-de-Marnes
Orches
Ingrandes
Preuilly-sur-Claise
Château d'Azay-le-Ferron
Azay-le-Ferron
Mézières-en-Brenne
Buzançais
Villedieu-sur-Indre
St. Varent
Airvault
Lencloître
Châtellerault
La Roche-Posay
Vendœuvres
Chiché
Mirebeau
Naintré
Pleumartin
Tournon-St. Martin
Claise
Brenne
Thénezay
Futuroscope
Bonneuil-Matours
Angles sur l'Anglin
Migné
Méobecq
Neuville-de-Poitou
St. Georges-lès-Baillargeaux
Ayron
La Ferrière-en-Parthenay
Vouillé
Parthenay
Le Blanc
St. Gaultier
Argenton-sur-Creuse
Poitiers
Église de Saint-Savin
Chauvigny
St. Savin
St. Julien-l'Ars
Bélâbre
Anglin
Mazières-en-Gâtine
Vausseroux
Fleuré
La Trimouille
St. Benoît-du-Sault
Éguzon-Chantôme
Lusignan
Rouillé
Vivonne
Lhommaizé
Montmorillon
Verrières
Tilly
St. Maixent-l'École
La Crèche
La Mothe-St. Héray
Lussac-les-Châteaux
Gençay
Bouresse
Lussac-les-Eglises
St. Sulpice-les-Feuilles
Dun-le-Palestel
Celles-sur-Belle
Prahecq
Couhé
Sommières-du-Clain
Usson-du-Poitou
L'Isle-Jourdain
Moulismes
Bussière-Poitevine
Magnac-Laval
La Souterraine
Lezay
Melle
Chaunay
Le Dorat
Vienne
Gartempe
Niort
Brioux-sur-Boutonne
Chef-Boutonne
Sauzé-Vaussais
Civray
Charroux
Pressac
Availles-Limouzine
Mézières-sur-Issoire
Châteauponsac
St. Etienne-de-Fursac
Bénévent-l'Abbaye
Bellac
Bessines-sur-Gartempe
Laurière
Vendée
Aubigné
La Villedieu
Surin
St. Germain-de-Confolens
Lesterps
Roussac
Razes
St. Sulpice-Laurière
Villefagnan
Ruffec
Confolens
Mortemart
Nantiat
La Jonchère-St. Maurice
Aulnay
Longré
Courcôme
Champagny-Mouton
Néré
Cherbonnières
Charente
Oradour-sur-Glane
Ambazac
Abbaye-de-St. Junien
St. Claud
Matha
Verdille
Aigre
Valence
Chabanais
St. Junien
Limoges
St. Léonard-de-Noblat
Mansle
Château de Rochechouart
Rochechouart
Maulde
Tourriers
Château de Rochefoucauld
Chasseneuil-sur-Bonnieure
St. Laurent-sur-Gorre
Aixe-sur-Vienne
Rouillac
Massignac
Oradour-sur-Vayres
Solignac
Angoumois
La Rochefoucauld
Tardoire
St Bonnet Briance
Cognac
Sigogne
Jarnac
Ruelle-sur-Touvre
Montbron
St. Mathieu
Nexon
Pierre-Buffière
Hiersac
Soyaux
Angoulême
Bussière-Badil
Périgord-Limousin
Dournazac
Châlus
Segonzac
Marthon
Augignac
Ladignac-le-Long
Magnac-Bourg
St. Germain-les-Belles
Châteauneuf-sur-Charente
Javerlhac
Dignac
Nontron
La Coquille
Meuzac
Masseret
Coussac-Bonneval
La Rochebeaucourt-et-Argentine
St. Pardoux-la-Rivière
St. Yrieix-la-Perche
Jumilhac-le-Grand
Barbezieux-St. Hilaire
Villebois-Lavalette
Blanzac
Mareuil
St. Jean-de-Côle
Thiviers
Lubersac
Arnac-Pompadour
Montmoreau-St. Cybard
Verteillac
Brantôme
Lanouaille
Vigeois
Baignes-Ste. Radegonde
Lizonne
Isle
Brossac
Chevanceaux
Aubeterre-sur-Dronne
Dronne
Sorges
Excideuil
Juillac
Auvézère
Montlieu-la-Garde
Chalais
Tocane-St. Apre
Ribérac
Château-l'Évêque
Trélissac
Sarliac-sur-l'Isle
Savignac-les-Églises
Château de Hautefort
Hautefort
Objat
Allassac
Donzenac
Montguyon
Berry
Marche
Limousin
A10
E05
E62
E09
A20
E603
E606
100
115
179
16
17
24
28
29
47°
46°

Orsennes
Ste. Sévère-sur-Indre
Préveranges
Estivareilles
Cosne d'Allier
Villefranche-d'Allier
St. Hilaire
Buxières-les-Mines
L'EGLISE DE L'ABBAYE DE ST. PIERRE ET ST. PAUL
Treban
Aigurande
La Chapelaude
Le Montet
Châtel-de-Neuvre
CHÂTEAU DE CROZANT
Treignat
Boussac
Domérat
Montluçon
Quinssaines
Doyet
Bezenet
Voussac
St. Pourçain-sur-Sioule
Dun-le-Palestel
Bonnat
Châtelus-Malvaleix
Néris-les Bains
Commentry
Montmarault
La Souterraine
St. Vaury
Chambon-sur-Voueize
Lapeyrouse
Chantelle
St. Etienne-de-Fursac
Ajain
Gouzon
Bellenaves
St. Eloy-les-Mines
Bénévent-l'Abbaye
Le-Grand-Bourg
Guéret
Évaux-les-Bains
Marcillat-en-Combraille
Montaigut
Fontanières
Lalizolle
Laurière
Chénerailles
Pionsat
Menat
Ebreuil
Gannat
St. Sulpice-Laurière
Ahun
St. Dizier-Leyrenne
Auzances
St. Gervais-d'Auvergne
Effiat
La Jonchère-St. Maurice
Pontarion
Aiguepers
Combronde
Thuret
Ambazac
Bourganeuf
Aubusson
Bellegarde-en-Marche
Montel-de-Gelat
St. Georges-de Mons
Manzat
Felletin
Châtel-Guyon
Riom
Maringues
Ennezat
Sauviat-sur-Vige
St. Léonard-de-Noblat
Royère-de-Vassivière
Crocq
St. Avit
Les Ancizes-Comps
Pontaumur
Volvic
Joze
Pontgibaud
Bromont-Lamothe
Clermont-Ferrand
Gerzat
Peyrat-le-Château
Gentioux
L. de Vassivière
Giat
Sauvagnat
VULCANIA
Royat
Pont-du-Château
St Bonnet Briance
Eymoutiers
Millevaches
Herment
Rochefort-Montagne
Puy-de-Dôme
Ceyrat
Châteauneuf la-Forêt
La Courtine
Plateau de Millevaches
Sornac
Eygurande
Bourg-Lastic
ST. JEAN
TEMPLE DE MERCURE
Cournon-d'Auvergne
Veyre-Monton
Mt. Gargan
St. Germain-les-Belles
Limousin
Millevaches
La Bourboule
St. Armant-Tallende
Vic-le
Magnac-Bourg
Bugeat
Le Mont-Dore
St. Nectaire
Chamberet
Tauves
Chambon-sur-Lac
Murol
Champeix
Masseret
Treignac
Meymac
Ussel
L'EGLISE HAUTE
Issoire
Puy de Sancy
Besse-en-Chandesse
Peyrissac
Mts. Dore
St. Angel
St. Germain-Lembron
Uzerche
Chamboulive
Egletons
Arnac-Pompadour
Champs-sur-Tarentaine
Égliseneuve-d'Entraigues
Ardes
Lempdes
Vigeois
Seilhac
Corrèze
Neuvic
Bort-les-Orgues
Condat
Ydes
Saignes
Anzat-le-Luguet
Blesle
Allassac
Tulle
Marcillac-la-Croisille
Marcenat
Riom-ès-Montagnes
Massiac
Laguenne
Donzenac
La Roche-Canillac
Trizac
Volcans d'Auvergne
Mauriac
Allanche
Molompize
St. Martin-la-Méanne
Ségur-les-Villas
Malemort
Neussargues-Moissac
Brive-la-Gaillarde
St. Chamant
Salers
Beynat
St. Privat
Pléaux
Talizat
Larche
Argentat
St. Martin-Valmeroux
Murat
Ussel
Viellespesse
Meyssac
St. Cernin
Plomb du Cantal
Roffiac
Cressensac
Thiezac
St. Flour
Les Ternes
Ruynes-en-Margeride
Vayrac
Beaulieu-sur-Dordogne
Laroquebrou
Jussac
Vic-sur-Cère
Martel
Souillac
Polminhac
Aurillac
Bretenoux
CHÂTEAU DE CASTELNAU-BRETENOUX
Arpajon-sur-Cère
Pierrefort
Raulhac
GROTTE DE LANCAVE
Sousceyrac
St. Céré
CHÂTEAU DE MONTAL
Le Rouget
St. Mamet-la-Salvetat
Chaudes-Aigues
Alvignac
Mur-de-Barrez
Fournels
Termes
Payrac
Rocamadour
Gramat
Latronquière
Lacroix-Barrez
St. Chély-d'Apcher
Causses
Calvinet
Cassuéjouls
Le Bourg
Lacapelle-Marival
Maurs
Montsalvy
St. Hippolyte
Laguiole
Nasbinals
Labastide-Murat
Livernon
Entraygues-sur-Truyère
Mts. d'Aubrac
Lamothe-Cassel
Grézec
Figeac
Conques
Aubrac
Lauzès
Capdenac-Gare
Decazeville
Firmi
Le Cayrol
St. Chély-d'Aubrac
Aubin
Espalion
St. Come-d'Olt
Montbazens
Chirac
Bourbonnais
Combrailles
Marche
Limousin
Monts du Cantal
Massif Central
0 10 20 30 km

Neuilly-le-Réal
Dompierre-sur-Besbre
Digoin
Paray-le-Monial
SACRÉ-COEUR
St. Bonnet-de-Joux
Lugny
St. Trivier-de-Courtes
Saligney-sur-Roudon
Coulanges
Molinet
St. Yan
Charolles
Beaubery
Cluny
ANCIENNE ABBAYE DE CLUNY
Pont-de-Vaux
St. Julien-sur-Reyssouze
St. Gérand-de-Vaux
Jaligny-sur-Besbre
Poisson
Matour
Pari-Gagné
Mâcon
Manziat
Marboz
Montrevel-en-Bresse
St. Loup
Varennes-sur-Allier
Trézelles
Le Donjon
CHÂTEAU DE LAPALISSE
Lapalisse
Montaiguët-en-Forez
Chambilly
Marcigny
St. Christophe-en-Brionnais
La Clayette
Crêches-sur-Saône
Pont-de-Veyle
St. Cyr-sur-Menthon
Bourg-en-Bresse
St. Gérand-le-Puy
St. Germain-des-Fossés
St. Martin-d'Estreaux
La Pacaudière
Châteauneuf
Iguerande
Chauffailles
Romanèche-Thorins
Mézériat
Le Breuil
Arfeuilles
Pouilly-sous-Charlieu
Charlieu
Belmont-de-la-Loire
Beaujeu
St. Didier
Châtillon-sur-Chalaronne
Neuville-les-Dames
Vichy
Cusset
Abrest
Changy
Châtel-Montagne
St. Germain-Lespinasse
ST. PHILIBERT
Cuinzier
Belleville
St. Paul-de-Varax
Le Mayet-de-Montagne
STE. MADELEINE
Mably
Cours-la-Ville
Lamure-sur-Azergues
St. Georges-de-Reneins
Marlieux
St. Trivier-sur-Moignans
St. Yorre
Ferrières-sur-Sichon
Renaison
Roanne
Bourg-de-Thizy
Thizy
Arnas
Ambérieux-en-Dombes
Villars-les-Dombes
Chalamont
Randan
Regny
Villemontais
Limons
Puy-Guillaume
Amplepuis
Villefranche-sur-Saône
Trévoux
St. Just-en-Chevalet
Cremeaux
St. Polgues
St. Symphorien-de-Lay
Valsonne
Tarare
Anse
St. André-de-Corcy
Meximieux
Lagnieu
Chabreloche
Neulise
Pontcharra-sur-Turdine
Montluel
Thiers
La Monnerie-le-Montel
Noirétable
Champoly
St. Germain-Laval
Néronde
Balbigny
Violay
L'Arbresle
Neuville-sur-Saône
Caluire-et-Cuire
Miribel
Villeurbanne
Pont-de-Dore
St. Julien-la-Vêtre
Panissières
Craponne
Pont-de-Chéruy
Vollore-Montagne
Boën
Feurs
St. Laurent-de-Chamousset
AQUEDUC ROMAIN
Oullins
Lyon
Meyzieu
St. Priest
Crémieu
Courpière
Chalmazel
CHÂTEAU DE LA BASTIE D'URFÉ
Ste. Foy-l'Argentière
Olliergues
St. Georges-en-Couzan
Montrond-les-Bains
St. Symphorien-sur-Coise
Thurins
Vénissieux
St. Dier-d'Auvergne
Champdieu
St. Martin-en-Haut
Mornant
St. Symphorien-d'Ozon
Villefontaine
Cunlhat
St. Amant-Roche-Savine
Chazelles-sur-Lyon
Diémoz
Bourgoin-Jallieu
Sugères
Sauxillanges
Montbrison
St. Galmier
Givors
Vienne
Livradois-Forez
Ambert
Andrézieux-Bouthéon
St. Jean-de-Bournay
Fournols
Sury-le-Comtal
St. Anthème
St. Chamond
Rive-de-Gier
Condrieu
Sarpoil
Marsac-en-Livradois
St. Marcellin-sur-Loire
St. Just-St. Rambert
La Grande-Croix
Les Roches
St. Germain-l'Herm
Viverols
St. Étienne
Pelussin
Cour-et-Buis
La Côte-St. André
Brassac-les-Mines
Arlanc
Champagnac-le-Vieux
Usson-en-Forez
St. Bonnet-le-Château
Le Chambon-Feugerolles
Pilat
Le Péage-de-Roussillon
Roussillon
Beaurepaire
Marcilloles
Auzon
Firminy
St. Genest-Malifaux
Le Bessat
Serrières
La Chaise-Dieu
L'ÉGLISE DE L'ABBAYE DE ST. ROBERT
Craponne-sur-Arzon
Monistrol-sur-Loire
St. Didier-en-Velay
St. Sauveur-en-Rue
Bourg-Argental
St. Rambert-d'Albon
Lens Lestang
Roybon
Hauterives
Collat
Ste. Sigolène
Riotord
Villevocance
Annonay
Andance
Paulhaguet
Allègre
Bellevue-la-Montagne
Vorey
Retournac
Montfaucon-en-Velay
Sarras
Montmiral
St. Georges-d'Aurac
St. Vallier
St. Marcellin
St. Paulien
Yssingeaux
Satillieu
Margès
Langeac
Siaugues-St. Romain
CHÂTEAU DE LAVOTE-POLIGNAC
St. Bonnet-le-Froid
Tain-l'Hermitage
St. Hilaire-du-Rosier
Chanteuges
Le Pertuis
Tence
Le Chambon-sur-Lignon
St. Félicien
CHÂTEAU CHAZOTTE
Arlebosc
Peyrins
Romans-sur-Isère
CHAPELLE ST. MICHEL D'AIGUILHE
Le Puy-en-Velay
St. Julien-Chapteuil
Tournon-sur-Rhône
Bourg-de-Péage
St. Nazaire-en-Royans
Bains
St. Agrève
Alixan
Saugues
Monistrol-d'Allier
Cayres
Le Monastier-sur-Gazeille
Laussonne
St. Martin-de-Valamas
Mt. Mézenc 1754
Lamastre
St. Péray
St. Marcel
Montelier
Valence
Costaros
Les Estables
Le Cheylard
Vernoux-en-Vivarais
Léoncel
Chabeuil
Portes-lès-Valence
Malzieu-Ville
Chanaleilles
Landos
Le Béage
Charmes-sur-Rhône
Montmeyran
Grandrieu
St. Pierreville
St. Sauveur-de-Montagut
La Voulte-sur-Rhône
Plan-de-Baix
St. Alban-sur-Limagnole
Pradelles
Coucouron
Mézilhac
Monts
Livron-sur-Drôme
Auroux
Privas
Crest
Langogne
Montpezat-sous-Bouzon
Loriol-sur-Drôme
Saillans
Serverette
Lanarce
Chomérac
St. Amans
Châteauneuf-de-Randon
Thueyts
Pont-de-Labeaume
Cruas
Mayres
Vals-les-Bains
Luc
Meysse
Cléon-d'Andran
La Bastide-Puylaurent
D'Ardèche
Aubenas
Rochemaure
Montélimar
Laubert
Valgorge
Lavilledieu
Villeneuve-de-Berg
Le Teil
Sauzet
La Bégude-de-Mazenc
Bourdeaux
Belvezet
Largentière
Vogüé
CHÂTEAU DE VOGÜÉ
Espeluche
Dieulefit
Mende
ERMITAGE DE ST. PRIVAT
Le Bleymard
Prevenchères
Joyeuse
BAPTISTRE DE MÉLAS
Viviers
Aleyrac
Bouvières
Beaujolais
Lyonnais
Monts du Forez
Mts du Velay
Dombes
Monts de la Margeride
Dauphiné
E62
E70
E15
E21
A40
A6
A46
A89
A72
A47
E611
A42
A432
A43
A7
E713
145
60
219
18
19
26
30
31

Romenay
Varennes-St. Sauveur
St. Trivier-de-Courtes
Cuiseaux
Orgelet
Lac de Vouglans
Morez
Les Rousses
Château d'Aubonne
Aubonne
Lausanne
Morges
St. Cergue
Rolle
Lac Léman
Evian-les-Bains
Thonon-les-Bains
Cormoz
St. Amour
Pont-de-Vaux
Domsure
St. Julien
Arinthod
Moirans-en-Montagne
St. Lupicin
Longchaumois
St. Claude
Divonne-les-Bains
Nyon
Coligny
St. Trivier-sur-Reyssouze
Marboz
Manziat
Montrevel-en-Bresse
St. Étienne-du-Bois
Haut-Jura
Col de la Faucille
Dortan
Crêt de la Neige 1718
Gex
Ferney-Voltaire
Versoix
Douvaine
Perrignier
Chablais
Abondance
Pont-de-Veyle
St. Cyr-sur-Menthon
Treffort
Oyonnax
Bourg-en-Bresse
Mézériat
Jasseron
Ceyzériat
Izernore
Chézery-Forens
St. Genis-Pouilly
Vernier
Genève
Geneva
St. Cergues
Bellevaux
Boëge
Annemasse
St. Germain-de-Joux
St. Julien-en-Genevois
St. Didier
Châtillon-sur-Chalaronne
Neuville-les-Dames
St. Martin-du-Frêne
Nantua
Bellegarde-sur-Valserine
Viry
St. Jeoire
Les Gets
St. Paul-de-Varax
Marlieux
Poncin
La Roche-sur-Foron
Taninges
Bonneville
Cluses
St. Trivier-sur-Moignans
Pont-d'Ain
Brénod
Frangy
Cruseilles
Scionzier
Ambérieux-en-Dombes
Villars-les-Dombes
Chalamont
Priay
Ambérieu-en-Bugey
Hauteville-Lompnès
Thorens-Glières
Le Petit-Bornand
Trévoux
St. Rambert-en-Bugey
Seyssel
La Balme-de-Sillingy
Le Grand-Bornand
La Clusaz
C. des Aravis 1486
Sallanches
St. André-de-Corcy
Meximieux
Lagnieu
Tenay
Artemare
Rumilly
Annecy
Thônes
Combloux
Montluel
Sault-Brénaz
Virieu-le-Grand
Culoz
Veyrier
Lac d'Annecy
Megève
Neuville-sur-Saône
Miribel
Caluire-et-Cuire
Montalieu-Vercieu
Serrières-de-Briord
Chazey-Bons
Sevrier
Talloires
Flumet
Villeurbanne
St. Jorioz
Les Contamines-Montjoie
Pont-de-Chéruy
Albens
Lyon
Meyzieu
St. Priest
Crémieu
Belley
Lac du Bourget
Massif des Bauges
Faverges
Ugine
Queige
Beaufort
Vénissieux
Trept
Morestel
Yenne
Aix-les-Bains
Lescheraines
Le Châtelard
Albertville
St. Symphorien-d'Ozon
Walibi Rhône-Alpes
Le Bourget-du-Lac
La Motte-Servolex
Grignon
La Bathie
Bourg St. Maurice
Villefontaine
Diémoz
La Tour-du-Pin
St. Genix-sur-Guiers
Novalaise
Les Déserts
St. Pierre-d'Albigny
Chambéry
Cevins
Vienne
Bourgoin-Jallieu
Pont-de-Beauvoisin
Cognin
Challes-les-Eaux
Ste. Hélène-sur-Isère
Aiguebelle
Aime
Bellentre
St. Jean-de-Bournay
Les Abrets
La Bridoire
Chamoux-sur-Gelon
La Plagne
Virieu
Montferrat
Col du Granier 1134
Montmélian
Epierre
Valmorel
Moûtiers
Cour-et-Buis
Chabons
Chapareillan
St. Pierre-d'Entremont
Le Touvet
Pontcharra
Allevard
St. Jean-de-Belleville
Courchevel
La Côte-St. André
Les Echelles
Chirens
Chartreuse
Voiron
St. Laurent-du-Pont
St. Pierre-d'Allevard
Méribel
St. Martin-de-Belleville
Pralognan-la-Vanoise
Roussillon
Beaurepaire
Marcilloles
Goncelin
La Chambre
St. Étienne-de-Cuines
Méribel Motraret
Les Ménuires
St. Rambert-d'Albon
Lens Lestang
St. Etienne-de-St. Geoirs
Rives
Moirans
St. Pierre-de-Chartreuse
Les Sept Laux
St. Jean-de-Maurienne
Hauterives
Roybon
Tullins
Voreppe
Froges
Belledonne
Maurienne
Val Thorens
St. Julien-Mont-Denis
Varacieux
St. Égrève
Meylan
Montmiral
Vinay
Domène
St. Sorlin-d'Arves
St. Marcellin
Grenoble
St. Martin-d'Hères
Echirolles
Valloire
St. Michel-de-Maurienne
Tunnel du Fréjus
Margès
St. Hilaire-du-Rosier
Rencurel
Chamrousse
Allemont
Valmeinier
Tain-l'Hermitage
Peyrins
Pont-en-Royans
Villard-de-Lans
Château de Vizille
Vizille
L'Alpe-d'Huez
Mt. Thabor 3181
Romans-sur-Isère
Le Bourg-d'Oisans
La Grave
Col du Galibier 2646
Bardonecchia
Bourg-de-Péage
St. Nazaire-en-Royans
Vif
Romanche
St. Georges-de-Commiers
Col d'Ornon 1318
Col du Lautaret 2058
Névache
St. Marcel
Alixan
St. Jean-en-Royans
La Chapelle-en-Vercors
Les Deux-Alpes
Montelier
Vercors
Monestier-de-Clermont
Le Monêtier-les-Bains
La Salle
Montgenèvre
Cesana
Valence
Chabeuil
Léoncel
Vassieux-en-Vercors
La Mure
Valbonnais
Ecrins
Serre-Chevalier
Ailefroide
Portes-lès-Valence
Massif du Pelvoux
Briançon
Montmeyran
Col de Rousset 1254
Clelles
Corps
Vallouise
St. Martin-de-Queyrières
Plan-de-Baix
Mens
St. Firmin
La Chapelle-en-Valgaudémar
Livron-sur-Drôme
Fortifications Gallo-Romaines
Die
Lalley
Loriol-sur-Drôme
Crest
Col de la Croix Haute 1179
L'Argentière-la-Bessée
Saillans
Vercheny
Châtillon-en-Diois
Agnières
Drôme
St. Bonnet
Orcières
Mont Dauphin
Guillestre
Pradelle
Luc-en-Diois
Col Bayard 1248
Cléon-d'Andran
Châteauroux-les-Alpes
Risoul
Sauzet
Montélimar
Bourdeaux
La Bégude-de-Mazenc
St. Nazaire
Beaurières
La Roche-des-Arnauds
Vars les Claux
Col de Vars 2109
Embrun
Espeluche
Aspres-sur-Buëch
Veynes
Gap
Chorges
Les Orres
Savines
0 10 20 30 km

Saanen
Gstaad
Adelboden
Kandersteg
Jungfrau
Finsteraarhorn
Münster
Furka Tunnel
Bedretto
Château-d'Oex
GSTAAD - SAANENLAND
Lenk
Lötschberg Basistunnel
Lötschberg Tunnel
Blatten
Aletschhorn
4195
Fiesch
San Carlo
CHÂTEAU DE VEVEY
Vevey
La Tour-de-Peilz
Montreux
CHILLON
Villeneuve
Col des Mosses
1445
Col du Pillon
1546
Leysin
Sépey
Les Diablerets
VILLARS
Vouvry
Aigle
Châtel
Monthey
Bex
St. Maurice
L'EGLISE DE L'ABBAYE DE ST. MAURICE
Champéry
CRANS MONTANA
Montana-Vermala
Leukerbad
Goppenstein
Leuk
Sierre
Turtmann
Visp
Stalden
Brig
Naters
STOCKALPER
Simplon P.
2005
Simplon
Simplon Tunnel
Formazza
Bignasco
Cévio
Góglio
Prémia
Cimalmotto
Crodo
Vergeletto
Iselle
Varzo
Crévola d'Ossola
Intragna
Ascona
Brissago
Masera
Santa Maria Maggiore
Bognanco Fonti
Domodóssola
Villadóssola
Val Grande
Cannóbio
Cánnero Riviera
Vogogna
Piedimulera
Antronapiana
Conthey
Sion
Vétroz
Vex
NENDAZ
Riddes
Fully
Vernayaz
Martigny
Verbier
Evolène
Les Haudères
Ayer
Zinal
St. Niklaus
Saas-Fee
Täsch
Zermatt
Ferpècle
Arolla
Orsières
Alpes Pennine
Berner Alpen
Alpi Lepontine
Matterhorn
4482
Dufourspitze
4634
Monte Rosa
Macugnaga
Breuil-Cervínia
Valtournenche
Chamonix-Mont Blanc
Les Praz
St-Gervais-les-Bains
Tunnel du Mt. Blanc
Mont Blanc
4807
COURMAYEUR
Courmayeur
Morgex
La Thuile
Col du Petit St-Bernard
2188
Ferret
Tunnel du Grd. St. Bernard
Étroubles
Bionaz
Valpelline
Aosta
Sarre
Nus
Châtillon
St. Vincent
CHÂTEAU DE CHÂTILLON
CHÂTEAU DE VERRÈS
Verrès
Mte. Emilius
3559
Issogne
Champorcher
Cogne
Valgrisenche
Valsavarenche
Rhêmes-Notre-Dame
Gran Paradiso
4061
Ronco Canavese
Alpi Graie
Pont
Champoluc
Brusson
Gressoney-la-Trinité
Gressoney-St.-Jean
Gaby
Alagna Valsésia
Balmuccia
MADONNA DI LORETO
Varallo
Scopello
L. d'Orta
Omegna
Forno
Gravellona Toce
Pallanza
Verbánia
Laveno
Stresa
Armeno
Meina
Angera
Arona
Vergiate
Borgosésia
Borgomanero
Piedicavallo
Trivero
SANTUARIO DI MARIA SANTISSIMA
Oropa
Serravalle
Valle Mosso
Gattinara
Romagnano Sésia
Oléggio
Pont-St. Martin
Settimo Vittone
ABBAZIA DI SETTIMO VITTONE
Biella
Cossato
Carpignano Sésia
Fara Novarese
Momo
Borgofranco d'Ivrea
Ivrea
Arbório
Buronzo
Biandrate
Novara
Salussola
Cavaglia
Formigliana
Santhià
San Germano Vercellese
Borgo Vercelli
Vespolate
Tronzano-Vercellese
Livorno Ferraris
Vercelli
Róbbio
Val-d'Isère
Col de l'Iseran
2764
Vanoise
Bonneval-sur-Arc
Lanslebourg-Mont-Cenis
Col du Mt.Cenis
2084
Ceresole-Reale
Locana
Pont Canavese
Cuorgnè
Castellamonte
Borgomasino
Caluso
Cigliano
Chialamberto
Forno Alpi-Gráie
Ala di Stura
Ceres
Balme
Cório
Busano
Rivarolo Canavese
Lanzo Torinese
Front
Ciriè
Usséglio
Viù
Margone
Fiano
Caselle Torinese
Venaria
Crescentino
Trino
Desana
Stroppiana
Chivasso
Brusasco
SAN GENUARIO
Casalborgone
Casale Monferrato
Cándia Lomellina
Sartirana Lomellina
Molaretto
Bussoleno
Susa
Condove
Almese
Alpignano
Chiomonte
Avigliana
Rívoli
Torino
Turin
Séttimo Torinese
ABBAZIA DI VEZZOLANO
Castelnuovo Don Bosco
Montiglio
Ozzano Monferrato
Occimiano
Moncalvo
Oulx
Fenestrelle
Pragelato
Forno
Villaretto
Giaveno
Trana
Orbassano
Chieri
Moncalieri
Montechiaro d'Asti
Calliano
Vignale
Valenza
SAN PIETRO
Montemagno
Quargnento
Alessandria
Sestriere
Perosa Argentina
Cumiana
Villar Perosa
Perrero
None
Poirino
Villanova d'Asti
Piemonte
Felizzano
Carignano
Villastellone
DUOMO DI SANTA MARIA ASSUNTA
Asti
Ghigo
Pinerolo
Torre Péllice
Bóbbio Pellice
Carmagnola
San Damiano d'Asti
Isola d'Asti
Oviglio
Bosco
Col d'Izoard
2360
Abriès
Aiguilles
Vigone
Pancalieri
Canale
Nizza Monferrato
Cavour
Moretta
Racconigi
Sommariva del Bosco
Costigliole d'Asti
Cassine
St. Véran
Crissolo
Barge
ABBAZIA DI SANTA MARIA DI STAFFARDA
Revello
Cavallermaggiore
Bra
Alba
Néive
Canelli
Acqui Terme
DUOMO
Mte. Viso
3841
Paesana
Chianale
Bubbio
Bistango
Visone
Ovada
Saluzzo
Savigliano
Cherasco
Diano d'Alba
Molare
CASTELLO DI MOLARE
Verzuolo
Genola
Narzole
Monforte d'Alba
Cortemilia
Casteldelfino
Sampéyre
Venasca
Costigliole Saluzzo
Fossano
Bene Vagienna
Bossolasco
Spigno Monferrato
San Damiano
Busca
Dogliani
Po
Dora Baltea
Dora Riparia
Rhône
Sesia
Tánaro
L. Maggiore

1
2
3
A
B
C
0
10
20
30 km
22
23
38
39
45°
44°
Côte des Landes
Côte d'Argent
Bassin d'Arcachon
Étang d'Hourtin-Carcans
Étang de Lacanau
Étang de Cazaux et de Sanguinet
Étang de Biscarrosse et de Parentis
Landes de Gascogne
Bassin
Aquitaine
Gascogne
Landes
Médoc
Garonne
Dordogne
Isle
Dronne
Dropt
Leyre
Ciron
Douze
Midouze
Midou
Adour
Luy
Luy-de-France
Luy-de-Béarn
Gabas
Bidouze
Vendays-Montalivet
Lesparre-Médoc
St. Christoly-Médoc
St. Ciers-sur-Gironde
St. Estèphe
Mirambeau
Baignes-Ste. Radegonde
Montendre
Chevanceaux
Brossac
Montlieu-la-Garde
Montguyon
Chalais
Aubeterre-sur-Dronne
St. Aulaye
La Roche-Chalais
Cissac-Médoc
Pauillac
Hourtin
St. Laurent-Médoc
Beychevelle
FORT MÉDOC
Blaye
Etauliers
St. Savin
Cavignac
Carcans
Carcans-Plage
Lamarque
Listrac-Médoc
Bourg
Guîtres
Coutras
St. Médard-de-Guizières
Lacanau-Océan
Castelnau-de-Médoc
Margaux
Macau
Ambès
St. André-de-Cubzac
Galgon
Lacanau
Ste. Hélène
Arsac
Le Porge-Océan
Blanquefort
Carbon-Blanc
Fronsac
Libourne
Lussac
Villefranche-de-Lonchat
Saumos
St. Médard-en-Jalles
Arveyres
St. Émilion
Castillon-la-Bataille
Le Porge
Mérignac
Bordeaux
Branne
Lamothe-Montravel
St. Jean-d'Illac
Pessac
Lège-Cap-Ferret
CATHÉDRAL ST-ANDRÉ
Pujols
Villenave-d'Ornon
Créon
Rauzan
Arès
Andernos-les-Bains
Lanton
Cestas
Targon
Pellegrue
Île aux Oiseaux
Audenge
La Brède
Portets
Sauveterre-de-Guyenne
Arcachon
Biganos
Marcheprime
Saucats
CHÂTEAU DE LA BRÈDE
Podensac
Cap Ferret
Pyla-sur-Mer
La Teste
Gujan-Mestras
Mios
Le Barp
Cabanac-et-Villagrains
Illats
Cadillac
Cérons
Monségur
Villagrains
La Réole
Salles
Guillos
Langon
St. Macaire
Cazaux
Sanguinet
Belin-Béliet
Hostens
Balizac
Auros
Mitton
Biscarrosse Plage
Villandraut
Bazas
St. Symphorien
Biscarrosse
Le Muret
Belhade
Préchac
Grignols
Parentis-en-Born
Moustey
Beaulac
Lerm-et-Musset
Casteljaloux
Gastes
Liposthey
Pissos
Sore
Captieux
Damazan
Pontenx-les-Forges
Luxey
St Michel-de-Castelnau
Mimizan-Plage
Labouheyre
Commensacq
Trensacq
Houeillès
Mimizan
Escource
Allons
Durance
Bias
Cap-de-Pin
Sabres
Contis-Plage
Onesse-et-Laharie
Labrit
Losse
Lapeyrade
St. Julien-en-Born
Mézos
Laharie
Morcenx
Garein
Brocas
Roquefort
Lit-et-Mixe
Uza
Arengosse
Sos
Gabarret
St. Girons-Plage
Ygos-St. Saturnin
St. Justin
Barbotan-les-Thermes
St. Girons
Le Souquet
Le Caloy
Castets
Rion-des-Landes
Villeneuve-de-Marsan
Cazaubon
Léon
Mont-de-Marsan
Estang
Laluque
Tartas
Meilhan
Eauze
Vieux-Boucau-les-Bains
Azur
Pontonx-sur-l'Adour
Souprosse
Grenade-sur-l'Adour
Manciet
Magescq
Le Houga
St. Paul-lès-Dax
Mugron
St. Sever
Nogaro
Soustons
Aire-sur-l'Adour
Vic-Fézensac
Aignan
Dax
Tosse
Hossegor
St. Geours-de-Maremne
Montfort-en-Chalosse
Hagetmau
Riscle
Capbreton
St. Vincent-de-Tyrosse
St. Lon-les-Mines
Pomarez
Geaune
Labenne
Puillon
Samadet
Plaisance
Tarnos
Boucau
Port de Lanne
Peyrehorade
Habas
Tilh
Amou
Sault-de-Navailles
Sarron
Garlin
Marciac
Bassoues
Anglet
Bayonne
Puyôo
Arzacq-Arraziguet
Biarritz
Bidart
Bidache
Salies-de-Béarn
Orthez
Thèze
Lembeye
Maubourguet
Briscous
Arthez-de-Béarn
Escos
Sauveterre-de-Béarn
Maslacq
Lacq
Artix
Uzein
Vic-en-Bigorre
Ustaritz
Hasparren
116
109
190
212
243
A630
A63
A660
A62
A65
A64
A89
E05
E70
E80
E72
E606
Canal latéral à la Garonne

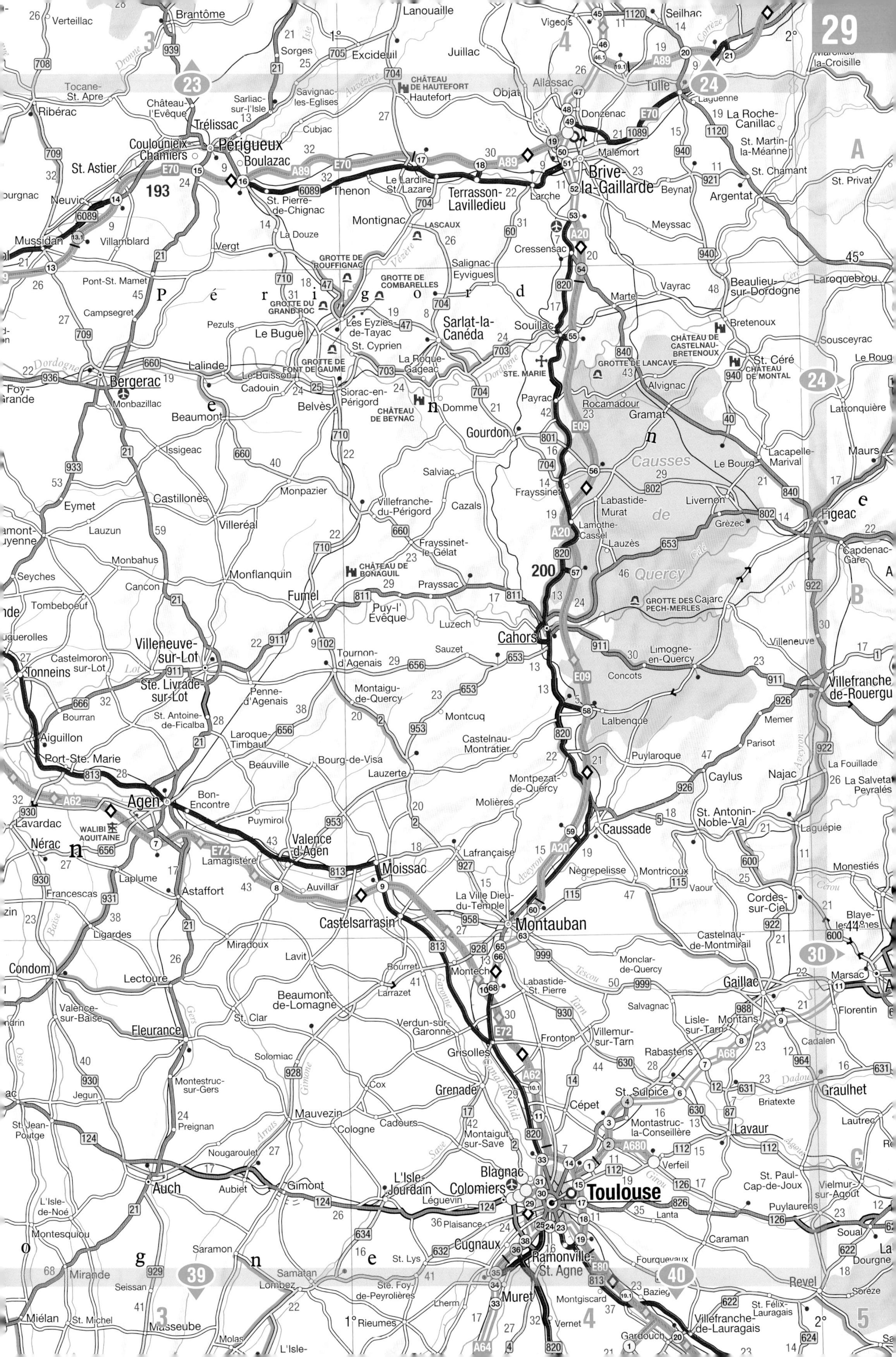
Verteillac
Brantôme
Lanouaille
Vigeois
Seilhac
Sorges
Excideuil
Juillac
Tocane-St. Apre
Ribérac
Château-l'Evêque
Sarliac-sur-l'Isle
Savignac-les-Eglises
CHÂTEAU DE HAUTEFORT
Hautefort
Objat
Allassac
Tulle
Laguenne
La Roche-Canillac
Trélissac
Coulounieix-Chamiers
Périgueux
Boulazac
Cubjac
Donzenac
Malemort
St. Martin-la-Méanne
St. Astier
Brive-la-Gaillarde
St. Chamant
St. Privat
Neuvic
Thenon
Le Lardin-St. Lazare
Terrasson-Lavilledieu
Larche
Beynat
Argentat
St. Pierre-de-Chignac
Montignac
LASCAUX
Meyssac
Mussidan
Villamblard
La Douze
Vergt
Cressensac
GROTTE DE ROUFFIGNAC
Salignac-Eyvigues
Pont-St. Mamet
GROTTE DE COMBARELLES
Vayrac
Martel
Beaulieu-sur-Dordogne
Laroquebrou
Campsegret
GROTTE DU GRAND ROC
Les Eyzies-de-Tayac
Sarlat-la-Canéda
Souillac
Bretenoux
Pezuls
Le Bugue
St. Cyprien
CHÂTEAU DE CASTELNAU-BRETENOUX
Sousceyrac
GROTTE DE FONT DE GAUME
La Roque-Gageac
GROTTE DE LANCAVE
St. Céré
CHÂTEAU DE MONTAL
Le Roug
Lalinde
Le Buisson
Dordogne
Bergerac
Cadouin
STE. MARIE
Alvignac
Siorac-en-Périgord
Monbazillac
Belvès
CHÂTEAU DE BEYNAC
Domme
Payrac
Rocamadour
Gramat
Latronquière
Beaumont
Gourdon
Issigeac
Causses
Maurs
Salviac
Le Bourg
Lacapelle-Marival
Monpazier
Castillonès
Frayssinet
Eymet
Villefranche-du-Périgord
Cazals
Labastide-Murat
Livernon
Figeac
Villeréal
Lauzun
Lamothe-Cassel
Lauzès
Grézec
Frayssinet-le-Gélat
Capdenac-Gare
Monbahus
CHÂTEAU DE BONAGUIL
Monflanquin
Seyches
Quercy
Cancon
Prayssac
Tombeboeuf
Fumel
Puy-l'Evêque
GROTTE DES PECH-MERLES
Cajarc
Luzech
Cahors
Villeneuve-sur-Lot
Villeneuve
Castelmoron-sur-Lot
Tonneins
Tournon-d'Agenais
Sauzet
Limogne-en-Quercy
Ste. Livrade-sur-Lot
Penne-d'Agenais
Concots
Villefranche-de-Rouergue
Montaigu-de-Quercy
Bourran
St. Antoine-de-Ficalba
Montcuq
Lalbenque
Memer
Aiguillon
Laroque-Timbaut
Castelnau-Montratier
Parisot
Port-Ste. Marie
Beauville
Bourg-de-Visa
Puylaroque
Lauzerte
Caylus
Najac
La Fouillade
La Salvetat-Peyralès
Montpezat-de-Quercy
Lavardac
Agen
Bon-Encontre
Molières
St. Antonin-Noble-Val
Caussade
WALIBI AQUITAINE
Puymirol
Nérac
Valence-d'Agen
Laguépie
Lafrançaise
Lamagistère
Moissac
Nègrepelisse
Montricoux
Monestiés
Laplume
Auvillar
Astaffort
Francescas
La Ville Dieu-du-Temple
Vaour
Cordes-sur-Ciel
Castelsarrasin
Montauban
Ligardes
Castelnau-de-Montmirail
Blaye-les-Mines
Miradoux
Lavit
Monclar-de-Quercy
Condom
Bourret
Montech
Labastide-St. Pierre
Gaillac
Marsac
Lectoure
Larrazet
Beaumont-de-Lomagne
Salvagnac
Florentin
Valence-sur-Baïse
St. Clar
Lisle-sur-Tarn
Montans
Fleurance
Verdun-sur-Garonne
Villemur-sur-Tarn
Fronton
Cadalen
Solomiac
Grisolles
Rabastens
Montestruc-sur-Gers
Cox
Grenade
Graulhet
Jegun
St. Sulpice
Briatexte
Cépet
Mauvezin
Montastruc-la-Conseillère
Lavaur
Lautrec
St. Jean-Poutge
Preignan
Cologne
Cadours
Montaigut-sur-Save
Nougaroulet
Verfeil
Auch
Aubiet
Gimont
Blagnac
L'Isle-Jourdain
Colomiers
Toulouse
St. Paul-Cap-de-Joux
Vielmur-sur-Agout
L'Isle-de-Noé
Léguevin
Puylaurens
Lanta
Montesquiou
Plaisance
Saramon
Cugnaux
Caraman
Soual
Dourgne
St. Lys
Ramonville-St. Agne
Fourquevaux
Mirande
Samatan
Revel
Seissan
Lombez
Ste. Foy-de-Peyrolières
Sorèze
Muret
Montgiscard
Baziege
Lherm
St. Félix-Lauragais
Miélan
St. Michel
Masseube
Rieumes
Vernet
Villefranche-de-Lauragais
Molas
L'Isle-
Gardouch
Lot
Garonne
Tarn
Aveyron
Gers
Baïse
Canal du Midi
Save
Vézère
Isle
Dronne
Corrèze
Tescou
Cérou
Dadou
Agout
Gimone
Arrats
Osse
Célé
A20
A62
A64
A68
A89
A680
E09
E70
E72
E80
23
24
30
39
40

Decazeville
Firmi
Capdenac-Gare
Aubin
Conques
Entraygues-sur-Truyère
Le Cayrol
Aubrac
St. Chély-d'Aubrac
Marvejols
Chirac
Mende
ERMITAGE DE ST. PRIVAT
Le Bleymard
Laubert
Belvezet
Villecomtal
Espalion
St. Come-d'Olt
St. Geniez-d'Olt
Montbazens
Roussennac
Marcillac-Vallon
Bozouls
Gabriac
Sebazac-Concourès
La Canourgue
Chanac
Col de Montmirat 1046
Villeneuve
Rignac
Villefranche-de-Rouergue
Rodez
Laissac
St. Saturnin-de-Lenne
Ste. Enimie
Ispagnac
Recoules-Prévinquières
Sévérac-le-Château
Le Massegros
La Malène
Florac
Cassagnas
Cévennes
Memer
Najac
La Fouillade
La Salvetat-Peyralès
Rieupeyroux
Baraqueville
La Primaube
Lac de Pont-de-Salars
Pont-de-Salars
Vézins-de-Lévézou
Les Vignes
Causse-Méjean
Barre-des-Cevennes
Lac de Pareloup
Salles-Curan
Salmiech
Mostuéjouls
Le Rozier
Rousses
Naucelle
Cassagnes-Bégonhès
Laguépie
Meyrueis
St. André-de-Valborgne
Mt. Aigoual 1567
St Beauzély
Aguessac
La Roque-Ste. Marguerite
Montjaux
Millau
Monestiés
Tanus
Carmaux
Villefranche-de-Panat
St. Georges-de-Luzençon
Creissels
Causse du Larzac
l'Esperou
Valleraugue
Blaye-les-Mines
Réquista
St. Rome-de-Tarn
Grands Causses
Nant
St. Jean-du-Bruel
Valence-d'Albigeois
Broquies
St. Rome-de-Cernon
La Cavalerie
Le Vigan
St. Hippolyte-du-Fort
St. Juéry
St. Izaire
L'Hospitalet-du-Larzac
Montdardier
Ganges
Marsac
Albi
Plaisance
St. Affrique
Florentin
Villefranche-d'Albigeois
Alban
St. Sernin-sur-Rance
St. Felix-de-Sorgues
Cornus
St. Maurice-Navacelles
St. Bauzille-de-Putois
Cadalen
Teillet
St. Pierre
Le Caylar
Col Notre-Dame 667
Causse-de-la-Selle
Camarès
Belmont-sur-Rance
Fayet
Ceilhes-et-Rocozels
Brusque
St. Pierre-de-la-Fage
St. Martin-de-Londres
Graulhet
Réalmont
Lodève
Montredon-Labessonnié
Lautrec
Vabre
Col de la Bassine 885
Lacaune
Murat-sur-Vèbre
Le Bousquet-d'Orb
Lunas
Aniane
Roquecourbe
Mts. de Lacaune
Lac du Salagou
Lac de Lauzas
Gignac
Montpellier
Vielmur-sur-Agout
Brassac
St. Gervais-sur-Mare
Hérépian
Clermont-l'Hérault
St. André-de-Sangonis
Pignan
Castres
Bédarieux
Cournonterral
Fabrègues
Soual
Labruguière
Dourgne
Anglès
La Salvetat-sur-Agout
Olargues
Haut-Languedoc
Poujol-sur-Orb
Canet
Paulhan
Revel
Sorèze
Mazamet
Montagne Noire
St. Amans-Soult
Labastide-Rouairoux
St. Pons-de-Thomières
Roquebrun
Roujan
Lezignan-la-Cèbe
Villeveyrac
Montagnac
Courniou
Col des Usclats 575
Murviel-lès-Béziers
Pézenas
Mèze
Frontignan
Col de Serières 681
St. Chinian
Cessenon
Cazouls-lès-Béziers
Servian
Florensac
Sète
Saissac
Mas-Cabardès
Castelnaudary
Puisserguier
Béziers
Bessan
Marseillan
Bassin de Thau
Caunes-Minervois
Aigues-Vives
Maureilhan
Agde
Montolieu
Peyriac-Minervois
Capestang
Alzonne
Bram
Conques-sur-Orbiel
Canal du Midi
Olonzac
Nissan-lez-Ensérune
Sérignan
Le Cap d'Agde
C. d'Agde
Côte d'A
Carcassonne
Fanjeaux
Montréal
Coursan
Fleury
Valras-Plage
Capendu
Lézignan-Corbières
Narbonne
Narbonne-Plage
Ferrals-les-Corbières
Thezar-les-Corbières
ABBAYE DE FONTFROIDE
Narbonnaise en Méditerranée
Gruissan
St. Hilaire
Lagrasse
St. Laurent-de-la-Cabrerisse
Limoux
Ajac
Sigean
Port-la-Nouvelle
Tanger
Nador
Chalabre
Alet-les-Bains
Vignevieille
Mouthoumet
Durban-Corbières
Villeneuve-les-Corbières
La Palme
Espéraza
Couiza
Rennes-les-Bains
Puivert
Leucate
Tuchan
Soulatgé
Corbières
Quillan
Paziols
Étang de Leucate
FORTERESS DE SALSES
Salses-le-Château
St. Paul-de-Fenouillet
Maury
Vingrau
Axat
Caudiès-de-Fenouillèdes
Rivesaltes
Le Barcarès
Usson-les-Bains
Agly
Estagel
St. Laurent-de-la-Salanque
Sournia
Millas
Perpignan
Quérigut
Ille-sur-Têt
Canet-en-Roussillon
Madrès

Vals-les-Bains
Aubenas
Montélimar
Luc-en-Diois
Aspres-sur-Buëch
Largentière
Villeneuve-de-Berg
Le Teil
Rochemaure
Meysse
Sauzet
Cléon-d'Andran
Pradelle
Bourdeaux
St. Nazaire-le-Désert
La Bégude-de-Mazenc
Dieulefit
Bellegarde-en-Diois
Vogüé
CHÂTEAU DE VOGÜÉ
BAPTISTRE DE MÉLAS
Espeluche
Aleyrac
Bouvières
La Motte-Chalançon
La Charce
Joyeuse
Viviers
Donzère
CHÂTEAU DE GRIGNAN
Taulignan
Grignan
Serres
Lablachère
Ruoms
St. Montant
Rémuzat
Rosans
L'Epine
Les Vans
Vallon-Pont-d'Arc
Pierrelatte
St. Paul-Trois-Châteaux
Valréas
Nyons
Verclause
Bourg-St. Andéol
Ste. Jalle
St. Paul-le-Jeune
Barjac
Orgnac-l'Aven
AVEN MARZAL-GROTTE, MUSÉE ET ZOO PREHISTORIQUE
Suze-la-Rousse
Tulette
Mirabel-aux-Baronnies
Laragne-Montéglin
Bessèges
St. Just
Vaison-la-Romaine
VILLE ROMAINE RUIN
Buis-les-Baronnies
La Rochette
Barret-le-Bas
Le Collet-de-Deze
St. Ambroix
Bollène
Pont-St. Esprit
St. André-de-Roquepertuis
Mondragon
Séderon
Les Omergues
La Grand-Combe
Les Mages
Bagnols-sur-Cèze
Camaret-sur-Aigues
Malaucène
Mt. Ventoux
Montbrun-les-Bains
Salindres
Lussan
Orange
Vacqueyras
Bédoin
Alès
Seynes
Connaux
Châteauneuf-du-Pape
Sault
Revest-du-Bion
St. Etienne-les-Orgues
St. Christol-lès-Alès
St. Quentin-la-Poterie
Roquemaure
Bédarrides
Mazan
Carpentras
Banon
ST. CHRISTOL
Anduze
Vézenobres
Serviers
Sorgues
St. Christol
Uzès
Villeneuve-lès-Avignon
Pernes-les-Fontaines
St. Saturnin-lès-Apt
Lédignan
Moussac
PONT DU GARD
Remoulins
Avignon
L'Isle-sur-la-Sorgue
Manosque
Sauve
Quissac
La Calmette
Aramon
Châteaurenard
Fontaine de Vaucluse
Rustrel
Reillanne
Montmirat
Barbentane
Apt
Cereste
Nîmes
Marguerittes
CHÂTEAU DE TARASCON
Noves
Sauteyrargues
Beaucaire
Tarascon
Graveson
Plan-d'Orgon
Cavaillon
Bonnieux
Luberon
La Bastide-des-Jourdans
Valflaunes
Sommières
Calvisson
Bouillargues
RUINES ROMAINES DE GLANUM
St. Rémy-de-Provence
Orgon
Lourmarin
Cucuron
Ste. Tulle
St. Mathieu-de-Tréviers
Boisseron
Alpilles
Sénas
Mallemort
Cadenet
La Tour d'Aigues
Uchaud
Bellegarde
Les Baux-de-Provence
Maussane-les-Alpilles
Eyguières
Vauvert
St. Gilles
Arles
Mouriès
Salon-de-Provence
Lambesc
Rognes
Pertuis
Peyrolles-en-Provence
Castries
Lunel
Aimargues
L'EGLISE DE L'ABBAYE DE ST. GILLES
St. Martin-de-Crau
Pélissanne
Le Puy-Ste. Réparade
St. Cannat
Meyrargues
St. Laurent-d'Aigouze
MURS DU MOYEN-AGE
Mauguio
Miramas
Venelles
Vauvenargues
Eguilles
Aix-en-Provence
Pérols
Aigues-Mortes
St. Chamas
Lançon-Provence
Châteauneuf-le-Rouge
Carnon Plage
La Grande-Motte
Le Grau-du-Roi
Palavas-les-Flots
Étang de Vaccarès
La Crau
Istres
Étang de Berre
Berre-l'Etang
Gardanne
Trets
Golfe d'Aigues-Mortes
Port-Camargue
Camargue
Fos-sur-Mer
Marignane
Martigues
St. Savournin
Auriol
Stes. Maries-de-la-Mer
STES. MARIES DE LA MER
Port-de-Bouc
Roquevaire
Allauch
Port-St.-Louis-du-Rhône
Carro
Carry-le-Rouet
Aubagne
Gémenos
C. Couronne
Sausset-les-Pins
CHÂTEAU D'IF
Marseille
Marseilles
Cassis
Cap Croisette
Calanques
La Ciotat
St. Cyr-sur-Mer
Sanary-sur-Mer
Rhône
Durance
Golfe du Lion
Oran
Alger
Annaba
Bejaia
Skikda
Tunis
Porto Tórres
Ajaccio
Bastia
l'Ile Rousse
Porto-Vecchio
Propriano
0
10
20
30 km
44°
43°
4°
5°
2
3
4
A
B
C

Luc-en-Diois
St. Bonnet
Orcières
Mont Dauphin
Guillestre
St. Véran
Châteauroux-les-Alpes
Risoul
Col Bayard 1248
Beaurières
St. Nazaire-le-Désert
Aspres-sur-Buëch
La Roche-des-Arnauds
Embrun
Vars Les Claux
Vars
Chorges
Col de Vars 2109
Bellegarde-en-Diois
Veynes
Gap
Les Orres
Savines-le-lac
La Motte-Chalançon
La Charce
Lac de Serre-Ponçon
Espinasses
St. Paul
Acceglio
Prazzo
Tallard
La Condamine-Châtelard
Col de Larche 1948
Serres
Savournon
Larche
Rémuzat
Rosans
L'Epine
Bréziers
Turriers
Le Lauzet-Ubaye
Jausiers
Argentera
Verclause
Ventavon
Selonnet
Seyne
Pra Loup
Barcelonette
Col de la Bonette 2802
St. Jalle
Eyguians
Durance
La Motte-du-Caire
Col de Maure 1347
Super Sauze
Col d'Allos 2247
Laragne-Montéglin
Le Poët
Bayons
Mt. Pelat 3052
Col de la Cayolle 2326
Buis-les-Baronnies
La Rochette
Barret-le-Bas
Barles
Le Vernet
St. Étienne-de-Tinée
St. Geniez
Authon
Allos
Séderon
Ribiers
Les Omergues
Beaujeu
Colmars
Mercantour
Ventoux
Montbrun-les-Bains
Sisteron
La Javie
Isola
Noyers-sur-Jabron
Le Brusquet
St. Martin-d'Entraunes
Sault
Château-Arnoux
Thorame-Haute
Revest-du-Bion
Cruis
Malijai
Digne-les-Bains
Thorame-Basse
Guillaumes
Valberg
Beuil
St. Etienne-les-Orgues
Banon
St. Christol
Peyruis
Châteauredon
Daluis
Les Mées
Le Fugeret
Forcalquier
St. André-les-Alpes
Puimichel
Annot
Puget-Théniers
St. Saturnin-lès-Apt
Mane
Barrême
Rustrel
La Brillanne
Bras d'Asse
Estoublon
Entrevaux
Reillanne
Oraison
Senez
St. Julien-du-Verdon
Apt
Volx
Puimoisson
Roquesteron
Cereste
Luberon
Valensole
Castellane
St. Auban
Brianconnet
La Bastide-des-Jourdans
Manosque
Moustiers-Ste. Marie
Mt. Cheiron 1776
Var
Ste. Tulle
Gréoux-les-Bains
Riez
Verdon
Soleils
Lourmarin
Cucuron
Cadenet
La Tour d'Aigues
Lac de Ste. Croix
Bramafan
Escragnolles
Vence
Le Bar-sur-Loup
Rognes
Vinon-sur-Verdon
Quinson
Comps-sur-Artuby
Pertuis
Ginasservis
St. Vallier-de-Thiey
Grasse
Cagnes-sur-Mer
Le Puy-Ste. Réparade
St. Cannat
Peyrolles-en-Provence
Montmeyan
Aups
Meyrargues
Fayence
Venelles
Montferrat
Bargemon
Eguilles
Rians
Esparron
Varages
Callas
Mougins
Vauvenargues
Aix-en-Provence
Brue-Auriac
Barjols
Salernes
Draguignan
Bagnols-en-Forêt
Cannes
Châteauneuf-le-Rouge
Flayosc
Trans-en-Provence
Mandelieu-la-Napoule
Gardanne
Lorgues
Le Muy
Trets
Carcès
Les Arcs
St. Maximin-la-Ste. Baume
Le Val
Cabasse
Abbaye du Thoronet
Vidauban
Puget-sur-Argens
Agay
St. Savournin
Auriol
Tourves
Brignoles
Le Luc
Fréjus
St. Raphaël
Roquevaire
Flassans-sur-Issole
St. Aygulf
Allauch
La Roquebrussanne
Gonfaron
Val d'Esquières
Aubagne
Gémenos
Garéoult
La Garde-Freinet
Côte de l'Esterel
Cuges-les-Pins
Signes
OK Corral
Puget-ville
Grimaud
Ste. Maxime
Marseille
Méounes-les-Montrieux
Collobrières
Cogolin
St. Tropez
Belgentier
Cuers
Maures
La Mole
Cassis
Le Beausset
Pierrefeu-du-Var
La Croix-Valmer
Cap Camarat
Cap Croisette
Calanques
Solliès-Pont
La Crau
Bormes-les-Mimosas
Cavalaire-sur-Mer
La Ciotat
St. Cyr-sur-Mer
Bandol
Toulon
Le Rayol
Hyères
La Londe-les-Maures
Le Lavandou
Sanary-sur-Mer
La Seyne-sur-Mer
Carqueiranne
Hyères Plage
C. Bénat
St. Mandrier-sur-Mer
Giens
Î. du Levant
Îs. d'Hyères
Porquerolles
Î. de Porquerolles
Î. de Port-Cros
Parc National de Port-Cros
Ajaccio
Bastia
l'Ile Rousse
Porto-Vecchio
Propriano
Porto Tórres
6°
7°
44°
43°
A
B
C
1
2
3
26
31

Paesana
Revello
Saluzzo
Savigliano
Verzuolo
Venasca
Costigliole Saluzzo
Busca
San Damiano Macra
Dronero
Caráglio
Centallo
Fossano
Genola
Cherasco
Narzole
Bene Vagienna
Dogliani
Carrù
Carmine
Morozzo
Monterosso Grana
Cuneo
Mondovì
Villanova Mondovì
Bòves
Borgo San Dalmazzo
Demonte
Vinadio
Valdieri
Peveragno
Chiusa di Pésio
Frabosa Soprana
Fontane
Certosa di Pésio
Vernante
Entrácque
Terme di Valdieri
Argentera
3297
Limone Piemonte
Colle di Tenda
1279
Tunnel de Tende
Tende
Alpes Maritimes
Mercantour
St. Martin-Vésubie
Roquebilière
Fontan
Saorge
Lantosque
Col de Turini
1604
St. Jean-la-Riviere
Moulinet
Col de Brouis
875
Breil-sur-Roya
Luceram
Sospel
Col de Braus
1002
L'Escarène
Airole
Ventimíglia
Menton
Palais Princier
Monte-Carlo
MONACO
Beaulieu-sur-Mer
Villefranche-sur-Mer
Nice
Cap Ferrat
Marineland
Antibes
Juan-les-Pins
Côte d'Azur
Bastia
I'lle Rousse
Ajaccio
Porto-Vecchio
Golfo Aranci
Alba
Diano d'Alba
Monforte d'Alba
Bubbio
Bistagno
Terme
Vésime
Cortemilia
Bossolasco
Murazzano
Piana Crixia
Monesiglio
Dego
Spigno Monferrato
Sassello
Pontinvrea
Cairo Montenotte
Cárcare
Millesimo
Ceva
San Michele Mondovì
Viola
Pamparato
Bagnasco
Calizzano
Garéssio
Ormea
Ponte di Nava
Erli
Borghetto d'Arróscia
Mónesi
Pieve di Teco
Arroscia
Triora
Pontedássio
Pigna
Badalucco
Dolceácqua
Seborga
Ospedaletti
Bordighera
San Remo
Taggia
Riva Ligure
San Lorenzo al Mare
Impéria
Diano Marina
Laiguéglia
Alássio
Albenga
Borghetto Santo Spirito
Loano
Pietra Ligure
Finale Lígure
Noli
C. di Noli
Spotorno
Vado Lígure
Savona
Albisola Marina
Celle Ligure
Varazze
Arenzano
Voltri
Pegli
Génova
Genoa
Nervi
Santa Margherita
Ovada
Molare
Castello di Molare
Gavi
Voltággio
Ronco Scrivia
Busalla
Rossiglione
Campo Ligure
Masone
Passo dei Giovi
Pontedécimo
Bolzaneto
Casella
Molassano
Appennino
Riviera di Ponente
Golfo di Génova
Bastia
Barcelona
Tanger
Palermo
Tunis
Skikda
Olbia
Porto Tórres
Árbatax
Barcelona
Tanger
MARE LIGURE
LIGURIAN SEA
44°
43°
8°
9°
0 10 20 30 km
3
4
A
B
C

1 2 3

A B C

0 10 20 30 km

C. Ortegal
Cariño
Ría de Ortigueira
Cedeira
Pantín
Ortigueira
Mera
Viveiro
Esteiro
Valdoviño
C. Prior
Cobas
Narón
Xubia
Ferrol
Neda
Doniños
Fene
Mugardos
Ares
A Capela
As Pontes de García Rodríguez
Espiñaredo
Ourol
Muras
Xistral 1032
Granas
Ría de Betanzos
Pontedeume
Eume
Cabreiros
Vilapedre
TORRE DE HERCULES
A Coruña
Mera
Lorbé
Santa Cruz
Sada
Miño
Oleiros
Candamil
Campo da Feira
Monfero
Is. Sisargas
Malpica de Bergantiños
Punta Nariga
Caion
Arteixo
Betanzos
Cambre
Villalba
Ría de Corme e Laxe
Ponteceso
Buño
Razo
Laracha
Carral
Coirós
Laxe
Carballo
Allóns
Cabana
Camelle
Cabo Vilán
Coristanco
Cerceda
Montesalgueiro
Baamonde
Camariñas
Dor
Baio
Agualada
Silva
Cesuras
Guitiriz
Ría de Camariñas
Muxía
Vimianzo
Zas
Curtis
Teixeiro
Curtis Santa Eulalia
Rábade
Outeiro de Rei
Moraime
C. Touriñán
Lanza
Vilasantar
Touriñán
Berdoias
Ordes
Sobrado
Santa Comba
Brandomil
Corredoiras
Lugo
43°
Friol
Emb. da Fervenza
A Baña
Cée
Corcubión
Portemouro
Sigueiro
Fisterra
Ezaro
Mazaricos
Pino de Val
Toques
C. Fisterra
O Pino
Arzúa
Santiago de Compostela
Negreira
Melide
Palas de Rei
Lousada
Guntín
O Pedrouzo
Carnota
Outes
Brión
Tambre
Serra de Outes
Bertamiráns
Boqueixón
Touro
Lariño
Tal
Muros
Urdilde
Noia
Ulla
Rio
Portomarín
Monterroso
Vila de Cruces
Padrón
Vedra
Teo
Agolada
Ría de Muros e Noia
Porto do Son
Pontecesures
Riobo
Chapa
Taboada
Embalse de Belesar
Catoira
A Estrada
Silleda
Lalín
Pobra do Caramiñal
Boiro
Rianxo
Cuntis
Rodeiro
Currelos
Corrubedo
Oleiros
Vilagarcía de Arousa
Caldas de Reis
Forcarei
Santa Uxía de Ribeira
Isla de Arousa
Chantada
Escairón
Cachafeiro
Cambados
Cerdedo
Soutelo de Montes
Carballeda
Emb. dos Peares
Ría de Arousa
Grove
Lérez
Regueiro
Piñor
Pantón
I. de Sálvora
Poio
Serra do Suido
Cea
Os Peares
Lanzada
Pontevedra
Vilamarín
A Peroxa
Illas
Sanxenxo
Ponte-Caldelas
Boboras
O Carballiño
Miño
Embalse de S. Esteban
I. de Ons
Portonovo
Marín
Maside
Luintra
Atlánticas
Mogor
San Amaro
Ría de Pontevedra
Bueu
Fornelos de Montes
Leiro
Peroxo de Aguiar
de
Estacas
Carballeda de Avia
Esgos
Cangas
Moaña
Redondela
Avión 1151
Ribadavia
Toén
Ourense
Xunqueira de Espadañedo
Galicia
Vigo
Barbadás
San Cibrao das Viñas
Maceda
Is. Cíes
Mondariz
Melón
Taboadela
Baños de Molgas
Ría de Vigo
Bouzas
Cortegada
A Merca
A Cañiza
S. MARTIÑO DE PAZO
Xunqueira de Ambia
O Porriño
Panxon
Ponteareas
Crecente
Allariz
Villar de Barrio
Baiona
Ramirás
A Bola
C. Silleiro
Gondomar
Celanova
Forriolo
As Neves
Melgaço
Vilar de Santos
Sarreaus
Tui
Lamas de Moaro
Rairiz de Veiga
Xinzo de Limia
Monção
Oia
Merufe
Trasmiras
42°
Seijo
Valença
Castro Laboreiro
Bande
Limia
São Pedro da Torre
Baixa
Tomiño
Sistelo
Blancos
Cualedro
São Bento
Limia-Sierra do Xurés
O Rosal
Cabreiro
Serra da Peneda
Mugueimes
Baltar
A Guarda
Vila Nova de Cerveira
Paredes de Coura
Fondevila
Randín
Coura
MONTE DE STA. TEGRA
Caminha
Lindoso
Vila Praia de Ancora
Moledo do Minho
Arcos de Valdevez
IGREJA ROMANICA DE BRAVES
Lima
Gerês
Montalegre
CASTELO DE MONTALEGRE
Orbacém
Ancora
Barragem do

42
42

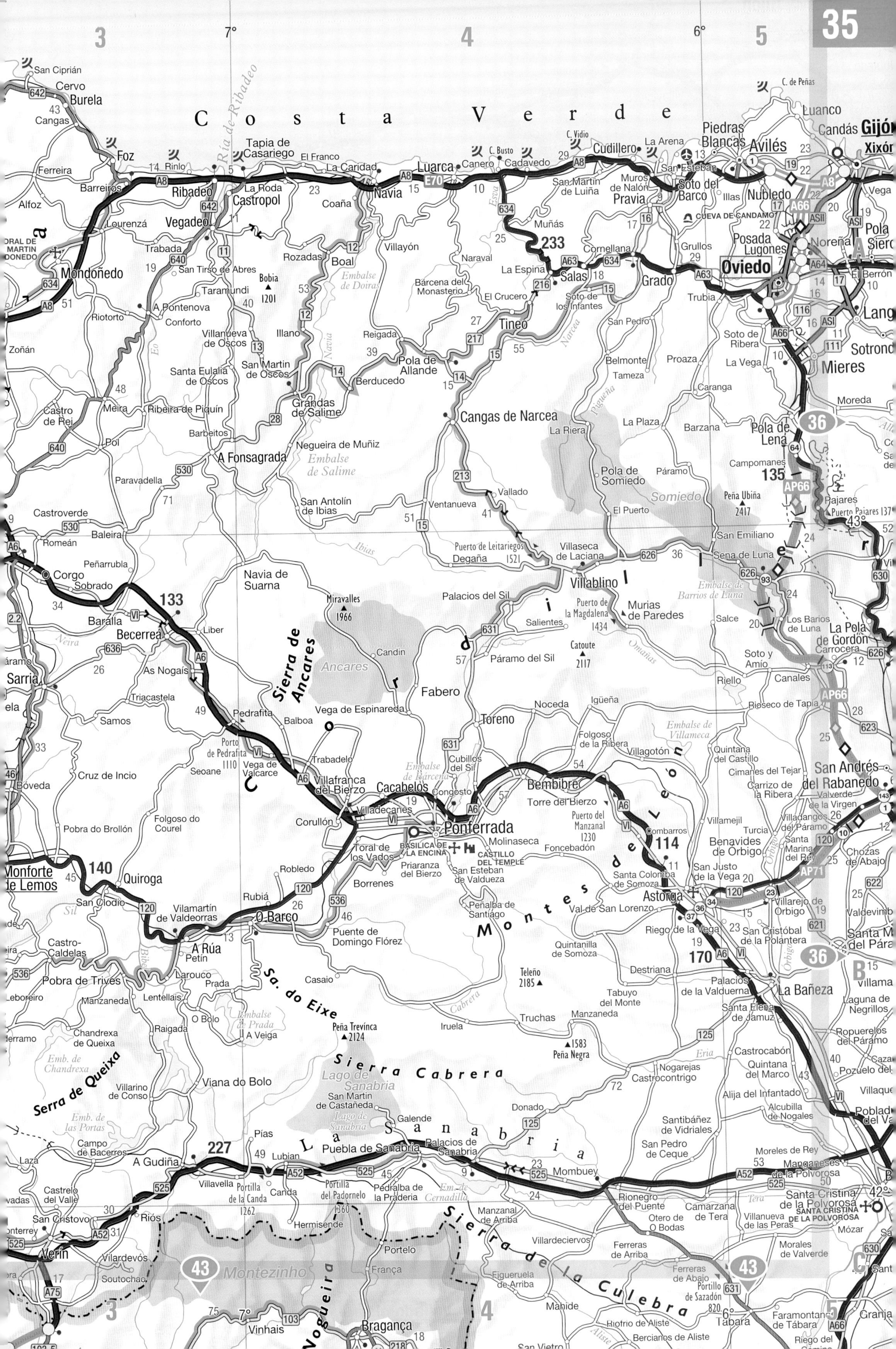

3
7°
4
6°
5
Costa Verde
San Ciprián
Cervo
Burela
Cangas
Foz
Ría de Ribadeo
Tapia de Casariego
El Franco
La Caridad
C. Busto
Luarca
Canero
Cadavedo
C. Vidio
Cudillero
La Arena
Piedras Blancas
Avilés
C. de Peñas
Luanco
Candás
Gijón
Xixón
Ferreira
Rinlo
Barreiros
Ribadeo
Vegadeo
La Roda
Castropol
Coaña
Navia
San Martín de Luiña
Muros de Nalón
Pravia
San Esteban
Soto del Barco
Illas
Nubledo
Alfoz
Lourenzá
Trabada
Villayón
Naraval
Muñás
Cornellana
CUEVA DE CANDAMO
Grullos
Posada
Lugones
Noreña
Pola Siero
Mondoñedo
San Tirso de Abres
Bobia 1201
Rozadas
Boal
Embalse de Doiras
Bárcena del Monasterio
El Crucero
La Espina
Salas
Soto de los Infantes
Grado
Trubia
Oviedo
El Berrón
Riotorto
Taramundi
A Pontenova
Conforto
Villanueva de Oscos
Illano
Reigada
Tineo
San Pedro
Langreo
Zoñán
Santa Eulalia de Oscos
San Martín de Oscos
Pola de Allande
Berducedo
Soto de Ribera
La Vega
Belmonte
Proaza
Sotrondio
Mieres
Tameza
Caranga
Castro de Rei
Meira
Ribeira de Piquín
Grandas de Salime
Cangas de Narcea
La Riera
La Plaza
Barzana
Pola de Lena
Moreda
Pol
Barbeitos
Negueira de Muñiz
Embalse de Salime
A Fonsagrada
Paravadella
Pola de Somiedo
Páramo
Campomanes
Somiedo
San Antolín de Ibias
Vallado
Ventanueva
El Puerto
Peña Ubiña 2417
Pajares
Puerto Pajares 1379
Castroverde
Baleira
Romeán
Ibias
Puerto de Leitariegos
Degaña 1521
Villaseca de Laciana
San Emiliano
Sena de Luna
Peñarrubla
Corgo
Sobrado
Navia de Suarna
Villablino
Embalse de Barrios de Luna
Miravalles 1966
Palacios del Sil
Puerto de la Magdalena 1434
Murias de Paredes
Baralla
Becerreá
Liber
Salientes
Salce
Los Barios de Luna
La Pola de Gordón
Neira
Sierra de Ancares
Candin
Ancares
Catoute 2117
Páramo del Sil
Omañas
Soto y Amío
Carrocera
Sarria
As Nogais
Riello
Canales
Fabero
Triacastela
Samos
Pedrafita
Balboa
Vega de Espinareda
Noceda
Igüeña
Rioseco de Tapia
Toreno
Porto de Pedrafita 1110
Trabadelo
Folgoso de la Ribera
Embalse de Villameca
Villagotón
Quintana del Castillo
Cruz de Incio
Seoane
Vega de Valcarce
Embalse de Bárcena
Cubillos del Sil
Cimanes del Tejar
San Andrés del Rabanedo
Bóveda
Villafranca del Bierzo
Cacabelos
Congosto
Bembibre
Carrizo de la Ribera
Valverde de la Virgen
Torre del Bierzo
Villadangos del Páramo
Villadecanes
Corullón
Puerto del Manzanal 1230
Villamejil
Turcia
Pobra do Brollón
Folgoso do Courel
Ponferrada
Molinaseca
Combarros
Benavides de Órbigo
Santa Marina del Rey
Chozas de Abajo
BASÍLICA DE LA ENCINA
CASTILLO DEL TEMPLE
Toral de los Vados
Fonsebadón
Priaranza del Bierzo
San Esteban de Valdueza
Monforte de Lemos
Quiroga
Robledo
Borrenes
Santa Colomba de Somoza
San Justo de la Vega
Montes de León
Astorga
San Clodio
Rubiá
Peñalba de Santiago
Val de San Lorenzo
Villarejo de Órbigo
Valdevimbre
Sil
Vilamartín de Valdeorras
O Barco
Riego de la Vega
San Cristóbal de la Polantera
Santa María del Páramo
Castro-Caldelas
A Rúa
Petín
Puente de Domingo Flórez
Quintanilla de Somoza
Pobra de Trives
Larouco
Sa. do Eixe
Casaio
Teleño 2185
Destriana
Palacios de la Valduerna
La Bañeza
Villamañán
Leboreiro
Manzaneda
Lentellais
Prada
Tabuyo del Monte
Laguna de Negrillos
O Bolo
Embalse de Prada
Cabrera
Truchas
Manzaneda
Santa Elena de Jamuz
Chandrexa de Queixa
Raigada
A Veiga
Peña Trevinca 2124
Iruela
Roperuelos del Páramo
Emb. de Chandrexa
1583 Peña Negra
Eria
Castrocabón
Pozuelo del Páramo
Serra de Queixa
Viana do Bolo
Sierra Cabrera
Lago de Sanabria
Nogarejas
Castrocontrigo
Quintana del Marco
Villarino de Conso
San Martín de Castañeda
Alija del Infantado
Villaquejida
Emb. de las Portas
Lago de Sanabria
Galende
Donado
Alcubilla de Nogales
Pobladura del Valle
Pías
La Sanabria
Santibáñez de Vidriales
Campo de Bacerros
Puebla de Sanabria
Palacios de Sanabria
San Pedro de Ceque
Moreles de Rey
Laza
A Gudiña
Lubián
Mombuey
Manganeses de la Polvorosa
Castrelo del Valle
Villavella
Portilla de la Canda 1262
Canda
Portilla del Padornelo 1360
Pedralba de la Pradería
Em. de Cernadilla
Rionegro del Puente
Otero de O Bodas
Camarzana de Tera
Tera
Villanueva de las Peras
Santa Cristina de la Polvorosa
SANTA CRISTINA DE LA POLVOROSA
Mózar
Ríos
San Cristovo
Hermisende
Manzanal de Arriba
Monterrey
Verín
Vilardevós
Villardeciervos
Ferreras de Arriba
Morales de Valverde
Soutochao
Montezinho
Portelo
França
Sierra de la Culebra
Ferreras de Abajo
Portillo de Sazadón 820
Figueruela de Arriba
Mahíde
Faramontanos de Tábara
Tábara
Granja
Vinhais
Nogueira
Bragança
Riofrío de Aliste
Bercianos de Aliste
Riego del Camino
San Vitero
Aliste
A
B
C
36
43

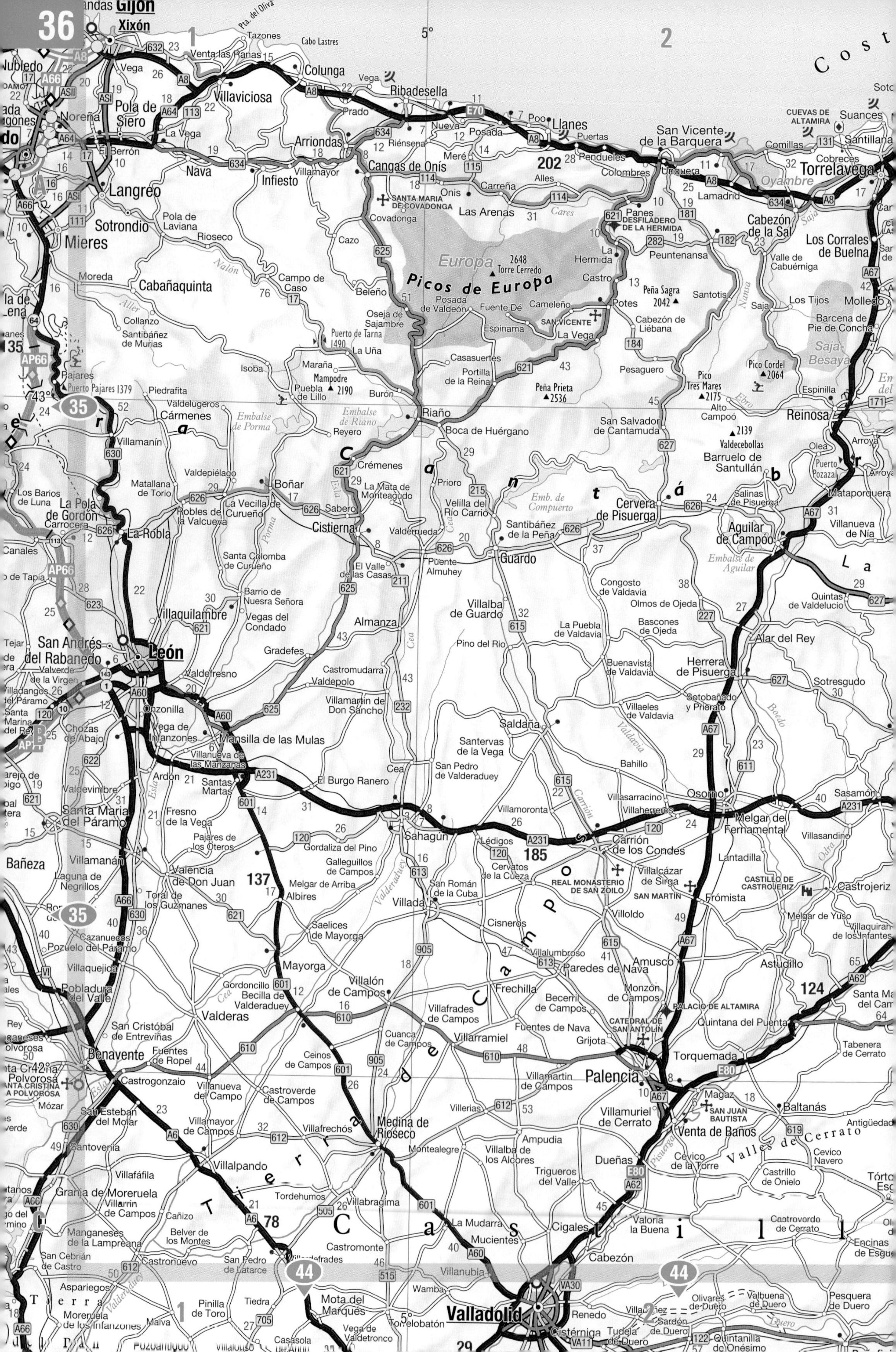

Montañesa
Plymouth
Portsmouth
Portsmouth
3°
0 10 20 30 km
Santander
C. de Ajo
C. de Quejo
Noja
Santoña
Laredo
Islares
Castro-Urdiales
C. de Matxitxako
Bermeo
Mundaka
Ibarranguelua
Lekeitio
Ondarroa
Mutriku
Zumaia
Zaraut
San Se
Gorliz
Plentzia
Bakio
Sopelana
Getxo
Portugalete
Mungia
Gernika-Lumo
Markina-Xemein
Deba
Zestoa
Aya
Somo
Ajo
Escalante
Beranga
Muriedas
El Astillero
Colindres
Solares
Solórzano
Entrambasaguas
Bedames
Ampuero
El Puente
Ciervana
PUENTE DE VIZCAYA
Santurtzi
Sestao
Barakaldo
Bilbao
Basauri
Muxilka- Ugarte
Muntibar
Amorebieta
Galdakao
Eibar
Elgoibar
Azpeitia
Régil
Vargas
Santa Maria de Cayón
Puente Viesgo
Riba
Rasines
Ramales de la Victoria
Mercadillo
El Callejo
Zalla
Güeñes
Arrigorriaga
Igorre
Durango
Ugarana
Zaldibar
Elorrio
Placencia
Azcoitia
Arredondo
San Roque de Riomera
Lanestosa
Balmaseda
Sodupe
Molinar
Llodio
Zeberio
Orozko
Urkiola
Bergara
Villacarriedo
La Concha
Entrambasmestas
Vega de Pas
Valnera 1718
Artziniega
Llanteno
Ceánuri
Arrasate
Zumárraga
Ordizia
Beasa
San Pedro del Romeral
Espinosa de los Monteros
Villasana de Mena
Bercedo
Villasante
Añes
Amurrio
Peña Gorbea 1475
Ubidea
Aretxabaleta
SANTUARIO DE LA VIRGEN DE ARANZAZU
San Miguel de Aguayo
Puerto del Escudo 1011
Corconte
Cilleruelo de Bezana
Santelices
Oteo
Quincoces de Yuso
Orduña
Murguia
Legutiano
Oñati
Arantzazu
Soncillo
La Cerca
Puerto de Orduña 900
Izarra
Embalse de Ullibarri
Ozaeta
Rozas
Puerto de Carrales 1020
Villarcayo
Medina de Pomar
Berberana
Durana
Manzanedo
Criales
Incinillas
Valdenoceda
Pedrosa de Tobalina
Villanueva de Valdegovia
Nanclares de la Oca
Vitoria-Gasteiz
Alegria
Salvatierra
Olazagutia
Sierra de Ur
Ruerrero
Escalada
Dobro
Trespaderne
Quintana-Martin Galindez
Espejo
Eulate
Pesadas de Burgos
Rucandio
Pobes
Puentelarra
Armiñón
Argote
San Vicente de Arana
San Felices
Sedano
La Oña
Bureba
La Aldea del Portillo del Busto
Arraia-Maeztu
Basconcillos del Tozo
Portillo del fresco 1028
Poza de la Sal
Cornudilla
Encio
Pancorvo
Miranda de Ebro
Santa Cruz de Campezo
Santa Maria Ribarredonda
Bujedo
Peñacerrada
Mendaz
La Nuez de Arriba
Masa
Cernégula
Terrazos
Sierra de Cantabria
Treviana
Haro
San Vicente de la Sonsierra
Cripán
Rubiacedo de Abajo
Briviesca
Casalarreina
Briones
Laguardia
Viana
Villante
Buezo
Cerezo de Riotirón
Herramelluri
Villadiego
Temiño
Monasterio de Rodilla
Castil de Peones
CATEDRAL DE SANTO DOMINGO DE LA CALZADA
San Asensio
Cenicero
Logroño
Quintanaortuño
Villamóndar
Mansilla de Burgos
Pedrosa del Rio Urbel
Puerto de la Brujula 981
Belorado
Santo Domingo de la Calzada
Nájera
Navarrete
Mendavia
Murillo de Río Leza
Alcanadr
CATEDRAL DE BURGOS
Quintanapalla
Villafranca-Montes de Oca
MONASTERIO DE SUSO
SANTA CRUZ
Albelda de Iregua
Tardajos
Burgos
Ibeas de Juarros
Santovenia
Ezcaray
Baños de Río Tobia
Ribafrecha
Arlanzón
Pradoluengo
San Millán de la Cogolla
Bobadilla
Nalda
Jubera
Iglesias
Carcedo de Burgos
CUEVA DE ATAPUERCA
SAN PEDRO DE CARDEÑA
Arcos
Fresneda de la Sierra Tiron
Torrecilla en Cameros
Villarobe
Sierra de la Demanda
SAN LORENZE
Robres del Castil
Estépar
Sarracín
San Lorenze 2271
Anguiano
San Juan
Tierra de Cameros
San Román de Cameros
Arnedillo
Mazuelo
Hontoria de la Cantera
Palazuelos de la Sierra
Pineda de la Sierra
Pampliega
Presencio
Ciadoncha
Barbadillo de Herreros
Tañabueyes
Brieva de Cameros
Enciso
Cuevas de San Clemente
Madrigalejo de Monte
Barbadillo del Pez
Huerta de Abajo
Villavelayo
Viniegra de Arriba
Picos de Urbión
Lumbreras
Villar del Río
Mecerreyes
Villahoz
Covarrubias
Hortiguela
Montenegro de Cameros
Puerto de Piqueras 1710
Neila
Urbión 2228
San Pedro Manrique
Lerma
Quintanilla de la Mata
Barbadillo del Mercado
Salas de los Infantes
Quintanar de la Sierra
La Póveda de Soria
Sierra Cebollera
Quintanilla del Coco
Puerto de Oncala 1454
Espinosa de Cerrato
Nebreda
Hacinas
Santo Domingo de Silos
Palacios de la Sierra
Canicosa de la Sierra
Covaleda
Vinuesa
Ventosa de la Sierra
Cilleruelo de Arriba
Almarza
Villafruela
Santa Maria de Mercadillo
Arauzo de Miel
Hontoria del Pinar
Embalse de la Cuerda del Pozo
El Royo
Tera
Castilfrio de la Sierra
Molinos de Duero
La Rubia
Bahabón de Esgueva
Torresandino
Huerta del Rey
Navaleno
Cidones
Garray
NUMANCIA ANTIQUÍSIMA
Almajano
Ventosilla
Sotillo de la Ribera
Gumiel de Hizán
Tubilla del Lago
Caleruega
Baños de Valdearados
San Leonardo de Yagüe
Cañón del Río Lobos
Casarejos
Muriel Viejo
Abejar
Soria
Aldea
Hontoria de Valdearados
Santa Maria de las Hoyas
Aldehuela de Calatañazor
Carbonera de Frentes
Los Rábanos
La Horra
Alcubilla de Avellaneda
Cubillos
Roa
SAN NICOLÁS DE BARI
Quemada
Ucero
Aranda de Duero
Peñaranda de Duero
Castrillo de la Vega
Valdocondes
Villálvaro
Torreblacos
Almenar de Soria
Fuentecén
La Vid
Lubia
Cubo de la Solana
Gómara
Fuentespina
Langa de Duero
El Burgo de Osma
Torralba de Burgo
Tardelcuende
Santa Cruz de la Salceda
Castilla y León
Cordillera Ibérica
38
45

0
10
20
30 km
Tarnos
Boucau
Bayonne
Anglet
Biarritz
Bidart
Côte Basque
Peyrehorade
Habas
Puyôo
Orthez
Salies-de-Béarn
Bidache
Briscous
Hasparren
Escos
Sauveterre-de-Béarn
Gave d'Oloron
Maslacq
St. Jean-de-Luz
Hendaye
Hondarribia
Irún
Ustaritz
St. Pée-sur-Nivelle
Ascain
Cambo-les-Bains
GROTTES D'ISTURITZ & OXOCELHAYA
St. Esteben
St. Palais
Mourenx
Navarrenx
Lekeitio
Ondarroa
Mutriku
Zumaia
Zarautz
Donostia-San Sebastián
CATEDRAL DEL BUEN PASTOR
Rentería
Oiartzun
Hernani
Sare
Vera de Bidasoa
Ainhoa
Urdax
Larceveau
Mauléon-Licharre
Markina
Deba
Zestoa
Lasarte
Andoain
Lesaka
Bidasoa
Maia
Erratzu
Eibar
Elgoibar
Azpeitia
Placencia
Régil
Villabona
Goizueta
Sunbilla
Elizondo
St. Etienne-de-Baigorry
St. Jean-Pied-de-Port
Musculdy
Barcus
Aramits
Azcoitia
Tolosa
Zubieta
Bergara
Zumárraga
Ordizia
Leitza
Puerto de Azpirotz 616
Donestebe-Santesteban
Irurita
Puerto de Belate 847
Aldudes
Arneguy
Tardets-Sorholus
SANTUARIO DE LA VIRGEN DE ARANZAZU
Oñati
Beasain
Lazkao
Idiazabal
Segura
Arantzazu
Lekunberri
Betelu
Orreaga-Roncesvalles
Puerto de Ibañeta 1057
Larrau
Ste. Engrâce
Embalse de Ullibarri
Ozaeta
SAN MIGUEL IN EXCELSIS
Araquil
Latasa
Irurzun
Olagüe
Auritz-Burguette
SANTA MARIA DE RONCESVALLES
Embalse de Irabia
Alsasua
Olazagutia
Etxarri-Aranatz
Ostiz
Zubiri
Erro
Aribe
Ochagavía
Ezcároz
Sierra de Urbasa
Sierra de Andia
Salvatierra
Alegria
Goñi
Ansoain
Burlada
Nagore
Isaba
Echauri
Barañain
Pamplona
Itoiz
Guesa
Roncal
Eulate
Cizur Mayor
Urroz
Aoiz
Noain
Ega
Arraia-Maeztu
San Vicente de Arana
Embalse de Alloz
Ansó
Hecho
Santa Cruz de Campezo
Estella
Puente la Reina
Monreal
Navascués
Burgui
Mañeru
EUNATE
Mendaza
IRACHE
Oteiza
Barasoain
Artajona
Lumbier
MONASTERIO DE LEYRE
Sigües
Arroniz
Aibar
Javier
Tiermas
Berdún
Embún
Cripán
Los Arcos
Allo
Larraga
Eslava
Sangüesa
Embalse de Yesa
Artieda
Viana
Tafalla
SANTA MARIA LA REAL DE SANGUESA
Puente la Reina de Jaca
Logroño
Lerín
San Martin de Unx
Cáseda
Peña 1069
Urries
Sos del Rey Católico
Sesma
Miranda de Arga
Ujué
Aragón
Bailó
Mendavia
Lodosa
Olite
Alcanadre
Murillo de Río Leza
Carcar
Andosilla
Albelda de Iregua
Falces
Santacara
Murillo el Fruto
Ribafrecha
Nalda
San Adrián
Peralta
Carcastillo
Castilisar
Luesia
Biel
Santa Maria
Jubera
El Villar de Arnedo
Calahorra
Marcilla
OLIVA
Caparroso
Uncastillo
Robres del Castillo
Villafranca
Milagro
Sádaba
El Frago
San Román de Cameros
Arnedillo
Arnedo
Quel
Rincón de Soto
Valtierra
DOÑA BLANCA DE NAVARRA
Farasdues
Biscarrués
Autol
Adeanueva de Ebro
Alfaro
Arguedas
Cidacos
Enciso
Castejón
Ebro
Ardisa
Corella
Ejea de los Caballeros
Luna
Villar del Río
Grávalos
Cintruénigo
Erla
Cornago
Igea
Fitero
Tudela
Cabanillas
Sierra de Luna
Alcalá de Gurrea
San Pedro Manrique
Cervera del Río Alhama
Alhama
Murchante
Fustiñana
Cascante
Ribaforada
Puerto de Oncala 1454
Valverde
Buñuel
Castejón de Valdejasa
Gurrea
Ventosa de la Sierra
CATEDRAL DE NUESTRA SEÑORA DE LA HUERTA
Cortes
El Temple
Castilfrío de la Sierra
Tarazona
La Rubia
Magaña
Castilruiz
El Buste
EL MISERICORDIA
CASTILLO DE BORJA
Mallén
Tauste
742 Esteban
Zuera
Garray
NUMANCIA ANTIQUISIMA
Almajano
Agreda
Vera de Moncayo
Borja
Gallur
Remolinos
San Mateo de Gállego
Ventosilla
Matalebreras
Sierra del Madero
Sierra del Moncayo
Magallon
Luceni
Soria
Aldeapozo
Olvega
Cueva de Agreda
Fuendejalón
Pedrola
Villanueva de Gállego
Los Rábanos
Alagón
Almenar de Soria
Borobia
Calcena
Tabuenca
Lumpiaque
Rueda de Jalón
Zaragoza
Cubo de la Solana
Gómara
Ciria
Aranda de Moncayo
Tierga
Épila
La Muela
Alfajarín
Almazul

Garlin
Marciac
Montesquiou
Saramon
Samatan
Lombez
Ste. Foy-de-Peyrolières
Lherm
Arzacq-Arraziguet
Thèze
Lembeye
Maubourguet
Tillac
Mirande
Seissan
Miélan
St. Michel
Masseube
Rieumes
Arthez-de-Béarn
Uzein
Vic-en-Bigorre
Rabastens-de-Bigorre
Molas
L'Isle-en-Dodon
Bérat
Artix
Lescar
Morlaàs
Trie-sur-Baïse
Boulogne-sur-Gesse
Pouy-de-Touges
Monein
Pau
Soumoulou
Andrest
Pouyastruc
Castelnau-Magnoac
Blajan
Le Fousseret
Angaïs
Tarbes
Galan
Aurignac
Cazères
Lasseube
Gan
Pontacq
Ossun
Juillan
Tournay
St. Plancard
St. Marcet
Martres Tolosane
Nay
Asson
St. Pé-de-Bigorre
Montgaillard
Villeneuve-de-Rivière
Boussens
St. Martory
Mazères-sur-Salat
Ste. Croix-Volvestre
Buzy
Arudy
Lourdes
Cieutat
Lannemezan
Pinas
Salies-du-Salat
Mane
Asasp
Louvie-Juzon
Capvern
Montréjeau
Valentine
St. Gaudens
Ferrières
Argelès-Gazost
GROTTES DE MÉDOUS
Bagnères-de-Bigorre
La Barthe-de-Neste
Barbazan
Accous
Laruns
Lesponne
Campan
Loures-Barousse
Aspet
Prat
Cazavet
St. Girons
Pic du Midi de Bigorre
Mauléon-Barousse
Sarrancolin
Col d'Aspin 1489
Eaux-Bonnes
Arrens-Marsous
Pierrefitte-Nestalas
Sengouagnet
Arbas
Col du Tourmalet 2114
2865
Cierp-Gaud
St. Béat
Orgibet
Castillon-en-Couserans
Barèges
Arreau
Granges-de Crouhens
Cadéac
Cauterets
2831 L'Arbizon
Fos
Pic du Midi d'Ossau 2884
Balaïtous 3146
Pont-d'Espagne
Luz-St.-Sauveur
Vielle-Aure
Col de Peyresourde 1565
Picde Bacanère 2193
Eylie
Mt. Valier 2839
Urdos
Col du Somport
Pyrénées
Pic Long 3192
Lés
Gèdre
St. Lary-Soulan
Bagnères-de-Luchon
Bossast
Tunnel du Somport
Sallent de Gállego
Vignemalle 3298
CHAOS DE COUMÉLY
Héas
Aragnouet
Candanchu
Balneario de Panticosa
Vall d'Aran
BAQUEIRA /BERET
Alos d'Ensil
Canfranc
Peña Collarada 2886
Panticosa
Gavarnie
Vielha
Salardú
Maladeta 3308
Tramacastilla de Tena
MONASTERIO DE SANTA ELENA
CIRQUE DE GAVARNIE
3355 Mte. Perdido
3371 Posets
3404 Pico de Aneto
Tunel de Vielha
Puerto de la Bonaigua 2072
Linas de Broto
Torla
CIRCA SOASA
Bielsa
Maladeta
Biescas
Broto
Ordesa y Monte Perdido
Salinas
Benasque
Caldas de Boi
BALNEARIO
Esterri d'Aneu
Espot
Jaca
Plan
Aigüestortes i Estany de Sant Maurici
Pirineos
Sabiñánigo
Yebra de Basa
Laspuña
Cotiella 2912
Castejón de Sos
Bono
Barruera
Montsent 2881
Cabdella
Llavorsí
Sierra Ferrera
Bernués
Hostal de Ipiés
Boltaña
Ainsa
Campo
Laspaules
La Torre de Cabdella
Llessui
Sort
Pont de Suert
Malpas
Gállego
Rasal
Caldearenas
Tierrantona
Torre la Ribera
Embalse de Escales
Embalse de Mediano
Senterada
Gerri de la Sal
Arcusa
Loarre
CASTILLO DE LOARRE
Nueno
Bolea
La Puebla de Roda
Pobla de Segur
Sierra de Guara
SANTUARIO S. COSME
Bárcabo
Embalse de el Grado
Igries
Esquedas
Emb. de Talarn-Tremp
Graus
Castilgaleu
Aguas
Naval
Laguarres
Puente de Montañana
Tremp
Boixols
Embalse de Barasona
Huesca
Alquézar
Figols
Isona
Embalse de la Sotonera
El Grado
Sietamo
Angües
Abiego
Tolva
Benabarre
Embalse de Canelles
Serra del Montsec
Emb. de Terradets
Monflorite
Pozán de Vero
Estadilla
Blecua
Barbastro
Peralta de la Sal
Fonz
Novales
Ager
Almudévar
Gállego
Estopiñán
Azanúy-Alins
Tardienta
Baells
Camporrells
Grañén
Ilche
Berbegal
Embalse Camarasa
Alberuela de Tubo
Selgua
San Esteban de Litera
Ballerias
Alcampell
Castillonroy
Artesa de Segre
Monzón
El Tormillo
Binefar
Tamarite de Litera
Camarasa
Robres
Poleñino
Flumen
La Masadera
Castelló de Farfaña
Montgai
Alcubierre
Sariñena
Binaced
Esplús
Alfarràs
Almenar
Leciñena
Balaguer
Termens
Berclaire d'Urgell
Lanaja
Alguaire
Linyola
Sierra de Alcubierre
Sena
Alcolea de Cinca
Albalate de Cinca
Almacelles
Rosselló
La Fulioala
Farlete
Pallaruelo de Monegros
Belver de Cinca
Bellvis
Anglesola
Lleida
Bell-lloc d'Urgell
Mollerussa
Torregrosa
Bellpuig d'Urgell
Monegrillo
Castejón de Monegros
Ballobar
Zaidín
Alcarraz

Toulouse
Blagnac
Lavaur
Castres
Mazamet
Labruguière
Revel
Castelnaudary
Carcassonne
Narbonne
Béziers
Pézenas
Bédarieux
Sérignan
Valras-Plage
Narbonne-Plage
Gruissan
Port-la-Nouvelle
Sigean
Leucate
Le Barcarès
Rivesaltes
Perpignan
Canet-en-Roussillon
St. Cyprien
Argelès-sur-Mer
Port-Vendres
Banyuls-sur-Mer
Cerbère
Portbou
Elne
Thuir
Céret
Le Perthus
La Jonquera
Ille-sur-Têt
Prades
Mont-Louis
Font-Romeu
Bourg-Madame
Puigcerdà
ANDORRA
Andorra La Vella
Encamp
Les Escaldes
St. Julià de Loria
Ax-les-Thermes
Tarascon-sur-Ariège
Foix
Pamiers
Mirepoix
Lavelanet
Quillan
Limoux
Espéraza
Couiza
Alet-les-Bains
Lézignan-Corbières
Capendu
Saverdun
Auterive
Muret
Ramonville-St. Agne
Cugnaux
St. Gaudens
St. Girons
Castillon-Len-Couserans
Villefranche-de-Lauragais
Côte Vermeille
Montagne Noire
Mts. de Lacaune
Haut-Languedoc
Méditerranée
Narbonnaise
Corbières
Roussillon
Pyrénées
Pyrén es Catalanes
Mts Albères
Cerdaña
Ariège
Pallars
Vall d'Aran
Vielha
Esterri d'Aneu
Sort
Aigüestortes i Estany de Sant Maurici
Pic d'Estats 3141
Pic de Montcalm 3078
Pic Carlit 2921
Canigou 2784
Madrès 2471
Puigmal 2910
Mt. Valier 2839
Pic des 3 Seigneurs 2199
Pic de St. Barthelemy 2348
Col de Puymorens 1915
Col de la Perche 1579
43°
1°
2°
3°
29
30
39
155
308
68

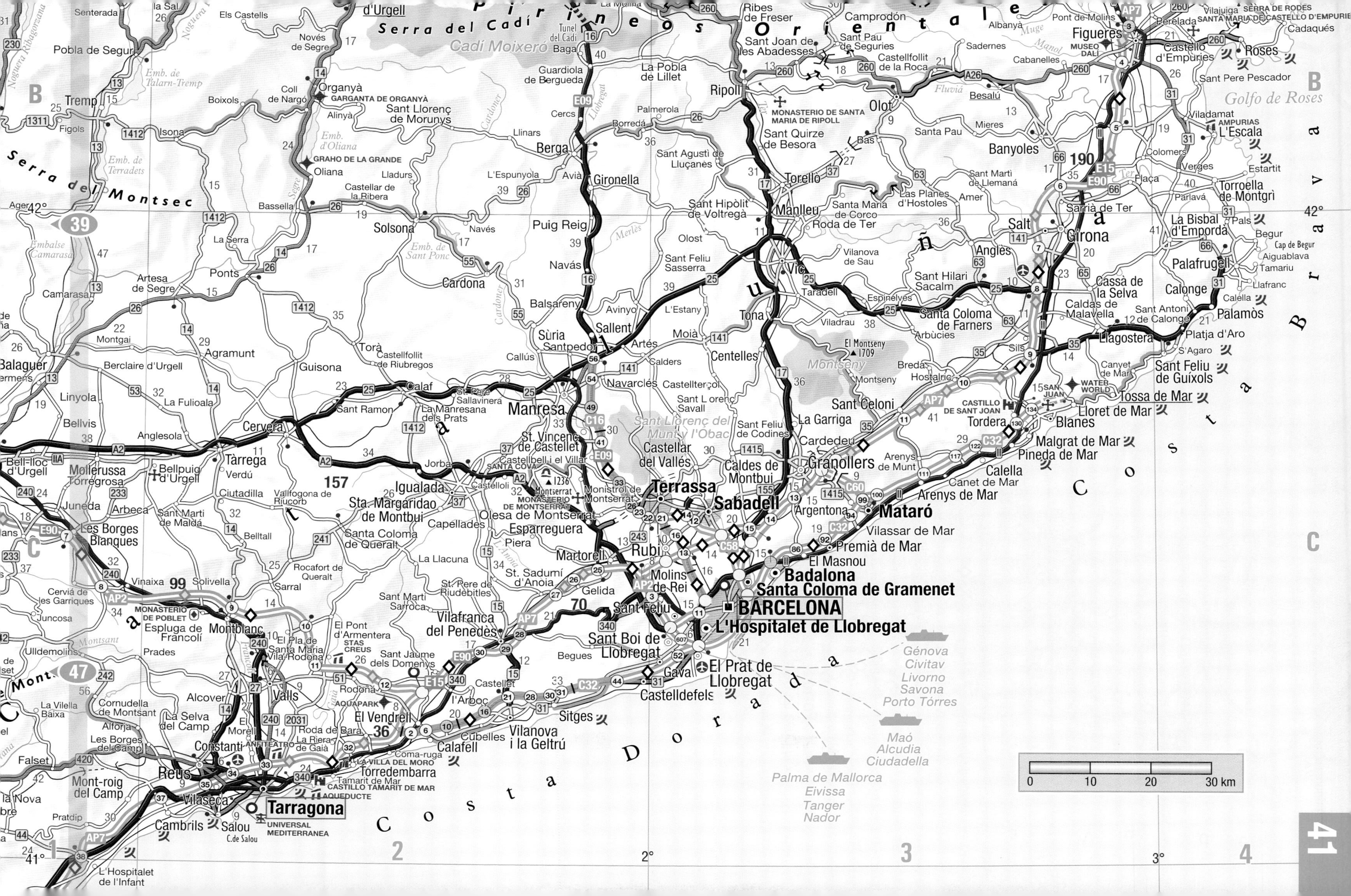

41
Pirineos Orientales
Serra del Cadí
Cadí Moixeró
Serra del Montsec
Costa Brava
Costa Dorada
Golfo de Roses
BARCELONA
L'Hospitalet de Llobregat
Santa Coloma de Gramenet
Badalona
El Masnou
Premià de Mar
Vilassar de Mar
Mataró
Arenys de Mar
Canet de Mar
Calella
Pineda de Mar
Malgrat de Mar
Blanes
Lloret de Mar
Tossa de Mar
Sant Feliu de Guíxols
S'Agaro
Platja d'Aro
Palamós
Calonge
Palafrugell
Begur
La Bisbal d'Empordà
Torroella de Montgrí
L'Escala
Roses
Cadaqués
Figueres
Castelló d'Empúries
Girona
Salt
Banyoles
Olot
Ripoll
Vic
Manlleu
Torelló
Granollers
Sabadell
Terrassa
Rubí
Manresa
Igualada
Martorell
Sant Feliu
Molins de Rei
Sant Boi de Llobregat
El Prat de Llobregat
Gavà
Castelldefels
Sitges
Vilanova i la Geltrú
Cubelles
Calafell
El Vendrell
Torredembarra
Tarragona
Salou
Cambrils
Reus
Vilaseca
Valls
Montblanc
Vilafranca del Penedès
Cervera
Tàrrega
Solsona
Cardona
Berga
Puig Reig
Sallent
Súria
Calaf
Mollerussa
Les Borges Blanques
Balaguer
Tremp
Organyà
Oliana
Ponts
Agramunt
Tordera
Sant Celoni
La Garriga
Cardedeu
Mont-roig del Camp
L'Hospitalet de l'Infant
Génova
Civitav
Livorno
Savona
Porto Tórres
Maó
Alcudia
Ciudadella
Palma de Mallorca
Eivissa
Tanger
Nador
0
10
20
30 km

O Rosal
A Guarda
Monte de Sta. Tegra
São Bento
Vila Nova de Cerveira
Paredes de Coura
Cabreiro
Serra da Peneda
Limia-Serra do Xurés
Mugueimes
Fondevila
Baltar
Verín
Oimbra
Randin
Caminha
Vila Praia de Ancora
Moledo do Minho
Coura
Labrujo
Igreja Romanica de Braves
Arcos de Valdevez
Lindoso
Lima
Montalegre
Castelo de Montalegre
Serra do Gerês
Peneda - Gerês
Ancora
Orbacém
Ponte da Barca
Touvedo
Barragem do Alto Cavado
Cortico
Chaves
Lanheses
Ponte de Lima
Terras do Bouro
Barragem de Salamonde
Barragem do Alto Rabagdo
Facha
Queljada
B. de Venda Nova
Serra do Barrosa
Boticas
Sapiãos
Viana do Castelo
Darque
Amorosa
Balugães
Caldelas
Barragem da Caniçada
Cabreira
Vilarandelo
Castelo do Neiva
Vila Verde
Amares
Soengas
Vieira do Minho
Salto
Campos
Vidago
Valpaços
Forjães
Prado
Cávado
Pinheiro
Serzedelo
Barragem de Guilhofrei
Rossas
Tâmega
Loivos
Marinhas
Esposende
Barcelos
Póvoa de Lanhoso
Arosa
Rio Douro
Ribeira da Pena
Carrazedo de Montenegro
Fão
Apúlia
Braga
Cabeceiras de Basto
São Torcato
Vila Pouca de Aguiar
Estela
Guimarães
Fafe
Gandarela
Cerva
Jou
A-Ver-o-Mar
Vila Nova de Famalicão
Fermil
Serra de Alvão
Alfarela de Jafes
Franco
Póvoa de Varzim
Celorico de Basto
Mondim de Basto
Murça
Caldas de Vizela
Parandaça
Alvão
Pópulo
Vila do Conde
Macieira
Felgueiras
Balsa
Abreiro
Santo Tirso
Villa Cova de Lixa
Trofa
Vila Real
Paços de Ferreira
Covas
Torgueda
Sabrosa
Alijó
Maia
Agua Longa
Alfena
Lousada
Amarante
Perafita
Ermezinde
Recezinhos
Padornelo
Marão
Serra de Marão
Santa Marta de Penaguião
Leca da Palmeira
Matosinhos
Paredes
Loivos do Monte
Aguas Santas
Tua
Porto
Rio Tinto
Valongo
Penafiel
Marco de Canevezes
Pinhão
Vila Nova de Gaia
Gondomar
Baião
Mesão Frio
Peso da Régua
São João da Pesqueira
Valbom
Lagares
Ancede
Lamego
Armamar
Tabuaco
Valadares
Avintes
Santa Leocadia
Resende
Miramar
Entre-os-Rios
Douro
Granja
Perozinho
Cinfães
Oliveira do Douro
Horta
Espinho
Raiva
Castelo de Paiva
Tarouca
Castelo de Penedono
Penedono
Montemuro
Corga de Lobão
Ezmoriz
Alvarenga
Moimenta da Beira
Barragem de Távora
Cortegaca
Caldas de San Jorge
Almofala
Arouca
Mosteiro de Santa Maria de Arouca
Santa Maria da Feira
Burgo
Rossas
Paiva
Castro Daire
Touro
Sernancelhe
Furadouro
São João da Madeira
Serra Gralheira
Ovar
Valega
Vale de Cambra
Moes
Quintela
Torre do Terranho
Figueiredo de Alva
Oliveira de Azeméis
Vila Nova de Paiva
Castelo de Aguiár da Beira
Torreira
Pinheiro
São João da Serra
Aguiar da Beira
Estarreja
São Pedro do Sul
Trancoso
Albergaria-a-Nova
Vouga
Oliveira de Frades
Douro Calvo
Murtosa
Sever do Vouga
Lordosa
Satão
Passegueiro
Vouzela
Cavernães
São Jacinto
Albergaria-a-Velha
Penalva do Castelo
Maceira
Ría de Aveiro
Barra
Angeja
Cambarinho
Viseu
Celorico da Beira
Aveiro
Costa Nova
Lamas
Talhadas
Dão
Ílhavo
Eixo
Fornos de Algodres
Varzielas
Baiuca
Mangualde
Vagos
Águeda
Guardão
Parada
Oiã
Silgueiros
Arcozelo
Cabra
Carrapichana
Palhaça
Serra de Caramulo
Nelas
Mondego
Nabais
Trinta
Praia de Mira
Tondela
Folgosinho
Mamarrosa
Anadia
Gouveia
Serra
Mira
Carregal do Sal
Oliveira do Conde
Lagares
Mealhada
Luso
Mortágua
Santa Comba Dão
Seia
Valhelhas
Palheiros da Tocha
Cantanhede
B. da Aguieira
Oliveira do Hospital
Candosa
Manteigas
Poço de Inferno
da Estrela
Belmonte
Pampilhosa
Tábua
Galizes
Tocha
Arazede
Penacova
Raiva
Moita
Mouronho
Vide
Covilhã
Catarruchos
Amieiro
Anca
Antuzede
São Martinho da Cortiça
Unhais da Serra
Pera Boa
Quiaios
Palheiros de Quiaios
Forte de Santa Catarina
Ervedal
Coimbra
Poiares
Tortosendo
C. Mondego
Lavaris
Serra da Estrela
Arganil
Maiorca
Montemor-o-Velho
Arzila
Capinha
Buarcos
Figueira da Foz
Alfarelos
Valonga
Ceira
Barco
Fundão
Semide
Portela
Góis
Silvares
Lavos
Condeixa
Vila Seca
Palácio dos Salazares
Barragem Sta. Luzia
Souto
Vale de Prazeres
Outeiro
Ruinas de Conimbriga
Lousã
Miranda do Corvo
Alpedrinha
Marinha das Ondas
Soure
Pampilhosa
Serra de Guardunha
Rego da Leiroa
Louriçal
Orvalho
Zêzere
São Miguel d'Acha
Proença-a
Mattos
Alvorge
Foz do Giraldo
Almaceda
Costa Verde
A
B
1
2
41°
40°
0
10
20
30 km

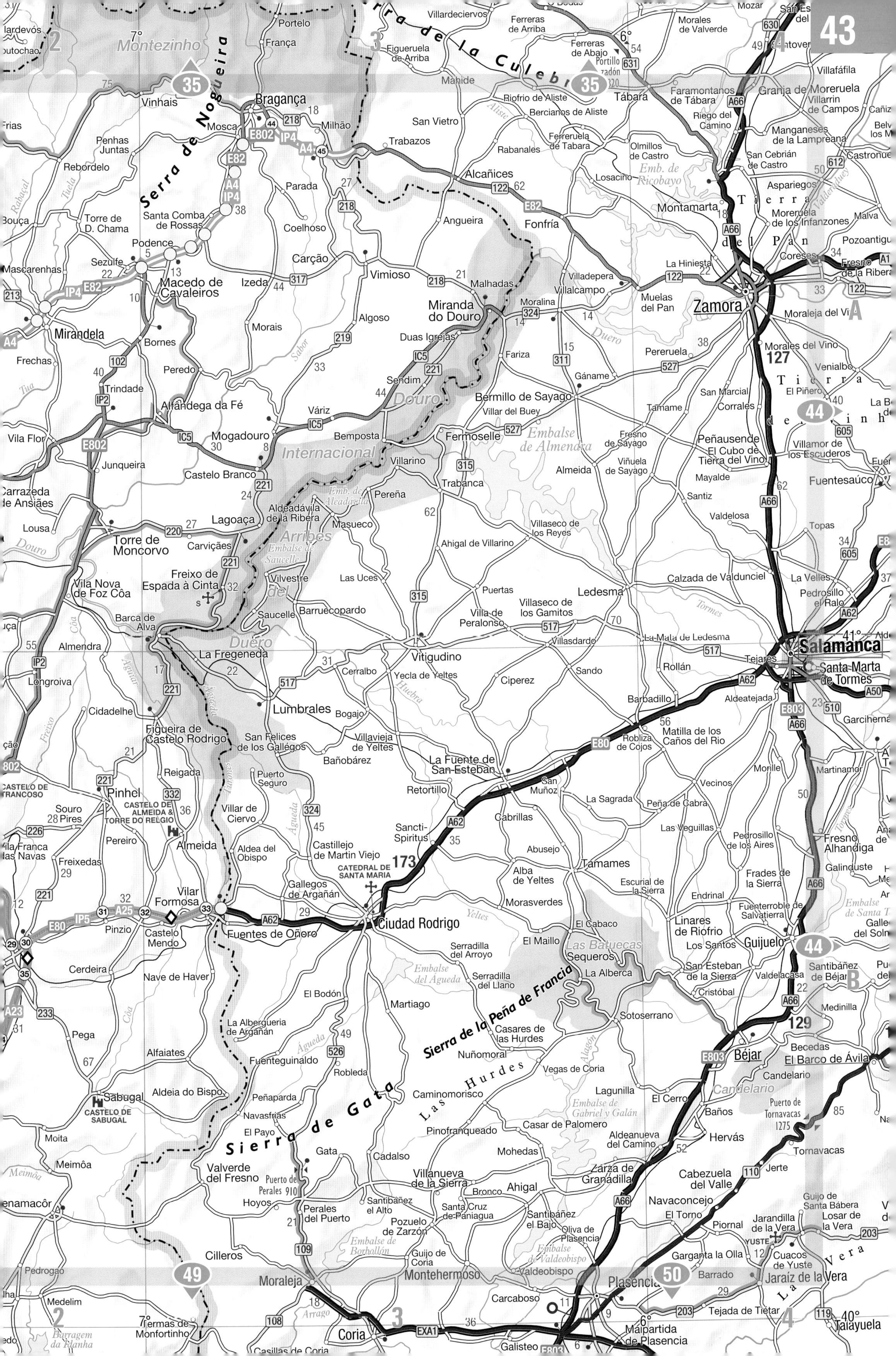
Montezinho
Serra de Nogueira
Sierra de la Culebra
Portelo
França
Villardeciervos
Ferreras de Arriba
Ferreras de Abajo
Portillo
Morales de Valverde
Mozar
Figueruela de Arriba
Mahide
Bragança
Vinhais
Mosca
Milhão
San Vietro
Riofrio de Aliste
Bercianos de Aliste
Tábara
Faramontanos de Tábara
Granja de Moreruela
Villafáfila
Villarrin de Campos
Riego del Camino
Manganeses de la Lampreana
San Cebrián de Castro
Castronue
Penhas Juntas
Rebordelo
Trabazos
Rabanales
Ferreruela de Tabara
Olmillos de Castro
Emb. de Ricobayo
Losacino
Parada
Alcañices
Asparіegos
Tierra del Pan
Montamarta
Moreruela de los Infanzones
Malva
Pozoantigu
Torre de D. Chama
Santa Comba de Rossas
Coelhoso
Angueira
Fonfría
Bouça
Podence
Carção
Vimioso
Coreses
Fresno de la Ribera
Mascarenhas
Sezulfe
Macedo de Cavaleiros
Izeda
Malhadas
La Hiniesta
Villadepera
Villalcampo
Muelas del Pan
Zamora
Moraleja del Vino
Mirandela
Miranda do Douro
Moralina
Bornes
Morais
Algoso
Duero
Morales del Vino
Frechas
Peredo
Duas Igrejas
Fariza
Pereruela
Venialbo
Trindade
Sendim
Gáname
Tierra del Vino
Alfândega da Fé
Douro
Bermillo de Sayago
Villar del Buey
San Marcial
Corrales
El Piñero
Vila Flor
Mogadouro
Váriz
Bemposta
Fermoselle
Embalse de Almendra
Tamame
Fresno de Sayago
Peñausende
El Cubo de Tierra del Vino
Villamor de los Escuderos
Internacional
Villarino
Viñuela de Sayago
Junqueira
Castelo Branco
Almeida
Mayalde
Fuentesaúco
Carrazeda de Ansiães
Trabanca
Santiz
Emb. de Aldeadávila
Pereña
Aldeadávila de la Ribera
Lagoaça
Valdelosa
Masueco
Topas
Lousa
Torre de Moncorvo
Carviçes
Arribes
Ahigal de Villarino
Villaseco de los Reyes
Embalse de Saucelle
Vilvestre
del
Freixo de Espada à Cinta
Las Uces
Calzada de Valdunciel
La Vellés
Vila Nova de Foz Côa
Puertas
Ledesma
Pedrosillo el Ralo
Saucelle
Barruecopardo
Villa de Peralonso
Villaseco de los Gamitos
Barca de Alva
Duero
Villasdardo
La Mata de Ledesma
Salamanca
Almendra
La Fregeneda
Vitigudino
Tejares
Santa Marta de Tormes
Tormes
Cerralbo
Yecla de Yeltes
Sando
Rollán
Ciperez
Longroiva
Lumbrales
Bogajo
Huebra
Barbadillo
Aldeatejada
Garcihernan
Cidadelhe
Figueira de Castelo Rodrigo
San Felices de los Gallegos
Villavieja de Yeltes
Robliza de Cojos
Matilla de los Caños del Rio
Bañobárez
La Fuente de San Esteban
Reigada
Puerto Seguro
San Muñoz
Morille
Martinamor
Castelo de Trancoso
Pinhel
Castelo de Almeida & Torre do Relgio
Retortillo
Vecinos
La Sagrada
Peña de Cabra
Souro Pires
Villar de Ciervo
Cabrillas
Las Veguillas
Pedrosillo de los Aires
Fresno Alhandiga
Vila Franca das Navas
Pereiro
Almeida
Aldea del Obispo
Sancti-Spiritus
Abusejo
Freixedas
Castillejo de Martin Viejo
Catedral de Santa Maria
Tamames
Galinduste
Frades de la Sierra
Alba de Yeltes
Escurial de la Sierra
Vilar Formosa
Gallegos de Argañán
Endrinal
Embalse de Santa T
Morasverdes
Fuenterroble de Salvatierra
Pinzio
Castelo Mendo
Fuentes de Oñoro
Ciudad Rodrigo
Yeltes
El Cabaco
Linares de Riofrio
Galle del Soln
Serradilla del Arroyo
El Maillo
Las Batuecas
Guijuelo
Sequeros
Los Santos
Cerdeira
Nave de Haver
Embalse del Águeda
Serradilla del Llano
La Alberca
San Esteban de la Sierra
Valdelacasa
Santibáñez de Béjar
El Bodón
Sierra de la Peña de Francia
Cristóbal
Martiago
Sotoserrano
Medinilla
Pega
La Albergueria de Argañán
Casares de las Hurdes
Béjar
Becedas
El Barco de Ávila
Alfaiates
Águeda
Nuñomoral
Candelario
Fuenteguinaldo
Robleda
Vegas de Coria
Las Hurdes
Lagunilla
El Cerro
Sabugal
Castelo de Sabugal
Aldeia do Bispo
Peñaparda
Caminomorisco
Embalse de Gabriel y Galán
Baños
Puerto de Tornavacas
Navasfrías
Sierra de Gata
Moita
El Payo
Pinofranqueado
Casar de Palomero
Aldeanueva del Camino
Hervás
Tornavacas
Meimôa
Gata
Cadalso
Mohedas
Jerte
Valverde del Fresno
Puerto de Perales
Villanueva de la Sierra
Zarza de Granadilla
Cabezuela del Valle
Ahigal
Bronco
Navaconcejo
Guijo de Santa Bábera
Losar de la Vera
Penamacôr
Hoyos
Santibáñez el Alto
Perales del Puerto
Pozuelo de Zarzón
Santa Cruz de Paniagua
Santibáñez el Bajo
Oliva de Plasencia
El Torno
Piornal
Jarandilla de la Vera
Embalse de Borbollón
Guijo de Coria
Embalse de Valdeobispo
Garganta la Olla
Cuacos de Yuste
Yuste
La Vera
Pedrogão
Cilleros
Moraleja
Montehermoso
Valdeobispo
Plasencia
Barrado
Jaraíz de la Vera
Medelim
Carcaboso
Tejada de Tiétar
Termas de Monfortinho
Arrago
Coria
Galisteo
Malpartida de Plasencia
Talayuela
Barragem da Idanha
Casillas de Coria
Bragança 35
44
49
50
Tierra de Vinh
A
B
2
3
4
7°
6°
41°
40°
127
129
173

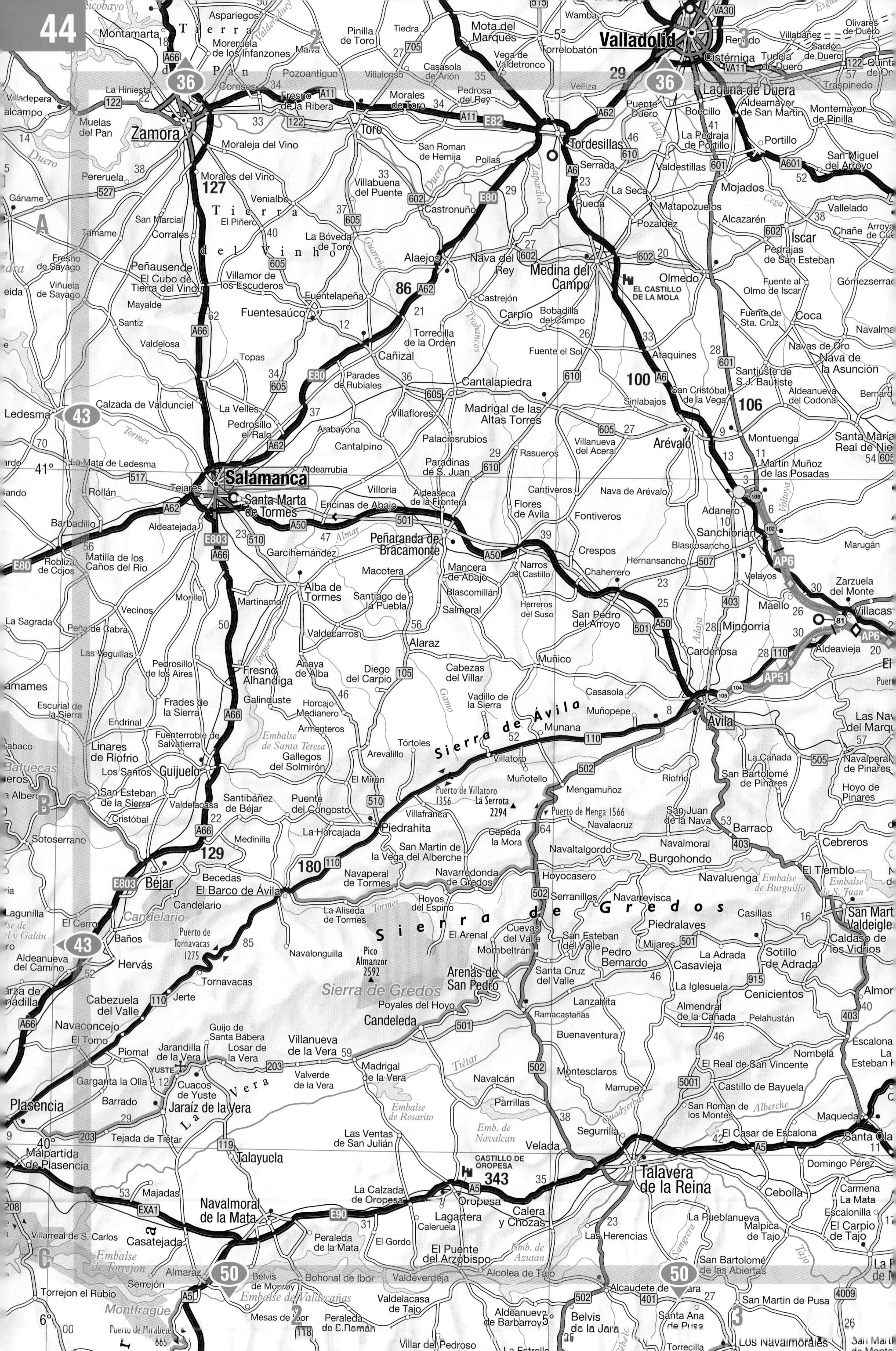

Montamarta
Tierra de Pan
Aspariegos
Moreruela de los Infanzones
Pinilla de Toro
Tiedra
Mota del Marqués
Wamba
Valladolid
Villanubla
Vega de Valdetronco
Torrelobatón
Cistérniga
Tudela de Duero
Renedo
Villabáñez
Olivares de Duero
Sardón de Duero
Quintanilla de Onésimo
Pozoantiguo
Villalonso
Casasola de Arión
Velliza
Laguna de Duera
Traspinedo
La Hiniesta
Villadepera
Almendra
Fresno de la Ribera
Morales de Toro
Pedrosa del Rey
Puente Duero
Boecillo
Aldeamayor de San Martín
Montemayor de Pinilla
Muelas del Pan
Zamora
Toro
Tordesillas
La Pedraja de Portillo
Portillo
San Miguel del Arroyo
Moraleja del Vino
San Roman de Hornija
Pollas
Serrada
Valdestillas
Pereruela
Morales del Vino
Villabuena del Puente
Castronuño
Rueda
La Seca
Mojados
Gáname
Venialbo
Tierra del Vino
Matapozuelos
Pozaldez
Alcazarén
Vallelado
San Marcial
El Piñero
Corrales
Tamame
La Bóveda de Toro
Alaejos
Nava del Rey
Medina del Campo
Olmedo
Íscar
Pedrajas de San Esteban
Chañe
Arroyo de Cuéllar
Fresno de Sayago
Peñausende
El Cubo de Tierra del Vino
Viñuela de Sayago
Villamor de los Escuderos
El Castillo de la Mola
Fuente al Olmo de Iscar
Gómezserracín
Mayalde
Fuentelapeña
Castrejón
Fuentesaúco
Carpio
Bobadilla del Campo
Fuente de Sta. Cruz
Coca
Santiz
Torrecilla de la Orden
Navalmanzano
Valdelosa
Topas
Cañizal
Fuente el Sol
Ataquines
Navas de Oro
Nava de la Asunción
Parades de Rubiales
Cantalapiedra
Santiuste de S.J. Bautiste
Calzada de Valdunciel
Ledesma
La Velles
Madrigal de las Altas Torres
San Cristóbal de la Vega
Sinlabajos
Aldeanueva del Codonal
Bernardos
Pedrosillo el Ralo
Arabayona
Villaflores
Palaciosrubios
Villanueva del Aceral
Arévalo
Montuenga
Santa María Real de Nieva
Cantalpino
Paradinas de S. Juan
Rasueros
Martín Muñoz de las Posadas
La Mata de Ledesma
Aldearrubia
Salamanca
Rollán
Tejares
Santa Marta de Tormes
Villoria
Aldeaseca de la Frontera
Cantiveros
Nava de Arévalo
Encinas de Abajo
Flores de Avila
Fontiveros
Adanero
Barbadillo
Aldeatejada
Peñaranda de Bracamonte
Sanchiorian
Marugán
Garcihernández
Crespos
Blascosancho
Matilla de los Caños del Rio
Robliza de Cojos
Macotera
Mancera de Abajo
Narros del Castillo
Hernansancho
Chaherrero
Velayos
Zarzuela del Monte
Alba de Tormes
Santiago de la Puebla
Blascomillán
Maello
Villacastín
Morille
Martinamor
Herreros del Suso
San Pedro del Arroyo
Vecinos
Salmoral
La Sagrada
Peña de Cabra
Valdecarros
Mingorria
Alaraz
Aldeavieja
Las Veguillas
Cardeñosa
Pedrosillo de los Aires
Fresno Alhandiga
Anaya de Alba
Diego del Carpio
Cabezas del Villar
Muñico
Tamames
Galinduste
Frades de la Sierra
Vadillo de la Sierra
Casasola
Escurial de la Sierra
Horcajo-Medianero
Gamo
Muñopepe
Ávila
Sierra de Ávila
Endrinal
Armenteros
Munana
Las Navas del Marqués
Fuenterroble de Salvatierra
Embalse de Santa Teresa
Tórtoles
Linares de Riofrio
Gallegos del Solmirón
Arevalillo
Villatoro
La Cañada
Navalperal de Pinares
Batuecas
Guijuelo
Los Santos
El Mirón
Muñotello
Riofrio
San Bartolomé de Pinares
San Esteban de la Sierra
Santibáñez de Béjar
Puente del Congosto
Puerto de Villatoro 1356
La Serrota 2294
Mengamuñoz
Hoyo de Pinares
Valdelacasa
Villafranca
Puerto de Menga 1566
Navalacruz
San Juan de la Nava
Cristóbal
Piedrahita
Cepeda la Mora
Barraco
Sotoserrano
Medinilla
La Horcajada
Navaltalgordo
Navalmoral
Cebreros
San Martín de la Vega del Alberche
Burgohondo
Navarredonda de Gredos
Hoyocasero
Navaluenga
Embalse de Burguillo
El Tiemblo
Embalse de S. Juan
Béjar
Becedas
El Barco de Ávila
Navaperal de Tormes
Serranillos
Navarrevisca
Lagunilla
Candelario
La Aliseda de Tormes
Hoyos del Espino
Sierra de Gredos
Casillas
San Martín de Valdeiglesias
El Cerro
Puerto de Tornavacas 1275
El Arenal
Cuevas del Valle
San Esteban del Valle
Piedralaves
Baños
Pico Almanzor 2592
Mombeltrán
Pedro Bernardo
Mijares
La Adrada
Sotillo de Adrada
Caldaso de los Vidrios
Aldeanueva del Camino
Hervás
Navalonguilla
Arenas de San Pedro
Santa Cruz del Valle
Casavieja
Tornavacas
La Iglesuela
Cenicientos
Cabezuela del Valle
Jerte
Poyales del Hoyo
Lanzahita
Almendral de la Cañada
Pelahustán
Almorox
Navaconcejo
Candeleda
Ramacastañas
El Torno
Guijo de Santa Bábera
Villanueva de la Vera
Buenaventura
Escalona
Piornal
Jarandilla de la Vera
Losar de la Vera
Nombela
Yuste
Madrigal de la Vera
El Real de San Vincente
Garganta la Olla
Cuacos de Yuste
Valverde de la Vera
Tiétar
Montesclaros
Navalcán
Marrupe
Castillo de Bayuela
Plasencia
Barrado
Jaraíz de la Vera
La Vera
Embalse de Rosarito
Parrillas
San Roman de los Montes
Alberche
Maqueda
Emb. de Navalcan
Segurrilla
Las Ventas de San Julián
Tejada de Tiétar
Velada
El Casar de Escalona
Santa Olalla
Malpartida de Plasencia
Talayuela
Castillo de Oropesa
Talavera de la Reina
Domingo Pérez
Majadas
La Calzada de Oropesa
Oropesa
Cebolla
Carmena
La Mata
Navalmoral de la Mata
Lagartera
Caleruela
Calera y Chozas
La Pueblanueva
Escalonilla
Villarreal de S. Carlos
Casatejada
Peraleda de la Mata
El Gordo
Las Herencias
Malpica de Tajo
El Carpio de Tajo
Embalse de Torrejon
El Puente del Arzobispo
Emb. de Azutan
Sangrera
Tajo
Almaraz
Serrejón
Belvis de Monroy
Bohonal de Ibor
Valdeverdeja
Alcolea de Tajo
San Bartolomé de las Abiertas
Torrejon el Rubio
Embalse de Valdecañas
Valdelacasa de Tajo
Alcaudete de la Jara
Santa Ana de Pusa
San Martín de Pusa
Montfragüe
Mesas de Ibor
Peraleda de S. Román
Aldeanueva de Barbarroya
Belvis de la Jara
Puerto de Mirabete
Villar del Pedroso
Torrecilla
Los Navalmorales
Duero
Tormes
Almar
Adaja
Voltoya
Cega
Eresma
Zapardiel
Trabancos
Guareña
Guadyerbas

Aranda de Duero
Peñaranda de Duero
Villálvaro
Torreblacos
Pesquera de Duero
Castrillo de la Vega
Valdocondes
La Vid
Langa de Duero
El Burgo de Osma
Torralba de Burgo
Tardelcuende
Fuentecén
Fuentespina
Santa Cruz de la Salceda
Peñafiel
Moradillo de Roa
Fuentelcésped
Lodares de Osma
Castrillo de Duero
San Esteban de Gormaz
Fuentepinilla
Parcilla
Castillejo de Robledo
Miño de San Esteban
Maderuelo
Hortezuela
Matamala
Sacramenia
Aldeasoña
Valtiendas
Sierra de Pradales
Embalse de Linares
Aldealuenga de Sta. Maria
Morcuera
Berlanga de Duero
Fuentidueña
Rubio 1377
232
Carabias
Cobertelade
Fuentesauco
San Miguel de Bernuy
Castroserracin
Grajera
Corral de Ayllón
Ayllón
Francos
Caltojar
Cuéllar
Torrecilla del Pinar
Liceros
Hontalbilla
Boceguillas
Montejo de Tiermes
Retortillo de Soria
Villasayas
Adradas
Sanchonuño
Embalse Burgomillodo
Sepúlveda
El Olmo
Madriguera
Castillejo de Mesleón
Riaza
Rio frio de Riaza
El Muyo
Miedes de Atienza
Barcones
Barahona
Lastras de Cuéllar
Zarzuela del Pinar
Villacadima
Cantalejo
Aldealcorvo
Perorrubio
Cerezo de Abajo
1510 Pico Grande
Galve de Sorbe
Paredes de Sigüenza
Fuentepelayo
Aguilafuente
Cabezuela
Condemios de Arriba
Condemios de Abajo
Atienza
Aldea Real
Escalona del Prado
Villarejo
Puerto de Somosierra 1404
Cercadillo
Imón
Medina
Carbonero el Mayor
Turégano
La Velilla
Pedraza
Somosierra
Sierra de Ayllon
Castillo de Turégano
Arcones
Maiaelrayo
Hiendelaencina
Sigüenza
Barbatona
Tabanera la Luenga
Navafriá
Colmenar de la Sierra
Las Cabezadas
La Salceda
Montejo de la Sierra
Embalse de El Vado
Congostrina
Embalse de Palmaces
Negredo
Torrecaballeros
Sierra de Guadarrama
Embalse de Puentes Viejas
Tamajón
Veguillas
Villaseca de Henares
La Torresaviñán
Algora
Segovia
Castillo de Lara
Lozoya
Buitrago del Lozoya
Cogolludo
Mandayona
Fuencemillán
Parque del Riofrios
Lozoyuela
Embalse de El Atazar
Jadraque
Almadrones
Rascafría
Alpedrete de la Sierra
Tortuero
Peñalara 2430
Canencia
El Berrueco
Puebla de Beleña
Alaminos
Revenga
Sierra de Guadarrama
Miralrio
Gajanejos
Otero de Herreros
Masegoso de Tajuña
Torrelaguna
Miraflores de la Sierra
Humanes
Cifuentes
Cuenca Alta del Manzanares
Siete Picos 2138
Malaguilla
Viñuelas
Torre del Burgo
Guadalix de la Sierra
El Vellón
Cercedilla
Navacerrada
Emb. de El Vellon
Yunquera de Henares
Brihuega
Fuentes de la Alcarria
Gárgoles de Abajo
Collado-Mediano
Soto del Real
Manzanares el Real
Embalse de Santillana
El Molar
El Casar
Torija
Trillo
Guadarrama 1516
Los Molinos
Cerceda
San Agustín de Guadalix
Valdetorres de Jarama
Galápagos
Marchamalo
Atanzón
Guadarrama
Valle de los Caidos
Collado Villalba
Torrejón del Rey
Guadalajara
Tomellosa
Budia
Santa Maria de la Alameda
Colmenar Viejo
Hoyo de Manzanares
Fuente el Saz de Jarama
Embalse de Entrepeñas
Peralveche
San Lorenzo de El Escorial
El Escorial
Torrelodones
San Sebastián de los Reyes
Algete
Azuqueca de Henares
Chiloeches
Horche
Chillarón del Rey
Escamilla
Pareja
Monasterio de El Escorial
Galapagar
Alcobendas
Camarma
Armuña de Tajuña
Alhóndiga
Los Santos de la Humosa
Valdemorillo
El Pardo
La Alcarria
Las Rozas
Aranzueque
Sacedón
Alcocer
Fresnedillas
Majadahonda
Alcalá de Henares
Pozo de Guadalajara
Valdeconcha
Torrejón de Ardoz
Pastrana
Cañaveruelas
Pozuelo de Alarcón
Coslada
Brunete
Boadilla del Monte
San Fernando de Henares
Torres de la Alameda
Embalse de Buendía
Sevilla la Nueva
Villaviciosa de Odón
Alcorcón
Loeches
Fuentenovilla
Sayatón
Buendia
Villalba del Rey
Aldea del Fresno
Villamantilla
Móstoles
Leganés
Velilla de S. Antonio
Campo Real
Mondéjar
Tinajas
Valdilecha
Albalete de Zorita
Arganda
Villamanta
Navalcarnero
Getafe
Madrid
Orusco
Albares
Villa del Prado
Fuenlabrada
Movie World
Perales de Tajuña
Carabaña
Garcinarro
La Peraleja
Méntrida
El Alamo
Pinto
San Martín de la Vega
Tielmes
Brea de Tajo
Estremera
Saceda del Rio
Griñón
Parla
Morata de Tajuña
Illana
Valmojado
Torrejón de la Calzada
Valdemoro
Villarejo de Salvanés
Valdaracete
Huete
Casarrubios del Monte
Carranque
Ciempozuelos
Barajes de Melo
Vellisca
Caracenilla
Illescas
Chinchón
Belmonte de Tajo
Fuentidueña de Tajo
Santa Cruz del Retamar
Esquivias
Seseña Nuevo
Colmenar de Oreja
Villaconejos
Cedillo del Condado
Borox
Palacio Real de Aranjuez
Loranca del Campo
Camarena
Yuncos
Belinchón
Paredes
Recas
Pantoja
Tarancón
Fuensalida
Alameda de la Sagra
Aranjuez
Nuestra Señora de los Remedios
Villarrubia de Santiago
Zarza de Tajo
Carrascosa del Campo
Horcajada
Villaluenga
Noblejas
Santo Domingo
Torrijos
Magán
Villaseca de la Sagra
Ocaña
Santa Cruz de la Zarza
Rozalén del Monte
Uclés
Saelices
Paloma
Barrindote
Bargas
Olias del Rey
Mocejón
Villarrubio
Montalbo
Burujón
Algodor
Villatobas
Toledo
Villasequilla de Yepes
Yepes
Cabañas de Yepes
Dosbarrios
Horcajo de Santiago
Huerta de Valdecarabanos
Cabezamesada
Guadamur
Villamuelas
Melgar
Villarejo
Cervera
Burguillos de Toledo
Polán
Almonacid de Toledo
La Guardia
Corral de Almaguer
Noez
Chueca
Villaminaya
Mascaraque
Villanueva de Bogas
Romeral
Lillo
Ajofrín
Pulgar
Castilla-La Mancha
Canal
0 10 20 30 km

Garray
NUMANCIA
ANTIQUISIMA
Almajano
Ventosilla
Soria
Carbonera de Frentes
Los Rábanos
Aldeapozo
Matalebreras
Olvega
Sierra del Madero
Sierra del Moncayo
Vera de Moncayo
Cueva de Agreda
Borja
Magallon
Anzón
Fuendejalón
Gallur
Remolinos
Luceni
Pedrola
Alagón
Ebro
Utebo
Canal Imperial de Aragon
Almenar de Soria
Jaray
Borobia
Calcena
Tabuenca
Lumpiaque
Rueda de Jalón
Lubia
Cubo de la Solana
Gómara
Ciria
Aranda de Moncayo
Tierga
Épila
La Muela
Tardelcuende
Duero
Tejado
Almazul
Torrelapaja
Illueca
Calatorao
Ricla
Matamala
Almazán
Escobasa de Almazán
Serón de Najima
Bijuesca
Deza
Villarroya de la Sierra
Morata de Jalón
Morés
La Almunia de Doña Godina
Cadr
Muel
Cobertelade
Morón de Almazán
Adradas
Villalengua
Cervera de la Cañada
Saviñán
El Frasno
Santa Cruz de Grío
Almonacid de la Sierra
Longares
Embalse de Mezalocha
Villanueva del Huerva
Villasayas
Monteagudo de las Vicarias
Calatayud
Ateca
Aguarón
Cariñena
Barahona
Ariza
Alhama de Aragón
Cetina
Mara
Miedes de Aragón
Codos
Puerto de Paniza
935
Embalse de las Torcas
Aguaviva de la Vega
Paredes de Siguenza
Santa María de Huerta
Emb. de la Tranquera
Morata de Jiloca
Fuentes de Jiloca
Herrera de los Navarros
Arcos de Jalón
Jalón
Cabolafuenta
Nuevalos
PIEDRA
Mainar
Medinaceli
Salinas de Medinaceli
Acered
Villafeliche
Villar de los Navarros
Laina
Campillo de Aragón
Santa Cruz
1423
Daroca
Badules
Mochales
Milmarcos
Cubel
Bádenas
Barbatona
Siguenza
Maranchón
Labros
Santed
Báguena
Ferreruela
Monforte de Moyuela
Alcolea del Pinar
Mazarete
Gallocanta
Fonfría
La Torresaviñán
Algora
Anquela del Ducado
Aragoncillo
1518
Tortuera
Tornos
Anadon
Laguna de Gallocanta
Riba de Saelices
Cillas
Bello
Cutanda
Abádanes
Cobeta
Calamocha
Rillo de Gallo
Odón
Torre los Negros
Masegoso de Tajuña
Sacecorbo
Huertahernando
Molina de Aragón
Caminreal
Bañon
Cifuentes
CASTILLO DE MOLINA DE ARAGON
Monreal del Campo
Tajo
Gallo
Zaorejas
El Pobo de Dueñas
Pozuel del Campo
Sierra Palomera
Gárgoles de Abajo
Pancrudo
Trillo
Valtablado del Rio
Terzaga
Villafranco del Campo
Tordesilos
Bueña
Visiedo
Villanueva de Alcorón
Ródenas
Embalse de Entrepeñas
Peralveche
Alustante
Alba
Perales de Alfambra
Escamilla
Pareja
Beteta
Perelejos de las Truchas
Checa
Orea
Sierra de Albarracín
Orihuela del Tremedal
Santa Eulalia
Salmerón
Pozondón
Alfambra
Valdeolivas
Vadillos
Bronchales
Guadiela
Serranía de Cuenca
Alcocer
Priego
Noguera
1856
Sierra Alta
Cella
Cañaveruelas
Cañamares
Villaconejos de Trabaque
Fresneda de la Sierra
Gea de Albarracín
Albarracín
Embalse de
Villalba del Rey
Cañaveras
Albalate de las Nogueras
Arcos de la Sierra
San Felipe
1835
Guadalaviar
Villar del Cobo
Tinajas
Tragacete
Montes Universales
Frías de Albarracín
Teruel
Gascueña
Torrecilla
Bezas
Terriente
Villastar
Bólliga
Villar de Domingo Garcia
Huélamo
Toril
La Peraleja
Villalba de la Sierra
Javalón
1695
Villel
Aldehuela
Sierra de Camarena
Losares
1388
CIUDAD ENCANTADA
La Toba
La Ventosa
Saceda del Rio
Mariana
Laguna del Marquesado
La Puebla de Valverde
Valdecabras
Cascante del Rio
Caracenilla
Villar del Saz de Navalón
Buenache de la Sierra
Valdemoro Sierra
Libros
Chillarón de Cuenca
El Hontanar
Rodeva
Naharros
Cuenca
Salvacañete
2020
Javalambre
Horcajada de la Torre
Cabrejas
Puerto de Cabrejas
1150
Júcar
Ademuz
Cañete
Sierra de Javalambre
Guadazaón
Arcos de las Salinas
Palomares del Campo
Fuentes
Cañada del Hoyo
Santa Cruz de Moya
Altarejos
Fuentelespino de Moya
Landete
Villareio-Periesteban
Reillo
Aras de Alpuente
San Lorenzo de la Parrilla
Carboneras de Guadazaón
Villar del Humo
La Ye

Zaragoza
Lleida
Balaguer
Fraga
Caspe
Alcañiz
Morella
Tortosa
Amposta
Sant Carles de la Ràpita
Vinaròs
Benicarló
Peñíscola
Castelló de la Plana
Vila-real de los Infantes
Burriana
Almassora
Benicàssim
Oropesa
Torreblanca
Alcalà de Xivert
Sierra de Alcubierre
Serra de Montsant
Sierra de San Just
Sierra de Gúdar
El Maestrat
Serra d'Irta
Delta de l'Ebre
Embalse de Mequinenza
Embalse de Caspe
Mequinenza
Flix
Gandesa
Mora d'Ebre
Valderrobres
Alcorisa
Andorra
Montalbán
Hijar
Belchite
Cantavieja
Mosqueruela
Rubielos de Mora
Sarrión
Onda
Vilafranca del Maestrat
Costa de Fora
Penyagolosa 1813
Peñarroya 2019
Espadán 1041
0 10 20 30 km
40°
41°

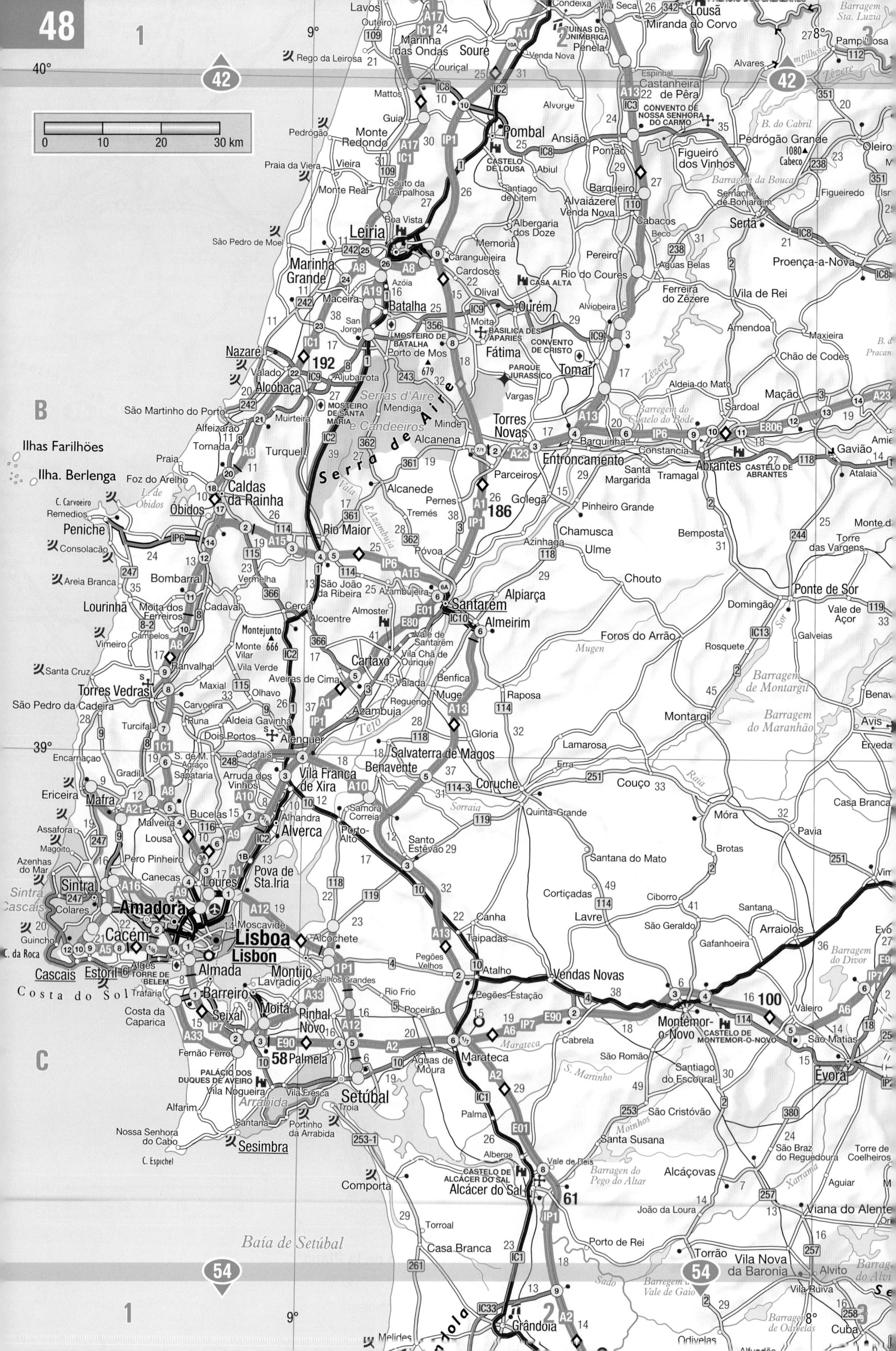

0 10 20 30 km
Lavos
Condeixa
Vila Seca
Lousã
Miranda do Corvo
Barragem Sta. Luzia
Marinha das Ondas
Soure
Rego da Leirosa
Penela
Venda Nova
Pampilhosa
Louriçal
Alvares
Castanheira de Pêra
Mattos
Convento de Nossa Senhora do Carmo
Alvorge
B. do Cabril
Guia
Monte Redondo
Pedrógão
Pombal
Ansião
Pedrógão Grande
Oleiros
Praia da Viera
Vieira
Castelo de Lousa
Abiul
Pontão
Figueiró dos Vinhos
Cabeço
Barragem da Bouca
Souto da Carpalhosa
Monte Real
Santiago de Litem
Barqueiro
Sernache de Bonjardim
Figueiredo
Alvaiázere
Venda Nova
Boa Vista
Albergaria dos Doze
Cabaços
Sertã
São Pedro de Moel
Leiria
Memória
Beco
Caranguejeira
Pereiro
Águas Belas
Proença-a-Nova
Marinha Grande
Azóia
Cardosos
Casa Alta
Rio do Coures
Maceira
Batalha
Olival
Ourém
Alviobeira
Ferreira do Zêzere
Vila de Rei
San Jorge
Mosteiro de Batalha
Porto de Mos
Moita
Basilica des Aparies
Fátima
Convento de Cristo
Amendoa
Maxieira
Nazaré
Tomar
Chão de Codes
Valado
Aljubarrota
Parque Jurassico
Zêzere
Aldeia-do-Mato
Alcobaça
Serras d'Aire
Mendiga
Vargas
Mação
São Martinho do Porto
Mosteiro de Santa Maria
e Candeeiros
Minde
Torres Novas
Barregem do Castelo do Bode
Sardoal
Alfeizarão
Muirteira
Tornada
Alcanena
Barquinha
Constancia
Gavião
Ilhas Farilhões
Turquel
Serra de Aire
Entroncamento
Abrantes
Castelo de Abrantes
Atalaia
Praia
Ilha. Berlenga
Foz do Arelho
Parceiros
Santa Margarida
Tramagal
L. de Óbidos
Caldas da Rainha
Alcanede
Golegã
Pinheiro Grande
C. Carvoeiro
Remedios
Óbidos
Pernes
Tremés
Peniche
Rio Maior
Chamusca
Bemposta
Monte da
Consolação
Azinhaga
Ulme
Torre das Vargens
Póvoa
Bombarral
Areia Branca
Vermelha
Chouto
Ponte de Sor
São João da Ribeira
Azambujeira
Santarém
Alpiarça
Lourinhã
Moita dos Ferreiros
Cadaval
Cercal
Alcoentre
Almoster
Almeirim
Domingão
Vale de Açor
Campelos
Montejunto
Vale de Santarém
Foros do Arrão
Galveias
Vimeiro
Monte Vilar
Vila Chã de Ourique
Mugen
Rosquete
Santa Cruz
Ranvalhal
Vila Verde
Cartaxo
Benfica
Barragem de Montargil
Aveiras de Cima
Valada
Raposa
Torres Vedras
Maxial
Olhavo
Reguengo
Muge
São Pedro da Cadeira
Carvoeira
Azambuja
Montargil
Barragem do Maranhão
Turcifal
Runa
Aldeia Gavinha
Tejo
Gloria
Avis
Dois Portos
Alenquer
Erveda
Encarnação
S. de M. Agraço
Cadafais
Salvaterra de Magos
Lamarosa
Sapataria
Benavente
Erra
Gradil
Arruda dos Vinhos
Vila Franca de Xira
Coruche
Couço
Ericeira
Mafra
Samora Correia
Sorraia
Quinta Grande
Móra
Casa Branca
Bucelas
Alhandra
Assafora
Malveira
Alverca
Porto-Alto
Pavia
Lousa
Santo Estêvão
Magoito
Brotas
Azenhas do Mar
Pero Pinheiro
Santana do Mato
Sintra
Canecas
Póvoa de Sta. Iria
Cascais
Loures
Corticadas
Ciborro
Colares
Amadora
Santana
Canha
Lavre
São Geraldo
Arraiolos
Guincho
Cacém
Moscavide
Taipadas
Gafanhoeira
Barragem do Divor
C. da Roca
Lisboa
Lisbon
Alcochete
Pegões Velhos
Atalho
Vendas Novas
Algés
Torre de Belém
Almada
Montijo
Cascais
Estoril
Lavradio
Sarilhos Grandes
Rio Frio
Pegões-Estação
Costa do Sol
Trafaria
Barreiro
Moita
Poceirão
Montemor-o-Novo
Castelo de Montemor-o-Novo
Valeiro
Costa da Caparica
Seixal
Pinhal Novo
São Matias
Fernão Ferro
Palmela
Marateca
Cabrela
São Romão
Évora
Palácio dos Duques de Aveiro
Águas de Moura
S. Martinho
Santiago do Escoural
Vila Nogueira
Vila Fresca
Setúbal
Alfarim
Arrábida
Troia
Palma
São Cristóvão
Nossa Senhora do Cabo
Santana
Portinho da Arrabida
Moinhos
Santa Susana
São Braz do Reguedoura
Torre de Coelheiros
Sesimbra
C. Espichel
Alberge
Vale de Reis
Comporta
Castelo de Alcácer do Sal
Alcácer do Sal
Barragen do Pego do Altar
Alcáçovas
Aguiar
Xarrama
João da Loura
Viana do Alentejo
Torroal
Baía de Setúbal
Casa Branca
Porto de Rei
Torrão
Vila Nova da Baronia
Alvito
Sado
Barregem de Vale de Gaio
Vila Ruiva
Grândola
Barragem de Odivelas
Cuba
Melides
Odivelas

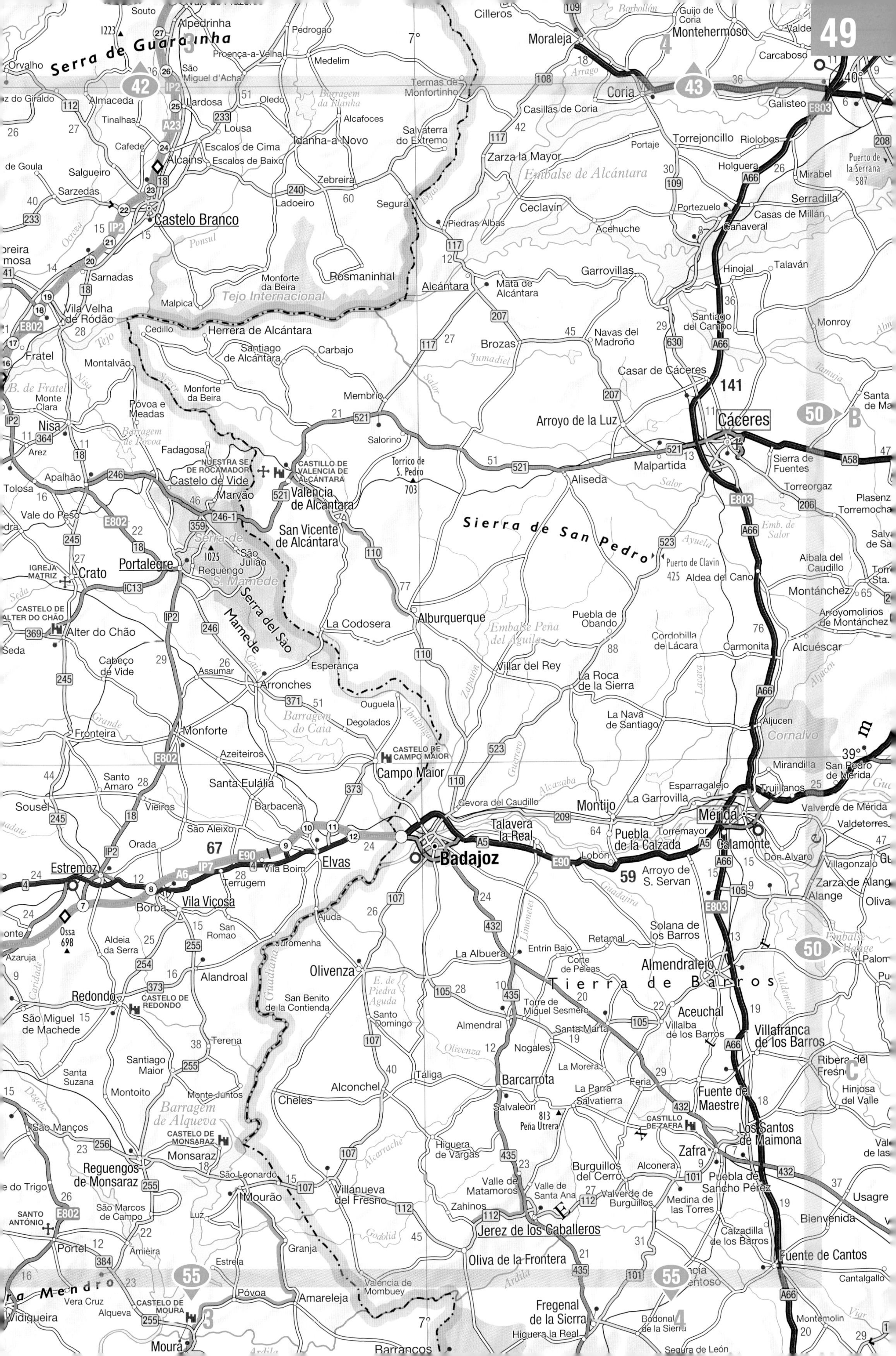
Serra de Guardunha
Castelo Branco
Cáceres
Badajoz
Mérida
Elvas
Portalegre
Estremoz
Coria
Alcántara
Sierra de San Pedro
Tierra de Barros
Almendralejo
Zafra
Jerez de los Caballeros
Olivenza
Campo Maior
Tejo Internacional
Embalse de Alcántara
Serra del São Mamede
Barragem de Alqueva
Reguengos de Monsaraz
Fregenal de la Sierra
Montijo
Alburquerque
Valencia de Alcántara
Idanha-a-Novo
Fuente de Cantos

Serrejón
Torrejon el Rubio
Montfragüe
Puerto de Mirabete 665
Embalse de Valdecañas
Mesas de Ibor
Peraleda de S.Román
Valdelacasa de Tajo
Aldeanueva de Barbarroya
Belvis de la Jara
Alcaudete de la Jara
Santa Ana de Pusa
Torrecilla de la Jara
Villar del Pedroso
Carrascalejo
La Nava de Ricomalillo
Espinoso del Rey
Los Navalu
Jaraicejo
Monroy
Almonte
Deleitosa
Castañar de Ibor
Aldeanueva de S. Bartolomé
Mohedas de la Jara
Puerto de S. Vicente
El Campillo de la Jara
Robledo del Mazo
Sevilleja de la Jara
Navaltoril
Robledo del Buey
Aldea de Trujillo
Torrecillas de la Tiesa
Robledollano
Santa Marta de Magasca
Aldeacentenera
Cabañas del Castillo
Navezuelas
Puerto de S. Vincente 807
Piedraescrita
Trujillo
Sierra de Fuentes
La Cumbre
Pico Villuercas 1601
MONASTERIO DE GUADALUPE
Guadalupe
Alia
Puerto Rey
Anchuras
Torreorgaz
Madroñera
Berzocana
Garciaz
Plasenzuela
Torremocha
Herguijuela
Sierra de Guadalupe
Puerto Llano 642
Pantano de Cijara
Emb. de Salor
Salvatierra de Santiago
Ruanes
Ibahernando
Conquista de la Sierra
Logrosán
Cañamero
Embalse de Garcia Sola
Horcajo de los Montes
Albala del Caudillo
Santa Cruz de la Sierra
Puerto de Santa Cruz
Santa Ana
Zorita
Castilblanco
Helechosa
Cijara
Embalse de Cíjara
Torre de Sta. Maria
Montánchez
Robledillo de Trujillo
Villamesias
Abertura
Alcollarin
Valdecaballeros
Arroyomolinos de Montánchez
Campo Lugar
Almoharin
Alcuéscar
Escurial
Miajadas
Peloche
Herrera del Duque
Villarta de los Montes
Madrigalejo
Casas de Don Pedro
Fuenlabrada de los Montes
Aljucen
Cornalvo
Villar de Rena
Gargaligas
Acedera
Navalvillar de Pela
Embalse de Orellana
Garbayuela
Santa Amalia
Orellana
Orellana de la Sierra
Talarrubias
Mirandilla
San Pedro de Mérida
Trujillanos
Guadiana
Villanueva de la Serena
Don Benito
La Coronada
Esparragosa del Caudillo
Puebla de Alcocer
Siruela
Tamurejo
Agudo
Valdemanco de Esteras
Saceruela
Valverde de Mérida
Valdetorres
La Haba
Magacela
Campanario
Embalse de La Serena
Garlitos
Don Alvaro
Villagonzalo
Guareña
Peñalsordo
Zarza de Alange
Alange
Manchita
Oliva de Mérida
La Serena
Zarza Capilla
Chillón
Almadén
Gargantiel
Fontan
Embalse de Alange
Palomas
Valle de la Serena
Quintana de la Serena
Castuera
Benquerencia de la Serena
Cabeza del Buey
Guadálmez
Almadenejos
Alamillo
Puebla de la Reina
Malpartida de la Serena
Higuera de la Serena
Zalamea de la Serena
Esparragossa de la Serena
Monterrubio de la Serena
Belalcázar
Santa Eufemia
Sierra de Pedrosa
Villafranca de los Barros
Hornachos
Ribera del Fresno
Hinojosa del Valle
Campillo de Llerena
Sierra del Pedrosa
848 Santa Inés
Peraleda del Zaucejo
Hinojosa del Duque
Los Pedroches
El Viso
Guijo
Los Santos de Maimona
Llera
Valencia de las Torres
Villaralto
Dos-Torres
Añora
Pedroche
Higuers de Llerena
Blázquez
Valsequillo
Villanueva del Duque
Usagre
Maguilla
La Granjuela
Alcaracejos
Pozoblanco
Bienvenida
Villagarcia de las Torres
Granja de Torrehermosa
Peñarroya-Pueblonuevo
Villanueva de Córdoba
Fuente de Cantos
Berlanga
Azuaga
Bélmez
Cantalgallo
Llerena
Ahillones
Fuente Obejuna
Casas de Reina
Valverde de Llerena
Argallón
Villanueva del Rey
Espiel
Montemolin
Trasierra
Ojuelos Altos
Sierra de los Santos
Fuente del Arco
Villaharta
Pallares
Puebla del Maestre
Malcocinado
La Cardanchosa
Obejo
Monesterio
Guadalcanal
Embalse de Puente Nuevo
Villaviciosa de Córdoba
Embalse de El Pintado
Alanís
Hoya de Santa Maria
Cerro Muriano
El Real de la Jara
San Nicolás del Puerto
Sierra Norte de Sevilla
LA PURISIMA CONCEPCION
San Calixto
Sierra de Hornachuelos
Santa Olalla
SANTA MARIA DE CONSOLACIÓN
Cazalla de la Sierra
Las Navas de la Concepción
Embalse del Bembézar
Santa Maria de Trassierra
Alcolea
Almadén de la Plata
Constantina
Embalse del Retortillo
La Quinlera
Embalse de la Breña
Almodóvar del Río
Córdoba
El Pedroso
Hornachuelos

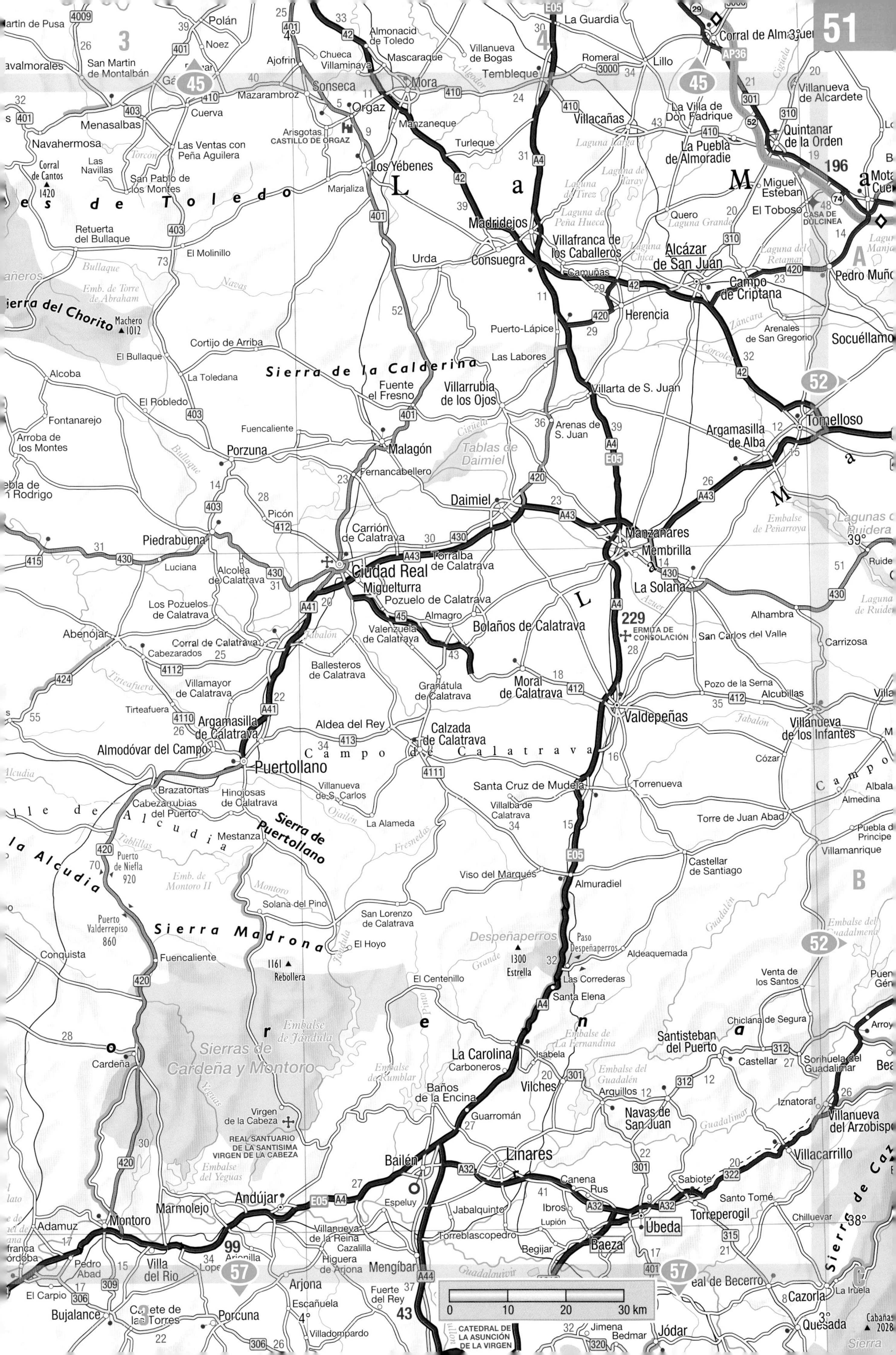
51
Martín de Pusa
Navalmorales
San Martín de Montalbán
Polán
Noez
Ajofrín
Almonacid de Toledo
Chueca
Villaminaya
Mascaraque
Villanueva de Bogas
La Guardia
Romeral
Lillo
Corral de Almaguer
Tembleque
Sonseca
Mazarambroz
Mora
Orgaz
Arisgotas
CASTILLO DE ORGAZ
Manzaneque
Cuerva
Menasalbas
Navahermosa
Las Ventas con Peña Aguilera
Corral de Cantos
1420
Las Navillas
San Pablo de los Montes
Turleque
Los Yébenes
Marjaliza
Villacañas
La Villa de Don Fadrique
La Puebla de Almoradiel
Quintanar de la Orden
Villanueva de Alcardete
Miguel Esteban
El Toboso
CASA DE DULCINEA
Quero
Laguna Grande
Laguna Larga
Laguna de Taray
Laguna del Tirez
Laguna de Peña Hueca
Montes de Toledo
La Mancha
Retuerta del Bullaque
El Molinillo
Madridejos
Villafranca de los Caballeros
Laguna Chica
Alcázar de San Juan
Camuñas
Campo de Criptana
Pedro Muñoz
Urda
Consuegra
Bullaque
Emb. de Torre de Abraham
Navas
Sierra del Chorito
Machero 1012
Herencia
Puerto-Lápice
Arenales de San Gregorio
Socuéllamos
Záncara
Corcoles
Cortijo de Arriba
El Bullaque
Las Labores
Sierra de la Calderina
Alcoba
La Toledana
Fuente el Fresno
Villarrubia de los Ojos
Villarta de S. Juan
El Robledo
Fontanarejo
Arroba de los Montes
Fuencaliente
Arenas de S. Juan
Argamasilla de Alba
Tomelloso
Malagón
Tablas de Daimiel
Cigüela
Porzuna
Fernancabellero
Puebla de Don Rodrigo
Daimiel
Picón
Carrión de Calatrava
Manzanares
Membrilla
Embalse de Peñarroya
Lagunas de Ruidera
39°
Piedrabuena
Luciana
Alcolea de Calatrava
Ciudad Real
Torralba de Calatrava
Miguelturra
La Solana
Ruidera
Pozuelo de Calatrava
Los Pozuelos de Calatrava
Almagro
Bolaños de Calatrava
Alhambra
229
ERMITA DE CONSOLACIÓN
San Carlos del Valle
Carrizosa
Abenójar
Corral de Calatrava
Cabezarados
Valenzuela de Calatrava
Jabalón
Ballesteros de Calatrava
Villamayor de Calatrava
Tirteafuera
Granátula de Calatrava
Moral de Calatrava
Pozo de la Serna
Alcubillas
Argamasilla de Calatrava
Aldea del Rey
Calzada de Calatrava
Valdepeñas
Villanueva de los Infantes
Almodóvar del Campo
Puertollano
Campo de Calatrava
Cózar
Brazatortas
Cabezarrubias del Puerto
Hinojosas de Calatrava
Villanueva de S. Carlos
Santa Cruz de Mudela
Torrenueva
Albaladejo
Almedina
Valle de Alcudia
Mestanza
Sierra de Puertollano
La Alameda
Villalba de Calatrava
Torre de Juan Abad
Puebla del Príncipe
Villamanrique
Puerto de Niefla 920
Emb. de Montoro II
Viso del Marqués
Castellar de Santiago
Almuradiel
Solana del Pino
San Lorenzo de Calatrava
Puerto Valderrepiso 860
Sierra Madrona
Conquista
El Hoyo
Despeñaperros
Paso Despeñaperros
Aldeaquemada
Embalse del Guadalmena
Fuencaliente
1161 Rebollera
1300 Estrella
El Centenillo
Las Correderas
Venta de los Santos
Santa Elena
Embalse de Jándula
Embalse de La Fernandina
Chiclana de Segura
Santisteban del Puerto
Cardeña
Sierras de Cardeña y Montoro
La Carolina
Carboneros
Isabela
Castellar
Sorihuela del Guadalimar
Embalse del Rumblar
Baños de la Encina
Vilches
Embalse del Guadalén
Arquillos
Iznatoraf
Navas de San Juan
Villanueva del Arzobispo
Virgen de la Cabeza
REAL SANTUARIO DE LA SANTISIMA VIRGEN DE LA CABEZA
Guarromán
Embalse del Yeguas
Bailén
Linares
Villacarrillo
Canena
Rus
Sabiote
Santo Tomé
Andújar
Marmolejo
Espeluy
Jabalquinto
Ibros
Lupión
Torreperogil
Úbeda
Chilluevar
Adamuz
Montoro
Villanueva de la Reina
Cazalilla
Torreblascopedro
Begíjar
Baeza
38°
Sierra de Cazorla
Pedro Abad
Villa del Río
Arjonilla
Lopera
Higuera de Arjona
Mengíbar
Guadalquivir
El Carpio
Arjona
Fuerte del Rey
Peal de Becerro
Cazorla
La Iruela
Bujalance
Cañete de las Torres
Porcuna
Escañuela
Villardompardo
Jimena
Bedmar
Jódar
Quesada
Cabañas 2028
0 10 20 30 km
CATEDRAL DE LA ASUNCIÓN DE LA VIRGEN

Huete
Vellisca
Caracenilla
Villar del Saz de Navalón
Chillarón de Cuenca
Mariana
Valdecabras
Buenache de la Sierra
Valdemoro Sierra
Laguna del Marquesado
Cuenca
Salvacañete
Tarancón
Carrascosa del Campo
Naharros
Horcajada de la Torre
Cabrejas
Puerto de Cabrejas 1150
Cañete
Uclés
Rozalén del Monte
Palomares del Campo
Saelices
Villarrubio
Fuentes
Cañada del Hoyo
Fuentelespino de Moya
Landete
Altarejos
Montalbo
Reillo
Carboneras de Guadazaón
Villar del Humo
Horcajo de Santiago
Villarejo-Periesteban
San Lorenzo de la Parrilla
Villares del Saz
Villarejo de Fuentes
Cervera del Llano
Valeria
Garaballa
Villar de Cañas
Olivares de Júcar
Valera de Abajo
Almodóvar del Pinar
Cardenete
Villamayor de Santiago
Mira
Valverde de Júcar
Fuentelespino de Haro
Embalse de Alarcón
Villanueva de Alcardete
Villalgordo del Marquesado
La Almarcha
Buenache de Alarcón
Enguídanos
Gabaldón
Campillo de Altobuey
Quintanar de la Orden
Honrubia
Los Hinojosos
Olmedilla de Alarcón
Villaescusa de Haro
Santa María del Campo Rus
Fuenterrobles
Embalse de Contreras
Belmonte
Cañadajuncosa
Motilla del Palancar
Villargordo del Cabriel
Miguel Esteban
Mota del Cuervo
Castillo de Belmonte
El Cañavete
Alarcón
Minglanilla
Graja de Iniesta
El Toboso
Casa de Dulcinea
El Pedernoso
La Alberca de Zancara
El Peral
Laguna de Manjavacas
Las Pedroñas
El Picazo
Villanueva de la Jara
Venta del Moro
Laguna del Retamar
Las Mesas
San Clemente
Rubielos Bajos
Iniesta
Pedro Muñoz
Villarta
Sisante
El Provencio
Casas de Fernando Alonso
Casasimarro
Pantano Muleteros
Hoces
Ledaña
Villamalea
Tabaqueros
Arenales San Gregorio
Casas de Haro
Quintanar del Rey
Villatoya
Socuéllamos
Villalgordo del Júcar
Tarazona de la Mancha
Casas-Ibáñez
Villarrobledo
Minaya
Madrigueras
Fuentealbilla
Tomelloso
La Roda
Mahora
Alcalá
Jorquera
Santa Marta
La Gineta
Valdeganga
Villavaliente
Alatoz
Canal de María Cristina
Casas del Juan Núñez
Embalse Peñarroya
Lagunas de Ruidera
Munera
Barrax
Sotuélamos
La Felipa
Ruidera
Ossa de Montiel
El Bonillo
Lezuza
Albacete
Hoya-Gonzalo
Higueruela
Lagunas de Ruidera
La Herrera
Chinchilla de Monte Aragón
Tiriez
Balazote
Laguna del Salobral
Villar de Chinchilla
Carrizosa
El Salobral
Horna
Bonete
Corral-Rubio
San Pedro
Pinilla
El Ballestero
Laguna de Pétrola
Pétrola
Jardín
Villahermosa
Viveros
Pozo Cañada
La Higuera
Robledo
Villanueva de los Infantes
Montiel
Montemayor
Peñas de San Pedro
Povedilla
Castillo de Alcaraz
Masegoso
Pinilla
Villanueva de la Fuente
Pozohondo
Fuente-Álamo
Peñascosa
Campo de Montiel
Alcaraz
Alcadozo
Albaladejo
Reolid
Santuario de la Encarnación
Almedina
Ontur
Tobarra
Sierra de Alcaraz
Puebla del Príncipe
Paterna del Madera
Bogarra
Albatana
Villamanrique
Almenara 1798
Ayna
Bienservida
Liétor
Riopar
Hellín
Guadalmena
Embalse de Talave
Mundo
Minateda
Molinicos
Embalse del Guadalmena
Elche de la Sierra
Agramón
Génave
Villaver de de Guadalimar
Embalse de Cenajo
Siles
Segura
Puente de Génave
Embalse de la Fuensanta
Letur
Yeste
El Arguellite
Montiras
Las Minas
Embalse de Camarillas
La Puerta de Segura
Parolis
Socovos
Arroyo del Ojanco
Cortijos Nuevos
Sorihuela del Guadalimar
Beas de Segura
Hornos
Calasparra
Cieza
Sierras de Cazorla
El Sabinar
Segura

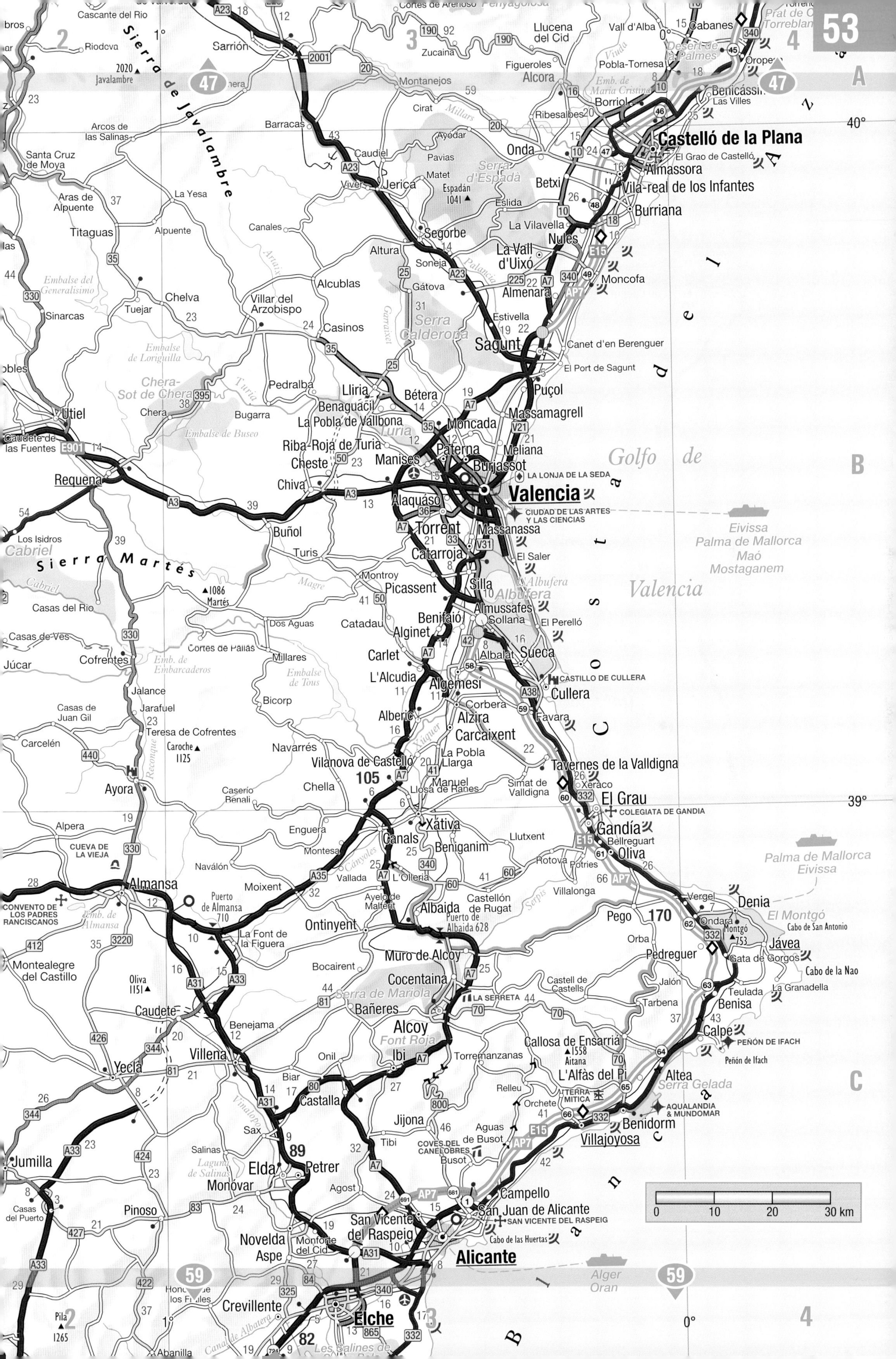
Sierra de Javalambre
Cascante del Rio
Riodeva
Sarrión
Javalambre 2020
Arcos de las Salinas
Santa Cruz de Moya
Aras de Alpuente
La Yesa
Titaguas
Alpuente
Canales
Embalse del Generalísimo
Chelva
Tuejar
Sinarcas
Villar del Arzobispo
Embalse de Loriguilla
Chera-Sot de Chera
Chera
Utiel
Caudete de las Fuentes
Requena
Los Isidros
Cabriel
Sierra Martés
1086 Martés
Casas del Rio
Casas de Ves
Cofrentes
Júcar
Emb. de Embarcaderos
Jalance
Jarafuel
Casas de Juan Gil
Teresa de Cofrentes
Carcelén
Caroche 1125
Ayora
Alpera
Cueva de la Vieja
Almansa
Convento de los Padres Franciscanos
Emb. de Almansa
Puerto de Almansa 710
Montealegre del Castillo
Oliva 1151
Caudete
Yecla
Villena
Jumilla
Casas del Puerto
Pinoso
Hondón de los Frailes
Pila 1265
Abanilla
Cortes de Arenoso
Penyagolosa
Llucena del Cid
Vall d'Alba
Cabanes
Zucaina
Figueroles
Alcora
Montanejos
Cirat
Barracas
Caudiel
Ayódar
Pavias
Onda
Matet
Serra d'Espadà
Espadán 1041
Viver
Jerica
Eslida
Segorbe
Altura
Soneja
Gátova
Serra Calderona
Alcublas
Casinos
Pedralba
Bugarra
Embalse de Buseo
Llíria
Benaguacil
La Pobla de Vallbona
Riba-Roja de Turia
Cheste
Chiva
Buñol
Turis
Montroy
Picassent
Dos Aguas
Catadau
Cortes de Pallás
Millares
Embalse de Tous
Bicorp
Navarrés
Chella
Caserío Benali
Enguera
Montesa
Navalón
Moixent
Vallada
La Font de la Figuera
Ontinyent
Bocairent
Serra de Mariola
Banyeres
Benejama
Sax
Salinas
Laguna de Salinas
Elda
Petrer
Monóvar
Novelda
Monforte del Cid
Aspe
Crevillente
Elche
Les Salines de Santa Pola
Desert de les Palmes
Pobla-Tornesa
Emb. de María Cristina
Oropesa
Benicàssim
Las Villes
Borriol
Ribesalbes
Castelló de la Plana
El Grao de Castelló
Almassora
Betxi
Vila-real de los Infantes
Burriana
La Vilavella
Nules
La Vall d'Uixó
Moncofa
Almenara
Estivella
Sagunt
Canet d'en Berenguer
El Port de Sagunt
Puçol
Bétera
Massamagrell
Moncada
Paterna
Meliana
Burjassot
Manises
La Lonja de la Seda
Valencia
Alaquàs
Ciudad de las Artes y las Ciencias
Torrent
Massanassa
Catarroja
El Saler
Silla
Albufera
L'Albufera
Almussafes
Sollana
El Perelló
Benifaió
Alginet
Carlet
Albalat
Sueca
L'Alcudia
Algemesí
Castillo de Cullera
Cullera
Corbera
Alberic
Alzira
Carcaixent
Favara
La Pobla Llarga
Vilanova de Castelló
Manuel
Llosa de Ranes
Tavernes de la Valldigna
Simat de Valldigna
Xeraco
El Grau
Colegiata de Gandia
Xàtiva
Canals
Beniganim
Llutxent
Gandía
Bellreguart
Oliva
Rotova
Potries
L'Olleria
Ayelo de Malferit
Albaida
Castellón de Rugat
Puerto de Albaida 628
Villalonga
Pego
Vergel
Ondara
Denia
El Montgó
Cabo de San Antonio
Montgó 753
Jávea
Gata de Gorgos
Cabo de la Nao
Orba
Pedreguer
Muro de Alcoy
Cocentaina
La Serreta
Castell de Castells
Jalón
Tarbena
Teulada
La Granadella
Benisa
Alcoy
Font Roja
Ibi
Onil
Torremanzanas
Callosa de Ensarria
1558 Aitana
Calpe
Peñón de Ifach
L'Alfàs del Pi
Altea
Serra Gelada
Relleu
Orcheta
Terra Mítica
Aqualandia & Mundomar
Benidorm
Villajoyosa
Castalla
Biar
Jijona
Tibi
Aguas de Busot
Coves del Canelobres
Busot
Agost
Campello
San Vicente del Raspeig
San Juan de Alicante
Cabo de las Huertas
Alicante
Golfo de Valencia
Costa del Azahar
Costa Blanca
Eivissa
Palma de Mallorca
Maó
Mostaganem
Alger
Oran
40°
39°
1°
0°
0 10 20 30 km

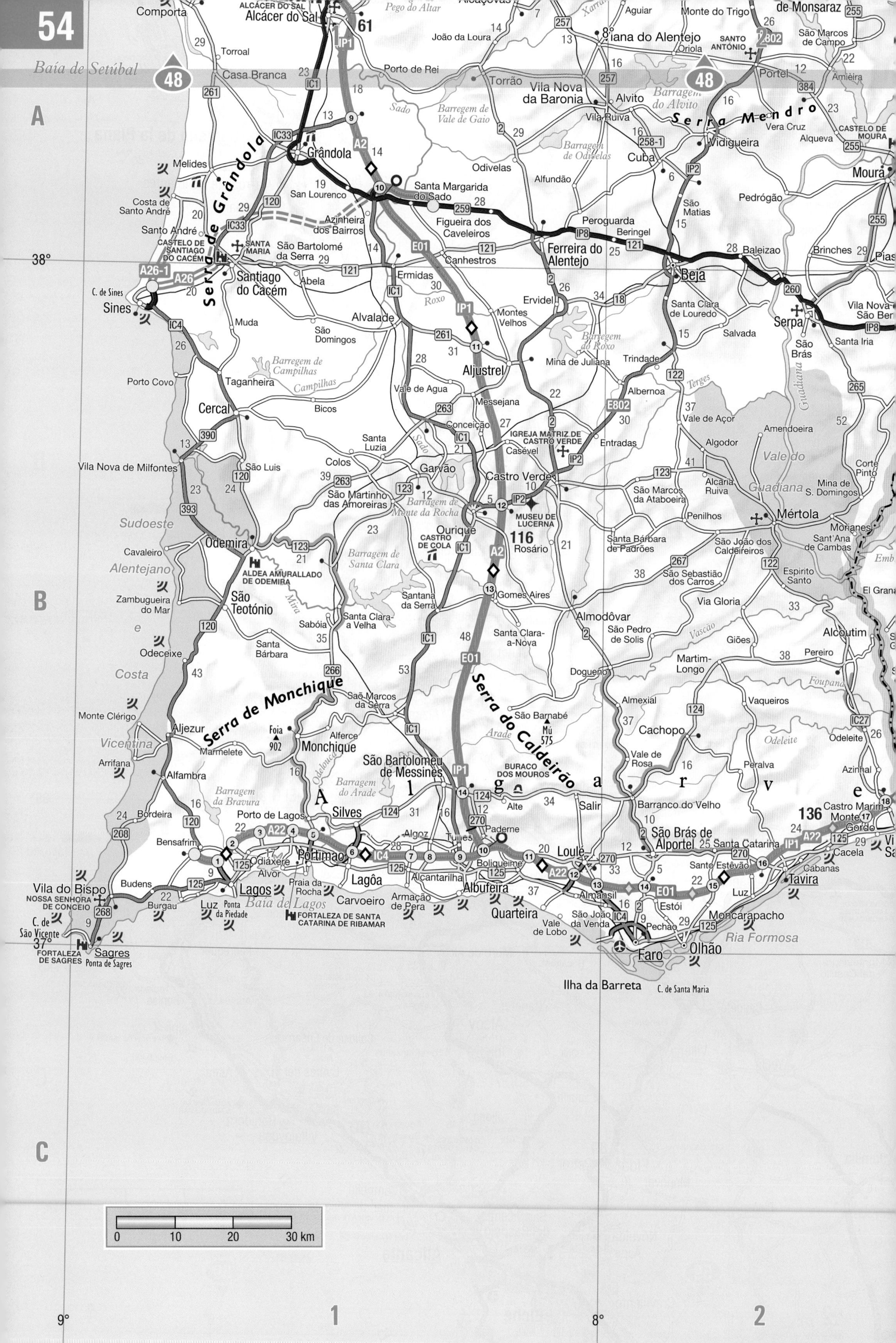
Baía de Setúbal
Comporta
Alcácer do Sal
Pego do Altar
João da Loura
Aguiar
Monte do Trigo
de Monsaraz
Viana do Alentejo
São Marcos de Campo
Torroal
Casa Branca
Porto de Rei
Torrão
Vila Nova da Baronia
Alvito
Barragem do Alvito
Portel
Amieira
Sado
Barregem de Vale de Gaio
Vila Ruiva
Serra Mendro
Vera Cruz
Alqueva
Castelo de Moura
Grândola
Cuba
Vidigueira
Moura
Melides
Serra de Grândola
Odivelas
Barragem de Odivelas
Alfundão
Santa Margarida do Sado
San Lourenco
Costa de Santo André
Pedrógão
São Matias
Azinheira dos Bairros
Figueira dos Caveleiros
Peroguarda
Beringel
Santo André
Castelo de Santiago do Cacém
Santa Maria
São Bartolomé da Serra
Canhestros
Ferreira do Alentejo
Baleizao
Brinches
38°
C. de Sines
Sines
Santiago do Cacém
Abela
Ermidas
Roxo
Beja
Ervidel
Santa Clara de Louredo
Serpa
Vila Nova São Bento
Muda
São Domingos
Alvalade
Montes Velhos
Barregem do Roxo
Salvada
Santa Iria
São Brás
Porto Covo
Taganheira
Barregem de Campilhas
Campilhas
Aljustrel
Mina de Juliana
Trindade
Vale de Agua
Albernoa
Terges
Guadiana
Cercal
Bicos
Messejana
Vale de Açor
Santa Luzia
Conceição
Igreja Matriz de Castro Verde
Entradas
Amendoeira
Vila Nova de Milfontes
São Luis
Colos
Garvão
Casével
Algodor
Vale do Guadiana
Corte Pinto
Castro Verde
São Marcos da Ataboeira
Alcaria Ruiva
Mina de S. Domingos
São Martinho das Amoreiras
Barragem de Monte da Rocha
Museu de Lucerna
Penilhos
Mértola
Sudoeste
Ourique
Castro de Cola
Rosário
Santa Bárbara de Padrões
São João dos Caldeireiros
Moriones
Sant'Ana de Cambas
Cavaleiro
Odemira
Alentejano
Aldea Amurallado de Odemira
Barragem de Santa Clara
São Sebastião dos Carros
Espirito Santo
Mira
Gomes Aires
El Granado
Zambugueira do Mar
São Teotónio
Santana da Serra
Via Gloria
Sabóia
Santa Clara-a-Velha
Almodôvar
São Pedro de Solis
Vascão
Alcoutim
Odeceixe
Santa Bárbara
Santa Clara-a-Nova
Giões
Pereiro
Costa
Martim-Longo
Dogueno
Foupana
Serra de Monchique
São Marcos da Serra
Serra do Caldeirão
Monte Clérigo
Almexial
Vaqueiros
São Barnabé
Aljezur
Foia 902
Alferce
Arade
Mú 575
Cachopo
Vicentina
Marmelete
Monchique
Odeleite
Arrifana
São Bartolomeu de Messines
Buraco dos Mouros
Vale de Rosa
Peralva
Alfambra
Odelouca
Barragem do Arade
Azinhal
Barragem da Bravura
Algarve
Alte
Salir
Barranco do Velho
Castro Marim
Monte Gordo
Bordeira
Porto de Lagos
Silves
Paderne
São Brás de Alportel
Santa Catarina
Algoz
Tunes
Bensafrim
Odiáxere
Portimão
Boliqueime
Loulé
Santo Estêvão
Cacela
Alvor
Lagôa
Alcantarilha
Cabanas
Tavira
Vila do Bispo
Nossa Senhora de Conceio
Budens
Lagos
Praia da Rocha
Albufeira
Almansil
Luz
Burgau
Luz
Ponta da Piedade
Baía de Lagos
Carvoeiro
Armação de Pera
Quarteira
Estói
Moncarapacho
C. de São Vicente
Fortaleza de Santa Catarina de Ribamar
São João da Venda
Pechão
Ria Formosa
37°
Fortaleza de Sagres
Sagres
Ponta de Sagres
Vale de Lobo
Faro
Olhão
Ilha da Barreta
C. de Santa Maria
A
B
C
0
10
20
30 km
9°
1
8°
2

Mourão
Villanueva del Fresno
Valle de Matamoros
Valle de Santa Ana
Zahinos
Jerez de los Caballeros
Valverde de Burguillos
Medina de las Torres
Puebla de Sancho Pérez
Usagre
Bienvenida
Llerena
Villagarcia de las Torres
Berlanga
Granja
Oliva de la Frontera
Valencia del Ventoso
Calzadilla de los Barros
Fuente de Cantos
Cantalgallo
Llerena
Ahillones
Casas de Reina
Valverde de Llerena
Estrela
Valencia de Mombuey
Póvoa
Amareleja
Ardila
Fregenal de la Sierra
Bodonal de la Sierra
Montemolin
Trasierra
Fuente del Arco
Higuera la Real
Segura de León
Calera de León
Pallares
Puebla del Maestre
Guadalcanal
Barrancos
Encinasola
Monesterio
Santo Amado
Safara
St. Aleixo
Cumbres de S. Bartolomé
Cumbres Mayores
Fuentes de León
Cabeza la Vaca
Tentudia 1110
Embalse de El Pintado
La Contienda
Cañaveral de León
Hoya de Santa Maria
Sobral da Adica
Picos de Aroche
Sierra de Aracena y Picas de Aroche
Hinojales
Arroyomolinos de León
Chanza
La Nava
Valdelarco
Cala
El Real de la Jara
Sierra Norte de
de Vargo
Rosal de la Frontera
Galaroza
Embalse de Aracena
Santa Olalla
Cazalla
Vila Verde de Filcalho
Aroche
Jabugo
Aracena
Corteconcepción
Almadén de la Plata
SANTA MARIA DE CONSOLACIÓN
Alcalaboza
Cortegana
Puerto Moral
Sierra de Aracena
Almonaster la Real
Alájar
Higuera de la Sierra
El Pedroso
Zufre
Chança
Arroya del Albahacar
Santa Barbara de Casa
San Telmo
Campofrio
Embalse de la Minilla
Huelva
Embalse de Cala
Cala
Viar
El Ronquillo
Cabezas Rubias
El Cerro de Andévalo
Nerva
Valdeflores
La Aulaga
Castilblanco de los Arroyos
Villanueva Río y Minas
Malagón
El Campillo
Minas de Riotinto
El Castillo de las Guardas
Zalamea la Real
El Madroño
El Alamo
Cantillana
Villaverde del Rio
Las Herreras
Calañas
El Garrobo
Burguillos
Puebla de Guzmán
Valverde del Camino
Berrocal
Las Pajanosas
Brenes
Tharsis
Alosno
Chanza
Dehesa
Oraque
Odiel
Gerena
Guillena
Alcalá del Río
El Almendro
Tinto
Aznalcóllar
La Rinconada
NEÁPOLIS ROMANA
Villanueva de los Castillejos
San Bartolome de la Torre
CIUDAD ANTIQUISIMA DE ITALICA
La Algaba
Paterna del Campo
Santiponce
ISLA MAGICA
Beas
DOLMEN DE SOTO
La Palma del Condado
Villalba del Alcor
Escacena del Campo
Olivares
Camas
Sevilla
Seville
El Viso del Alcor
Silvestre Guzmán
Tariquejas
Gibraleón
Trigueros
CASTILLO DE NIEBLA
Niebla
Villarrasa
Manzanilla
Sanlúcar la Mayor
Castilleja
Alcalá de Guadaira
Emb. de Piedras
Piedras
Carrión
Benacazón
Bollullos
Bormujos
Villablanca
Lepe
Cartaya
Aljaraque
Bonares
Lucena
Bollullos par del Condado
Pilas
Mairena de Aljarafe
Gelves
ALCAZAR DE ALCALA DE GUADAIRA
MONASTERIO DE SANTA CLARA
Rociana del Condado
Aznalcázar
La Puebla del Río
Coria del Río
Dos Hermanas
La Redondela
El Rompido
Huelva
Moguer
MONASTERIO DE SANTA MARIA DE LA RABIDA
Almonte
Hinojos
Villamanrique de la Condesa
Ayamonte
La Antillas
Palos de la Frontera
Utrera
Isla Cristina
Isla Canela
Real de Santo Antonio
Punta Umbria
Isla de Saltes
Mazagón
Los Palacios y Villafranca
El Rocio
Villafranco del Guadalquivir
Entorno de Doñana
Queipo
Madre de las Marismas
Parque Nacional de Doñana
Golfo de Cádiz
Matalascanas
Entorno de Doñana
Guadalquivir
Las Cabezas de San Juan
Lebrija
Las Palmas de Gran Canaria
Santa Cruz de Tenerife
Costa de la Luz
Trebujena
El Cuervo
Sanlúcar de Barrameda
Bonanza
Chipiona
Arcos de la Frontera
Jerez de la Frontera
La Barca de la Florida
Embalse de Guadalcacín
Laguna de Medina
Rota
El Puerto de Santa Maria
Bahía de Cádiz
Arrecife
Las Palmas de Gran Canaria
Santa Cruz de Tenerife
Santa Cruz de la Palma
Puerto Real
Cádiz
Baños
Paterna de
Medina Sidonia
Chiclana de la Frontera
San Fernando
A
B
C
2
3
4
7°
6°
37°
38°
49
56

Santa Olalla
Cazalla de la Sierra
Las Navas de la Concepción
Embalse del Bembézar
Almadén de la Plata
Constantina
Embalse del Retortillo
La Puebla de los Infantes
Hornachuelos
Almodóvar del Río
El Pedroso
Posadas
Guadalcázar
El Ronquillo
Embalse de Cala
Embalse de la Minilla
Peñaflor
Palma del Río
Fuente Palmera
La Carlota
Castilblanco de los Arroyos
Villanueva del Río y Minas
Lora del Río
El Castillo de las Guardas
Cantillana
Villaverde del Río
Alcolea del Río
Cañada Rosal
El Garrobo
Burguillos
Tocina
La Campana
Las Pajanosas
Brenes
Écija
Santaella
Gerena
Guillena
La Luisiana
Alcalá del Río
Aznalcóllar
Fuentes de Andalucía
Ciudad Antiquísima de Itálica
Necrópolis Romana
La Rinconada
Paterna del Campo
Carmona
La Algaba
Santiponce
Camas
Sevilla
Seville
El Viso del Alcor
Sanlúcar la Mayor
Castilleja
Marinaleda
Carrión
Benacazón
Bormujos
Mairena del Alcor
Herrera
Bollullos
Mairena de Aljarafe
Gelves
Alcalá de Guadaira
Alcázar de Alcalá de Guadaira
La Lantejuela
El Rubio
Marchena
Hinojos
Aznalcázar
La Puebla del Río
Coria del Río
Dos Hermanas
Paradas
Arahal
Estepa
Villamanrique de la Condesa
Osuna
Gilena
Pedrera
Aguadulce
La Puebla de Cazalla
La Roda de Andalucía
Utrera
El Rocío
Los Palacios y Villafranca
Villafranco del Guadalquivir
Los Morales
Sierra de Yeguas
El Coronil
Morón de la Frontera
El Saucejo
Queipo
Parque Nacional de Doñana
Martín de la Jara
Los Corrales
Embalse de la Torre del Águila
Villanueva de S. Juan
Las Cabezas de San Juan
Montellano
Campillos
Almargen
Teba
Coripe
La Encarnación
Pruna
Castillo de Olvera
Olvera
Cañete la Real
Lebrija
Puerto Serrano
Alcalá del Valle
Trebujena
Algodonales
Espera
Villamartín
El Cuervo
Zahara
El Gastor
Setenil
Ardales
Cuevas del Becerro
Bonanza
Bornos
Embalse de Zahara
El Burgo
Arcos de la Frontera
Prado del Rey
Embalse de Bornos
Arriate
Grazalema
Jerez de la Frontera
El Bosque
Sierra de Grazalema
Benaocaz
Benaoján
Cueva de la Pileta
Castillo de Ronda
Ronda
Serranía de Ronda
Yunquera
Embalse de los Hurones
Sierra de las Nieves
Tolox
Rota
La Barca de la Florida
Algar
Ubrique
Jimera de Líbar
Guaro
El Puerto de Santa María
Laguna de Medina
Embalse de Guadalcacín
Cortes de la Frontera
Monda
Garcisobaco
Bahía de Cádiz
Istán
Cádiz
Puerto Real
Algatocín
Jubrique
Benarrabá
Ojén
El Comenar
Sierra Bermeja
Baños de Gigonza
Paterna de Rivera
Gaucín
Marbella
Medina Sidonia
Alcalá de los Gazules
San Fernando
Chiclana de la Frontera
Castillo de Jimena de la Frontera
Casares
San Pedro de Alcántara
Sancti-Petri
Jimena de la Frontera
Los Alcornocales
Embalse de Barbate
Estepona
La Barrosa
Campano
Benalup
Manilva
San Martín del Tesorillo
Embalse de Celemín
Castellar de la Frontera
San Enrique
Cabo Roche
Conil de la Frontera
Castillo de Castellar Viejo
Almoraima
Guadiaro
Vejer de la Frontera
Embalse de Palmones
Charco-Redondo
San Roque
Los Caños de Meca
Castillo Árabe
Barbate
Los Barrios
La Línea de la Concepción
C. Trafalgar
Puente Mayorga
Zahara de los Atunes
Facinas
Algeciras
Gibraltar (U.K.)
Castillo de Almadrabas
Pta. de Europa
Baelo Claudia
Bahía de Algeciras
Tanger
Castillo de Guzmán el Bueno
Tanger Ceuta
Tarifa
Punta Marroqui
36°
37°
5°
6°
1
2
3
A
B
C

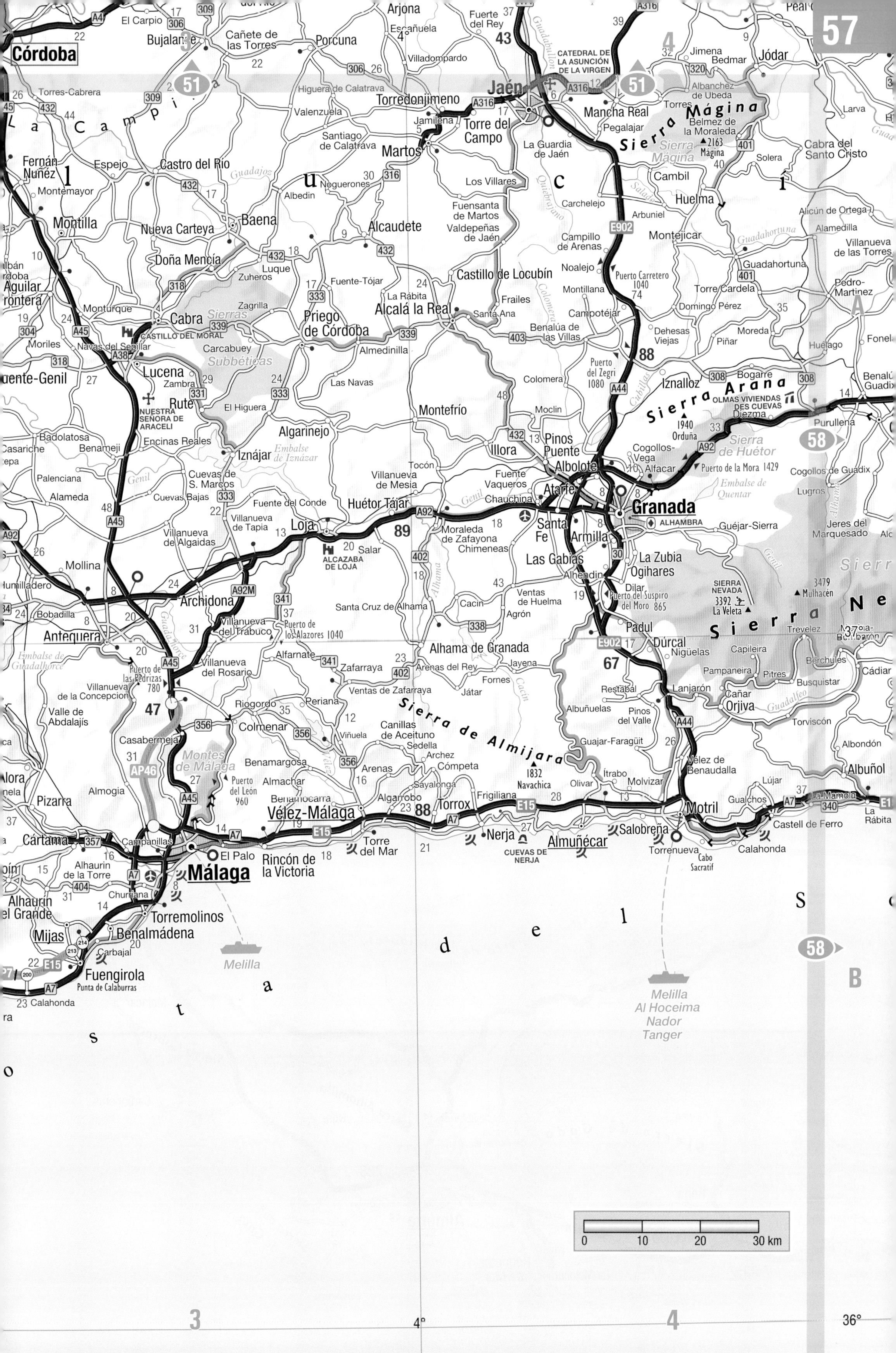

Puebla del Principe
Villamanrique
Sierra de
Almenara 1798
Paterna del Madera
Bogarra
Ayna
Bienservida
Riopar
Liétor
Hellín
52
Embalse del Guadalmena
Génave
Villaver de Guadalimar
Molinicos
Elche de la Sierra
Embalse de Talave
Minateda
Agramón
Embalse de Cenajo
uemada
236
Venta de los Santos
Puente de Génave
Siles
La Puerta de Segura
El Arguellite
Montiras 1897
Parolis
Yeste
Embalse de la Fuensanta
Letur
Socovos
Las Minas
Orcera
Santisteban del Puerto
Chiclana de Segura
Arroyo del Ojanco
Castellar
Sorihuela del Guadalimar
Cortijos Nuevos
Beas de Segura
Hornos
Sierras de Cazorla Segura y Las Villas
El Sabinar
Calasparra
Moratalla
Iznatoraf
Villanueva del Arzobispo
Embalse del Tranco de Beas
Pontones
Sierra de Segura
Sierra de Taibilla
Nerpio
Cehegín
Villacarrillo
Sierra de Cazorla
1831 Blanquilla
Santiago de la Espade
Caravaca de la Cruz
Archivel
Bullas
Sabiote
Santo Tomé
Torreperogil
Chilluevar
La Sagra 2381
Almudena
51
Puebla de Don Fadrique
Peal de Becerro
Cazorla
La Iruela
Royos
Casas Nuevas
Zarzadilla de Totana
Quesada
Cabañas 2028
Sierra de Castril
Embalse de La Bolera
Topares
Zarcilla de Ramos
La Paca
Embalse de Valdeinfierno
CASTILLO DE ALE
Huéscar
Castril
Larva
Huesa
Castillejar
Galera
Embalse de Puentes
Fuensanta
Cabra del Santo Cristo
Pozo Alcón
Orce
Maria
Velez Blanco
Sierra de María-Los Vélez
Lorca
Cortes de Baza
Vélez Rubio
Cuevas del Campo
Dehesas de Guadix
Alicún de Ortega
Alamedilla
Villanueva de las Torres
Benamaurel
Cúllar
Sierra de María
CASTILLO DE NOGALTE
Embalse de Negratín
COLEGIATA CONCATEDRAL DE LA ENCARNACIÓN
181
Chirivel
Puerto Lumbreras
Zújar
Pedro-Martinez
Los Cerricos
Sierra de las Estancias
Baza
Gorafe
Caniles
Oria
Santa Maria de Nieva
Huélago
Fonelas
Mt. Santa Bárbara 2271
El Hijate
Lúcar
Urracal
Olula del Rio
Albox
Pulpi
Benalúa de Guadix
Somontin
Huércal-Overa
Emb. de Cuevas de Almanzora
Gor
Sierra de Baza
Purullena
Guadix
Alcontar
Serón
Tíjola
Purchena
Cantoria
Zurgena
Cuevas del Almanzora
Macael
Albánchez
Alcudia de Guadix
Bacares
Cogollos de Guadix
Antas
Vera
Palomares
Lugros
57
Sierra de los Filabres
Tahal
Lubrin
Lacalahorra
Huéneja
Senés
Velefique
Bédar
Los Gallardos
Garrucha
Jeres del Marquesado
Aldeire
Fiñana
Uleila del Campo
Abla
Mojacar
Sierra Nevada
Gérgal
Sorbas
3479 Mulhacén
Ohanes
Sierra Cabrera
Tabernas
Lucainena de las Torres
Mecina-Bombaron
Válor
Laujar de Andarax
Canjáyar
Ugíjar
Sierra Alhamilla
Carboneras
Bérchules
Illar
Alcolea
Gádor
Rioja
Níjar
Cádiar
Busquistar
Sierra de Gádor
Morrón 2242
Alhama de Almería
Benahadux
Fernán Peréz
Punta de la Media Naranja
Murtas
Turón
Félix
Huércal de Almería
Viator
228
Las Negras
Albondón
Berja
Dalias
Vícar
El Alquián
Cabo de Gata-Nijar
Albuñol
Aguadulce
Almería
Punta del Río
La Mamola
El Ejido
Roquetas de Mar
Cabo de Gata
Sierra del Cabo de Gata
La Rábita
Adra
Golfo de Almería
de Ferro
Balerma
La Mojonera
San José
Almerimar
Guardias Viejas
San Agustín
Cabo de Gata
Melilla Oran Nador Ghazaouet
Punta del Sabinar
1
2
3
A
B
C
M u r
a
3°
2°
37°
38°
E15
A7
A92
A92-N
A91
A334
A1051
AL12
340a
341
332
315
326
330
334
712
711
730
715
714
510
3217
3228
412
322
312
308
340
15
11

Jumilla
Casas del Puerto
Pinoso
Salinas
Sax
Elda
Petrer
Monóvar
Castalla
Jijona
Tibi
Agost
Novelda
Aspe
Monforte del Cid
San Vicente del Raspeig
Campello
San Juan de Alicante
SAN VICENTE DEL RASPEIG
Alicante
Cabo de las Huertas
Benidorm
Villajoyosa
Orchete
Aguas de Busot
Busot
COVES DEL CANELOBRES
Hondón de los Frailes
Crevillente
Elche
Les Salines de Santa Pola
El Fondo
Santa Pola
Cabo de Santo Pola
Nueva Tabarca
Alger
Oran
Pila
1265
Cieza
Abarán
Blanca
Fortuna
Abanilla
Albatera
Catral
Dolores
Callosa de Segura
Orihuela
Almoradí
Guardamar del Segura
Rojales
Benejúzar
Bigastro
Salinas de la Mata
Lagunas de la Mata -Torrevieja
Salinas de Torrevieja
Torrevieja
Archena
Lorquí
Ceutí
Molina de Segura
Santomera
Monteagudo
Mula
Pliego
Alguazas
Alcantarilla
Murcia
Emb. de la Pedrera
San Miguel de Salinas
Pilar de la Horadada
El Palmer
El Valle
Sangonera la Verde
Puerto de la Cadena
372
Corvera
Sucina
San Javier
San Pedro del Pinatar
Lo Pagán
Santiago de la Ribera
Sierra de Espuña
Librilla
Torre-Pacheco
Los Alcázares
Mar Menor
Fuente-Álamo de Murcia
Albujón
Aljorra
La Pinilla
El Algar
Los Nietos
Cabo de Palos
Los Dolores
La Unión
Cartagena
Portman
Escombreras
Cabo Tiñoso
Mazarrón
Puerto de Mazarrón
Campico López
879
Talayón
Puntas de Calnegre
Golfo de Mazarrón
Cope
Cabo Cope
Costa Blanca
38°
37°
1°
0°
A
B
C
3
4
0
10
20
30 km

1 2° 2

A

40°

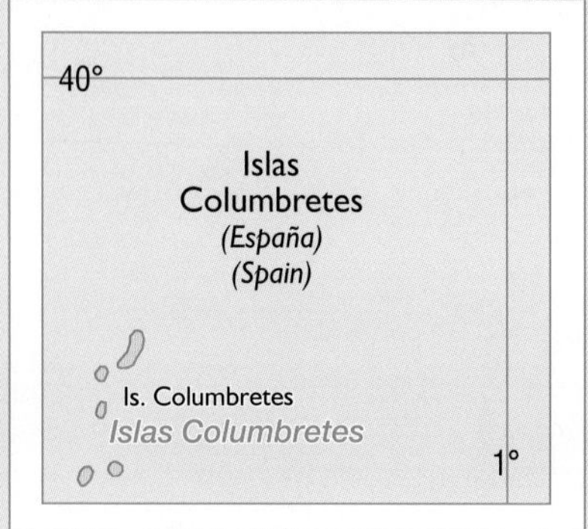


ISLAS BALEARES

BALEARIC ISLANDS

B

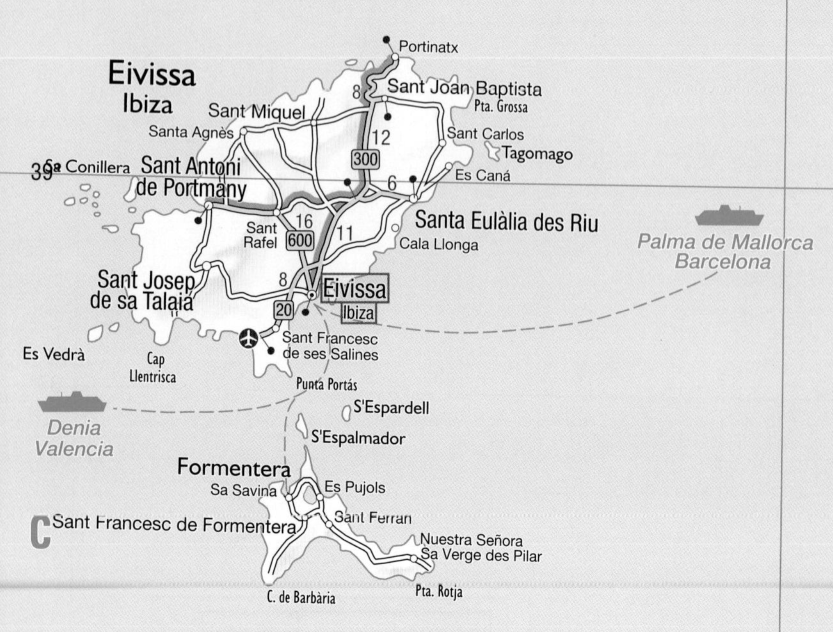


39°

C

1 2° 2

Barcelona
Capo de Cavalleria
Fornells
Punta Nati
Cala Morell
Cap de Favàritx
Ciudadela de Menorca
Es Mercadal
Ferreries
358 Toro
Alaior
Cala Galdana
Es Migjorn Gran
C. de Artrutx
Son Bou
Maó
Menorca
Minorca
Sant Climent
Pta. de s'Esperó
Es Castell
Sant Luis
Punta Prima
I. de l'Aire
Palma de Mallorca
Valencia
Cap de Formentor
Punta Beca
Port de Pollença
B. de Pollença
Pollença
Cap des Pinar
Alcúdia
Es Port d'Alcúdia
B. d'Alcúdia
Puig Major 1445
Sa Pobla
C'an Picafort
Cap Ferrutx
562 Morey
Cap des Freu
Selva
Lloseta
Inca
Muro
Santa Margalida
Artà
Cala Ratjada
Capdepera
CUEVAS DE ARTA
Sta. Maria del Camí
Sencelles
Sineu
Sant Llorenç des Carctassar
Cap des Pinar
Son Servera
Petra
Montuïri
Cala Millor
Punta de n'Amer
Algaida
MONASTERIO DE CORA
Manacor
Porto Cristo
CUEVAS DEL DRACH
Porreres
Llucmajor
Felanitx
Cales de Mallorca
SAN SALVADOR (MONASTERIO)
Campos del Port
Porto Colom
Cala d'Or
Porto Petro
Sa Rapita
Ses Salines
Santanyí
Colònia de Sant Jordi
Cap de ses Salines
I. des Conills
Archipiélago de Cabrera
Cabrera
40°
39°
3°
4°
0 10 20 30 km

Corse
Corsica
(France)
Parc Naturel Régional de Corse
Bastia
Ajaccio
Corte
Calvi
Porto-Vecchio
Bonifacio
Sartène
Propriano
L'Île-Rousse
St. Florent
Aléria
Ghisonaccia
Solenzara
Capraia
Marseille Toulon Nice Génova Savona Livorno
Livorno
Nice Marseille
Nice Toulon Marseille
Marseille
Porto Tórres
G. de St. Florent
Golfe de Porto
Golfe de Sagone
Golfe d'Ajaccio
G. de Valinco
Bouches de Bonifacio
Arcipélago della Maddalena
la Maddalena
Santa Teresa Gallura
Palau
Caprera
Costa
C. Corse
Mte. Cinto 2706
Mte. Rotondo 2622
L'Incudine 2136
Pte. d'Ovace 1340
COUVENT ANCIEN DE SANTA CATALINA
GROTTE DES VEAUX MARINS
GROTTE DE SCAFFA
MUSEO NAZIONALE DEL COMPENDIO GARIBALDINO DI CAPRERA
0 10 20 30 km

## City plans • Plans de villes
## Stadtpläne • Piante di città

Motorway – Autoroute
Major through route – Route principale majeur
Through route – Route principale
Secondary road – Route secondaire
Dual carriageway – Chaussées séparées
Other road – Autre route
Tunnel – Tunnel
Limited access / pedestrian road – Rue réglementée / rue piétonne
One-way street – Sens unique
Parking – Parc de stationnement
Motorway number A7 – Numéro d'autoroute
National road number 447 – Numéro de route nationale
European road number E45 – Numéro de route européenne
Destination GENT – Destination
Car ferry – Bac passant les autos
Railway – Chemin de fer
Rail / bus station – Gare / gare routière
Underground, metro station – Station de métro
Cable car – Téléférique
Abbey, cathedral – Abbaye, cathédrale
Church of interest – Église intéressante
Synagogue – Synagogue
Hospital – Hôpital
Police station – Police
Post office – Bureau de poste
Tourist information – Office de tourisme
Place of interest – Theatre – Autre curiosité
Autobahn – Autostrada
Hauptstrecke – Strada di grande communicazione
Schnellstrasse – Strada d'importanza regionale
Nebenstrasse – Strada d'interesse locale
Zweispurig Schnellstrasse – Strada a carreggiate doppie
Nebenstrecke – Altra strada
Tunnel – Galleria stradale
Beschränkter Zugang/ Fussgängerzone – Strada pedonale / a accesso limitato
Einbahnstrasse – Senso unico
Parkplatz – Parcheggio
Autobahnnummer A7 – Numero di autostrada
Nationalstrassen-nummer 447 – Numero di strada nazionale
Europäische Strassennummer E45 – Numero di strada europea
Ziel GENT – Destinazione
Autofähre – Traghetto automobili
Eisenbahn – Ferrovia
Bahnhof / Busstation – Stazione ferrovia / pullman
U-Bahnstation – Metropolitano
Drahtseilbahn – Funivia
Abtei, Kloster, Kathedrale – Abbazia, duomo
Interessante Kirche – Chiesa da vedere
Synagoge – Sinagoga
Krankenhaus – Ospedale
Polizeiwache – Polizia
Postamt – Ufficio postale
Informationsbüro – Ufficio informazioni turistiche
Sonstige Sehenswürdigkeit – Theatre – Luogo da vedere

## Approach maps • Agglomérations
## Carte régionale • Regionalkarte

Toll motorway – with motorway number A10 – Autoroute à péage – avec numéro d'autoroute
Toll-free motorway – with European road number E51 – Autoroute – avec numéro de route européenne
Pre-pay motorway – vignette required – Autoroute – 'vignette'
Motorway services – Aire de service
Motorway junction – full access, restricted access 24 – Échangeur d'autoroute – accès libre, accès reglémenté
Under construction – En construction
Tunnel – Tunnel
Major route – dual carriageway, single carriageway 14 – Route principale – chausées séparées, chausée sans séparation
Secondary route – dual carriageway, single carriageway 96 – Route secondaire – chausées séparées, chausée sans séparation
Other road – Autre route
Car ferry – Bac passant les autos
Destination GIRONA – Destination
Railway – Chemin de fer
Railway station Estación Central – Gare
Height – in metres 234 – Altitude – en mètres
Airport – Aéroport principal
Airfield – Autre aéroport
City plan coverage area – Région de plan de ville
Gebührenpflichtige Autobahn – mit Autobahnnummer A10 – Autostrada a pedaggio – con numero
Gebührenfreie Autobahn – Europäische Strassennummer E51 – Autostrada – con numero di strada europea
Autobahn – 'vignette' – Autostrada – 'vignette'
Autobahnservice – Area di servizio autostradale
Autobahnkreuz – voller/begrenzter Zugang 24 – Raccordi autostradali – completo/parziali
Im Bau – In construzione
Tunnel – Galleria stradale
Hauptstrecke – zweispurige Schnellstrasse 14 – Strada di grande communicazione – carreggiata doppia, carreggiata unica
Nebenstrasse – zweispurige Schnellstrasse 96 – Strada d'interesse locale – carreggiata doppia, carreggiata unica
Nebenstrecke – Altra strada
Autofähre – Traghetto automobili
Ziel GIRONA – Destinazione
Eisenbahn – Ferrovia
Hauptbahnhof Estación Central – Stazione ferrovia
Höhe – über dem Meeresspiegel 234 – Altezza in metri
Flughafen – Aeroporto
Flugplatz – Aerodromo/ campo d'aviazione
Vom Stadtplan abgedecktes Gebiet – Area della pianta della città

## Alicante

0 km 0.5

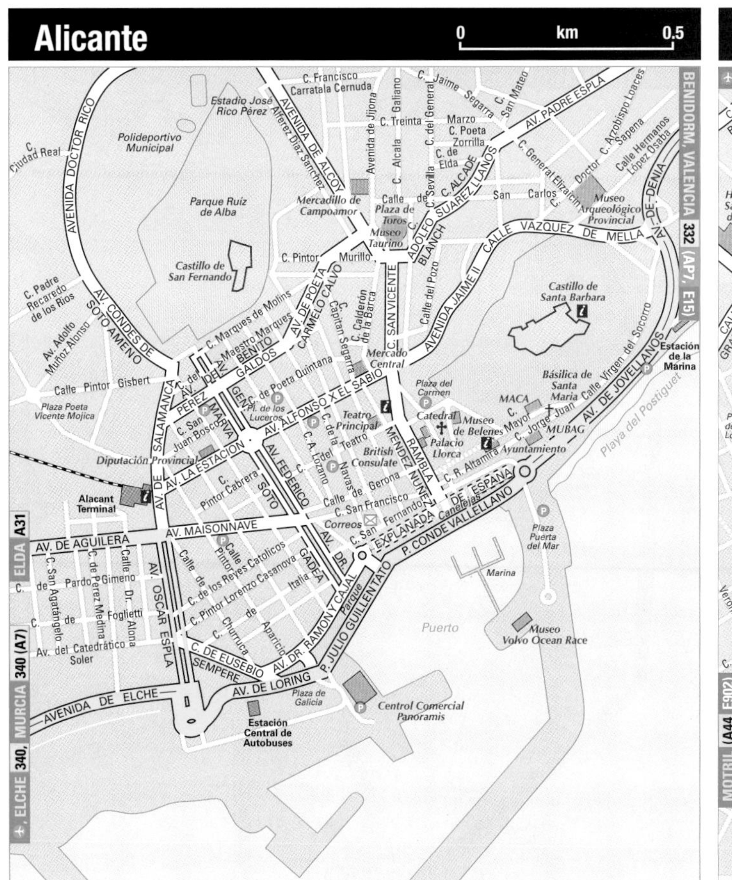
Estadio José Rico Pérez
Polideportivo Municipal
Parque Ruiz de Alba
Castillo de San Fernando
Castillo de Santa Barbara
Mercadillo de Campoamor
Plaza de Toros
Museo Taurino
Museo Arqueológico Provincial
Mercado Central
Teatro Principal
Catedral
Museo de Belenes
Palacio Llorca
Ayuntamiento
Basílica de Santa María
MACA
MUBAG
British Consulate
Diputación Provincial
Alacant Terminal
Correos
Marina
Puerto
Museo Volvo Ocean Race
Centro Comercial Panoramis
Estación Central de Autobuses
Estación de la Marina
Playa del Postiguet
AVENIDA DE ALCOY
AV. PADRE ESPLA
AV. DE JOVELLANOS
AV. DE SALAMANCA
AV. ALFONSO X EL SABIO
AV. MAISONNAVE
AV. DE AGUILERA
AV. OSCAR ESPLA
AVENIDA DE ELCHE
AV. DE LORING
AVENIDA DOCTOR RICO
AV. CONDES DE SOTO AMEINO
RAMBLA MENDEZ NUÑEZ
EXPLANADA DE ESPAÑA
P. CONDE VALLELLANO
P. JULIO GUILLENTATO
AVENIDA JAIME II
CALLE VAZQUEZ DE MELLA
BENIDORM, VALENCIA 332 (AP7, E15)
ELDA A31
MURCIA 340 (A7)
ELCHE 340,

## Granada

0 km 0.5

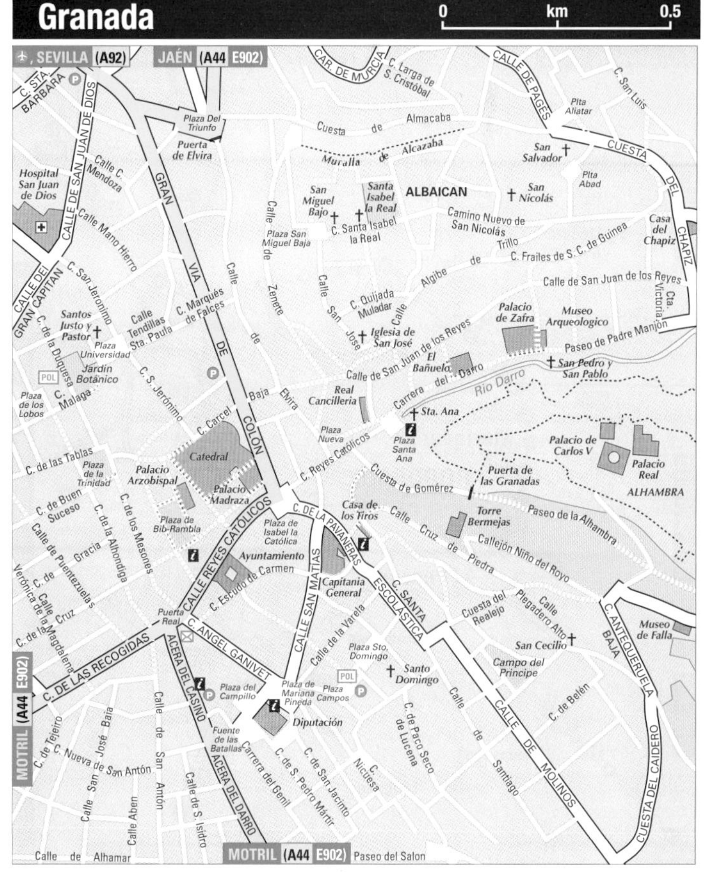
SEVILLA (A92)
JAÉN (A44 E902)
MOTRIL (A44 E902)
Hospital San Juan de Dios
Puerta de Elvira
Plaza Del Triunfo
Muralla
Alcazaba
Almacaba
ALBAICAN
San Miguel Bajo
San Nicolás
San Salvador
Palacio de Zafra
Museo Arqueologico
Iglesia de San José
El Bañuelo
Rio Darro
Sta. Ana
Real Cancilleria
Catedral
Palacio Arzobispal
Palacio Madraza
Capilla Real
Universidad
Jardín Botánico
Ayuntamiento
Capitania General
Casa de los Tiros
Puerta de las Granadas
Torre Bermejas
Palacio de Carlos V
Palacio Real
ALHAMBRA
Santo Domingo
Diputación
Museo de Falla
San Cecilio
Campo del Principe
GRAN VIA DE COLÓN
CALLE REYES CATOLICOS
ACERA DEL CASINO
C. DE LAS RECOGIDAS
CALLE DE SAN JUAN DE DIOS
CUESTA DEL CHAPIZ
Paseo de la Alhambra
Paseo del Salon

## Barcelona

0 km 5

TERRASSA, MANRESA | GIRONA | TERRASSA, MANRESA (C16) | GIRONA, FIGUERES (AP7) | MATARÓ (C32) | LLEIDA (AP2) VALENCIA | VILANOVA I LA GELTRÚ TARRAGONA (AP7)

Rubí, Ripollet, Sant Cugat del Vallès, Valldoreix, Madrona, La Floresta, El Papiol, Santa Cruz de Olorde, Tibidabo, Molins de Rei, Vallvidrera, Sant Vicenç dels Horts, San Pedro Mártir, Sant Just Desvern, Pedralbes, Sarrià, Putxet, Gràcia, Sant Feliu de Llobregat, Esplugas, Sant Joan Despí, Colonia Güell, La Ribera, L'Hospitalet de Llobregat, Cornellà, Sant Boi de Llobregat, S. Clemente del Llobregat, Viladecans, Gavà, El Prat de Llobregat, Aeropuerto de Barcelona Prat, La Pineda, Sta. Coloma de Gramanet, Badalona, Sant Adrià de Besós, BARCELONA, Barceloneta, MAR MEDITERRÁNEO

## Barcelona

0 km 1

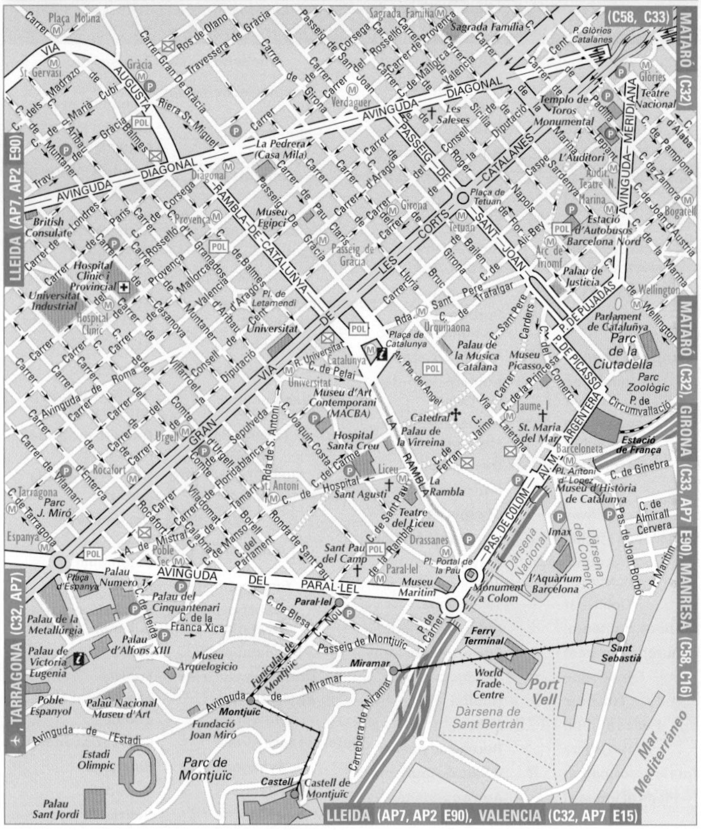

LLEIDA (AP7, AP2 E90) | MATARÓ (C32) | MATARÓ (C32), GIRONA (C33, AP7 E90), MANRESA (C58, C16) | TARRAGONA (C32, AP7) | LLEIDA (AP7, AP2 E90), VALENCIA (C32, AP7 E15)

Sagrada Familia, Avinguda Diagonal, La Pedrera (Casa Milà), Passeig de Gràcia, Rambla de Catalunya, Gran Via de les Corts Catalanes, Plaça de Catalunya, Palau de la Música Catalana, Museu Picasso, Parc de la Ciutadella, Parc Zoològic, Estació de França, Catedral, La Rambla, Museu d'Art Contemporani (MACBA), Hospital Santa Creu, Teatre del Liceu, Monument a Colom, L'Aquàrium Barcelona, Port Vell, World Trade Centre, Parc de Montjuïc, Fundació Joan Miró, Estadi Olímpic, Palau Sant Jordi, Palau Nacional Museu d'Art, Poble Espanyol, Plaça d'Espanya, Avinguda del Paral·lel, Mar Mediterràneo

## Bordeaux

0 km 5

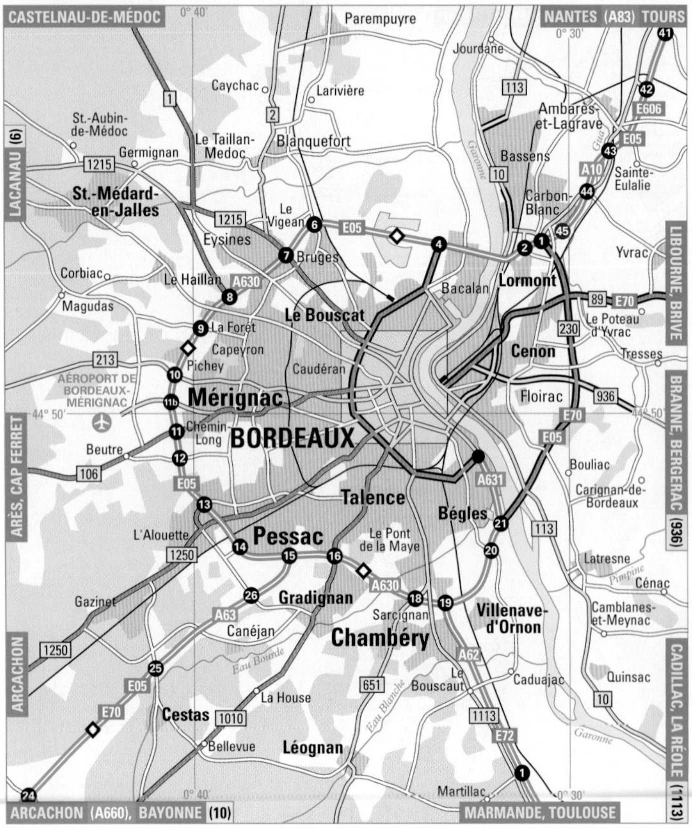

CASTELNAU-DE-MÉDOC | NANTES (A83) TOURS | LACANAU (6) | LIBOURNE BRIVE | BRANNE, BERGERAC (936) | CADILLAC, LA RÉOLE (1113) | ARÈS, CAP FERRET | ARCACHON | ARCACHON (A660), BAYONNE (10) | MARMANDE, TOULOUSE

Parempuyre, Caychac, Larivière, St.-Aubin-de-Médoc, Le Taillan-Médoc, Blanquefort, St.-Médard-en-Jalles, Eysines, Le Vigean, Bruges, Le Haillan, Le Bouscat, Bassens, Ambarès-et-Lagrave, Sainte-Eulalie, Carbon-Blanc, Lormont, Yvrac, Cenon, Floirac, Mérignac, BORDEAUX, Talence, Pessac, Bègles, Gradignan, Villenave-d'Ornon, Chambéry, Cestas, Léognan, Martillac

## Bordeaux

0 km 1

LACANAU (D6) | SAINTES, POITIERS (A10 E05) | PÉRIGUEUX, CLERMONT FERRAND N89 E70 | CAP FERRET D106 | ARCACHON D1250 | BAYONNE (N10 E05 E70)

Quai des Chartrons, Musée du Vin et du Négoce, Jardin Public, Cours de Verdun, Allées de Tourny, Grand Théâtre, Place de la Bourse, Miroir d'Eau, Cathédrale, Palais de Justice, Cours Victor Hugo, Pont de Pierre, La Garonne, Quai Richelieu, Cours de l'Argonne, Cours de la Marne, Boulevard Antoine Gautier

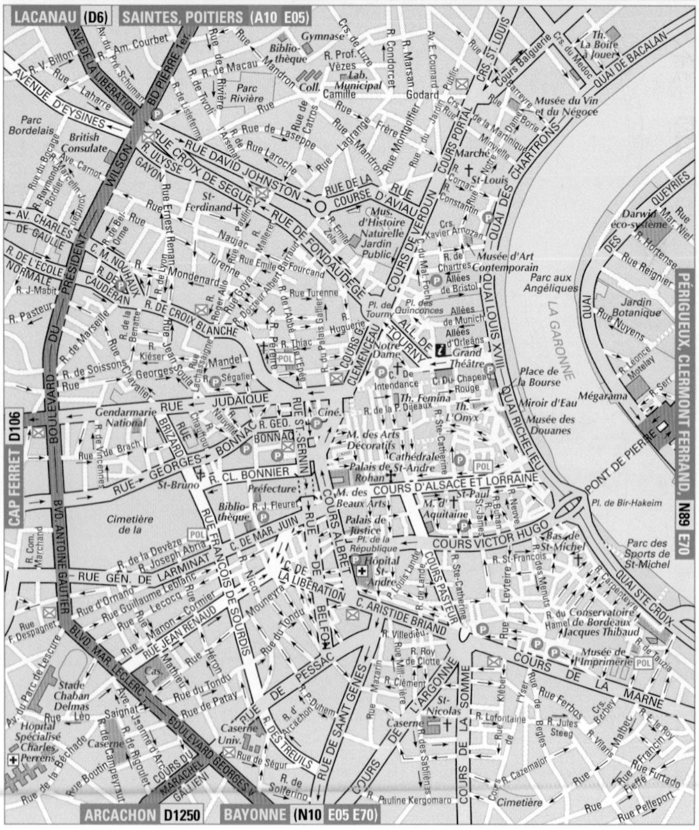

## Lisboa Lisbon

0 km 5

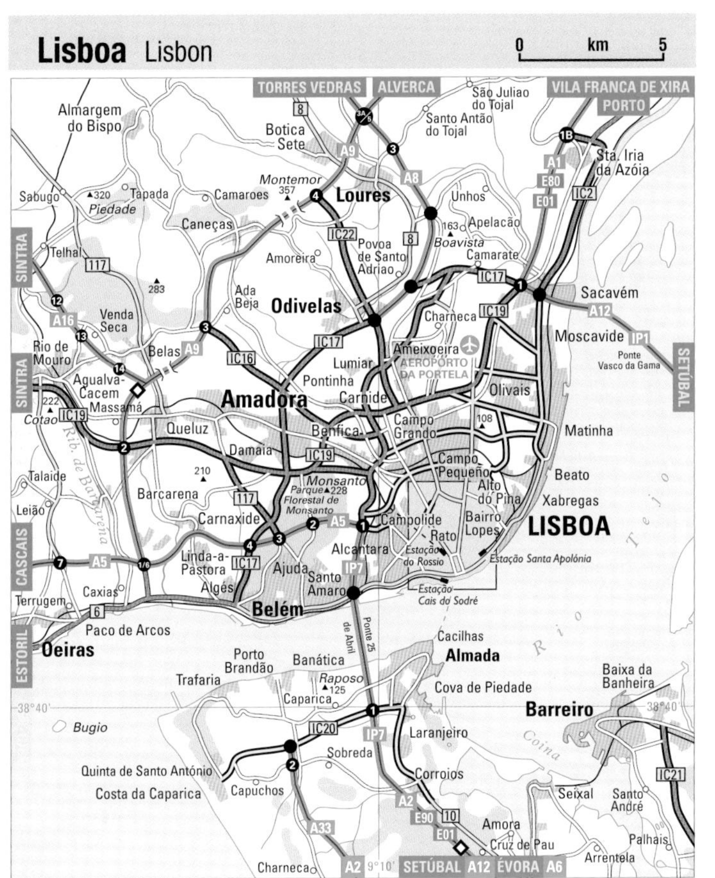


## Lisboa Lisbon

0 km 1

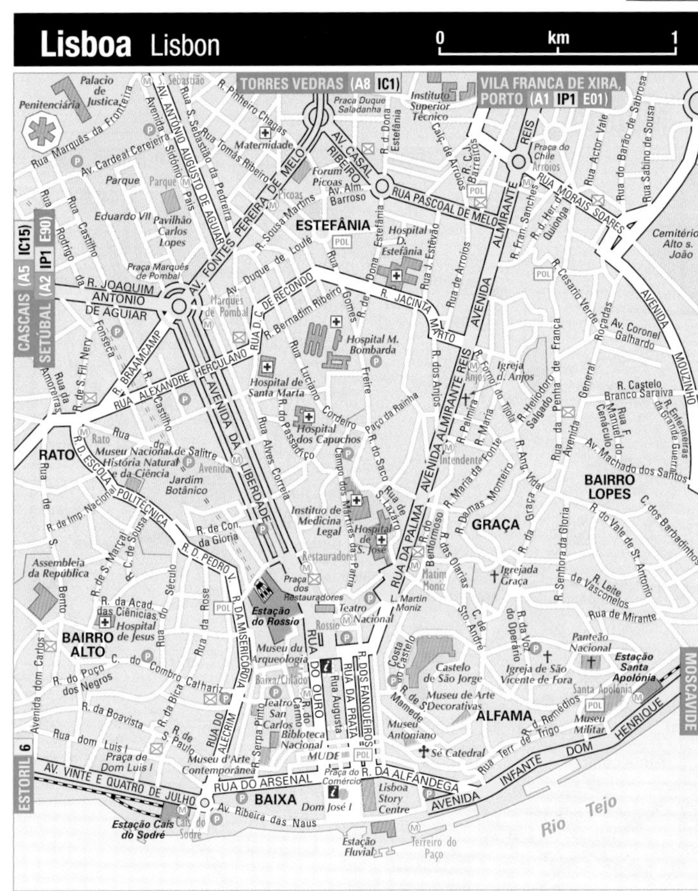


## Lyon

0 km 5

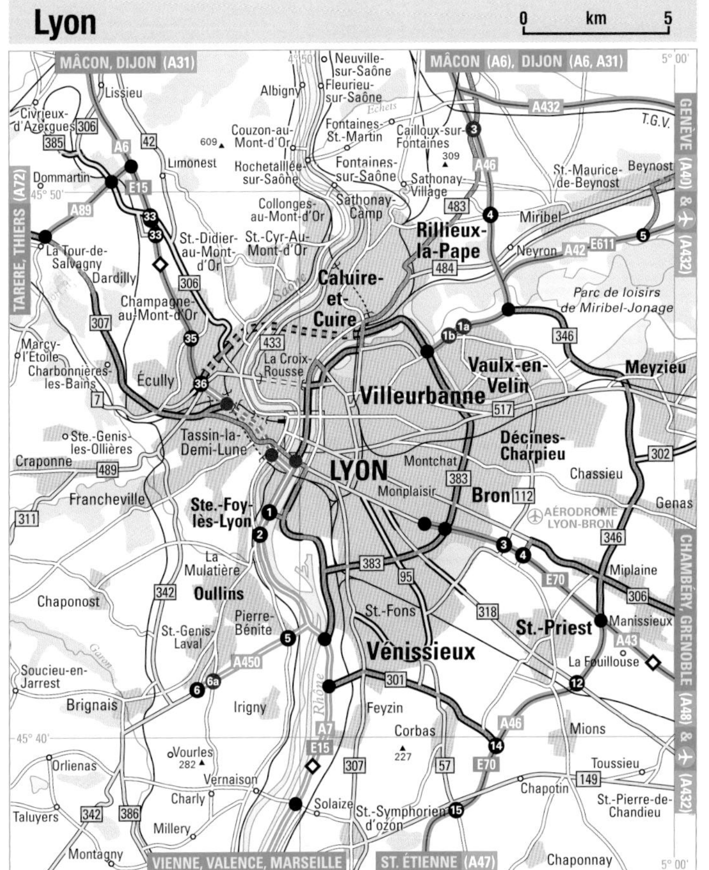


## Lyon

0 km 1

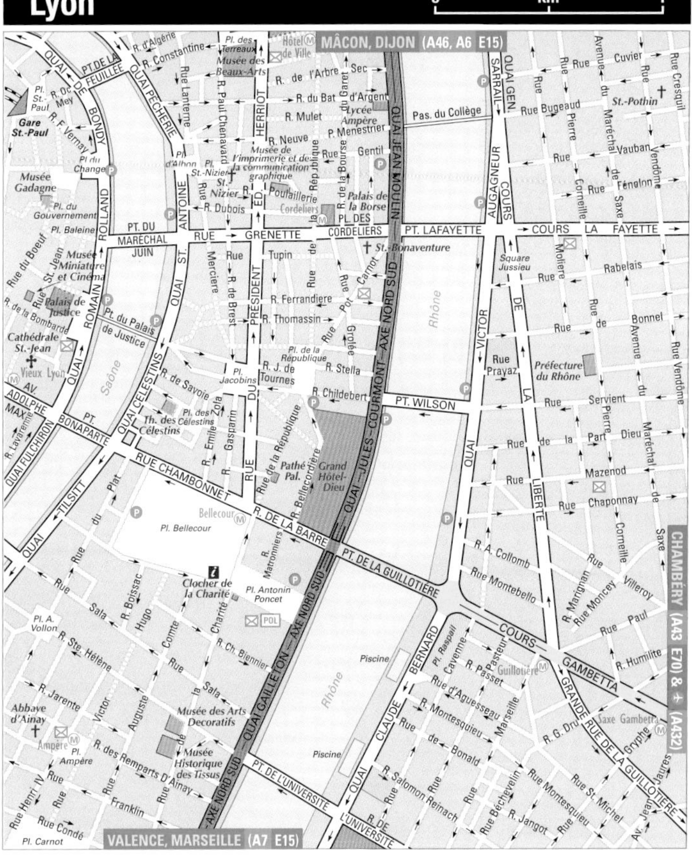

## Madrid

0 km 5

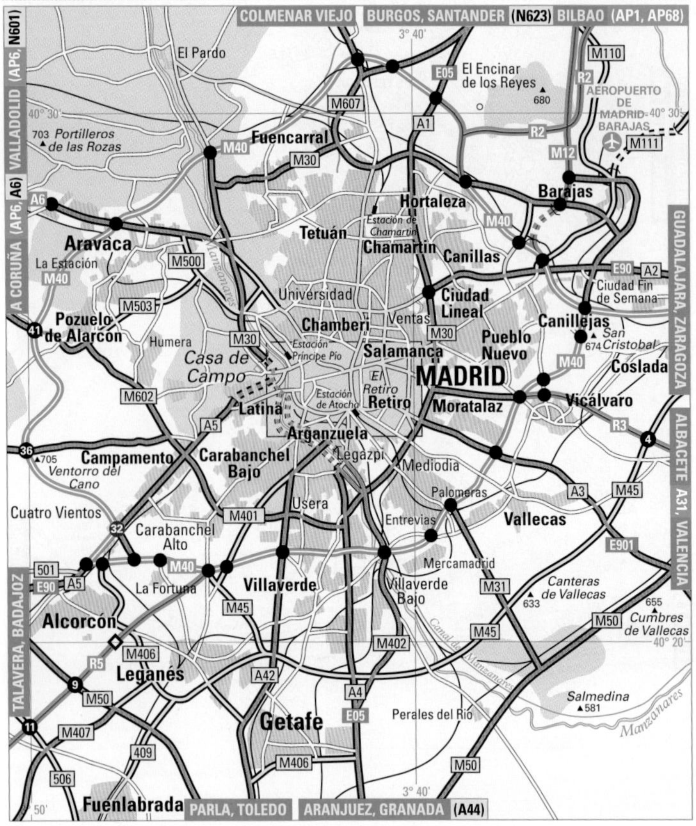

COLMENAR VIEJO | BURGOS, SANTANDER (N623) | BILBAO (AP1, AP68)

GUADALAJARA, ZARAGOZA | ALBACETE A31, VALENCIA

PARLA, TOLEDO | ARANJUEZ, GRANADA (A44)

TALAVERA, BADAJOZ | A CORUÑA (AP6, A6) VALLADOLID (AP6, N601)

## Marseille / Marseilles

0 km 0.5

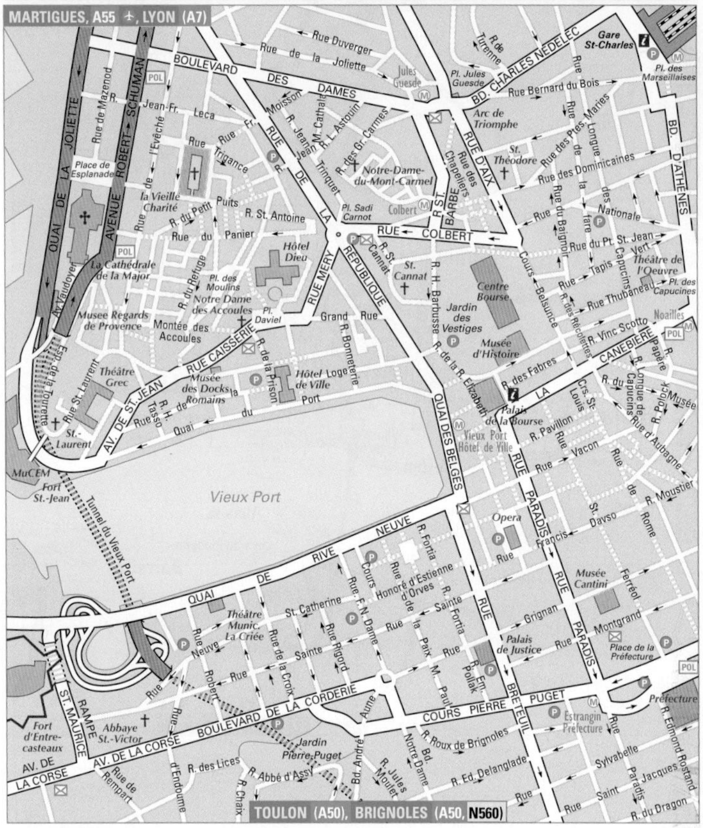

MARTIGUES, A55 | LYON (A7)

TOULON (A50), BRIGNOLES (A50, N560)

## Madrid

0 km 1

ARÉVALO (A6, A6) | COLMENAR (M607) | (A2, E90) ALCALÁ (A2)

ZARAGOZA (M40, A2) A2 E90 | ARGANDA, VALENCIA A3 E901

TOLEDO M30 (A42) | M30 | TOLEDO A42 | ARANJUEZ A4 E05 | ARANJUEZ M30 (A4)

TALAVERA DE LA REINA A5 E90 | A CORUÑA M30 (AP6, A6)

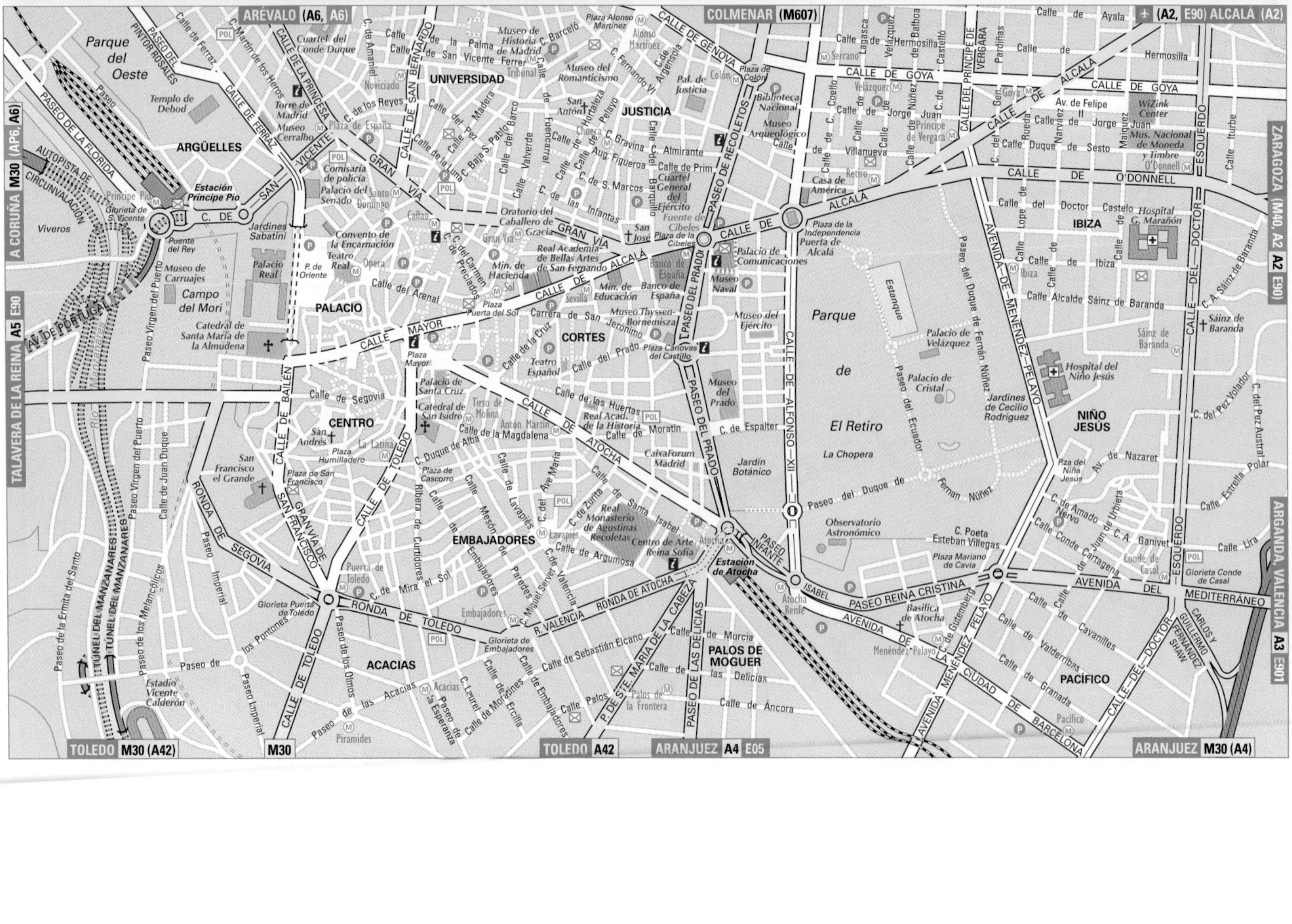

# Paris

0 km 5

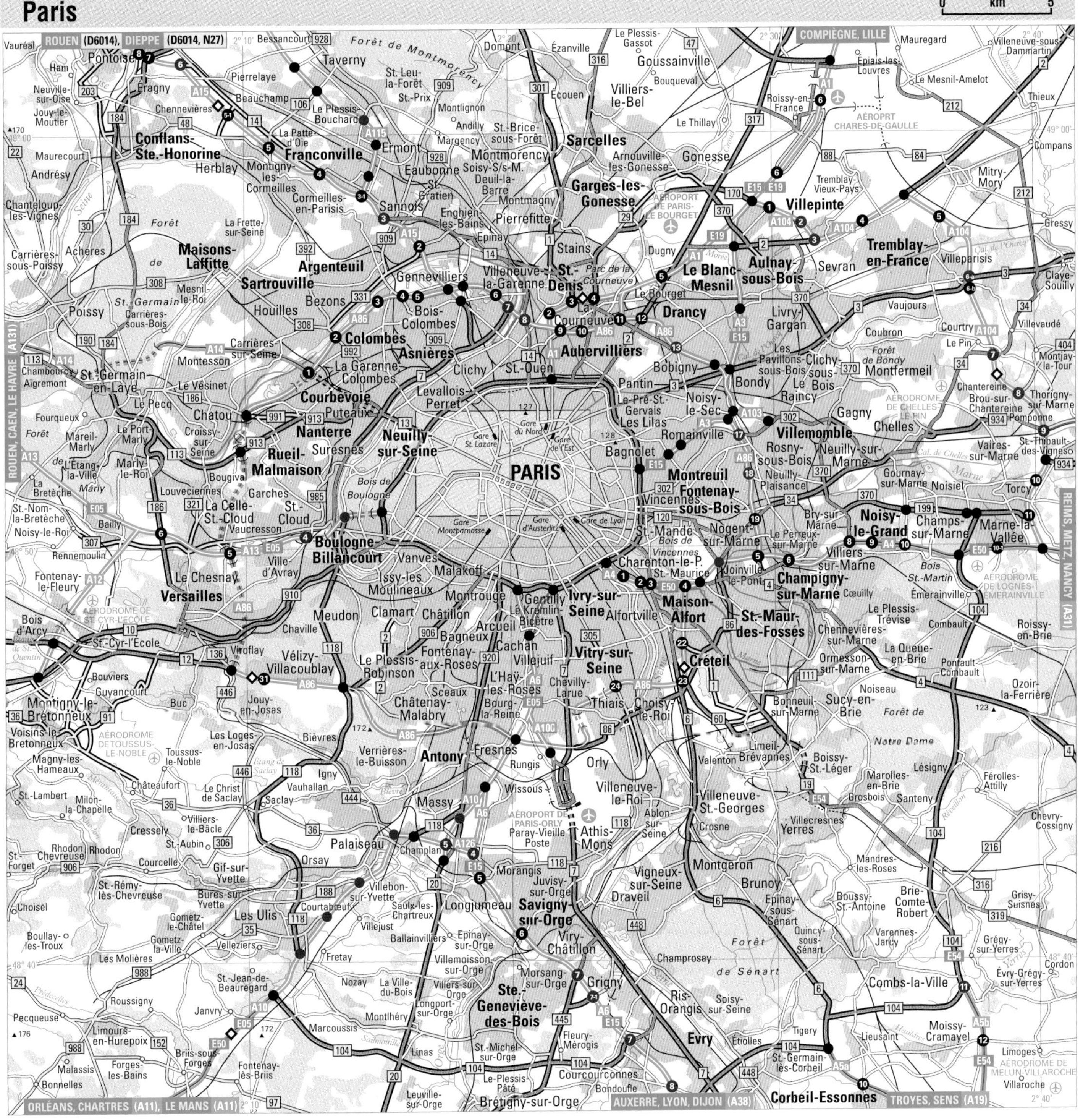
ROUEN (D6014), DIEPPE (D6014, N27)
COMPIÈGNE, LILLE
ROUEN, CAEN, LE HAVRE (A13)
REIMS, METZ, NANCY (A31)
ORLÉANS, CHARTRES (A11), LE MANS (A11)
AUXERRE, LYON, DIJON (A38)
TROYES, SENS (A19)
PARIS
Pontoise
Taverny
Sarcelles
Conflans-Ste.-Honorine
Franconville
Herblay
Ermont
Montmorency
Garges-lès-Gonesse
Villepinte
Maisons-Laffitte
Argenteuil
Sartrouville
St.-Denis
Le Blanc-Mesnil
Aulnay-sous-Bois
Tremblay-en-France
Drancy
Colombes
Asnières
Aubervilliers
Courbevoie
Nanterre
Neuilly-sur-Seine
Rueil-Malmaison
Villemomble
Montreuil
Fontenay-sous-Bois
Noisy-le-Grand
Boulogne-Billancourt
Champigny-sur-Marne
Versailles
Ivry-sur-Seine
Maison-Alfort
St.-Maur-des-Fossés
Créteil
Vitry-sur-Seine
Antony
Savigny-sur-Orge
Ste.-Geneviève-des-Bois
Evry
Corbeil-Essonnes
Forêt de Montmorency
Forêt de Sénart
AÉROPORT CHARLES-DE-GAULLE
AÉROPORT DE PARIS-LE BOURGET
AÉROPORT DE PARIS-ORLY
Bois de Boulogne
Bois de Vincennes

## Paris

0 km 1

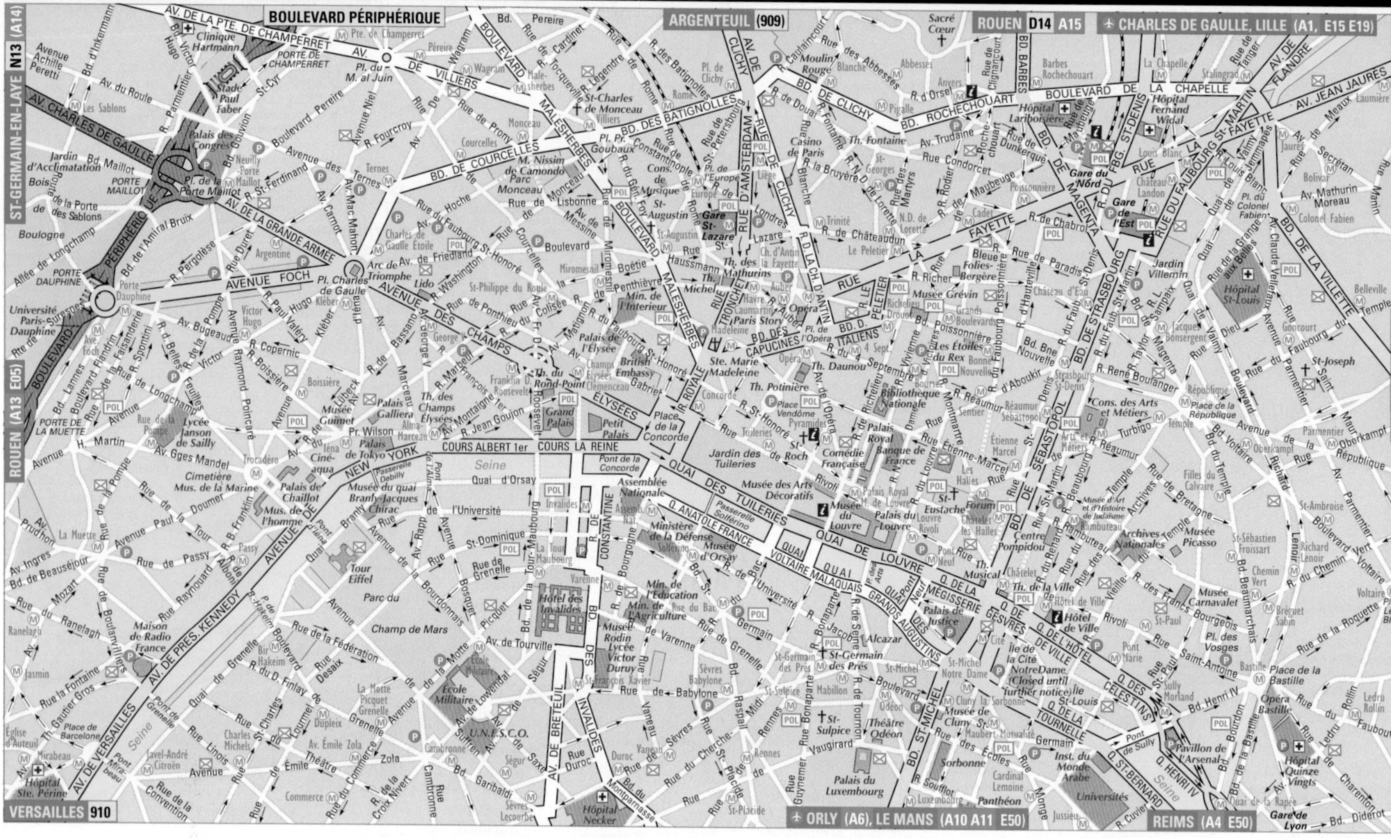

BOULEVARD PÉRIPHÉRIQUE · ARGENTEUIL (909) · ROUEN D14 A15 · CHARLES DE GAULLE, LILLE (A1, E15 E19) · MEAUX (N3) · NOISY-LE-SEC (A3) · REIMS (A4 E50) · ORLY (A6), LE MANS (A10 A11 E50) · VERSAILLES 910 · ROUEN (A13 E05) · ST-GERMAIN-EN-LAYE N13 (A14)

## Sevilla Seville

0 km 0.5

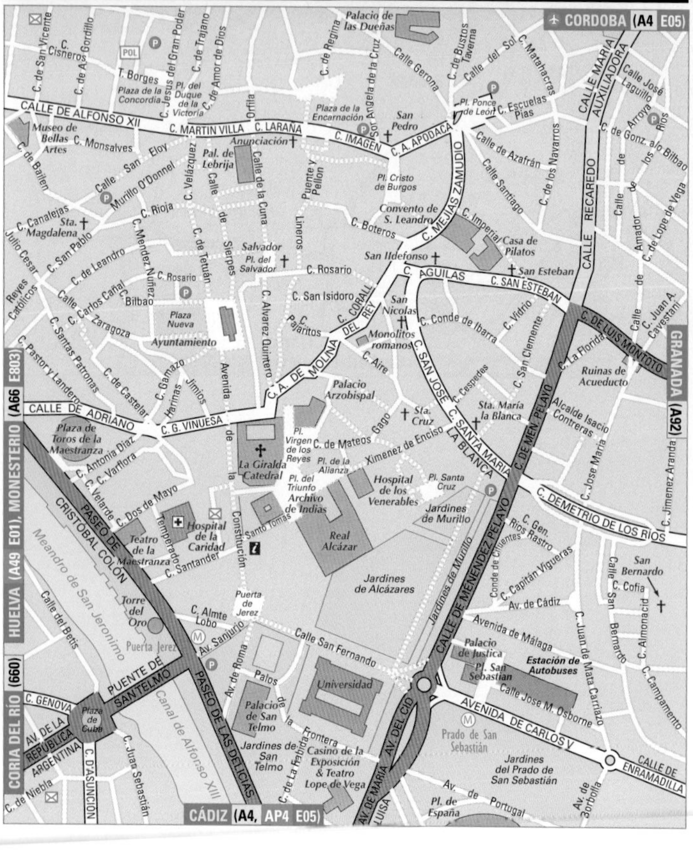

CORDOBA (A4 E05) · GRANADA (A92) · CÁDIZ (A4, AP4 E05) · CORIA DEL RIO (660) · HUELVA (A49 E01), MONESTERIO (A66 E803)

## Strasbourg

0 km 0.5

METZ A4 E25 · BISCHHEIM A350 · KEHL (28), OFFENBURG (A5) · KEHL (28) · ERSTEIN, SÉLESTAT (A35 D1083) · SAVERNE, NANCY (A351 D1004, N4) · SÉLESTAT, MULHOUSE A35

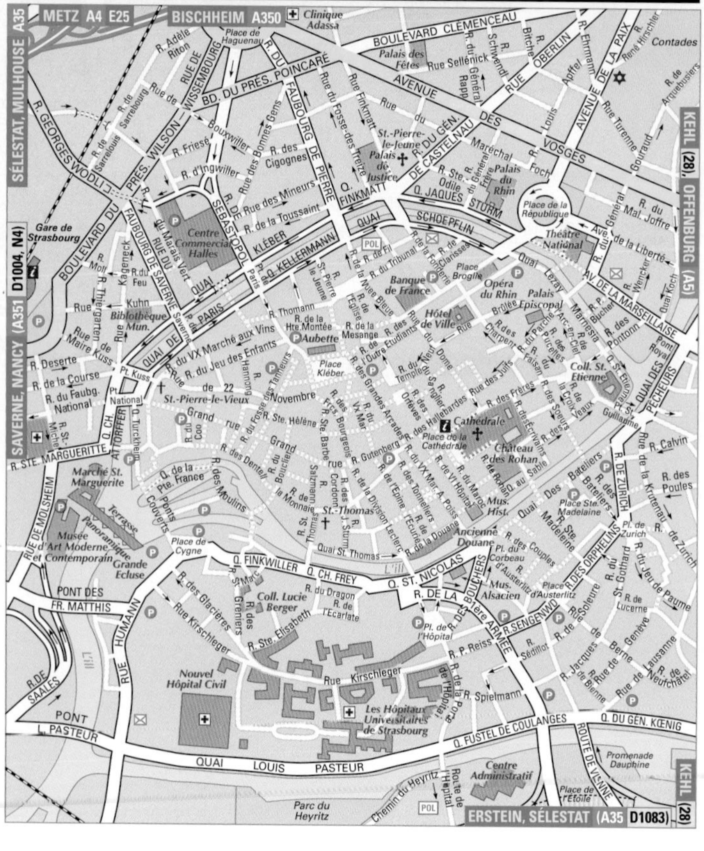

| (A) Austria | Autriche | Österreich | Austria |
|---|---|---|---|
| (AND) Andorra | Andorre | Andorra | Andorra |
| (B) Belgium | Belgique | Belgien | Bélgica |
| (CH) Switzerland | Suisse | Schweiz | Suiza |
| (D) Germany | Allemagne | Deutschland | Alemania |
| (E) Spain | Espagne | Spanien | España |
| (F) France | France | Frankreich | Francia |
| (FL) Liechtenstein | Liechtenstein | Liechtenstein | Liechtenstein |

| (GBZ) Gibraltar | Gibraltar | Gibraltar | Gibraltar |
|---|---|---|---|
| (I) Italy | Italie | Italien | Italia |
| (L) Luxembourg | Luxembourg | Luxemburg | Luxemburgo |
| (MC) Monaco | Monaco | Monaco | Mónaco |
| (NL) Netherlands | Pays-Bas | Niederlande | Países Bajos |
| (P) Portugal | Portugal | Portugal | Portugal |
| (UK) United Kingdom | Royaume Uni | Grossbritannien und Nordirland | Reino Unido |



## A

Aach D 21 B4
Aalst B 7 B4
Aalter B 7 A3
Aarau CH 20 B3
Aarberg CH 20 B2
Aarburg CH 20 B2
Aardenburg NL 7 A3
Aarschot B 7 B4
Abádanes E 46 B1
Abades E 45 B3
Abadin E 35 A3
A Baña E 34 B2
Abanilla E 59 A3
Abarán E 59 A3
Abbeville F 10 A1
Abejar E 37 C4
Abela P 54 B1
Abenójar E 51 B3
Abertura E 50 A2
Abiego E 39 B3
Abiul P 48 B2
Abla E 58 B2
Ablis F 10 C1
A Bola E 34 B3
Abondance F 26 A3
Abrantes P 48 B2
Abreiro P 42 A2
Abreschviller F 12 C3
Abrest F 25 A3
Abriès F 27 C3
Abusejo E 43 B3
A Cañiza E 34 B2
A Capola E 34 A2
Accéglio I 32 A2
Accous F 39 A3
Acedera E 50 A2
Acehuche E 49 B4
Acered E 46 A2
Aceuchal E 49 C4
Achene B 7 B5
Achern D 13 C4
Acheux-en-Amienois F 10 A2
A Coruña E 34 A2
Acqua Doria F 62 B1
Acquigny F 9 A5
Ácqui Terme I 27 C5
Acy-en-Multien F 10 B2
Adamuz E 51 B3
Adanero E 44 B3
Adeanueva de Ebro E 38 B2
Adelboden CH 20 C2
Ademuz E 46 B2
Adinkerke B 6 A2
Adliswil CH 21 B3
Adra E 58 C1
Adradas E 46 A1
Adrall E 41 B2
Adzaneta E 47 B3
Aesch CH 20 B2
A Estrada E 34 B2
Affoltern CH 20 B3
A Fonsagrada E 35 A3
Agay F 32 B2
Agde F 30 B2
Agen F 29 B3
Ager E 39 C4
Agnières F 26 C2
Agolada E 34 B2
Agon Coutainville F 8 A2
Agost E 59 A4
Agramón E 52 C2
Agramunt E 41 C2
Agreda E 38 C2
Agrón E 57 A4
Aguadulce
*Almería* E 58 C2
*Sevilla* E 56 A3
Agualada E 34 A2
Agua Longa P 42 A1
A Guarda E 34 C2
Aguarón E 46 A2
Aguas E 39 B3
Aguas Belas P 48 B2
Aguas de Busot E 53 C3
Aguas de Moura P 48 C2
Águas Frias P 42 A2
Aguas Santas P 42 A1
Aguaviva E 47 B3
Aguaviva de la Vega E 46 A1
A Gudiña E 35 B3
Agudo E 50 B3
Águeda P 42 B1
Aguessac F 30 A2
Aguiar P 48 C3
Aguiàr da Beira P 42 B2
Aguilafuente E 45 A3
Aguilar de Campóo E 36 B2
Aguilar de la Frontera E 57 A3
Aguilas E 58 B3
Ahigal E 43 B3
Ahigal de Villarino E 43 A3
Ahillones E 50 B2
Ahun F 24 A2
Aibar E 38 B2
Aigle CH 27 A3
Aignan F 28 C3
Aignay-le-Duc F 18 B3
Aigre F 23 C4
Aigrefeuille-d'Aunis F 22 B3
Aigrefeuille-sur-Maine F 15 B4
Aiguablava E 41 C4
Aiguebelle F 26 B3
Aigueperse F 24 A3
Aigues-Mortes F 31 B3
Aigues-Vives F 30 B1
Aiguilles F 27 C3
Aiguillon F 29 B3
Aigurande F 17 C3
Ailefroide F 26 C3
Aillant-sur-Tholon F 18 B2
Ailly-sur-Noye F 10 B2
Ailly-sur-Somme F 10 B2
Aimargues F 31 B3
Aime F 26 B3
Ainhoa F 38 A2
Ainsa E 39 B4
Airaines F 10 B1
Aire-sur-l'Adour F 28 C2
Aire-sur-la-Lys F 6 B2
Airole I 33 B3
Airolo CH 21 C3
Airvault F 16 C1
Aisey-sur-Seine F 18 B3
Aïssey F 19 B5
Aisy-sur-Armançon F 18 B3
Aitona E 47 A4
Aitrach D 21 B5
Aix-en-Othe F 18 A2
Aix-en-Provence F 31 B4
Aixe-sur-Vienne F 23 C5
Aix-les-Bains F 26 B2
Aizenay F 22 B2
Ajac F 40 A3
Ajaccio F 62 B1
Ajain F 24 A1
Ajo E 37 A3
Ajofrín E 51 A4
Ajuda P 49 C3
Ala di Stura I 27 B4
Alaejos E 44 A2
Alagna Valsésia I 27 B4
Alagón E 38 C2
Alaior E 61 B4
Alájar E 55 B3
Alameda E 57 A3
Alameda de la Sagra E 45 B4
Alamedilla E 57 A4
Alamillo E 50 B3
Alaminos E 45 B5
Alandroal P 49 C3
Alange E 50 B1
Alanís E 50 B2
Alaquáso E 53 B3
Alaraz E 44 B2
Alarcón E 52 B1
Alar del Rey E 36 B2
Alaró E 61 B2
Alássio I 33 A4
Alatoz E 52 B2
Alba
E 46 B2
I 27 C5
Albacete E 52 C2
Alba de Tormes E 44 B2
Alba de Yeltes E 43 B3
Albaida E 53 C3
Albaladejo E 52 C1
Albala del Caudillo E 50 A1
Albalat E 53 B3
Albalate de Cinca E 39 C4
Albalate del
Arzobispo E 47 A3
Albalate de las
Nogueras E 46 B1
Albalete de Zorita E 45 B5
Alban F 30 B1
Albánchez E 58 B2
Albanchez de Ubeda E 57 A4
Albanyà E 41 B3
Albares E 45 B4
Albarracín E 46 B2
Albatana E 52 C2
Albatarrec E 47 A4
Albatera E 59 A4
Albbruck D 20 B3
Albedin E 57 A3
Albelda de Iregua E 37 B4
Albenga I 33 A4
Albens F 26 B2
Albergaria-a-Nova P 42 B1
Albergaria-a-Velha P 42 B1
Albergaria dos Doze P 48 B2
Alberge P 48 C2
Alberic E 53 B3
Albernoa P 54 B2
Albert F 10 A2
Albertville F 26 B3
Alberuela de Tubo E 39 C3
Albi F 30 B1
Albires E 36 B1
Albisola Marina I 33 A4
Albocácer E 47 B4
Albolote E 57 A4
Albondón E 58 C1
Alborea E 52 B2
Albox E 58 B2
Albstadt D 21 A4
Albufeira P 54 B1
Albuñol E 58 C1
Albuñuelas E 57 B4
Alburquerque E 49 B3
Alcácer do Sal P 48 C2
Alcáçovas P 48 C2
Alcadozo E 52 C2
Alcafoces P 49 B3
Alcains P 49 B3
Alcaláde Guadaira E 56 A2
Alcaláde Gurrea E 38 B3
Alcaláde Henares E 45 B4
Alcaláde la Selva E 47 B3
Alcaládel Júcar E 52 B2
Alcaláde los Gazules E 56 B2
Alcaládel Río E 56 A2
Alcaládel Valle E 56 B2
Alcaláde Xivert E 47 B4
Alcalála Real E 57 A4
Alcampell E 39 C4
Alcanadre E 38 B1
Alcanar E 47 B4
Alcanede P 48 B2
Alcanena P 48 B2
Alcañices E 43 A3
Alcántara E 49 B4
Alcantarilha P 54 B1
Alcantarilla E 59 B3
Alcañz E 47 A3
Alcaracejos E 50 B3
Alcaraz E 52 C1
Alcaria Ruiva P 54 B2
Alcarraz E 47 A4
Alcaudete E 57 A3
Alcaudete de la Jara E 44 C3
Alcázar de San Juan E 51 A4
Alcazarén E 44 A3
Alcoba E 51 A3
Alcobaça P 48 B1
Alcobendas E 45 B4
Alcocer E 45 B5
Alcochete P 48 C2
Alcoentre P 48 B2
Alcolea
*Almería* E 58 C2
*Córdoba* E 50 C3
Alcolea de Calatrava E 51 B3
Alcolea de Cinca E 39 C4
Alcolea del Pinar E 46 A1
Alcolea del Rio E 56 A2
Alcolea de Tajo E 44 C2
Alcollarin E 50 A2
Alconchel E 49 C3
Alconera E 49 C4
Alcontar E 58 B2
Alcora E 47 B3
Alcorcón E 45 B4
Alcorisa E 47 B3
Alcossebre E 47 B4
Alcoutim P 54 B2
Alcover E 41 C2
Alcoy E 53 C3
Alcubierre E 39 C3
Alcubilla de
Avellaneda E 37 C3
Alcubilla de Nogales E 35 B5
Alcubillas E 51 B4
Alcublas E 53 B3
Alcúdia E 61 B3
Alcudia de Guadix E 58 B1
Alcuéscar E 49 B4
Aldeacentenera E 50 A2
Aldeadávila de
la Ribera E 43 A3
Aldea del Cano E 49 B4
Aldea del Fresno E 45 B3
Aldea del Obispo E 43 B3
Aldea del Rey E 51 B4
Aldea de Trujillo E 50 A2
Aldealcorvo E 45 A4
Aldealuenga de
Santa Maria E 45 A4
Aldeamayor de
San Martin E 44 A3
Aldeanueva de
Barbarroya E 44 C2
Aldeanueva del
Camino E 43 B4
Aldeanueva del
Codonal E 44 A3
Aldeanueva de San
Bartolomé E 50 A2
Aldeapozo E 38 C1
Aldeaquemada E 51 B4
Aldea Real E 45 A3
Aldearrubia E 44 A2
Aldeaseca de la
Frontera E 44 B2
Aldeasoña E 45 A3
Aldeatejada E 44 B2
Aldeavieja E 44 B3
Aldehuela E 46 B2
Aldehuela de
Calatañazor E 37 C4
Aldeia da Serra P 49 C3
Aldeia do Bispo P 43 B3
Aldeia do Mato P 48 B2
Aldeia Gavinha P 48 B1
Aldeire E 58 B1
Aldudes F 38 A2
Aledo E 59 B3
Alegria E 37 B4
Alençon F 9 B4
Alenquer P 48 B1
Alenya F 40 B3
Aléria F 62 A2
Alès F 31 A3
Alet-les-Bains F 40 B3
Aleyrac F 31 A3
Alfacar E 57 A4
Alfaiates P 43 B3
Alfajarin E 47 A3
Alfambra
E 46 B2
P 54 B1
Alfândega da Fé P 43 A3
Alfarela de Jafes P 42 A2
Alfarelos P 42 B1
Alfarim P 48 C1
Alfarnate E 57 B3
Alfaro E 38 B2
Alfarràs E 39 C4
Alfaz del Pi E 53 C3
Alfeizarão P 48 B1
Alfena P 42 A1
Alferce P 54 B1
Alforja E 41 C1
Alfoz E 35 A3
Alfundão P 54 A1
Algaida E 61 B2
Algar E 56 B2
Algarinejo E 57 A3
Algarrobo E 57 B3
Algatocin E 56 B2
Algeciras E 56 B2
Algemesí E 53 B3
Algés P 48 C1
Algete E 45 B4
Alginet E 53 B3
Algodonales E 56 B2
Algodor
E 45 C4
P 54 B2
Algora E 45 B5
Algoso P 43 A3
Algoz P 54 B1
Alguaire E 39 C4
Alguazas E 59 A3
Alhama de Almeria E 58 C2
Alhama de Aragón E 46 A2
Alhama de Granada E 57 B4
Alhama de Murcia E 59 B3
Alhambra E 51 B4
Alhandra P 48 C1
Alhaurin de la Torre E 57 B3
Alhaurin el Grande E 57 B3
Alhendin E 57 A4
Alhóndiga E 45 B5
Alia E 50 A2
Aliaga E 47 B3
Alicante E 59 A4
Alicún de Ortega E 58 B1
Alija del Infantado E 35 B5
Alijó P 42 A2
Alinyà E 41 B2
Aliseda E 49 B4
Alixan F 25 C5
Aljaraque E 55 B3
Aljezur P 54 B1
Aljorra E 59 B3
Aljubarrota P 48 B2
Aljucen E 49 B4
Aljustrel P 54 B1
Alken B 7 B5
Allaines F 17 A3
Allaire F 15 B3
Allanche F 24 B2
Allariz E 34 B3
Allassac F 29 A4
Allauch F 31 B4
Allègre F 25 B3
Allemont F 26 B3
Allepuz E 47 B3
Alles E 36 A2
Allevard F 26 B3
Allmannsdorf D 21 B4
Allo E 38 B1
Allogny F 17 B4
Allones
*Eure et Loire* F 10 C1
*Maine-et-Loire* F 16 B2
Allonnes F 16 B2
Allons F 28 B2
Allos F 32 A2
Almaceda P 49 B3
Almacelles E 39 C4
Almachar E 57 B3
Almada P 48 C1
Almadén E 50 B3
Almadén de la Plata E 55 B3
Almadenejos E 50 B3
Almadrones E 45 B5
Almagro E 51 B4
Almajano E 38 C1
Almansa E 53 C2
Almansil P 54 B1
Almanza E 36 B1
Almaraz E 44 C2
Almargen E 56 B2
Almarza E 37 C4
Almassora E 53 B3
Almazán E 46 A1
Almazul E 46 A1
Almedina E 52 C1
Almedinilla E 57 A3
Almeida
E 43 A3
P 43 B3
Almeirim P 48 B2
Almenar E 39 C4
Almenara E 53 B3
Almenar de Soria E 46 A1
Almendra P 43 B2
Almendral E 49 C4
Almendral de
la Cañada E 44 B3
Almendralejo E 49 C4
Almería E 58 C2
Almerimar E 58 C2
Almese I 27 B4
Almexial P 54 B2
Almodôvar P 54 B1
Almodóvar
del Campo E 51 B3
Almodóvar del Pinar E 52 B2
Almodóvar del Río E 56 A2
Almofala P 42 B2
Almogia E 57 B3
Almoharin E 50 A1
Almonacid de
la Sierra E 46 A2
Almonacid de Toledo E 51 A4
Almonaster la Real E 55 B3
Almonte E 55 B3
Almoradí E 59 A4
Almoraima E 56 B2
Almorox E 44 B3
Almoster P 48 B2
Almudena E 58 A3
Almudévar E 39 B3
Almuñécar E 57 B4
Almuradiel E 51 B4
Almussafes E 53 B3
Álora E 57 B3
Alos d'Ensil E 40 B2
Alosno E 55 B2
Alozaina E 56 B3
Alpedrete de la Sierra E 45 B4
Alpedrinha P 42 B2
Alpera E 53 C2
Alpiarça P 48 B2
Alpignano I 27 B4
Alpirsbach D 13 C4
Alpuente E 53 B2
Alqueva P 54 A2
Alquézar E 39 B4
Alsasua E 38 B1
Altarejos E 52 B1
Altdorf CH 21 C3
Alte P 54 B1
Altea E 53 C3
Altenheim D 13 C3
Altensteig D 13 C4
Alter do Chão P 49 B3
Altkirch F 20 B2
Alto Campoó E 36 A2
Altshausen D 21 B4
Altstätten CH 21 B4
Altura E 53 B3
Altusried D 21 B5
Alustante E 46 B2
Alvaiázere P 48 B2
Alvalade P 54 B1
Alvarenga P 42 B1
Alvares P 48 A2
Alverca P 48 C1
Alvignac F 29 B4
Alvimare F 9 A4
Alviobeira P 48 B2
Alvito P 54 A2
Alvor P 54 B1
Alvorge P 48 B2
Alzénau D 13 A5
Alzey D 13 B4
Alzira E 53 B3
Alzonne F 40 A3
Amadora P 48 C1
Amance F 19 B5
Amancey F 19 B5
Amarante P 42 A1
Amareleja P 55 A2
Amares P 42 A1
Amay B 7 B5
Ambazac F 23 C5
Ambérieu-en-Bugey F 26 B2
Ambérieux-en-
Dombes F 25 A4
Ambert F 25 B3
Ambès F 28 A2
Ambleteuse F 6 B1
Amboise F 16 B2
Ambrières-les-Vallées F 8 B3
Amden CH 21 B4
Amélie-les-
Bains-Palalda F 40 B3
Amendoa P 48 B2
Amendoeira P 54 B2
Amer E 41 B3
A Merca E 34 B3
Amièira P 49 C3
Amieira P 48 B3
Amieiro P 42 B1
Amiens F 10 B2
Amorebieta E 37 A4
Amorosa P 42 A1
Amou F 28 C2
Amplepuis F 25 B4
Amposta E 47 B4
Ampudia E 36 C2
Ampuero E 37 A3
Amriswil CH 21 B4
Amtzell D 21 B4
Amurrio E 37 A4
Amusco E 36 B2
Anadia P 42 B1
Anadon E 46 B2
Anaya de Alba E 44 B2
Ança P 42 B1
Ancede P 42 A1
Ancenis F 15 B4
Ancerville F 11 C5
Anchuras E 50 A3
Ancora P 42 A1
Ancy-le-Franc F 18 B3
Andance F 25 B4
Andeer CH 21 C4
Andelfingen CH 21 B3
Andelot-Blanchville F 19 A4
Andelot-en-Montagne F 19 C4
Andenne B 7 B5
Anderlues B 7 B4
Andermatt CH 21 C3
Andernos-les-Bains F 28 B1
Andoain E 38 A1
Andolsheim F 20 A2
Andorra E 47 B3
Andorra La Vella AND 40 B2
Andosilla E 38 B2
Andratx E 60 B2
Andrest F 39 A4
Andrezieux-Bouthéon F 25 B4
Andújar E 51 B3
Anduze F 31 A2
Añes E 37 A3
Anet F 10 C1
Angaïs F 39 A3
Angeja P 42 B1
Angers F 16 B1
Angerville F 10 C2
Anglès E 41 C3
Anglés F 30 B1
Angles F 22 B2
Anglesola E 41 C2
Angles sur l'Anglin F 23 B4
Anglet F 28 C1
Anglure F 11 C3
Angoulême F 23 C4
Angoulins F 22 B2
Angueira P 43 A3
Angües E 39 B3
Anguiano E 37 B4
Anhée B 7 B4
Aniane F 30 B2
Aniche F 6 B3
Anizy-le-Château F 11 B3
Anlezy F 18 C2
Annecy F 26 B3
Annemasse F 26 A3
Annevoie-Rouillon B 7 B4
Annonay F 25 B4
Annot F 32 B2
Annweiler D 13 B3
Añora E 50 B3
Anould F 20 A1
Anquela del Ducado E 46 B1
Anse F 25 B4
Anseroeul B 7 B3
Ansião P 48 B2
Ansó E 38 B3
Ansoain E 38 B2
Antas E 58 B3
Antequera E 57 A3
Antibes F 32 B3
Antigüedad E 36 C2
Antoing B 7 B3
Antrain F 8 B2
Antronapiana I 27 A5
Antuzede P 42 B1
Antwerp = Antwerpen B 7 A4
Antwerpen = Antwerp B 7 A4
Anvin F 6 B2
Anzat-le-Luguet F 24 B3
Anzón E 38 C2
Aoiz E 38 B2
Aosta I 27 B4

Apalhão P 49 B3
A Peroxa E 34 B3
A Pontenova E 35 A3
Appenzell CH 21 B4
Appoigny F 18 B2
Apremont-la-Forêt F 12 C1
Apt F 31 B4
Apúlia P 42 A1
Arabayona E 44 A2
Aracena E 55 B3
Aragnouet F 39 B4
Arahal E 56 A2
Aramits F 38 A3
Aramon F 31 B3
Aranda de Duero E 37 C3
Aranda de Moncayo E 46 A2
Aranjuez E 45 B4
Arantzazu E 37 B4
Aranzueque E 45 B4
Aras de Alpuente E 53 B2
Arauzo de Miel E 37 C3
Arazede P 42 B1
Arbas F 39 B4
Arbeca E 41 C1
Arbois F 19 C4
Arbon CH 21 B4
Arbório I 27 B5
Arbùcies E 41 C3
Arbuniel E 57 A4
Arcachon F 28 B1
Arc-en-Barrois F 19 B3
Arces-Dilo F 18 A2
Arc-et-Senans F 19 B4
Arcey F 20 B1
Archena E 59 A3
Archez E 57 B4
Archiac F 23 C3
Archidona E 57 A3
Archivel E 58 A3
Arcis-sur-Aube F 11 C4
Arc-lès-Gray F 19 B4
Arcones E 45 A4
Arcos E 37 B3
Arcos de Jalón E 46 A1
Arcos de la Frontera E 56 B2
Arcos de la Sierra E 46 B1
Arcos de las Salinas E 53 B2
Arcos de Valdevez P 42 A1
Arcozelo P 42 B2
Arc-sur-Tille F 19 B4
Arcusa E 39 B4
Arcy-sur-Cure F 18 B2
Ardales E 56 B3
Ardentes F 17 C3
Ardes F 24 B3
Ardez CH 21 C5
Ardisa E 38 B3
Ardón E 36 B1
Ardooie B 6 B3
Ardres F 6 B1
Areia Branca P 48 B1
Arenales de San Gregorio E 51 A4
Arenas E 57 B3
Arenas de Iguña E 36 A2
Arenas del Rey E 57 B4
Arenas de San Juan E 51 A4
Arenas de San Pedro E 44 B2
Arendonk B 7 A5
Arengosse F 28 B2
Arenys de Mar E 41 C3
Arenys de Munt E 41 C3
Arenzano I 33 A4
Areo E 40 B2
Ares E 34 A2
Arès F 28 B1
Ares del Maestrat E 47 B3
Arette F 38 A3
Aretxabaleta E 37 A4
Arevalillo E 44 B2
Arévalo E 44 A3
Arez P 49 B3
Arfeuilles F 25 A3
Argallón E 50 B2
Argamasilla de Alba E 51 A4
Argamasilla de Calatrava E 51 B3
Arganda E 45 B4
Arganil P 42 B1
Argelès-Gazost F 39 A3
Argelès-sur-Mer F 40 B4
Argentan F 9 B3
Argentat F 24 B1
Argentera I 32 A2
Argenteuil F 10 C2
Argenthal D 13 B3
Argentona E 41 C3
Argenton-Château F 16 C1
Argenton-sur-Creuse F 17 C3
Argentré F 16 A1
Argentré-du-Plessis F 15 A4
Argent-sur-Sauldre F 17 B4
Argote E 37 B4
Arguedas E 38 B2
Argueil F 10 B1
Aribe E 38 B2
Ariño E 47 A3
Arinthod F 26 A2
Arisgotas E 51 A4
Ariza E 46 A1
Arjona E 51 C3
Arjonilla E 51 C3
Arlanc F 25 B3
Arlanzón E 37 B3
Arlebosc F 25 B4
Arles F 31 B3
Arles-sur-Tech F 40 B3
Arlon B 12 B1
Armação de Pera P 54 B1
Armamar P 42 A2
Armeno I 27 B5
Armenteros E 44 B2
Armentières F 6 B2
Armilla E 57 A4
Armiñón E 37 B4
Armuña de Tajuña F 45 B4
Arnac-Pompadour F 23 C5
Arnage F 16 B2
Arnas F 25 A4
Arnay-le-Duc F 18 B3
Arnedillo E 38 B1
Arnedo E 38 B1
Arneguy F 38 A2
Arnés E 47 B4
Aroche E 55 B3
Arolla CH 27 A4
Arona I 27 B5
Arosa
CH 21 C4
P 42 A1
Arouca P 42 B1
Arpajon F 10 C2
Arpajon-sur-Cère F 24 C2
Arques F 6 B2
Arques-la-Bataille F 9 A5
Arquillos E 51 B4
Arraia-Maeztu E 37 B4
Arraiolos P 48 C2
Arrancourt F 12 C2
Arras F 6 B2
Arrasate E 37 A4
Arreau F 39 B4
Arredondo E 37 A3
Arrens-Marsous F 39 B3
Arriate E 56 B2
Arrifana P 54 B1
Arrigorriaga E 37 A4
Arriondas E 36 A1
Arroba de los Montes E 51 A3
Arromanches-les-Bains F 8 A3
Arronches P 49 B3
Arroniz E 38 B1
Arrou F 17 A3
Arroya E 36 B2
Arroya de Cuéllar E 44 A3
Arroyal E 36 B2
Arroyo de la Luz E 49 B4
Arroyo del Ojanco E 58 A2
Arroyo de San Servan E 49 C4
Arroyomolinos de León E 55 A3
Arroyomolinos de Montánchez E 50 A1
Arruda dos Vinhos P 48 C1
Arsac F 28 B2
Ars-en-Ré F 22 B2
Ars-sur-Moselle F 12 B2
Artà E 61 B3
Artajona E 38 B2
Arteixo E 34 A2
Artemare F 26 B2
Artenay F 17 A3
Artés E 41 C2
Artesa de Segre E 41 C2
Arth CH 21 B3
Arthez-de-Béarn F 39 A3
Arthon-en-Retz F 15 B4
Artieda E 38 B3
Artix F 39 A3
Artziniega E 37 A3
A Rúa E 35 B3
Arudy F 39 A3
Arveyres F 28 B2
Arvieux F 26 C3
Arzacq-Arraziguet F 28 C2
Arzano F 14 B2
Arzila P 42 B1
Arzúa E 34 B2
Asasp F 39 A3
Ascain F 38 A2
Aschaffenburg D 13 B5
Ascó E 47 A4
Asco F 62 A2
Ascoux F 17 A4
Asfeld F 11 B4
As Neves E 34 B2
As Nogais E 35 B3
Aspariegos E 43 A4
Aspe E 59 A4
Aspet F 39 A4
As Pontes de García Rodríguez E 34 A3
Aspres-sur-Buëch F 32 A1
Assafora P 48 C1
Asse B 7 B4
Asselborn L 12 A1
Assenede B 7 A3
Assesse B 7 B5
Asson F 30 A3
Assumar P 49 B3
Astaffort F 29 B3
Asti I 27 C5
Astorga E 35 B4
Astudillo E 36 B2
Atalaia P 48 B3
Atalho P 48 C2
Atanzón E 45 B4
Ataquines E 44 A3
Atarfe E 57 A4
Ateca E 46 A2
A Teixeira E 35 B3
Ath B 7 B3
Athies F 10 B2
Athies-sous-Laon F 11 B3
Atienza E 45 A5
Attichy F 10 B3
Attigny F 11 B4
Au A 21 B4
Aubagne F 32 B1
Aubange B 12 B1
Aubenas F 25 C4
Aubenton F 11 B4
Auberive F 19 B4
Aubeterre-sur-Dronne F 28 A3
Aubiet F 29 C3
Aubigné F 23 B3
Aubigny F 22 B2
Aubigny-au-Bac F 6 B3
Aubigny-en-Artois F 6 B2
Aubigny-sur-Nère F 17 B4
Aubin F 30 A1
Aubonne CH 19 C5
Aubrac F 24 C2
Aubusson F 24 B2
Auch F 29 C3
Auchy-au-Bois F 6 B2
Audenge F 28 B1
Auderville F 8 A2
Audierne F 14 A1
Audincourt F 20 B1
Audruicq F 6 B2
Audun-le-Roman F 12 B1
Audun-le-Tiche F 12 B1
Augignac F 23 C4
Aulendorf D 21 B4
Aullène F 62 B2
Aulnay F 23 B3
Aulnoye-Aymeries F 7 B3
Ault F 10 A1
Aulus-les-Bains F 40 B2
Aumale F 10 B1
Aumetz F 12 B1
Aumont-Aubrac F 24 C3
Aunay-en-Bazois F 18 B2
Aunay-sur-Odon F 8 A3
Auneau F 10 C1
Auneuil F 10 B1
Aups F 32 B2
Auray F 14 B3
Aurignac F 39 A4
Aurillac F 24 C2
Auriol F 32 B1
Auritz-Burguette E 38 B2
Auros F 28 B2
Auroux F 25 C3
Auterive F 40 A2
Autheuil-Authouillet F 9 A5
Authon F 32 A2
Authon-du-Perche F 16 A2
Autol E 38 B2
Autreville F 12 C1
Autrey-lès-Gray F 19 B4
Autun F 18 C3
Auty-le-Châtel F 17 B4
Auvelais B 7 B4
Auvillar F 29 B3
Auxerre F 18 B2
Auxi-le-Château F 6 B2
Auxon F 18 A2
Auxonne F 19 B4
Auxy F 18 C3
Auzances F 24 A2
Auzon F 25 B3
Availles-Limouzine F 23 B4
Avallon F 18 B2
A Veiga E 35 B3
Aveiras de Cima P 48 B2
Aveiro P 42 B1
Avelgem B 7 B3
Avenches CH 20 C2
A-Ver-o-Mar P 42 A1
Avesnes-le-Comte F 6 B2
Avesnes-sur-Helpe F 11 A3
Avià E 41 B2
Avigliana I 27 B4
Avignon F 31 B3
Ávila E 44 B3
Avilés E 35 A5
Avilley F 19 B5
Avintes P 42 A1
Avinyo E 41 C2
Avioth F 12 B1
Avis P 48 B3
Avize F 11 C4
Avon F 10 C2
Avord F 17 B4
Avranches F 8 B2
Avril F 12 B1
Avrillé F 16 B1
Awans B 7 B5
Axat F 40 B3
Axel NL 7 A3
Ax-les-Thermes F 40 B2
Ay F 11 B4
Aya E 38 A1
Ayamonte E 55 B2
Ayelo de Malferit E 53 C3
Ayer CH 27 A4
Ayerbe E 38 B3
Ayette F 6 B2
Ayllón E 45 A4
Ayna E 52 C1
Ayódar E 53 B3
Ayora E 53 B2
Ayron F 23 B4
Azaila E 47 A3
Azambuja P 48 B2
Azambujeira P 48 B2
Azannes-et-Soumazannes F 12 B1
Azanúy-Alins E 39 C4
Azaruja P 49 C3
Azay-le-Ferron F 23 B5
Azay-le-Rideau F 16 B2
Azcoitia E 37 A4
Azé F 25 A4
Azeiteiros P 49 B3
Azenhas do Mar P 48 C1
Azinhaga P 48 B2
Azinhal P 54 B2
Azinheira dos Bairros P 54 A1
Aznalcázar E 55 B3
Aznalcóllar E 55 B3
Azóia P 48 B2
Azpeitia E 38 A1
Azuaga E 50 B2
Azuara E 47 A3
Azuqueca de Henares E 45 B4
Azur F 28 C1

## B

Baad A 21 B5
Baamonde E 34 A3
Baar CH 21 B3
Baarle-Nassau B 7 A4
Babenhausen
*Bayern* D 21 A5
*Hessen* D 13 B4
Bacares E 58 B2
Baccarat F 12 C2
Bacharach D 13 A3
Bacqueville-en-Caux F 9 A5
Badajoz E 49 C4
Badalona E 41 C3
Badalucco I 33 B3
Bad Bergzabern D 13 B3
Bad Buchau D 21 A4
Bad Dürkheim D 13 B4
Bad Dürrheim D 21 A3
Baden CH 20 B3
Bádenas E 46 A2
Baden-Baden D 13 C4
Badenweiler D 20 B2
Bad Friedrichshall D 13 B5
Bad Herrenalb D 13 C4
Bad Innerlaterns A 21 B4
Bad Kemmeriboden CH 20 C2
Bad König D 13 B5
Bad Kreuznach D 13 B3
Bad Krozingen D 20 B2
Bad Liebenzell D 13 C4
Badolatosa E 57 A3
Badonviller F 12 C2
Bad Peterstal D 13 C4
Bad Ragaz CH 21 C4
Bad Rappenau D 13 B5
Bad Säckingen D 20 B2
Bad Schönborn D 13 B4
Bad Schussenried D 21 A4
Badules E 46 A2
Bad Waldsee D 21 B4
Bad Wurzach D 21 B4
Baells E 39 C4
Baena E 57 A3
Baeza E 51 C4
Baga E 41 B2
Bagnasco I 33 A4
Bagnères-de-Bigorre F 39 A4
Bagnères-de-Luchon F 39 B4
Bagnoles-de-l'Orne F 9 B3
Bagnols-en-Forêt F 32 B2
Bagnols-sur-Cèze F 31 A3
Bâguena E 46 A2
Bahabón de Esgueva E 37 C3
Bahillo E 36 B2
Baião P 42 A1
Baiersbronn D 13 C4
Baignes-Ste Radegonde F 23 C3
Baigneux-les-Juifs F 18 B3
Bailén E 51 B4
Baileux B 11 A4
Bailleul F 6 B2
Baillonville B 7 B5
Bailó E 38 B3
Bain-de-Bretagne F 15 B4
Bains F 25 B3
Bains-les-Bains F 19 A5
Baio E 34 A2
Baiona E 34 B2
Bais F 9 B3
Baiuca P 42 B2
Bakio E 37 A4
Balaguer E 39 C4
Balazote E 52 C1
Balbigny F 25 B4
Balboa E 35 B4
Baleira E 35 A3
Baleizao P 54 A2
Balen B 7 A5
Balerma E 58 C2
Balingen D 21 A3
Balizac F 28 B2
Ballancourt-sur-Essonne F 10 C2
Ballerias E 39 C3
Balleroy F 8 A3
Ballesteros de Calatrava E 51 B4
Ballobar E 47 A4
Ballon F 16 A2
Balmaseda E 37 A3
Balme I 27 B4
Balmuccia I 27 B5
Balneario de Panticosa E 39 B3
Balsa P 42 A2
Balsareny E 41 C2
Balsthal CH 20 B2
Baltanás E 36 C2
Baltar E 34 C3
Balugães P 42 A1
Bande
B 7 B5
E 34 B3
Bandol F 32 B1
Bañeres E 53 C3
Bangor F 14 B2
Bannalec F 14 B2
Bannes F 11 C3
Bañobárez E 43 B3
Bañon E 46 B2
Banon F 32 A1
Baños E 43 B4
Baños de Gigonza E 56 B2
Baños de la Encina E 51 B4
Baños de Molgas E 34 B3
Baños de Rio Tobia E 37 B4
Baños de Valdearados E 37 C3
Bantheville F 11 B5
Bantzenheim F 20 B2
Banyalbufar E 60 B2
Banyoles E 41 B3
Banyuls-sur-Mer F 40 B4
Bapaume F 10 A2
Barahona E 45 A5
Barajes de Melo E 45 B5
Barakaldo E 37 A4
Baralla E 35 B3
Barañain E 38 B2
Baraqueville F 30 A1
Barasoain E 38 B2
Barbacena P 49 C3
Barbadás E 34 B3
Barbadillo E 43 B4
Barbadillo de Herreros E 37 B3
Barbadillo del Mercado E 37 B3
Barbadillo del Pez E 37 B3
Barbastro E 39 B4
Barbate E 56 B2
Barbatona E 46 A1
Barbâtre F 22 B1
Barbazan F 39 A4
Barbeitos E 35 A3
Barbentane F 31 B3
Barbezieux-St Hilaire F 23 C3
Barbonne-Fayel F 11 C3
Barbotan-les-Thermes F 28 C2
Bárcabo E 39 B4
Barca de Alva P 43 A3
Barcarrota E 49 C4
Barcelona E 41 C3
Barcelonette F 32 A2
Barcelos P 42 A1
Bárcena del Monasterio E 35 A4
Barcena de Pie de Concha E 36 A2
Barco P 42 B2
Barcones E 45 A5
Barcus F 38 A3
Bardonécchia I 26 B3
Barèges F 39 B4
Barentin F 9 A4
Barenton F 8 B3
Barfleur F 8 A2
Bargas E 45 C3
Barge I 27 C4
Bargemon F 32 B2
Barjac F 31 A3
Barjols F 32 B1
Barjon F 19 B3
Bar-le-Duc F 11 C5
Barles F 32 A2
Barneville-Carteret F 8 A2
Baron F 10 B2
Barqueiro P 48 B2
Barquinha P 48 B2
Barr F 13 C3
Barra P 42 B1
Barracas E 53 A3
Barraco E 44 B3
Barrado E 44 B2
Barranco do Velho P 54 B2
Barrancos P 55 A3
Barrax E 52 B1
Barre-des-Cevennes F 30 A2
Barreiro P 48 C1
Barreiros E 35 A3
Barrême F 32 B2
Barret-le-Bas F 32 A1
Barrio de Nuesra Señora E 36 B1
Barruecopardo E 43 A3
Barruelo de Santullán E 36 B2
Barruera E 39 B4
Bar-sur-Aube F 18 A3
Bar-sur-Seine F 18 A3
Barzana E 35 A5
Bas E 41 B3
Basauri E 37 A4
Basconcillos del Tozo E 37 B3
Bascones de Ojeda E 36 B2
Basécles B 7 B3
Basel CH 20 B2
Bassecourt CH 20 B2
Bassella E 41 B2
Bassou F 18 B2
Bassoues F 28 C3
Bastelica F 62 A2
Bastelicaccia F 62 B1
Bastia F 62 A2
Bastogne B 12 A1
Batalha P 48 B2
Batea E 47 A4
Bätterkinden CH 20 B2
Baud F 14 B2
Baudour B 7 B3
Baugé F 16 B1
Baugy F 17 B4
Bauma CH 21 B3
Baume-les-Dames F 19 B5
Baumholder D 13 B3
Bavay F 7 B3
Bavilliers F 20 B1
Bayel F 19 A3
Bayeux F 8 A3
Bayon F 12 C2
Bayonne F 28 C1
Bayons F 32 A2
Baza E 58 B2
Bazas F 28 B2
Baziege F 40 A2
Bazoches-les-Gallerandes F 17 A4
Bazoches-sur-Hoëne F 9 B4
Beade E 34 B2
Beas E 55 B3
Beasain E 38 A1
Beas de Segura E 58 A2
Beaubery F 25 A4
Beaucaire F 31 B3
Beaufort F 26 B3
Beaufort-en Vallée F 16 B1
Beaugency F 17 B3
Beaujeu
*Alpes-de-Haute-Provence* F 32 A2
*Rhône* F 25 A4
Beaulac F 28 B2
Beaulieu F 17 B4
Beaulieu-sous-la-Roche F 22 B2
Beaulieu-sur-Dordogne F 29 B4
Beaulieu-sur-Mer F 33 B3
Beaulon F 18 C2
Beaumesnil F 9 A4
Beaumetz-lès-Loges F 6 B2
Beaumont
B 7 B4
F 29 B3
Beaumont-de-Lomagne F 29 C3
Beaumont-du-Gâtinais F 17 A4
Beaumont-en-Argonne F 11 B5
Beaumont-Hague F 8 A2
Beaumont-la-Ronce F 16 B2
Beaumont-le-Roger F 9 A4
Beaumont-sur-Oise F 10 B2
Beaumont-sur-Sarthe F 16 A2
Beaune F 19 B3
Beaune-la-Rolande F 17 A4
Beaupréau F 15 B5
Beauraing B 11 A4
Beaurepaire F 25 B5
Beaurepaire-en-Bresse F 19 C4
Beaurières F 32 A1
Beauvais F 10 B2
Beauval F 10 A2
Beauville F 29 B3
Beauvoir-sur-Mer F 22 B1
Beauvoir-sur-Niort F 22 B3
Becedas E 44 B2
Beceite E 47 B4
Becerreá E 35 B3
Becerril de Campos E 36 B2
Bécherel F 15 A4
Becilla de Valderaduey E 36 B1
Beco P 48 B2
Bécon-les-Granits F 16 B1
Bedames E 37 A3
Bédar E 58 B3
Bédarieux F 30 B2
Bédarrides F 31 A3
Bédée F 15 A4
Bedmar E 57 A4
Bédoin F 31 A4
Bedretto CH 21 C3
Beerfelden D 13 B4
Beernem B 6 A3
Beflelay CH 20 B2
Bégard F 14 A2
Begijar E 51 C4
Begijnendijk B 7 A4
Begues E 41 C2
Begur E 41 C4
Beine-Nauroy F 11 B4
Beinwil CH 20 B3
Beja P 54 A2
Béjar E 43 B4
Belâbre F 23 B5
Belalcázar E 50 B2
Belcaire F 40 B2
Belchite E 47 A3
Beleño E 36 A1
Bélesta F 40 B2
Belfort F 20 B1
Belgentier F 32 B1
Belgodère F 62 A2
Belhade F 28 B2
Belin-Bèliet F 28 B2
Belinchón E 45 B4
Bellac F 23 B5
Belleau F 10 B3
Bellegarde
*Gard* F 31 B3
*Loiret* F 17 B4
Bellegarde-en-Diois F 32 A1
Bellegarde-en-Marche F 24 B2
Bellegarde-sur-Valserine F 26 A2
Belle-Isle-en-Terre F 14 A2
Bellême F 9 B4
Bellenaves F 24 A3
Bellentre F 26 B3
Bellevaux F 26 A3
Bellevesvre F 19 C4
Belleville F 25 A4
Belleville-sur-Vie F 22 B2
Bellevue-la-Montagne F 25 B3
Belley F 26 B2
Bellheim D 13 B4
Bell-lloc d'Urgell E 47 A4
Bello E 46 B2
Bellpuig d'Urgell E 41 C2
Bellreguart E 53 C3
Belltall E 41 C2
Bellver de Cerdanya E 40 B2
Bellvis E 41 C1
Bélmez E 50 B2
Belmez de la Moraleda E 57 A4
Belmont-de-la-Loire F 25 A4
Belmonte
*Asturias* E 35 A4
*Cuenca* E 52 B1
P 42 B2
Belmonte de San José E 47 B3
Belmonte de Tajo E 45 B4
Belmont-sur-Rance F 30 B1
Beloeil B 7 B3
Belorado E 37 B3
Belp CH 20 C2
Belpech F 40 A2
Belver de Cinca E 47 A4
Belver de los Montes E 36 C1
Belvès F 29 B3
Belvezet F 30 A2
Belvis de la Jara E 44 C3
Belvis de Monroy E 44 C2
Belz F 14 B2
Bembibre E 35 B4
Bemposta
*Bragança* P 43 A3
*Santarém* P 48 B2
Benabarre E 39 B4
Benacazón E 55 B3
Benaguacil E 53 B3
Benahadux E 58 C2
Benalmádena E 57 B3
Benalúa de Guadix E 58 B1
Benalúa de las Villas E 57 A4
Benalup E 56 B2
Benamargosa E 57 B3
Benamaurel E 58 B2
Benameji E 57 A3
Benamocarra E 57 B3
Benaocaz E 56 B2
Benaoján E 56 B2
Benarrabá E 56 B2
Benasque E 39 B4
Benavente
E 36 B1
P 48 C2
Benavides de Órbigo E 35 B5
Benavila P 48 B3
Benejama E 53 C3
Benejúzar E 59 A4
Bénestroff F 12 C2
Benet F 22 B3
Bene Vagienna I 33 A3
Bénévent-l'Abbaye F 24 A1
Benfeld F 13 C3
Benfica P 48 B2
Benicarló E 47 B4
Benicássim E 47 B4
Benidorm E 53 C3
Benifaió E 53 B3
Beniganim E 53 C3
Benisa E 53 C4
Bénodet F 14 B1
Benquerencia de la Serena E 50 B2
Bensafrim P 54 B1
Bensheim D 13 B4
Beranga E 37 A3
Bérat F 40 A2
Berbegal E 39 C3
Berberana E 37 B3
Bercedo E 37 A3
Bercenay-le-Hayer F 11 C3
Berchem B 7 B3
Bérchules E 57 B4
Bercianos de Aliste E 43 A3
Berck F 6 B1
Berclaire d'Urgell E 41 C1
Berdoias E 34 A1

Berducedo E 35 A4
Berdún E 38 B3
Berga E 41 B2
Bergara E 37 A4
Bergen op Zoom NL 7 A4
Bergerac F 29 B3
Bergères-lés-Vertus F 11 C4
Bergeyk NL 7 A5
Berghausen D 13 C4
Bergues F 6 B2
Bergün Bravuogn CH 21 C4
Beringel P 54 A2
Beringen B 7 A5
Berja E 58 C2
Berkheim D 21 A5
Berlanga E 50 B2
Berlanga de Duero E 45 A5
Bermeo E 37 A4
Bermillo de Sayago E 43 A3
Bern CH 20 C2
Bernardos E 44 A3
Bernau D 20 B3
Bernaville F 10 A2
Bernay F 9 A4
Bernkastel-Kues D 12 B3
Bernués E 39 B3
Beromünster CH 20 B3
Berre-l'Etang F 31 B4
Berrocal E 55 B3
Bertamiráns E 34 B2
Berthelming F 12 C2
Bertincourt F 10 A2
Bertogne B 12 A1
Bertrix B 11 B5
Berville-sur-Mer F 9 A4
Berzocana E 50 A2
Besalú E 41 B3
Besançon F 19 B5
Besenfeld D 13 C4
Besigheim D 13 C5
Besle F 15 B4
Bessais-le-Fromental F 17 C4
Bessan F 30 B2
Besse-en-Chandesse F 24 B2
Bessèges F 31 A3
Bessé-sur-Braye F 16 B2
Bessines-sur-Gartempe F 23 B5
Best NL 7 A5
Betanzos E 34 A2
Betelu E 38 A2
Bétera E 53 B3
Beteta E 46 B1
Béthenville F 11 B4
Béthune F 6 B2
Beton-Bazoches F 10 C3
Bettembourg L 12 B2
Betterdorf L 12 B2
Betxi E 53 B3
Betz F 10 B2
Beuil F 32 A2
Beuzeville F 9 A4
Beveren B 7 A4
Bex CH 27 A4
Beychevelle F 28 A2
Beynat F 29 A4
Bezas E 46 B2
Bezau A 21 B4
Bèze F 19 B4
Bezenet F 24 A2
Béziers F 30 B2
Biandrate I 27 B5
Biar E 53 C3
Biarritz F 38 A2
Bias F 28 B1
Biberach
*Baden-Württemberg* D 13 C4
*Baden-Württemberg* D 21 A4
Biblis D 13 B4
Bicorp E 53 B3
Bicos P 54 B1
Bidache F 28 C1
Bidart F 38 A2
Biel E 38 B3
Biel / Bienne CH 20 B2
Biella I 27 B5
Bielsa E 39 B4
Bienservida E 52 C1
Bienvenida E 50 B1
Bierné F 16 B1
Bierwart B 7 B5
Biescas E 39 B3
Bietigheim-Bissingen D 13 C5
Bièvre B 11 B5
Biganos F 28 B2
Bigas P 42 B2
Bigastro E 59 A4
Bignasco CH 27 A5
Biguglia F 62 A2
Bijuesca E 46 A2
Bilbao E 37 A4
Billom F 24 B3
Binaced E 39 C4
Binche B 7 B4
Binefar E 39 C4
Bingen D 13 B3
Binic F 14 A3
Bionaz I 27 B4
Birkenfeld
*Baden-Württemberg* D 13 C4
*Rheinland-Pfalz* D 12 B3
Bisbal de Falset E 47 A4
Biscarosse F 28 B1
Biscarosse Plage F 28 B1
Biscarrués E 38 B3
Bischheim F 13 C3
Bischofszell CH 21 B4
Bischwiller F 13 C3
Bisingen D 13 C4
Bissen L 12 B2
Bistango I 27 C5
Bitburg D 12 B2
Bitche F 13 B3
Bitschwiller F 20 B2
Biville-sur-Mer F 9 A5
Biwer L 12 B2
Blacy F 11 C4
Blagnac F 29 C4
Blaichach D 21 B5
Blain F 15 B4
Blainville-sur-l'Eau F 12 C2
Blajan F 39 A4
Blâmont F 12 C2
Blanca E 59 A3
Blancos E 34 C3
Blanes E 41 C3
Blangy-sur-Bresle F 10 B1
Blankenberge B 6 A3
Blanquefort F 28 B2
Blanzac F 23 C4
Blanzy F 18 C3
Blascomillán E 44 B2
Blascosancho E 44 B3
Blatten CH 27 A4
Blaye F 28 A2
Blaye-les-Mines F 30 A1
Blázquez E 50 B2
Blecua E 39 B3
Bléneau F 18 B1
Blérancourt F 10 B3
Bléré F 16 B2
Blesle F 24 B3
Blet F 17 C4
Bletterans F 19 C4
Blieskastel D 12 B3
Bligny-sur-Ouche F 18 B3
Blois F 17 B3
Blonville-sur-Mer F 9 A4
Bludenz A 21 B4
Blumberg D 21 B3
Boal E 35 A4
Boa Vista P 48 B2
Bobadilla
*Logroño* E 37 B4
*Málaga* E 57 A3
Bobadilla del Campo E 44 A2
Bobadilla del Monte E 45 B4
Bóbbio Pellice I 27 C4
Bobigny F 10 C2
Böblingen D 13 C5
Boboras E 34 B2
Boca de Huérgano E 36 B2
Bocairent E 53 C3
Boceguillas E 45 A4
Bocognano F 62 A2
Bodonal de la Sierra E 55 A3
Boecillo E 44 A3
Boëge F 26 A3
Boën F 25 B3
Bogajo E 43 B3
Bogarra E 52 C1
Bogarre E 57 A4
Bognanco Fonti I 27 A5
Bohain-en-Vermandois F 11 B3
Bohonal de Ibor E 44 C2
Boiro E 34 B2
Bois-d'Amont F 19 C5
Boisseron F 31 B3
Boixols E 41 B2
Bolaños de Calatrava E 51 B4
Bolbec F 9 A4
Bolea E 39 B3
Boliqueime P 54 B1
Bollène F 31 A3
Bólliga E 46 B1
Bollullos E 55 B3
Bollullos par del Condado E 55 B3
Bologne F 19 A4
Boltaña E 39 B4
Boltigen CH 20 C2
Bolzaneto I 33 A4
Bombarral P 48 B1
Bona F 18 B2
Bonaduz CH 21 C4
Bonanza E 55 C3
Boñar E 36 B1
Bonares E 55 B3
Bondorf D 13 C4
Bon-Encontre F 29 B3
Bonete E 52 C2
Bonifacio F 62 B2
Bonigen CH 20 C2
Bonnat F 24 A1
Bonndorf D 20 B3
Bonnétable F 16 A2
Bonnétage F 20 B1
Bonneuil-les-Eaux F 10 B2
Bonneuil-Matours F 23 B4
Bonneval F 17 A3
Bonneval-sur-Arc F 27 B4
Bonneville F 26 A3
Bonnières-sur-Seine F 10 B1
Bonnieux F 31 B4
Bönnigheim D 13 B5
Bonny-sur-Loire F 17 B4
Bono E 39 B4
Boom B 7 A4
Boos F 9 A5
Boqueixón E 34 B2
Boran-sur-Oise F 10 B2
Borba P 49 C3
Bordeaux F 28 B2
Bordeira P 54 B1
Bordighera I 33 B3
Bordón E 47 B3
Borghetto d'Arróscia I 33 A3
Borghetto Santo Spirito I 33 A4
Borgloon B 7 B5
Borgo F 62 A2
Borgofranco d'Ivrea I 27 B4
Borgomanero I 27 B5
Borgomasino I 27 B4
Borgo San Dalmazzo I 33 A3
Borgosésia I 27 B5
Borgo Vercelli I 27 B5
Borja E 38 C2
Bormes-les-Mimosas F 32 B2
Bórmio I 21 C5
Bormujos E 55 B3
Bornes P 43 A2
Bornos E 56 B2
Borobia E 46 A2
Borox E 45 B4
Borredá E 41 B2
Borrenes E 35 B4
Borriol E 53 A3
Bort-les-Orgues F 24 B2
Bossast E 39 B4
Bossolasco I 33 A4
Bot E 47 A4
Boticas P 42 A2
Bötzingen D 20 A2
Bouaye F 15 B4
Bouça P 43 A2
Boucau F 28 C1
Bouchain F 6 B3
Bouchoir F 10 B2
Boudreville F 19 B3
Boudry CH 20 C1
Bouesse F 17 C3
Bouguenais F 15 B4
Bouhy F 18 B2
Bouillargues F 31 B3
Bouillon B 11 B5
Bouilly F 18 A2
Bouin F 22 B2
Boulay-Moselle F 12 B2
Boulazac F 29 A3
Boule-d'Amont F 40 B3
Bouligny F 12 B1
Boulogne-sur-Gesse F 39 A4
Boulogne-sur-Mer F 6 B1
Bouloire F 16 B2
Bouquemaison F 6 B2
Bourbon-Lancy F 18 C2
Bourbon-l'Archambault F 18 C2
Bourbonne-les-Bains F 19 B4
Bourbourg F 6 B2
Bourbriac F 14 A2
Bourcefranc-le-Chapus F 22 C2
Bourdeaux F 31 A4
Bouresse F 23 B4
Bourg F 28 A2
Bourg-Achard F 9 A4
Bourganeuf F 24 B1
Bourg-Argental F 25 B4
Bourg-de-Péage F 25 B5
Bourg-de-Thizy F 25 A4
Bourg-de-Visa F 29 B3
Bourg-en-Bresse F 26 A2
Bourges F 17 B4
Bourg-et-Comin F 11 B3
Bourg-Lastic F 24 B2
Bourg-Madame F 40 B2
Bourgneuf-en-Retz F 22 A2
Bourgogne F 11 B4
Bourgoin-Jallieu F 26 B2
Bourg-St Andéol F 31 A3
Bourg-St Maurice F 27 B3
Bourgtheroulde F 9 A4
Bourgueil F 16 B2
Bourmont F 19 A4
Bourneville F 9 A4
Bournezeau F 22 B2
Bourran F 29 B3
Bourret F 29 C4
Bourron-Marlotte F 10 C2
Boussac F 24 A2
Boussens F 39 A4
Boutersem B 7 B4
Bouttencourt F 10 B1
Bouvières F 31 A4
Bouvron F 15 B4
Bouxwiller F 13 C3
Bouzas E 34 B2
Bouzonville F 12 B2
Bóveda E 35 B3
Boves F 10 B2
Bóves I 33 A3
Boxtel NL 7 A5
Bozouls F 30 A1
Bra I 27 C4
Bracieux F 17 B3
Brackenheim D 13 B5
Braga P 42 A1
Bragança P 43 A3
Braine F 11 B3
Braine-le-Comte B 7 B4
Braives B 7 B5
Brakel B 7 B3
Bram F 40 A3
Bramafan F 32 B2
Brand A 21 B4
Brando F 62 A2
Brandomil E 34 A2
Branne F 28 B2
Brantôme F 23 C4
Bras d'Asse F 32 B2
Brasparts F 14 A2
Brassac F 30 B1
Brassac-les-Mines F 24 B3
Brasschaat B 7 A4
Bray Dunes F 6 A2
Bray-sur-Seine F 10 C3
Bray-sur-Somme F 10 B2
Brazatortas E 51 B3
Brazey-en-Plaine F 19 B4
Brea de Tajo E 45 B4
Brécey F 8 B2
Brecht B 7 A4
Brécy F 17 B4
Breda
E 41 C3
NL 7 A4
Bregenz A 21 B4
Bréhal F 8 B2
Breidenbach F 13 B3
Breil-sur-Roya F 33 B3
Breisach D 20 A2
Breitenbach CH 20 B2
Bremgarten CH 20 B3
Brem-sur-Mer F 22 B2
Brenes E 56 A2
Brénod F 26 A2
Brensbach D 13 B4
Breskens NL 7 A3
Bresles F 10 B2
Bressuire F 16 C1
Brest F 14 A1
Bretenoux F 29 B4
Breteuil
*Eure* F 9 B4
*Oise* F 10 B2
Brétigny-sur-Orge F 10 C2
Bretten D 13 B4
Bretteville-sur-Laize F 9 A3
Breuil-Cervinia I 27 B4
Bréziers F 32 A2
Brezolles F 9 B5
Briançon F 26 C3
Brianconnet F 32 B2
Briare F 17 B4
Briatexte F 29 C4
Briaucourt F 19 A4
Bricquebec F 8 A2
Briec F 14 A1
Brie-Comte-Robert F 10 C2
Brienne-le-Château F 11 C4
Brienon-sur-Armançon F 18 B2
Brienz CH 20 C3
Brieva de Cameros E 37 B4
Briey F 12 B1
Brig CH 27 A5
Brignogan-Plage F 14 A1
Brignoles F 32 B2
Brihuega E 45 B5
Brillon-en-Barrois F 11 C5
Brinches P 54 A2
Brinon-sur-Beuvron F 18 B2
Brinon-sur-Sauldre F 17 B4
Brión E 34 B2
Briones E 37 B4
Brionne F 9 A4
Brioude F 25 B3
Brioux-sur-Boutonne F 23 B3
Briouze F 9 B3
Briscous F 38 A2
Brissac-Quincé F 16 B1
Brive-la-Gaillarde F 29 A4
Briviesca E 37 B3
Brocas F 28 B2
Broglie F 9 B4
Bromont-Lamothe F 24 B2
Bronchales E 46 B2
Bronco E 43 B3
Broons F 15 A3
Broquies F 30 A1
Brossac F 23 C3
Brotas P 48 C2
Broto E 39 B3
Brou F 17 A3
Brouage F 22 C2
Broût-Vernet F 24 A3
Brouvelieures F 20 A1
Brouwershaven NL 7 A3
Brozas E 49 B4
Bruay-la-Buissière F 6 B2
Bruchsal D 13 B4
Brue-Auriac F 32 B1
Bruen CH 21 C3
Bruère-Allichamps F 17 C4
Brugg CH 20 B3
Brugge B 6 A3
Bruinisse NL 7 A4
Brûlon F 16 B1
Brumath F 13 C3
Brunehamel F 11 B4
Brunete E 45 B3
Brunnen CH 21 C3
Brusasco I 27 B5
Brusque F 30 B1
Brussels = Bruxelles B 7 B4
Brusson I 27 B4
Bruxelles = Brussels B 7 B4
Bruyères F 20 A1
Bruz F 15 A4
Buarcos P 42 B1
Bubbio I 27 C5
Bubry F 14 B2
Bucelas P 48 C1
Buchboden A 21 B4
Buchenberg D 21 B5
Buchères F 18 A3
Buchs CH 21 B4
Buchy F 9 A5
Bucy-lés-Pierreport F 11 B3
Budens P 54 B1
Budia E 45 B5
Bueña E 46 B2
Buenache de Alarcón E 52 B1
Buenache de la Sierra E 46 B2
Buenaventura E 44 B3
Buenavista de Valdavia E 36 B2
Buendia E 45 B5
Bueu E 34 B2
Buezo E 37 B3
Bugarra E 53 B3
Bugeat F 24 B1
Bühl
*Baden-Württemberg* D 13 C4
*Bayern* D 21 B5
Bühlertal D 13 C4
Buis-les-Baronnies F 31 A4
Buitrago del Lozoya E 45 B4
Bujalance E 51 C3
Bujaraloz E 47 A3
Bujedo E 37 B3
Bülach CH 21 B3
Bulgnéville F 19 A4
Bullas E 58 A3
Bulle CH 20 C2
Buño E 34 A2
Buñol E 53 B3
Bunsbeek B 7 B4
Buñuel E 38 C2
Bunyola E 60 B2
Burdons-sur-Rognon F 19 A4
Burela E 35 A3
Büren an der Aare CH 20 B2
Burgau P 54 B1
Burgdorf CH 20 B2
Burgo P 42 B1
Burgohondo E 44 B3
Burgos E 37 B3
Burgui E 38 B3
Burguillos E 56 A2
Burguillos del Cerro E 49 C4
Burguillos de Toledo E 45 C4
Burie F 22 C3
Burjassot E 53 B3
Burlada E 38 B2
Burladingen D 21 A4
Burón E 36 A1
Buronzo I 27 B5
Burret F 40 B2
Burriana E 53 B3
Bürs A 21 B4
Bürstadt D 13 B4
Burujón E 45 C3
Busano I 27 B4
Busca I 33 A3
Busot E 53 C3
Busquistar E 57 B4
Bussang F 20 B1
Bussière-Badil F 23 C4
Bussière-Poitevine F 23 B4
Bussoleno I 27 B4
Bütschwil CH 21 B4
Buxières-les-Mines F 18 C1
Buxy F 18 C3
Buzançais F 17 C3
Buzancy F 11 B4
Buzy F 39 A3


## C


Cabacos P 48 B2
Cabana E 34 A2
Cabanac-et-Villagrains F 28 B2
Cabañaquinta E 36 A1
Cabanas P 54 B2
Cabañas del Castillo E 50 A2
Cabañas de Yepes E 45 C4
Cabanelles E 41 B3
Cabanes E 47 B4
Cabanillas E 38 B2
Cabasse F 32 B2
Cabdella E 40 B2
Cabeceiras de Basto P 42 A1
Cabeço de Vide P 49 B3
Cabeza del Buey E 50 B2
Cabeza la Vaca E 55 A3
Cabezamesada E 45 C4
Cabezarados E 51 B3
Cabezarrubias del Puerto E 51 B3
Cabezas del Villar E 44 B2
Cabezas Rubias E 55 B2
Cabezón E 36 C2
Cabezón de la Sal E 36 A2
Cabezón de Liébana E 36 A2
Cabezuela E 45 A4
Cabezuela del Valle E 43 B4
Cabo de Gata E 58 C2
Cabo de Palos E 59 B4
Cabolafuenta E 46 A1
Cabourg F 9 A3
Cabra
E 57 A3
P 42 B2
Cabra del Santo Cristo E 57 A4
Cabreiro P 34 C2
Cabreiros E 34 A3
Cabrejas E 46 B1
Cabrela P 48 C2
Cabrillas E 43 B3
Cacabelos E 35 B4
Cacela P 54 B2
Cacém P 48 C1
Cáceres E 49 B4
Cachafeiro E 34 B2
Cachopo P 54 B2
Cacin E 57 A4
Cadafais P 48 C1
Cadalen F 29 C5
Cadalso E 43 B3
Cadaqués E 41 B4
Cadaval P 48 B1
Cadavedo E 35 A4
Cadéac F 39 B4
Cadenet F 31 B4
Cadeuil F 22 C3
Cádiar E 58 C1
Cadillac F 28 B2
Cádiz E 56 B1
Cadouin F 29 B3
Cadours F 29 C4
Cadrete E 46 A3
Caen F 9 A3
Cafede P 49 B3
Cagnes-sur-Mer F 32 B3
Cahors F 29 B4
Caion E 34 A2
Cairo Montenotte I 33 A4
Cajarc F 29 B4
Cala E 55 B3
Calaceite E 47 B4
Calacuccia F 62 A2
Cala d'Or E 61 B3
Calaf E 41 C2
Calafell E 41 C2
Cala Galdana E 61 B3
Calahonda
*Granada* E 57 B4
*Málaga* E 57 B3
Calahorra E 38 B2
Calais F 6 B1
Cala Llonga E 60 C1
Cala Millor E 61 B3
Calamocha E 46 B2
Calamonte E 49 C4
Cala Morell E 61 A3
Calañas E 55 B3
Calanda E 47 B3
Cala Ratjada E 61 B3
Calasparra E 58 A3
Calatayud E 46 A2
Calatorao E 46 A2
Calcena E 46 A2
Caldas da Rainha P 48 B1
Caldas de Boi E 39 B4
Caldas de Malavella E 41 C3
Caldas de Reis E 34 B2
Caldas de San Jorge P 42 B1
Caldas de Vizela P 42 A1
Caldaso de los Vidrios E 44 B3
Caldearenas E 39 B3
Caldelas P 42 A1
Calders E 41 C2
Caldes de Montbui E 41 C3
Calella
*Barcelona* E 41 C3
*Girona* E 41 C4
Calenzana F 62 A1
Calera de León E 55 A3
Calera y Chozas E 44 C3
Caleruega E 37 C3
Caleruela E 44 C2
Cales de Mallorca E 61 B3
Calizzano I 33 A4
Callac F 14 A2
Callas F 32 B2
Calliano I 27 B5
Callosa de Ensarriá E 53 C3
Callosa de Segura E 59 A4
Callús E 41 C2
Calmbach D 13 C4
Calonge E 41 C4
Calpe E 53 C4
Caltojar E 45 A5
Caluire-et-Cuire F 25 B4
Caluso I 27 B4
Calvi F 62 A1
Calviá E 60 B2
Calvinet F 24 C2
Calvisson F 31 B3
Calw D 13 C4
Calzada de Calatrava E 51 B4
Calzada de Valdunciel E 44 A2
Calzadilla de los Barros E 49 C4
Camarasa E 39 C4
Camarena E 45 B3
Camarès F 30 B1
Camaret-sur-Aigues F 31 A3
Camaret-sur-Mer F 14 A1
Camarillas E 47 B3
Camariñas E 34 A1
Camarma E 45 B4
Camarzana de Tera E 35 B4
Camas E 56 A1
Cambados E 34 B2
Cambarinho P 42 B1
Cambil E 57 A4
Cambligeu F 6 B2
Cambo-les-Bains F 38 A2
Cambrai F 6 B3
Cambre E 34 A2
Cambrils E 41 C2
Cameleño E 36 A2
Camelle E 34 A1
Caminha P 42 A1
Caminomorisco E 43 B3
Caminreal E 46 B2
Camors F 14 B3
Campan F 39 A4
Campanario E 50 B2
Campanillas E 57 B3
Campano E 56 B1
Campaspero E 45 A3
Campello E 59 A4
Campelos P 48 B1
Campico López E 59 B3
Campillo de Altobuey E 52 B2
Campillo de Aragón E 46 A2
Campillo de Arenas E 57 A4
Campillo de Llerena E 50 B2
Campillos E 56 A3
Campo E 39 B4
Campo da Feira E 34 A3
Campo de Bacerros E 35 B3
Campo de Caso E 36 A1
Campo de Criptana E 51 A4
Campofrio E 55 B3
Campo Ligure I 33 A4
Campo Lugar E 50 A2
Campo Maior P 49 B3
Campomanes E 35 A5
Campo Molino I 33 A3
Campomono F 62 B1
Campo Real E 45 B4
Camporrells E 39 C4
Camporrobles E 52 B2
Campos P 42 A2
Camposa P 42 A1
Campos del Port E 61 B3
Camposines E 47 A4
Campotéjar E 57 A4
Camprodón E 41 B3
Campsegret F 29 B3
Camuñas E 51 A4
Cañada del Hoyo E 52 B2
Cañadajuncosa E 52 B1
Cañada Rosal E 56 A2
Canale I 27 C4
Canales
*Asturias* E 35 B5
*Castellón de la Plana* E 53 B3
Canals E 53 C3
Cañamares E 46 B1
Cañamero E 50 A2
Cañar E 57 B4
Cañate la Real E 56 B2
Cañaveral E 49 B4
Cañaveral de León E 55 A3
Cañaveras E 46 B1
Cañaveruelas E 45 B5
Cancale F 8 B2
Cancon F 29 B3
Canda E 35 B4
Candamil E 34 A3
Candanchu E 39 B3
Candas E 35 A5
Candasnos E 47 A4
Candé F 15 B4
Candelario E 44 B2
Candeleda E 44 B2
Candin E 35 B4
Candosa P 42 B2
Canecas P 48 C1
Canelli I 27 C5
Canena E 51 B4
Canencia E 45 B4
Canero E 35 A4
Canet F 30 B2
Canet de Mar E 41 C3
Canet d'en Berenguer E 53 B3
Cañete E 52 A2
Cañete de las Torres E 57 A3
Canet-en-Roussillon F 40 B4
Canfranc E 39 B3
Cangas
*Lugo* E 35 A3
*Pontevedra* E 34 B2
Cangas de Narcea E 35 A4
Cangas de Onís E 36 A1
Canha P 48 C2
Canhestros P 54 A1
Canicosa de la Sierra E 37 C3
Caniles E 58 B2
Canillas de Aceituno E 57 B3
Canisy F 8 A2
Cañizal E 44 A2
Cañizo E 36 C1
Canjáyar E 58 C2
Cannes F 32 B3
Can Pastilla E 60 B2
C'an Picafort E 61 B3
Cantalapiedra E 44 A2
Cantalejo E 45 A4
Cantalgallo E 55 A3
Cantalpino E 44 A2
Cantanhede P 42 B1
Cantavieja E 47 B3
Cantillana E 56 A2
Cantiveros E 44 B3
Cantoria E 58 B2

Cany-Barville F 9 A4
Canyet de Mar E 41 C3
Caparroso E 38 B2
Capbreton F 28 C1
Capdenac-Gare F 24 C2
Capdepera E 61 B3
Cap-de-Pin F 28 B2
Capellades E 41 C2
Capendu F 40 A3
Capestang F 30 B2
Cap Ferret F 28 B1
Capileira E 57 B4
Capinha P 42 B2
Captieux F 28 B2
Capvern F 39 A4
Carabaña E 45 B4
Carabias E 45 A4
Caracenilla E 46 B1
Caráglio I 33 A3
Caraman F 40 A2
Caranga E 35 A4
Caranguejeira P 48 B2
Carantec F 14 A2
Caravaca de la Cruz E 58 A3
Carbajal E 57 B3
Carbajo E 49 B3
Carballeda E 34 B3
Carballeda de Avia E 34 B2
Carballo E 34 A2
Carbon-Blanc F 28 B2
Carbonera de Frentes E 37 C4
Carboneras E 58 C3
Carboneras de Guadazaón E 52 B2
Carbonero el Mayor E 45 A3
Carboneros E 51 B4
Carbonne F 40 A2
Carcaboso E 43 B3
Carcabuey E 57 A3
Carcaixent E 53 B3
Carcans F 28 A1
Carcans-Plage F 28 A1
Carção P 43 A3
Carcar E 38 B2
Cárcare I 33 A4
Carcassonne F 40 A3
Carcastillo E 38 B2
Carcedo de Burgos E 37 B3
Carcelén E 53 B2
Carcès F 32 B2
Carchelejo E 57 A4
Cardedeu E 41 C3
Cardeña E 51 B3
Cardenete E 52 B2
Cardeñosa E 44 B3
Cardona E 41 C2
Cardosos P 48 B2
Carentan F 8 A2
Carentoir F 15 B3
Cargèse F 62 A1
Carhaix-Plouguer F 14 A2
Caria P 42 B2
Carignan F 11 B5
Carignano I 27 C4
Cariñena E 46 A2
Cariño E 34 A3
Carlepont F 10 B3
Carlet E 53 B3
Carmagnola I 27 C4
Carmaux F 30 A1
Carmena E 44 C3
Cármenes E 36 B1
Carmine I 33 A3
Carmona E 56 A2
Carmonita E 49 B4
Carnac F 14 B2
Carnon Plage F 31 B2
Carnota E 34 B1
Carolles F 8 B2
Carpentras F 31 A4
Carpignano Sésia I 27 B5
Carpio E 44 A2
Carquefou F 15 B4
Carqueiranne F 32 B2
Carral E 34 A2
Carranque E 45 B4
Carrapichana P 42 B2
Carrascalejo E 50 A2
Carrascosa del Campo E 45 B5
Carratraca E 56 B3
Carrazeda de Ansiães P 42 A2
Carrazedo de Montenegro P 42 A2
Carregal do Sal P 42 B1
Carreña E 36 A2
Carrión E 55 B3
Carrión de Calatrava E 51 A4
Carrión de los Condes E 36 B2
Carrizo de la Ribera E 35 B5
Carrizosa E 51 B5
Carro F 31 B4
Carrocera E 36 B1
Carros F 33 B3
Carrouge CH 20 C1
Carrouges F 9 B3
Carrù I 33 A3
Carry-le-Rouet F 31 B4
Cartagena E 59 B4
Cártama E 57 B3
Cartaxo P 48 B2
Cartaya E 55 B2
Carteret F 8 A2
Cartes E 36 A2
Carviçães P 43 A3
Carvin F 6 B2
Carvoeira P 48 B1
Carvoeiro P 54 B1
Casabermeja E 57 B3
Casa Branca
*Portalegre* P 48 C3
*Setúbal* P 48 C2
Casaio E 35 B4
Casalarreina E 37 B4
Casalborgone I 27 B4
Casale Monferrato I 27 B5
Casamozza F 62 A2
Casarabonela E 56 B3
Casar de Cáceres E 49 B4
Casar de Palomero E 43 B3
Casarejos E 37 C3
Casares E 56 B2
Casares de las Hurdes E 43 B3
Casariche E 57 A3
Casarrubios del Monte E 45 B3
Casas de Don Pedro E 50 A2
Casas de Fernando Alonso E 52 B1
Casas de Haro E 52 B1
Casas de Juan Gil E 53 B2
Casas del Juan Núñez E 52 B2
Casas del Puerto E 53 C2
Casas del Rio E 53 B2
Casas de Millán E 49 B4
Casas de Reina E 50 B2
Casas de Ves E 53 B2
Casas-Ibáñez E 52 B2
Casasimarro E 52 B1
Casas Nuevas E 58 B3
Casasola E 44 B3
Casasola de Arión E 44 A2
Casasuertes E 36 A2
Casatejada E 44 C2
Casavieja E 44 B3
Cascais P 48 C1
Cascante E 38 C2
Cascante del Rio E 46 B2
Cáseda E 38 B2
Caselle Torinese I 27 B4
Caseres E 47 A4
Caserío Benali E 53 B3
Casével P 54 B1
Casillas E 44 B3
Casillas de Coria E 49 B4
Casinos E 53 B3
Caspe E 47 A3
Cassàde la Selva E 41 C3
Cassagnas F 30 A2
Cassagnes-Bégonhès F 30 A1
Cassel F 6 B2
Cassine I 27 C5
Cassis F 32 B1
Cassuéjouls F 24 C2
Castalla E 53 C3
Castañar de Ibor E 50 A2
Castanheira de Pêra P 48 A2
Casteição P 42 B2
Castejón E 38 B2
Castejón de Monegros E 47 A3
Castejón de Sos E 39 B4
Castejón de Valdejasa E 38 C3
Castel de Cabra E 47 B3
Casteldelfino I 32 A3
Casteljaloux F 28 B3
Castellamonte I 27 B4
Castellane F 32 B2
Castellar E 51 B4
Castellar de la Frontera E 56 B2
Castellar de la Ribera E 41 B2
Castellar del Vallès E 41 C3
Castellar de Santiago E 51 B4
Castellbell i Villar E 41 C2
Castelldans E 47 A4
Castell de Cabres E 47 B4
Castell de Castells E 53 C3
Castelldefels E 41 C2
Castell de Ferro E 57 B4
Castellet E 41 C2
Castellfollit de la Roca E 41 B3
Castellfollit de Riubregos E 41 C2
Castellfort E 47 B3
Castellóde Farfaña E 39 C4
Castellóde la Plana E 53 B3
Castello d'Empùries E 41 B4
Castelloli E 41 C2
Castellón de Rugat E 53 C3
Castellote E 47 B3
Castellterçol E 41 C3
Castelmoron-sur-Lot F 29 B3
Castelnaudary F 40 A2
Castelnau-de-Médoc F 28 A2
Castelnau-de-Montmirail F 29 C4
Castelnau-Magnoac F 39 A4
Castelnau-Montratier F 29 B4
Castelnou E 47 A3
Castelnuovo Don Bosco I 27 B4
Castelo Branco
*Bragança* P 43 A3
*Castelo Branco* P 49 B3
Castelo de Paiva P 42 A1
Castelo de Vide P 49 B3
Castelo do Neiva P 42 A1
Castelo Mendo P 43 B3
Castelsarrasin F 29 B4
Castelserás E 47 B3
Castets F 28 C1
Castilblanco E 50 A2
Castilblanco de los Arroyos E 55 B4
Castil de Peones E 37 B3
Castilfrío de la Sierra E 38 C1
Castilgaleu E 39 B4
Castilisar E 38 B2
Castilleja E 55 B3
Castillejar E 58 B2
Castillejo de Martin Viejo E 43 B3
Castillejo de Mesleón E 45 A4
Castillejo de Robledo E 45 A4
Castillo de Bayuela E 44 B3
Castillo de Locubín E 57 A4
Castillonès F 29 B3
Castillon-la-Bataille F 28 B2
Castillon-en-Couserans F 40 B2
Castillonroy E 39 C4
Castilruiz E 38 C1
Castirla F 62 A2
Castrejón E 44 A2
Castrelo del Valle E 35 B3
Castres F 30 B1
Castries F 31 B2
Castril E 58 B2
Castrillo de Duero E 45 A4
Castrillo de la Vega E 37 C3
Castrillo de Onielo E 36 C2
Castro E 36 A2
Castrocabón E 35 B5
Castro-Caldelas E 35 B3
Castrocontrigo E 35 B4
Castro Daire P 42 B2
Castro del Río E 57 A3
Castro de Rey E 35 A3
Castrogonzaio E 36 B1
Castrojeriz E 36 B2
Castro Laboreiro P 34 B2
Castro Marim P 54 B2
Castromonte E 36 C1
Castromudarra E 36 B1
Castronuevo E 36 C1
Castronuño E 44 A2
Castropol E 35 A3
Castroserracin E 45 A4
Castro-Urdiales E 37 A3
Castroverde E 35 A3
Castro Verde P 54 B1
Castroverde de Campos E 36 C1
Castroverde de Cerrato E 36 C2
Castuera E 50 B2
Catadau E 53 B3
Catarroja E 53 B3
Catarruchos P 42 B1
Cati E 47 B4
Catillon F 11 A3
Catoira E 34 B2
Catral E 59 A4
Caudebec-en-Caux F 9 A4
Caudete E 53 C3
Caudete de las Fuentes E 53 B2
Caudiel E 53 B3
Caudiès-de-Fenouillèdes F 40 B3
Caudry F 11 A3
Caulnes F 15 A3
Caumont-l'Evente F 8 A3
Caunes-Minervois F 40 A3
Cauro F 62 B1
Caussade F 29 B4
Causse-de-la-Selle F 30 B2
Cauterets F 39 B3
Cavaglia I 27 B5
Cavaillon F 31 B4
Cavalaire-sur-Mer F 32 B2
Cavaleiro P 54 B1
Cavallermaggiore I 27 C4
Cavernães P 42 B2
Cavignac F 28 A2
Cavour I 27 C4
Cayeux-sur-Mer F 6 B1
Caylus F 29 B4
Cayres F 25 C3
Cazalilla E 51 C4
Cazalla de la Sierra E 50 C2
Cazals F 29 B4
Cazanuecos E 36 B1
Cazaubon F 28 C2
Cazaux F 28 B1
Cazavet F 40 A2
Cazères F 40 A2
Cazis CH 21 C4
Cazo E 36 A1
Cazorla E 58 B2
Cazouls-lès-Béziers F 30 B2
Cea
*León* E 36 B1
*Orense* E 34 B3
Ceánuri E 37 A4
Ceauce F 8 B3
Cebolla E 44 C3
Cebreros E 44 B3
Ceclavín E 49 B4
Cedeira E 34 A2
Cedillo E 49 B3
Cedillo del Condado E 45 B4
Cedrillas E 47 B3
Cée E 34 B1
Cehegín E 58 A3
Ceilhes-et-Rocozels F 30 B2
Ceinos de Campos E 36 B1
Ceira P 42 B1
Celanova E 34 B3
Cella E 46 B2
Celle Ligure I 33 A4
Celles B 7 B4
Celles-sur-Belle F 23 B3
Celorico da Beira P 42 B2
Celorico de Basto P 42 A1
Cenicero E 37 B4
Cenicientos E 44 B3
Censeau F 19 C5
Centallo I 33 A3
Centelles E 41 C3
Cepeda la Mora E 44 B2
Cépet F 29 C4
Cérans Foulletourte F 16 B2
Cerbère F 40 B4
Cercadillo E 45 A5
Cercal
*Lisboa* P 48 B1
*Setúbal* P 54 B1
Cerceda E 45 B4
Cercedilla E 45 B3
Cercs E 41 B2
Cercy-la-Tour F 18 C2
Cerdedo E 34 B2
Cerdeira P 43 B2
Cerdon F 17 B4
Ceres I 27 B4
Ceresole-Reale I 27 B4
Cereste F 32 B1
Céret F 40 B3
Cerezo de Abajo E 45 A4
Cerezo de Riotirón E 37 B3
Cerfontaine B 7 B4
Cergy F 10 B2
Cérilly F 17 C4
Cerisiers F 18 A2
Cerizay F 22 B3
Cernay F 20 B2
Cernégula E 37 B3
Cérons F 28 B2
Cerralbo E 43 B3
Cerro Muriano E 50 B3
Certosa di Pésio I 33 A3
Cerva P 42 A2
Cervatos de la Cueza E 36 B2
Cervera E 41 C2
Cervera de la Cañada E 46 A2
Cervera del Llano E 52 B1
Cervera del Río Alhama E 38 B2
Cervera de Pisuerga E 36 B2
Cerviàde les Garrigues E 41 C1
Cervione F 62 A2
Cervo E 35 A3
Cervon F 18 B2
Cesana Torinese I 27 C3
Cessenon F 30 B2
Cesson-Sévigné F 15 A4
Cestas F 28 B2
Cesuras E 34 A2
Cetina E 46 A2
Ceuti E 59 A3
Ceva I 33 A4
Cevico de la Torre E 36 C2
Cevico Navero E 36 C2
Cevins F 26 B3
Cévio CH 27 A5
Ceyrat F 24 B3
Ceyzériat F 26 A2
Chaam NL 7 A4
Chabanais F 23 C4
Chabeuil F 25 C5
Chablis F 18 B2
Châbons F 26 B2
Chabreloche F 25 B3
Chabris F 17 B3
Chagny F 19 C3
Chaherrero E 44 B3
Chailland F 8 B3
Chaillé-les-Marais F 22 B2
Chailles F 17 B3
Chailley F 18 A2
Chalabre F 40 B3
Chalais F 28 A3
Chalamont F 26 B2
Châlette-sur-Loing F 17 A4
Chalindrey F 19 B4
Challans F 22 B2
Challes-les-Eaux F 26 B2
Chalmazel F 25 B3
Chalmoux F 18 C2
Chalonnes-sur-Loire F 16 B1
Châlons-en-Champagne F 11 C4
Chalon-sur-Saône F 19 C3
Châlus F 23 C4
Cham CH 20 B3
Chamberet F 24 B1
Chambéry F 26 B2
Chambilly F 25 A4
Chambley F 12 B1
Chambly F 10 B2
Chambois F 9 B4
Chambon-sur-Lac F 24 B2
Chambon-sur-Voueize F 24 A2
Chambord F 17 B3
Chamborigaud F 31 A2
Chamboulive F 24 B1
Chamonix-Mont-Blanc F 27 B3
Chamoux-sur-Gelon F 26 B3
Champagnac-le-Vieux F 25 B3
Champagney F 20 B1
Champagnole F 19 C4
Champagny-Mouton F 23 B4
Champaubert F 11 C3
Champdeniers-St-Denis F 22 B3
Champdieu F 25 B4
Champdôtre F 19 B4
Champeix F 24 B3
Champéry CH 27 A3
Champigne F 16 B1
Champignelles F 18 B2
Champigny-sur-Veude F 16 B2
Champlitte-et-le-Prelot F 19 B4
Champoluc I 27 B4
Champoly F 25 B3
Champorcher I 27 B4
Champrond-en-Gâtine F 9 B5
Champs-sur-Tarentaine F 24 B2
Champs-sur-Yonne F 18 B2
Champtoceaux F 15 B4
Chamrousse F 26 B2
Chamusca P 48 B2
Chanac F 30 A2
Chanaleilles F 25 C3
Chandrexa de Queixa E 35 B3
Chañe E 44 A3
Changy F 25 A3
Channes F 18 B3
Chantada E 34 B3
Chantelle F 24 A3
Chantenay-St Imbert F 18 C2
Chanteuges F 25 B3
Chantilly F 10 B2
Chantonnay F 22 B2
Chão de Codes P 48 B2
Chaource F 18 A3
Chapa E 34 B2
Chapareillan F 26 B2
Chapelle Royale F 17 A3
Chapelle-St Laurent F 16 C1
Charbonnat F 18 C3
Charenton-du-Cher F 17 C4
Charleroi B 7 B4
Charleville-Mézières F 11 B4
Charlieu F 25 A4
Charly F 10 C3
Charmes F 12 C2
Charmes-sur-Rhône F 25 C4
Charmey CH 20 C2
Charmont-en-Beauce F 17 A4
Charny F 18 B2
Charolles F 25 A4
Chârost F 17 C4
Charquemont F 20 B1
Charrin F 18 C2
Charroux F 23 B4
Chartres F 10 C1
Chasseneuil-sur-Bonnieure F 23 C4
Chassigny F 19 B4
Château-Arnoux F 32 A2
Châteaubernard F 23 C3
Châteaubourg F 15 A4
Châteaubriant F 15 B4
Château-Chinon F 18 B2
Château-d'Oex CH 20 C2
Château-d'Olonne F 22 B2
Château-du-Loir F 16 B2
Châteaudun F 17 A3
Châteaugiron F 15 A4
Château-Gontier F 16 B1
Château-Landon F 17 A4
Château-la-Vallière F 16 B2
Château-l'Evêque F 29 A3
Châteaulin F 14 A1
Châteaumeillant F 17 C4
Châteauneuf
*Nièvre* F 18 B2
*Saône-et-Loire* F 25 A4
Châteauneuf-de-Randon F 25 C3
Châteauneuf-d'Ille-et-Vilaine F 8 B2
Châteauneuf-du-Faou F 14 A2
Châteauneuf-du-Pape F 31 A3
Châteauneuf-en-Thymerais F 9 B5
Châteauneuf la-Forêt F 24 B1
Châteauneuf-le-Rouge F 32 B1
Châteauneuf-sur-Charente F 23 C3
Châteauneuf-sur-Cher F 17 C4
Châteauneuf-sur-Loire F 17 B4
Châteauneuf-sur-Sarthe F 16 B1
Châteauponsac F 23 B5
Château-Porcien F 11 B4
Châteauredon F 32 A2
Châteaurenard
*Bouches du Rhône* F 31 B3
*Loiret* F 18 B1
Château-Renault F 16 B2
Châteauroux F 17 C3
Châteauroux-les-Alpes F 26 C3
Château-Salins F 12 C2
Château-Thierry F 11 B3
Châteauvillain F 19 A3
Châtel F 27 A3
Châtelaillon-Plage F 22 B2
Châtelaudren F 14 A3
Châtel-Censoir F 18 B2
Châtel-de-Neuvre F 24 A3
Châtelet B 7 B4
Châtel-Guyon F 24 B3
Châtellerault F 23 B4
Châtel-Montagne F 25 A3
Châtel-St Denis CH 20 C1
Châtel-sur-Moselle F 12 C2
Châtelus-Malvaleix F 24 A2
Châtenois F 19 A4
Châtenois-les-Forges F 20 B1
Châtillon I 27 B4
Châtillon-Coligny F 17 B4
Châtillon-en-Bazois F 18 B2
Châtillon-en-Diois F 26 C2
Châtillon-sur-Chalaronne F 25 A4
Châtillon-sur-Indre F 17 C3
Châtillon-sur-Loire F 17 B4
Châtillon-sur-Marne F 11 B3
Châtillon-sur-Seine F 18 B3
Châtres F 11 C3
Chauchina E 57 A4
Chaudes-Aigues F 24 C3
Chaudrey F 11 C4
Chauffailles F 25 A4
Chaulnes F 10 B2
Chaument Gistoux B 7 B4
Chaumergy F 19 C4
Chaumont F 19 A4
Chaumont-en-Vexin F 10 B1
Chaumont-Porcien F 11 B4
Chaumont-sur-Aire F 11 C5
Chaumont-sur-Loire F 17 B3
Chaunay F 23 B4
Chauny F 10 B3
Chaussin F 19 C4
Chauvigny F 23 B4
Chavagnes-en-Paillers F 22 B2
Chavanges F 11 C4
Chaves P 42 A2
Chavignon F 11 B3
Chazelles-sur-Lyon F 25 B4
Chazey-Bons F 26 B2
Checa E 46 B2
Chef-Boutonne F 23 B3
Cheles E 49 C3
Chella E 53 B3
Chelles F 10 C2
Chelva E 53 B2
Chémery F 17 B3
Chemery-sur-Bar F 11 B4
Chemillé F 16 B1
Chemin F 19 C4
Chénerailles F 24 A2
Cheniménil F 19 A5
Chenonceaux F 17 B3
Chenôve F 19 B3
Chera E 53 B3
Cherasco I 27 C4
Cherbonnières F 23 C3
Cherbourg F 8 A2
Chéroy F 18 A1
Chessy-lès-Pres F 18 A2
Cheste E 53 B3
Chevagnes F 18 C2
Chevanceaux F 23 C3
Chevillon F 11 C5
Chevilly F 17 A3
Chézery-Forens F 26 A2
Chialamberto I 27 B4
Chianale I 27 C4
Chiché F 16 C1
Chiclana de la Frontera E 56 B1
Chiclana de Segura E 58 A1
Chieri I 27 B4
Chillarón de Cuenca E 46 B1
Chillarón del Rey E 45 B5
Chilleurs-aux-Bois F 17 A4
Chillón E 50 B3
Chilluevar E 58 B1
Chiloeches E 45 B4
Chimay B 11 A4
Chimeneas E 57 A4
Chinchilla de Monte Aragón E 52 C2
Chinchón E 45 B4
Chinon F 16 B2
Chiomonte I 27 B3
Chipiona E 55 C3
Chirac F 30 A2
Chirens F 26 B2
Chirivel E 58 B2
Chissey-en-Morvan F 18 B3
Chiusa di Pésio I 33 A3
Chiva E 53 B3
Chivasso I 27 B4
Cholet F 22 A3
Chomérac F 25 C4
Chorges F 32 A2
Chouilly F 11 B4
Chouto P 48 B2
Chouzy-sur-Cisse F 17 B3
Chozas de Abajo E 36 B1
Chueca E 51 A4
Chur CH 21 C4
Churriana E 57 B3
Churwalden CH 21 C4
Ciadoncha E 37 B3
Ciborro P 48 C2
Cidadelhe P 43 B2
Cidones E 37 C4
Ciempozuelos E 45 B4
Cierp-Gaud F 39 B4
Ciervana E 37 A3
Cieutat F 39 A4
Cieza E 59 A3
Cifuentes E 45 B5
Cigales E 36 C2
Cigliano I 27 B5
Cillas E 46 B2
Cilleros E 43 B3
Cilleruelo de Arriba E 37 C3
Cilleruelo de Bezana E 37 B3
Cimalmotto CH 27 A5
Cimanes del Tejar E 35 B5
Cinctorres E 47 B3
Ciney B 7 B5
Cinfães P 42 A1
Cinq-Mars-la-Pile F 16 B2
Cintegabelle F 40 A2
Cintruénigo E 38 B2
Ciperez E 43 B3
Cirat E 47 B3
Cirey-sur-Vezouze F 12 C2
Ciria E 46 A2
Ciriè I 27 B4
Ciry-le-Noble F 18 C3
Cisneros E 36 B2
Cissac-Médoc F 28 A2
Cistérniga E 44 A3
Cistierna E 36 B1
Ciudadela de Menorca E 61 B3
Ciudad Real E 51 B4
Ciudad Rodrigo E 43 B3
Ciutadilla E 41 C2
Civray F 23 B4
Cizur Mayor E 38 B2
Clairvaux-les-Lacs F 19 C4
Clamecy F 18 B2
Claye-Souilly F 10 C2
Cléder F 14 A1
Clefmont F 19 A4
Cléguérec F 14 A2
Clelles F 26 C2
Cléon-d'Andran F 25 C4
Cléré-les-Pins F 16 B2
Clères F 9 A5
Clermont F 10 B2
Clermont-en-Argonne F 11 B5
Clermont-Ferrand F 24 B3
Clermont-l'Hérault F 30 B2
Clerval F 19 B5
Clervaux L 12 A2
Cléry-St André F 17 B3
Clisson F 15 B4
Clohars-Carnoët F 14 B2
Cloyes-sur-le-Loir F 17 B3
Cluis F 17 C3
Cluny F 25 A4
Cluses F 26 A3
Coaña E 35 A4
Cobas E 34 B2
Cobertelade E 45 A5
Cobeta E 46 B1
Cobreces E 36 A2
Coca E 44 A3
Cocentaina E 53 C3
Codos E 46 A2
Coelhoso P 43 A3
Cofrentes E 53 B2
Cogeces del Monte E 44 A3
Cognac F 23 C3
Cogne I 27 B4
Cognin F 26 B2
Cogolin F 32 B2
Cogollos de Guadix E 58 B1
Cogollos-Vega E 57 A4
Cogolludo E 45 B4
Coimbra P 42 B1
Coin E 57 B3
Coirós E 34 A2
Colares P 48 C1
Colera E 40 B4
Coligny F 26 A2
Colindres E 37 A3
Collado-Mediano E 45 B3
Collado Villalba E 45 B4
Collanzo E 36 A1
Collat F 25 B3
Coll de Nargó E 41 B2
Collinée F 15 A3
Collobrières F 32 B2
Colmar F 20 A2
Colmars F 32 A2
Colmenar E 57 B3
Colmenar de la Sierra E 45 A4
Colmenar de Oreja E 45 B4
Colmenar Viejo E 45 B4
Cologne F 29 C3
Colombey-les-Belles F 12 C1
Colombey-les-deux-Églises F 19 A3
Colombres E 36 A2
Colomera E 57 A4
Colomers E 41 B3
Colomiers F 29 C4
Colònia de Sant Jordi E 61 B3
Colos P 54 B1
Colunga E 36 A1
Coma-ruga E 41 C2

Combarros E 35 B4
Combeaufontaine F 19 B4
Combloux F 26 B3
Combourg F 8 B2
Combronde F 24 B3
Comillas E 36 A2
Comines F 6 B3
Commensacq F 28 B2
Commentry F 24 A2
Commercy F 12 C1
Cómpeta E 57 B4
Compiègne F 10 B2
Comporta P 48 C2
Comps-sur-Artuby F 32 B2
Concarneau F 14 B2
Conceição P 54 B1
Conches-en-Ouche F 9 B4
Concots F 29 B4
Condat F 24 B2
Condé-en-Brie F 11 C3
Condeixa P 42 B1
Condemios de Abajo E 45 A4
Condemios de Arriba E 45 A4
Condé-sur-l'Escaut F 7 B3
Conde-sur-Marne F 11 B4
Condé-sur-Noireau F 8 B3
Condom F 29 C3
Condove I 27 B4
Condrieu F 25 B4
Conflans-sur-Lanterne F 19 B5
Confolens F 23 B4
Conforto E 35 A3
Congosto E 35 B4
Congosto de Valdavia E 36 B2
Congostrina E 45 A4
Conil de la Frontera E 56 B1
Conlie F 16 A1
Conliège F 19 C4
Connantre F 11 C3
Connaux F 31 A3
Connerré F 16 A2
Conques F 24 C2
Conques-sur-Orbiel F 40 A3
Conquista E 51 B3
Conquista de la Sierra E 50 A2
Consenvoye F 11 B5
Consolacão P 48 B1
Constancia P 48 B2
Constanti E 41 C2
Constantina E 56 A2
Consuegra E 51 A4
Contay F 10 B2
Conthey CH 27 A4
Contis-Plage F 28 B1
Contres F 17 B3
Contrexéville F 19 A4
Conty F 10 B2
Coole F 11 C4
Cope E 59 B3
Coray F 14 A2
Corbeil Essonnes F 10 C2
Corbeny F 11 B3
Corbera E 53 B3
Corbie F 10 B2
Corbigny F 18 B2
Corbion B 11 B4
Corconte E 37 A3
Corcubión E 34 B1
Cordes-sur-Ciel F 29 B4
Córdoba E 50 C3
Cordobilla de Lácara E 49 B4
Corella E 38 B2
Coreses E 44 A2
Corga de Lobão P 42 B1
Coria E 49 B4
Coria del Río E 56 A1
Cório I 27 B4
Coripe E 56 B2
Coristanco E 34 A2
Corlay F 14 A2
Cormainville F 17 A3
Cormatin F 18 C3
Cormeilles F 9 A4
Cormery F 16 B2
Cormoz F 26 A2
Cornago E 38 B1
Cornellana E 35 A4
Cornimont F 20 B1
Cornudella de Montsant E 41 C1
Cornudilla E 37 B3
Cornus F 30 B2
Corps F 26 C2
Corps Nuds F 15 B4
Corral de Almaguer E 51 A4
Corral de Ayllon E 45 A4
Corral de Calatrava E 51 B3
Corrales E 43 A4
Corral-Rubio E 52 C2
Corredoiras E 34 A2
Corrèze F 24 B1
Corrubedo E 34 B1
Corte F 62 A2
Corteconcepción E 55 B3
Corte de Peleas E 49 C4
Cortegaca P 42 B1
Cortegada E 34 B2
Cortegana E 55 B3
Cortemilia I 33 A4
Corte Pinto P 54 B2
Cortes E 38 C2
Cortes de Aragón E 47 B3
Cortes de Arenoso E 47 B3
Cortes de Baza E 58 B2
Cortes de la Frontera E 56 B2
Cortes de Pallás E 53 B3
Cortiçadas P 48 C2
Cortico P 42 A2
Cortijo de Arriba E 51 A3
Cortijos Nuevos E 58 A2
Coruche P 48 C2
Corullón E 35 B4
Corvera E 59 B3
Coslada E 45 B4
Cosne-Cours-sur-Loire F 18 B1
Cosne d'Allier F 17 C4
Cospeito E 34 A3
Cossato I 27 B5
Cossaye F 18 C2
Cossé-le-Vivien F 15 B5
Cossonay CH 19 C5
Costa da Caparica P 48 C1
Costa de Santo André P 54 A1
Costa Nova P 42 B1
Costaros F 25 C3
Costigliole d'Asti I 27 C5
Costigliole Saluzzo I 33 A3
Coublanc F 19 B4
Couches F 18 C3
Couço P 48 C2
Coucouron F 25 C3
Coucy-le-Château-Auffrique F 10 B3
Couëron F 15 B4
Couflens F 40 B2
Couhé F 23 B4
Couiza F 40 B3
Coulanges F 18 C2
Coulanges-la-Vineuse F 18 B2
Coulanges-sur-Yonne F 18 B2
Couleuvre F 18 C1
Coulmier-le-Sec F 18 B3
Coulommiers F 10 C3
Coulonges-sur-l'Autize F 22 B3
Coulounieix-Chamiers F 29 A3
Coupéville F 11 C4
Couptrain F 9 B3
Coura P 34 C2
Courcelles B 7 B4
Courcelles-Chaussy F 12 B2
Courchevel F 26 B3
Cour-Cheverny F 17 B3
Courcôme F 23 C4
Courçon F 22 B3
Cour-et-Buis F 25 B4
Courgenay CH 20 B2
Courmayeur I 27 B3
Courniou F 30 B1
Cournon-d'Auvergne F 24 B3
Cournonterral F 30 B2
Courpière F 25 B3
Coursan F 30 B2
Courseulles-sur-Mer F 9 A3
Cours-la-Ville F 25 A4
Courson-les-Carrières F 18 B2
Courtalain F 17 A3
Courtenay F 18 A2
Courtomer F 9 B4
Courville
*Eure-et-Loire* F 9 B5
*Marne* F 11 B3
Coussac-Bonneval F 23 C5
Coutances F 8 A2
Couterne F 9 B3
Coutras F 28 A2
Couvet CH 20 C1
Couvin B 11 A4
Couzon F 18 C2
Covadonga E 36 A1
Covaleda E 37 C4
Covarrubias E 37 B3
Covas P 42 A1
Covilha P 42 B2
Cox F 29 C4
Cózar E 51 B4
Cozes F 22 C3
Cozzano F 62 B2
Craon F 15 B5
Craonne F 11 B3
Craponne F 25 B4
Craponne-sur-Arzon F 25 B3
Crato P 49 B3
Crecente E 34 B2
Crèches-sur-Saône F 25 A4
Crécy-en-Ponthieu F 6 B1
Crécy-la-Chapelle F 10 C2
Crécy-sur-Serre F 11 B3
Creil F 10 B2
Creissels F 30 A2
Cremeaux F 25 B3
Crémenes E 36 B1
Crémieu F 26 B2
Creney F 11 C4
Créon F 28 B2
Crépey F 12 C1
Crépy F 11 B3
Crépy-en-Valois F 10 B2
Crescentino I 27 B5
Crespos E 44 B3
Cressensac F 29 A4
Cressia F 19 C4
Crest F 25 C5
Cresta CH 21 C4
Créteil F 10 C2
Creully F 8 A3
Creutzwald F 12 B2
Crèvecoeur-le-Grand F 10 B2
Crevillente E 59 A4
Crévola d'Ossola I 27 A5
Criales E 37 B3
Criel-sur-Mer F 10 A1
Crillon F 10 B1
Cripán E 37 B4
Criquetot-l'Esneval F 9 A4
Crissolo I 27 C4
Cristóbal E 43 B4
Crocq F 24 B2
Crodo I 27 A5
Cronat F 18 C2
Crouy F 10 B3
Crozon F 14 A1
Cruas F 25 C4
Cruis F 32 A1
Cruseilles F 26 A3
Cruz de Incio E 35 B3
Cuacos de Yuste E 44 B2
Cualedro E 34 C3
Cuanca de Campos E 36 B1
Cuba P 54 A2
Cubel E 46 A2
Cubelles E 41 C2
Cubillos E 37 C4
Cubillos del Sil E 35 B4
Cubjac F 29 A3
Cubo de la Solana E 46 A1
Cucuron F 31 B4
Cudillero E 35 A4
Cuéllar E 45 A3
Cuenca E 46 B1
Cuers F 32 B2
Cuerva E 51 A3
Cueva de Agreda E 38 C2
Cuevas Bajas E 57 A3
Cuevas del Almanzora E 58 B3
Cuevas del Becerro E 56 B2
Cuevas del Campo E 58 B2
Cuevas del Valle E 44 B2
Cuevas de San Clemente E 37 B3
Cuevas de San Marcos E 57 A3
Cuges-les-Pins F 32 B1
Cugnaux F 29 C4
Cuinzier F 25 A4
Cuiseaux F 19 C4
Cuisery F 19 C4
Culan F 17 C4
Culemborg NL 7 A5
Cúllar E 58 B2
Cullera E 53 B3
Cully CH 20 C1
Culoz F 26 B2
Cumbres de San Bartolomé E 55 A3
Cumbres Mayores E 55 A3
Cumiana I 27 C4
Cúneo I 33 A3
Cunlhat F 25 B3
Cuntis E 34 B2
Cuorgnè I 27 B4
Currelos E 34 B3
Curtis E 34 A2
Curtis Santa Eulalia E 34 A2
Cusset F 25 A3
Cussy-les-Forges F 18 B3
Custines F 12 C2
Cutanda E 46 B2
Cuts F 10 B3
Cuvilly F 10 B2


## D


Dabo F 12 C3
Dagmersellen CH 20 B2
Dahn D 13 B3
Daimiel E 51 A4
Dalaas A 21 B5
Dalheim L 12 B2
Dalias E 58 C2
Daluis F 32 A2
Damazan F 29 B3
Damgan F 15 B3
Dammarie-les-Lys F 10 C2
Dammartin-en-Goële F 10 B2
Dampierre F 19 B4
Dampierre-sur-Salon F 19 B4
Damüls A 21 B4
Damville F 9 B5
Damvillers F 12 B1
Dangers F 9 B5
Dangé-St Romain F 16 C2
Dangeul F 9 B4
Danjoutin F 20 B1
Dannemarie F 20 B2
Daoulas F 14 A1
Darmstadt D 13 B4
Darney F 19 A5
Daroca E 46 A2
Darque P 42 A1
Daumeray F 16 B1
Davos CH 21 C4
Dax F 28 C1
Deauville F 9 A4
Deba E 37 A4
Decazeville F 30 A1
Decize F 18 C2
Degaña E 35 B4
Dego I 33 A4
Degolados P 49 B3
De Haan B 6 A3
Dehesas de Guadix E 58 B1
Dehesas Viejas E 57 A4
Deia E 60 B2
Deinze B 7 B3
Deleitosa E 50 A2
Delémont CH 20 B2
Delle F 20 B2
Delme F 12 C2
Demigny F 19 C3
Demonte I 33 A3
Denain F 6 B3
Dender-monde B 7 A4
Denia E 53 C4
Déols F 17 C3
De Panne B 6 A2
Derval F 15 B4
Desana I 27 B5
Descartes F 16 C2
Destriana E 35 B4
Desvres F 6 B1
Dettingen D 21 B4
Dettwiller F 13 C3
Deza E 46 A1
Diano d'Alba I 27 C5
Diano Marina I 33 B4
Die F 26 C2
Diebling F 12 B2
Dieburg D 13 B4
Diego del Carpio E 44 B2
Diekirch L 12 B2
Diélette F 8 A2
Diémoz F 26 B2
Diepenbeck B 7 B5
Dieppe F 9 A5
Diest B 7 B5
Dietikon CH 20 B3
Dietzenbach D 13 A4
Dieue-sur-Meuse F 12 B1
Dieulefit F 31 A4
Dieulouard F 12 C2
Dieuze F 12 C2
Diezma E 57 A4
Differdange L 12 B1
Dignac F 23 C4
Digne-les-Bains F 32 A2
Digny F 9 B5
Digoin F 18 C2
Dijon F 19 B4
Diksmuide B 6 A2
Dilar E 57 A4
Dillingen D 12 B2
Dinan F 15 A3
Dinant B 7 B4
Dinard F 15 A3
Diou F 18 C2
Dirksland NL 7 A4
Disentis CH 21 C3
Ditzingen D 13 C5
Dives-sur-Mer F 9 A3
Divion F 6 B2
Divonne les Bains F 26 A3
Dixmont F 18 A2
Dizy-le-Gros F 11 B4
Doade E 35 B3
Dobro E 37 B3
Dogliani I 33 A3
Dogueno P 54 B2
Doische B 11 A4
Dois Portos P 48 B1
Dolancourt F 18 A3
Dolceácqua I 33 B3
Dol-de-Bretagne F 8 B2
Dole F 19 B4
Dollot F 18 A2
Dolores E 59 A4
Domat-Ems CH 21 C4
Dombasle-sur-Meurthe F 12 C2
Domène F 26 B2
Domérat F 24 A2
Domfessel F 12 C3
Domfront F 8 B3
Domfront-en-Champagne F 16 A2
Domingão P 48 B2
Domingo Pérez
*Granada* E 57 A4
*Toledo* E 44 C3
Dommartin F 11 C4
Dommartin-le-Franc F 11 C4
Domme F 29 B4
Domodóssola I 27 A5
Dompaire F 19 A5
Dompierre-du-Chemin F 8 B2
Dompierre-sur-Besbre F 18 C2
Dompierre-sur-Mer F 22 B2
Domrémy-la-Pucelle F 12 C1
Domsure F 26 A2
Donado E 35 B4
Don Alvaro E 49 C4
Doña Mencía E 57 A3
Donaueschingen D 20 B3
Don Benito E 50 B2
Donestebe-Santesteban E 38 A2
Donges F 15 B3
Doniños E 34 A2
Donnemarie-Dontilly F 10 C3
Donostia-San Sebastián E 38 A2
Donzenac F 29 A4
Donzère F 31 A3
Donzy F 18 B2
Dor E 34 A1
Dordrecht NL 7 A4
Dormans F 11 B3
Dornbirn A 21 B4
Dornecy F 18 B2
Dornes F 18 C2
Dornhan D 13 C4
Dortan F 26 A2
Dos Aguas E 53 B3
Dosbarrios E 45 C4
Dos Hermanas E 56 A2
Dos-Torres E 50 B3
Dottignies B 6 B3
Döttingen CH 20 B3
Douai F 6 B3
Douarnenez F 14 A1
Douchy F 18 B2
Douchy-les-Mines F 6 B3
Doucier F 19 C4
Doudeville F 9 A4
Doué-la-Fontaine F 16 B1
Doulaincourt-Saucourt F 11 C5
Doulevant-le-Château F 11 C4
Doullens F 10 A2
Dour B 7 B3
Dourdan F 10 C2
Dourgne F 40 A3
Dournazac F 23 C4
Douro Calvo P 42 B2
Douvaine F 26 A3
Douvres-la-Délivrande F 9 A3
Douzy F 11 B5
Doyet F 24 A2
Dozule F 9 A3
Draguignan F 32 B2
Dreieich D 13 A4
Dreisen D 13 B4
Dreux F 9 B5
Dronero I 33 A3
Droué F 17 A3
Drulingen F 12 C3
Drunen NL 7 A5
Duas Igrejas P 43 A3
Dübendorf CH 21 B3
Ducey F 8 B2
Duclair F 9 A4
Dueñas E 36 C2
Duffel B 7 A4
Dugny-sur-Meuse F 12 B1
Dunkerque = Dunkirk F 6 A2
Dunkirk = Dunkerque F 6 A2
Dun-le-Palestel F 24 A1
Dun-les-Places F 18 B3
Dunningen D 21 A3
Dun-sur-Auron F 17 C4
Dun-sur-Meuse F 11 B5
Durach D 21 B5
Durana E 37 B4
Durance F 28 B3
Durango E 37 A4
Duras F 28 B3
Durban-Corbières F 40 B3
Dürbheim D 21 A3
Durbuy B 7 B5
Dúrcal E 57 B4
Durlach D 13 C4
Dürrboden CH 21 C4
Dürrenboden CH 21 C3
Durtal F 16 B1
Dusslingen D 13 C5


## E


Ea E 37 A4
Eaux-Bonnes F 39 B3
Eauze F 28 C3
Eberbach D 13 B4
Ebnat-Kappel CH 21 B4
Ebreuil F 24 A3
Echallens CH 20 C1
Echauri E 38 B2
Echiré F 22 B3
Échirolles F 26 B2
Echourgnac F 28 A3
Echternach L 12 B2
Ecija E 56 A2
Éclaron F 11 C4
Écommoy F 16 B2
Écouché F 9 B3
Ecouis F 10 B1
Écueillé F 17 B3
Edenkoben D 13 B4
Edesheim D 13 B4
Eekloo B 7 A3
Eersel NL 7 A5
Effiat F 24 A3
Egg
A 21 B4
D 21 A5
Éghezée B 7 B4
Égletons F 24 B2
Eglisau CH 21 B3
Égliseneuve-d'Entraigues F 24 B2
Eglofs D 21 B4
Eguilles F 31 B4
Eguilly-sous-Bois F 18 A3
Éguzon-Chantôme F 17 C3
Ehrang D 12 B2
Eibar E 37 A4
Eindhoven NL 7 A5
Einsiedeln CH 21 B3
Einville-au-Jard F 12 C2
Eisenberg D 13 B4
Eivissa = Ibiza E 60 C1
Eixo P 42 B1
Ejea de los Caballeros E 38 B2
Ejulve E 47 B3
Eke B 7 B3
El Alamo
*Madrid* E 45 B4
*Sevilla* E 55 B3
El Algar E 59 B4
El Almendro E 55 B2
El Alquián E 58 C2
Élancourt F 10 C1
El Arenal E 44 B2
El Arguellite E 58 A2
El Astillero E 37 A3
El Ballestero E 52 C1
El Barco de Ávila E 44 B2
El Berrón E 36 A1
El Berrueco E 45 B4
Elbeuf F 9 A4
El Bodón E 43 B3
El Bonillo E 52 C1
El Bosque E 56 B2
El Bullaque E 51 A3
El Burgo E 56 B3
El Burgo de Ebro E 47 A3
El Burgo de Osma E 45 A4
El Burgo Ranero E 36 B1
El Buste E 38 C2
El Cabaco E 43 B3
El Callejo E 37 A3
El Campillo E 55 B3
El Campillo de la Jara E 50 A2
El Cañavete E 52 B1
El Carpio E 51 C3
El Carpio de Tajo E 44 C3
El Casar E 45 B4
El Casar de Escalona E 44 B3
El Castillo de las Guardas E 55 B3
El Centenillo E 51 B4
El Cerro E 43 B4
El Cerro de Andévalo E 55 B3
Elche E 59 A4
Elche de la Sierra E 52 C1
El Comenar E 56 B2
El Coronil E 56 A2
El Crucero E 35 A4
El Cubo de Tierra del Vino E 43 A4
El Cuervo E 56 B1
Elda E 53 C3
El Ejido E 58 C2
El Escorial E 45 B3
El Espinar E 45 B3
El Frago E 38 B3
El Franco E 35 A4
El Frasno E 46 A2
El Garrobo E 55 B3
El Gastor E 56 B2
Elgoibar E 37 A4
El Gordo E 44 C2
El Grado E 39 B4
El Granado E 55 B2
El Grao de Castelló E 53 B4
El Grau E 53 C3
El Higuera E 57 A3
El Hijate E 58 B2
El Hontanar E 46 B2
El Hoyo E 51 B4
Elizondo E 38 A2
Ellezelles B 7 B3
Elm CH 21 C4
El Madroño E 55 B3
El Maillo E 43 B3
El Masnou E 41 C3
El Mirón E 44 B2
El Molar E 45 B4
El Molinillo E 51 A3
El Morell E 41 C2
Elmstein D 13 B3
El Muyo E 45 A4
Elne F 40 B3
El Olmo E 45 A4
Elorrio E 37 A4
Éloyes F 19 A5
El Palo E 57 B3
El Pardo E 45 B4
El Payo E 43 B3
El Pedernoso E 52 B1
El Pedroso E 56 A2
El Peral E 52 B2
El Perelló
*Tarragona* E 47 B4
*Valencia* E 53 B3
El Picazo E 52 B1
El Pinell de Bray E 47 A4
El Piñero E 44 A2
El Pla de Santa Maria E 41 C2
El Pobo E 47 B3
El Pobo de Dueñas E 46 B2
El Pont d'Armentera E 41 C2
El Port de la Selva E 41 B4
El Port de Llançà E 40 B4
El Port de Sagunt E 53 B3
El Prat de Llobregat E 41 C3
El Provencio E 52 B1
El Puente E 37 A3
El Puente del Arzobispo E 44 C2
El Puerto E 35 A4
El Puerto de Santa María E 56 B1
El Real de la Jara E 55 B3
El Real de San Vincente E 44 B3
El Robledo E 51 A3
El Rocío E 55 B3
El Rompido E 55 B2
El Ronquillo E 55 B3
El Royo E 37 C4
El Rubio E 56 A3
El Sabinar E 58 A2
El Saler E 53 B3
El Salobral E 52 C2
El Saucejo E 56 A2
Els Castells E 41 B2
Elsenfeld D 13 B5
El Serrat AND 40 B2
El Temple E 38 C3
El Tiemblo E 44 B3
El Toboso E 51 A5
El Tormillo E 39 C3
El Torno E 43 B4
Eltville D 13 A4
El Valle de las Casas E 36 B1
Elvas P 49 C3
El Vellón E 45 B4
Elven F 15 B3
El Vendrell E 41 C2
El Villar de Arnedo E 38 B1
El Viso E 50 B3
El Viso del Alcor E 56 A2
Elzach D 20 A3
Embrun F 32 A2
Embún E 38 B3
Emmen CH 20 B3
Emmendingen D 20 A2
Encamp AND 40 B2
Encarnação P 48 C1
Encinas de Abajo E 44 B2
Encinas de Esgueva E 36 C2
Encinasola E 55 A3
Encinas Reales E 57 A3
Encio E 37 B3
Enciso E 38 B1
Endingen D 20 A2
Endrinal E 43 B4
Engelberg CH 20 C3
Engen D 21 B3
Enghien B 7 B4
Enguera E 53 C3
Enguidanos E 52 B2
Enkenbach D 13 B3
Ennezat F 24 B3
Ensisheim F 20 B2
Entlebuch CH 20 B3
Entrácque I 33 A3
Entradas P 54 B1
Entrains-sur-Nohain F 18 B2
Entrambasaguas E 37 A3
Entrambasmestas E 37 A3
Entraygues-sur-Truyère F 24 C2
Entre-os-Rios P 42 A1
Entrevaux F 32 B2
Entrin Bajo E 49 C4
Entroncamento P 48 B2
Entzheim F 13 C3
Envermeu F 9 A5
Enzklösterle D 13 C4
Épagny F 10 B3
Epalinges CH 20 C1
Epannes F 22 B3
Épernay F 11 B3
Épernon F 10 C1
Epfig F 13 C3
Epierre F 26 B3
Épila E 46 A2
Épinac F 18 C3
Épinal F 19 A5
Epoisses F 18 B3
Eppenbrunn D 13 B3
Eppingen D 13 B4
Erbach D 13 B4
Erbalunga F 62 A2
Ericeira P 48 C1
Eriswil CH 20 B2
Erla E 38 B3
Erli I 33 A4
Ermenonville F 10 B2
Ermezinde P 42 A1
Ermidas P 54 A1
Ernée F 8 B3
Erolzheim D 21 A5
Erquelinnes B 7 B4
Erquy F 15 A3
Erra P 48 C2
Erratzu E 38 A2
Erro E 38 B2
Ersa F 62 A2
Erstein F 13 C3
Erstfeld CH 21 C3
Ertingen D 21 A4
Ervedal
*Coimbra* P 42 B1
*Portalegre* P 48 B3
Ervidel P 54 B1
Ervy-le-Châtel F 18 A2
Esbly F 10 C2
Escacena del Campo E 55 B3
Escairón E 34 B3
Escalada E 37 B3
Escalante E 37 A3
Escalona E 44 B3
Escalona del Prado E 45 A3
Escalonilla E 44 C3
Escalos de Baixo P 49 B3
Escalos de Cima P 49 B3
Escamilla E 46 B1
Es Caná E 60 B1

Escañuela E 51 C3
Es Castell E 61 B4
Escatrón E 47 A3
Eschach D 21 B4
Eschenz CH 21 B3
Esch-sur-Alzette L 12 B1
Esch-sur-Sûre L 12 B1
Escobasa de Almazán E 46 A1
Escoeuilles F 6 B1
Escombreras E 59 B4
Escos F 38 A2
Escource F 28 B1
Escragnolles F 32 B2
Escurial E 50 A2
Escurial de la Sierra E 43 B4
Esgos E 34 B3
Eslava E 38 B2
Eslida E 53 B3
Es Mercadal E 61 B4
Es Migjorn Gran E 61 B4
Espalion F 30 A1
Esparragalejo E 49 C4
Esparragosa del Caudillo E 50 B2
Esparragossa de la Serena E 50 B2
Esparreguera E 41 C2
Esparron F 32 B1
Espejo
*Alava* E 37 B3
*Córdoba* E 57 A3
Espeluche F 31 A3
Espeluy E 51 B4
Espera E 56 B2
Esperança P 49 B3
Espéraza F 40 B3
Espiel E 50 B2
Espinama E 36 A2
Espiñaredo E 34 A3
Espinasses F 32 A2
Espinelves E 41 C3
Espinhal P 48 A2
Espinho P 42 A1
Espinilla E 36 A2
Espinosa de Cerrato E 37 C3
Espinosa de los Monteros E 37 A3
Espinoso del Rey E 50 A3
Espirito Santo P 54 B2
Espluga de Francolí E 41 C2
Esplús E 39 C4
Espolla E 40 B3
Esporles E 60 B2
Es Port d'Alcúdia E 61 B3
Esposende P 42 A1
Espot E 40 B2
Es Pujols E 60 C1
Esquedas E 39 B3
Esquivias E 45 B4
Essay F 9 B4
Essen B 7 A4
Essertaux F 10 B2
Es Soleràs E 47 A4
Essoyes F 18 A3
Estacas E 34 B2
Estadilla E 39 B4
Estagel F 40 B3
Estaires F 6 B2
Estang F 28 C2
Estarreja P 42 B1
Estartit E 41 B4
Estavayer-le-Lac CH 20 C1
Esteiro E 34 A2
Estela P 42 A1
Estella E 38 B1
Estellencs E 60 B2
Estepa E 56 A3
Estépar E 37 B3
Estepona E 56 B2
Esternay F 11 C3
Esterri d'Aneu E 40 B2
Estissac F 18 A2
Estivadas E 34 B3
Estivareilles F 24 A2
Estivella E 53 B3
Estói P 54 B2
Estopiñán E 39 C4
Estoril P 48 C1
Estoublon F 32 B2
Estrée-Blanche F 6 B2
Estrées-St Denis F 10 B2
Estrela P 49 C3
Estremera E 45 B4
Estremoz P 49 C3
Esyres F 16 B2
Etables-sur-Mer F 14 A3
Étain F 12 B1
Étalans F 19 B5
Etalle B 12 B1
Étampes F 10 C2
Etang-sur-Arroux F 18 C3
Étaples F 6 B1
Etauliers F 28 A2
Etoges F 11 C3
Etréaupont F 11 B3
Étréchy F 10 C2
Étrépagny F 10 B1
Étretat F 9 A4
Étroeungt F 11 A3
Étroubles I 27 B4
Ettelbruck L 12 B2
Etten NL 7 A4
Ettenheim D 20 A2
Ettlingen D 13 C4
Etuz F 19 B4
Etxarri-Aranatz E 38 B1
Eu F 10 A1
Eulate E 38 B1
Europoort NL 7 A4
Évaux-les-Bains F 24 A2
Evergem B 7 A3
Évian-les-Bains F 26 A3
Evisa F 62 A1
Evolène CH 27 A4
Évora P 40 C3
Evoramonte P 49 C3
Evran F 15 A4
Evrecy F 9 A3
Évreux F 9 A5
Évron F 16 A1
Évry F 10 C2
Excideuil F 23 C5
Exmes F 9 B4
Eyguians F 32 A1
Eyguières F 31 B4
Eygurande F 24 B2
Eylie F 39 B4
Eymet F 29 B3
Eymoutiers F 24 B1
Ezaro E 34 B1
Ezcaray E 37 B4
Ezcároz E 38 B2
Ezmoriz P 42 B1


## F


Fabara E 47 A4
Fabero E 35 B4
Fabrègues F 30 B2
Facha P 42 A1
Facinas E 56 B2
Fadagosa P 49 B3
Fafe P 42 A1
Fagnières F 11 C4
Faido CH 21 C3
Fains-Véel F 11 C5
Falaise F 9 B3
Falces E 38 B2
Falset E 41 C1
Fanjeaux F 40 A3
Fão P 42 A1
Faramontanos de Tábara E 43 A4
Fara Novarese I 27 B5
Farasdues E 38 B2
Fariza E 43 A3
Farlete E 47 A3
Faro P 54 B2
Fátima P 48 B2
Faucogney-et-la-Mer F 19 B5
Fauguerolles F 28 B3
Faulquemont F 12 B2
Fauquembergues F 6 B2
Fauville-en-Caux F 9 A4
Fauvillers B 12 B1
Favara E 53 B3
Faverges F 26 B3
Faverney F 19 B5
Fay-aux-Loges F 17 B4
Fayence F 32 B2
Fayet F 30 B1
Fayl-Billot F 19 B4
Fayón E 47 A4
Fécamp F 9 A4
Felanitx E 61 B3
Feldkirch A 21 B4
Felgueiras P 42 A1
Félix E 58 C2
Felizzano I 27 C5
Felletin F 24 B2
Fene E 34 A2
Fenestrelle I 27 B4
Fénétrange F 12 C3
Feneu F 16 B1
Fère-Champenoise F 11 C3
Fère-en-Tardenois F 11 B3
Feria E 49 C4
Fermil P 42 A2
Fermoselle E 43 A3
Fernancabellero E 51 A4
Fernán Nuñéz E 57 A3
Fernán Peréz E 58 C2
Fernão Ferro P 48 C1
Fernay-Voltaire F 26 A3
Ferpécle CH 27 A4
Ferrals-les-Corbières F 40 A3
Ferreira E 35 A3
Ferreira do Alentejo P 54 A1
Ferreira do Zêzere P 48 B2
Ferreras de Abajo E 35 C4
Ferreras de Arriba E 35 C4
Ferreries E 61 B4
Ferreruela E 46 A2
Ferreruela de Tabara E 43 A3
Ferret CH 27 B4
Ferrette F 20 B2
Ferrière-la-Grande F 7 B3
Ferrières
*Hautes-Pyrénées* F 39 A3
*Loiret* F 17 A4
*Oise* F 10 B2
Ferrières-sur-Sichon F 25 A3
Ferrol E 34 A2
Festieux F 11 B3
Feuges F 11 C4
Feuquières F 10 B1
Feurs F 25 B4
Fiano I 27 B4
Fiesch CH 27 A5
Figari F 62 B2
Figeac F 24 C2
Figols E 39 B4
Figueira da Foz P 42 B1
Figueira de Castelo Rodrigo P 43 B3
Figueira dos Caveleiros P 54 A1
Figueiredo P 48 B3
Figueiredo de Alva P 42 B2
Figueiródos Vinhos P 48 B2
Figueres E 41 B3
Figueroles E 47 B3
Figueruela de Arriba E 35 C4
Filisur CH 21 C4
Finale Ligure I 33 A4
Fiñana E 58 B2
Firmi F 30 A1
Firminy F 25 B4
Fischbach D 13 B3
Fischen D 21 B5
Fismes F 11 B3
Fisterra E 34 B1
Fitero E 38 B2
Flaça E 41 B3
Flace F 25 A4
Flaine F 26 A3
Flamatt CH 20 C2
Flassans-sur-Issole F 32 B2
Flavigny-sur-Moselle F 12 C2
Flavy-le-Martel F 10 B3
Flawil CH 21 B4
Flayosc F 32 B2
Flehingen D 13 B4
Flers F 8 B3
Fleurance F 29 C3
Fleuré F 23 B4
Fleurier CH 19 C5
Fleurus B 7 B4
Fleury
*Hérault* F 30 B2
*Yonne* F 18 B2
Fleury-les-Aubrais F 17 B3
Fleury-sur-Andelle F 9 A5
Fleury-sur-Orne F 9 A3
Flims CH 21 C4
Flines-lèz-Raches F 6 B3
Flirey F 12 C1
Flix E 47 A4
Flixecourt F 10 A2
Flize F 11 B4
Flobecq B 7 B3
Flogny-la-Chapelle F 18 B2
Flonheim D 13 B4
Florac F 30 A2
Floreffe B 7 B4
Florennes B 7 B4
Florensac F 30 B2
Florentin F 29 C5
Florenville B 11 B5
Flores de Avila E 44 B2
Flörsheim D 13 A4
Flühli CH 20 C3
Flumet F 26 B3
Flums CH 21 B4
Foix F 40 B2
Folelli F 62 A2
Folgosinho P 42 B2
Folgoso de la Ribera E 35 B4
Folgoso do Courel E 35 B3
Foncebadón E 35 B4
Foncine-le-Bas F 19 C5
Fondevila E 34 C2
Fonelas E 58 B1
Fonfria
*Teruel* E 46 B2
*Zamora* E 43 A3
Fontaine F 11 C4
Fontainebleau F 10 C2
Fontaine de Vaucluse F 31 B4
Fontaine-Française F 19 B4
Fontaine-le-Dun F 9 A4
Fontan F 33 A3
Fontanarejo E 51 A3
Fontane I 33 A3
Fontanières F 24 A2
Fontanosas E 51 B3
Fontenay-le-Comte F 22 B3
Fontenay-Trésigny F 10 C2
Fontevrault-l'Abbaye F 16 B2
Fontiveros E 44 B3
Fontoy F 12 B1
Fontpédrouse F 40 B3
Font-Romeu F 40 B3
Fonz E 39 B4
Forbach
D 13 C4
F 12 B2
Forcall E 47 B3
Forcalquier F 32 B1
Forcarei E 34 B2
Forges-les-Eaux F 10 B1
Forjães P 42 A1
Formazza I 27 A5
Formerie F 10 B1
Formigliana I 27 B5
Formiguères F 40 B3
Fornalutx E 60 B2
Fornells E 61 A4
Fornelos de Montes E 34 B2
Fornes E 57 B4
Forno
*Piemonte* I 27 B4
*Piemonte* I 27 B5
Forno Alpi-Gráie I 27 B4
Fornos de Algodres P 42 B2
Foros do Arrão P 48 B2
Forriolo E 34 B3
Fortanete E 47 B3
Fort-Mahon-Plage F 6 B1
Fortuna E 59 A3
Fos F 39 B4
Fossano I 33 A3
Fosse-la-Ville B 7 B4
Fos-sur-Mer F 31 B3
Fouchères F 18 A3
Fouesnant F 14 B1
Foug F 12 C1
Fougères F 15 A4
Fougerolles F 19 B5
Foulain F 19 A4
Fouras F 22 C2
Fourchambault F 18 B2
Fourmies F 11 A4
Fournels F 24 C3
Fournols F 25 B3
Fourques F 40 B3
Fourquevaux F 40 A2
Fours F 18 C2
Foz E 35 A3
Foz do Arelho P 48 B1
Foz do Giraldo P 49 B3
Frabosa Soprana I 33 A3
Frades de la Sierra E 43 B4
Fraga E 47 A4
Frailes E 57 A4
Fraire B 7 B4
Fraize F 20 A1
França P 35 C4
Francaltroff F 12 C2
Francescas F 29 B3
Franco P 42 A2
Francos E 45 A4
Frangy F 26 A2
Frankenthal D 13 B4
Frasne F 19 C5
Frasnes-lez-Anvaing B 7 B3
Frasseto F 62 B2
Frastanz A 21 B4
Fratel P 49 B3
Frauenfeld CH 21 B3
Frayssinet F 29 B4
Frayssinet-le-Gélat F 29 B4
Frechas P 43 A2
Frechilla E 36 B2
Fregenal de la Sierra E 55 A3
Freiburg D 20 B2
Freisen D 12 B3
Freixedas P 43 B2
Freixo de Espada à Cinta P 43 A3
Fréjus F 32 B2
Fresnay-sur-Sarthe F 9 B4
Fresneda de la Sierra E 46 B1
Fresneda de la Sierra Tiron E 37 B3
Fresnedillas E 45 B3
Fresnes-en-Woevre F 12 B1
Fresne-St Mamès F 19 B4
Fresno Alhandiga E 44 B2
Fresno de la Ribera E 44 A2
Fresno de la Vega E 36 B1
Fresno de Sayago E 43 A4
Fresnoy-Folny F 10 B1
Fresnoy-le-Grand F 11 B3
Fressenville F 10 A1
Fréteval F 17 B3
Fretigney F 19 B4
Freudenstadt D 13 C4
Freux B 12 B1
Frévent F 6 B2
Freyming-Merlebach F 12 B2
Frias de Albarracin E 46 B2
Fribourg CH 20 C2
Frick CH 20 B3
Friedrichshafen D 21 B4
Friesenheim D 13 C3
Frigiliana E 57 B4
Friol E 34 A3
Froges F 26 B2
Froissy F 10 B2
Frómista E 36 B2
Fronsac F 28 B2
Front I 27 B4
Fronteira P 49 B3
Frontenay-Rohan-Rohan F 22 B3
Frontignan F 30 B2
Fronton F 29 C4
Frouard F 12 C2
Fruges F 6 B2
Frutigen CH 20 C2
Fuencaliente
*Ciudad Real* E 51 A4
*Ciudad Real* E 51 B3
Fuencemillán E 45 B4
Fuendejalón E 38 C2
Fuengirola E 57 B3
Fuenlabrada E 45 B4
Fuenlabrada de los Montes E 50 A3
Fuensalida E 45 B3
Fuensanta E 58 B3
Fuensanta de Martos E 57 A4
Fuente-Alamo E 52 C2
Fuente-Álamo de Murcia E 59 B3
Fuentealbilla E 52 B2
Fuente al Olmo de Iscar E 44 A3
Fuentecén E 45 A4
Fuente Dé E 36 A2
Fuente de Cantos E 49 C4
Fuente del Arco E 50 B2
Fuente del Conde E 57 A3
Fuente del Maestre E 49 C4
Fuente de Santa Cruz E 44 A3
Fuente el Fresno E 51 A4
Fuente el Saz de Jarama E 45 B4
Fuente el Sol E 44 A3
Fuenteguinaldo E 43 B3
Fuentelapeña E 44 A2
Fuentelcésped E 45 A4
Fuentelespino de Haro E 52 B1
Fuentelespino de Moya E 52 B2
Fuentenovilla E 45 B4
Fuente Obejuna E 50 B2
Fuente Palmera E 56 A2
Fuentepelayo E 45 A3
Fuentepinilla E 45 A5
Fuenterroble de Salvatierra E 44 B2
Fuenterrobles E 52 B2
Fuentes E 52 B1
Fuentesauco E 45 A3
Fuentesaúco E 44 A2
Fuentes de Andalucía E 56 A2
Fuentes de Ebro E 47 A3
Fuentes de Jiloca E 46 A2
Fuentes de la Alcarria E 45 B5
Fuentes de León E 55 A3
Fuentes de Nava E 36 B2
Fuentes de Oñoro E 43 B3
Fuentes de Ropel E 36 B1
Fuentespalda E 47 B4
Fuentespina E 45 A4
Fuente-Tójar E 57 A3
Fuente Vaqueros E 57 A4
Fuentidueña E 45 A4
Fuentidueña de Tajo E 45 B4
Fuerte del Rey E 51 C4
Fully CH 27 A4
Fumay F 11 B4
Fumel F 29 B3
Fundão P 42 B2
Furadouro P 42 B1
Fürth D 13 B4
Furtwangen D 20 A3
Fusio CH 21 C3
Fustiñana E 38 B2


## G


Gabaldón E 52 B2
Gabarret F 28 C2
Gabriac F 30 A1
Gaby I 27 B4
Gacé F 9 B4
Gadmen CH 20 C3
Gádor E 58 C2
Gael F 15 A3
Gafanhoeira P 48 C2
Gaggenau D 13 C4
Gaillac F 29 C4
Gaillefontaine F 10 B1
Gaillon F 9 A5
Gaja-la-Selve F 40 A2
Gajanejos E 45 B5
Galan F 39 A4
Galapagar E 45 B3
Galápagos E 45 B4
Galaroza E 55 B3
Galdakao E 37 A4
Galende E 35 B4
Galera E 58 B2
Galéria F 62 A1
Galgon F 28 B2
Galinduste E 44 B2
Galisteo E 49 B4
Galizes P 42 B2
Gallardon F 10 C1
Gallegos de Argañán E 43 B3
Gallegos del Solmirón E 44 B2
Galleguillos de Campos E 36 B1
Gallocanta E 46 B2
Gallur E 38 C2
Galtür A 21 C5
Galve de Sorbe E 45 A4
Galveias P 48 B2
Gálvez E 51 A3
Gamaches F 10 B1
Gammertingen D 21 A4
Gams CH 21 B4
Gan F 39 A3
Gáname E 43 A3
Gandarela P 42 A1
Gandesa E 47 A4
Gandía E 53 C3
Ganges F 30 B2
Gannat F 24 A3
Gannay-sur-Loire F 18 C2
Gap F 32 A2
Garaballa E 52 B2
Garbayuela E 50 A2
Garciaz E 50 A2
Garcihernández E 44 B2
Garcillán E 45 B3
Garcinarro E 45 B5
Garcisobaco E 56 B2
Gardanne F 31 B4
Gardouch F 40 A2
Garein F 28 B2
Garéoult F 32 B2
Garéssio I 33 A4
Gargaligas E 50 A2
Gargallo E 47 B3
Garganta la Olla E 44 B2
Gargantiel E 50 B3
Gargellen A 21 C4
Gargilesse-Dampierre F 17 C3
Gárgoles de Abajo E 46 B1
Garlin F 28 C2
Garlitos E 50 B2
Garnat-sur-Engièvre F 18 C2
Garray E 37 C4
Garriguella E 40 B4
Garrovillas E 49 B4
Garrucha E 58 B3
Garvão P 54 B1
Gaschurn A 21 C5
Gascueña E 46 B1
Gasny F 10 B1
Gastes F 28 B1
Gata E 43 B3
Gata de Gorgos E 53 C4
Gátova E 53 B3
Gattinara I 27 B5
Gaucín E 56 B2
Gava E 41 C3
Gavarnie F 39 B3
Gavião P 48 B3
Gavray F 8 B2
Gea de Albarracin E 46 B2
Géaudot F 11 C4
Geaune F 28 C2
Gedinne B 11 B4
Gèdre F 39 B4
Geel B 7 A4
Geetbets B 7 B5
Geinsheim D 13 B4
Geisenheim D 13 B4
Geisingen D 21 B3
Geldermalsen NL 7 A5
Gelida E 41 C2
Gelsa E 47 A3
Gelterkinden CH 20 B2
Gelves E 56 A1
Gembloux B 7 B4
Gemeaux F 19 B4
Gémenos F 32 B1
Gémozac F 22 C3
Gemünden D 13 B3
Genappe B 7 B4
Génave E 58 A2
Gençay F 23 B4
Genelard F 18 C3
Geneva = Genève CH 26 A3
Genève = Geneva CH 26 A3
Genevriéres F 19 B4
Gengenbach D 13 C4
Genillé F 17 B3
Genlis F 19 B4
Gennes F 16 B1
Genola I 33 A3
Gensingen D 13 B3
Gent = Ghent B 7 A3
Gentioux F 24 B1
Geraards-bergen B 7 B3
Gérardmer F 20 A1
Gerbéviller F 12 C2
Gerena E 55 B3
Gérgal E 58 B2
Gergy F 19 C3
Gerindote E 44 C3
Germay F 12 C1
Germersheim D 13 B4
Gernika-Lumo E 37 A4
Gernsbach D 13 C4
Gernsheim D 13 B4
Gerpinnes B 7 B4
Gerri de la Sal E 41 B2
Gerzat F 24 B3
Gespunsart F 11 B4
Gesté F 15 B4
Getafe E 45 B4
Getxo E 37 A4
Gevora del Caudillo E 49 C4
Gevrey-Chambertin F 19 B3
Gex F 26 A3
Ghent = Gent B 7 A3
Ghigo I 27 C4
Ghisonaccia F 62 A2
Ghisoni F 62 A2
Giat F 24 B2
Giaveno I 27 B4
Gibraleón E 55 B3
Gibraltar GBZ 56 B2
Gien F 17 B4
Giens F 32 B2
Giffaumont-Champaubert F 11 C4
Gignac F 30 B2
Gijón = Xixón E 36 A1
Gilena E 56 A3
Gilley F 19 B5
Gilley-sur-Loire F 18 C2
Gilocourt F 10 B2
Gilze NL 7 A4
Gimont F 29 C3
Ginasservis F 32 B1
Gingelom B 7 B5
Giões P 54 B2
Giromagny F 20 B1
Girona E 41 C3
Gironcourt-sur-Vraine F 12 C1
Gironella E 41 B2
Gironville-sous-les-Côtes F 12 C1
Gisors F 10 B1
Gistel B 6 A2
Giswil CH 20 C3
Givet F 11 A4
Givors F 25 B4
Givry
B 7 B4
F 18 C3
Givry-en-Argonne F 11 C4
Gizeux F 16 B2
Gland CH 19 C5
Glarus CH 21 B4
Gletsch CH 20 C3
Glomel F 14 A2
Gloria P 48 B2
Goderville F 9 A4
Goes NL 7 A3
Goetzenbrück F 13 C3
Góglio I 27 A5
Goirle NL 7 A5
Góis P 42 B1
Goizueta E 38 A2
Goldach CH 21 B4
Goldbach D 13 A5
Golegã P 48 B2
Gómara E 46 A1
Gomaringen D 13 C5
Gomes Aires P 54 B1
Gómezserracin E 44 A3
Goncelin F 26 B2
Gondomar
E 34 B2
P 42 A1
Gondrecourt-le-Château F 12 C1
Gondrin F 28 C3
Gonfaron F 32 B2
Goñi E 38 B2
Gooik B 7 B4
Goppenstein CH 27 A4
Gor E 58 B2
Gorafe E 58 B1
Gordaliza del Pino E 36 B1
Gordoncillo E 36 B1
Gorey UK 8 A1
Gorinchem NL 7 A4
Górliz E 37 A4
Gorron F 8 B3
Gossau CH 21 B4
Götzis A 21 B4
Gouarec F 14 A2
Gourdon F 29 B4
Gourgançon F 11 C4
Gourin F 14 A2
Gournay-en-Bray F 10 B1
Gouveia P 42 B2
Gouzeacourt F 10 A3
Gouzon F 24 A2
Gozee B 7 B4
Grabs CH 21 B4
Graçay F 17 B3
Gradefes E 36 B1
Gradil P 48 C1
Grado E 35 A4
Graja de Iniesta E 52 B2
Grajera E 45 A4
Gramat F 29 B4
Granada E 57 A4
Grañas E 34 A3
Granátula de Calatrava E 51 B4
Grancey-le-Château F 19 B4
Grandas de Salime E 35 A4
Grandcamp-Maisy F 8 A2
Grand-Champ F 14 B3
Grand Couronne F 9 A5
Grand-Fougeray F 15 B4
Grândola P 54 A1
Grandpré F 11 B4
Grandrieu
B 7 B4
F 25 C3
Grandson CH 20 C1
Grandvillars F 20 B1
Grandvilliers F 10 B1
Grañén E 39 C3
Granges-de Crouhens F 39 B4
Granges-sur-Vologne F 20 A1
Granja
*Évora* P 49 C3
*Porto* P 42 A1
Granja de Moreruela E 36 C1
Granja de Torrehermosa E 50 B2
Granollers E 41 C3
Granville F 8 B2
Grasse F 32 B2
Graulhet F 29 C4
Graus E 39 B4
Grávalos E 38 B2
Gravelines F 6 A2
Gravellona Toce I 27 B5
Graveson F 31 B3
Gray F 19 B4
Grazalema E 56 B2
Grenade F 29 C4
Grenade-sur-l'Adour F 28 C2
Grenchen CH 20 B2
Grenoble F 26 B2
Gréoux-les-Bains F 32 B1
Gressoney-la-Trinité I 27 B4
Gressoney-St.-Jean I 27 B4
Grevenmacher L 12 B2
Grez-Doiceau B 7 B4
Grèzec F 29 B4
Grez-en-Bouère F 16 B1
Griesheim D 13 B4

Grignan F 31 A3
Grignols F 28 B2
Grignon F 26 B3
Grijota E 36 B2
Grimaud F 32 B2
Grimbergen B 7 B4
Grimmialp CH 20 C2
Grindelwald CH 20 C3
Griñón E 45 B4
Grisolles F 29 C4
Groix F 14 B2
Grönenbach D 21 B5
Gross-Gerau D 13 B4
Grosshöchstetten CH 20 C2
Grossostheim D 13 B5
Gross Umstadt D 13 B4
Grostenquin F 12 C2
Grove E 34 B2
Gruissan F 30 B2
Grullos E 35 A4
Grünstadt D 13 B4
Gruyères CH 20 C2
Gstaad CH 20 C2
Gsteig CH 27 A4
Guadahortuna E 57 A4
Guadalajara E 45 B4
Guadalaviar E 46 B2
Guadalcanal E 50 B2
Guadalcázar E 56 A3
Guadalix de la Sierra E 45 B4
Guadálmez E 50 B3
Guadalupe E 50 A2
Guadamur E 45 C3
Guadarrama E 45 B3
Guadiaro E 56 B2
Guadix E 58 B1
Guagno F 62 A1
Guajar-Faragüit E 57 B4
Gualchos E 57 B4
Guarda P 43 B2
Guardamar del Segura E 59 A4
Guardão P 42 B1
Guardias Viejas E 58 C2
Guardiola de Bergueda E 41 B2
Guardo E 36 B2
Guareña E 50 B1
Guaro E 56 B3
Guarromán E 51 B4
Guebwiller F 20 B2
Guéjar-Sierra E 57 A4
Guémené-Penfao F 15 B4
Guémené-sur-Scorff F 14 A2
Güeñes E 37 A3
Guer F 15 B3
Guérande F 15 B3
Guéret F 24 A1
Guérigny F 18 B2
Guesa E 38 B2
Gueugnon F 18 C3
Guia P 48 B2
Guichen F 15 B4
Guignes F 10 C2
Guijo E 50 B3
Guijo de Coria E 43 B3
Guijo de Santa Bábera E 44 B2
Guijuelo E 44 B2
Guillaumes F 32 A2
Guillena E 56 A1
Guillestre F 26 C3
Guillos F 28 B2
Guilvinec F 14 B1
Guimarães P 42 A1
Guincho P 48 C1
Guînes F 6 B1
Guingamp F 14 A2
Guipavas F 14 A1
Guiscard F 10 B3
Guiscriff F 14 A2
Guise F 11 B3
Guisona E 41 C2
Guitiriz E 34 A3
Guîtres F 28 A2
Gujan-Mestras F 28 B1
Gumiel de Hizán E 37 C3
Gundel-fingen D 20 A2
Gundelsheim D 13 B5
Gunderschoffen F 13 C3
Guntersblum D 13 B4
Guntin E 34 B3
Gurrea de Gállego E 38 B3
Guttannen CH 20 C3
Güttingen CH 21 B4
Gy F 19 B4
Gyé-sur-Seine F 18 A3
Gypsera CH 20 C2

## H

Haacht B 7 B4
Haamstede NL 7 A3
Habas F 28 C2
Habay B 12 B1
Habsheim F 20 B2
Hacinas E 37 C3
Hagenbach D 13 B4
Hagetmau F 28 C2
Hagondange F 12 B2
Haguenau F 13 C3
Haigerloch D 13 C4
Halle B 7 B4
Halluin F 6 B3
Ham F 10 B3
Hambach F 12 B3
Hamme B 7 A4
Hannut B 7 B5
Hardelot Plage F 6 B1
Hardt D 20 A3
Harfleur F 9 A4
Hargicourt F 10 B3
Hargnies F 11 A4
Haro E 37 B4
Haroué F 12 C2
Hartennes F 10 B3
Haslach D 20 A3
Hasparren F 38 A2
Hasselt B 7 B5
Hassloch D 13 B4
Hastière-Lavaux B 7 B4
Hatten F 13 C3
Hattstatt F 20 A2
Haudainville F 12 B1
Hausach D 20 A3
Hautefort F 29 A4
Hauterives F 25 B5
Hauteville-Lompnès F 26 B2
Haut-Fays B 11 A5
Hautmont F 7 B3
Hautrage B 7 B3
Havelange B 7 B5
Hayange F 12 B2
Hazebrouck F 6 B2
Héas F 39 B4
Hechingen D 13 C4
Hecho E 38 B3
Hechtel B 7 A5
Hédé F 15 A4
Heidelberg D 13 B4
Heilbronn D 13 B5
Heinerscheid L 12 A2
Heist-op-den-Berg B 7 A4
Helchteren B 7 A5
Helechosa E 50 A3
Hellevoetsluis NL 7 A4
Hellín E 52 C2
Héming F 12 C2
Hendaye F 38 A2
Hénin-Beaumont F 6 B2
Hennebont F 14 B2
Henrichemont F 17 B4
Heppenheim D 13 B4
Herbault F 17 B3
Herbeumont B 11 B5
Herbignac F 15 B3
Herbisse F 11 C4
Herbitzheim F 12 B3
Herbolzheim D 20 A2
Herencia E 51 A4
Herent B 7 B4
Herentals B 7 A4
Hérépian F 30 B2
Herguijuela E 50 A2
Héric F 15 B4
Héricourt F 20 B1
Héricourt-en-Caux F 9 A4
Hérimoncourt F 20 B1
Herisau CH 21 B4
Hérisson F 17 C4
Herk-de-Stad B 7 B5
Herment F 24 B2
Hermeskeil D 12 B2
Hermisende E 35 C4
Hermonville F 11 B3
Hernani E 38 A2
Hernansancho E 44 B3
Herramelluri E 37 B3
Herrenberg D 13 C4
Herrera E 56 A3
Herrera de Alcántara E 49 B3
Herrera del Duque E 50 A2
Herrera de los Navarros E 46 A2
Herrera de Pisuerga E 36 B2
Herreros del Suso E 44 B2
Herrlisheim F 13 C3
Herselt B 7 A4
Hervás E 43 B4
Herxheim D 13 B4
Herzogenbuchsee CH 20 B2
Hesdin F 6 B2
Hettange-Grande F 12 B2
Heuchin F 6 B2
Heudicourt-sous-les-Côtes F 12 C1
Heunezel F 19 A5
Heuqueville F 9 A4
Hiendelaencina E 45 A5
Hiersac F 23 C4
Higuera de Arjona E 51 C4
Higuera de Calatrava E 57 A3
Higuera de la Serena E 50 B2
Higuera de la Sierra E 55 B3
Higuera de Vargas E 49 C4
Higuera la Real E 55 A3
Higuers de Llerena E 50 B1
Higueruela E 52 C2
Híjar E 47 A3
Hilvarenbeek NL 7 A5
Hindelbank CH 20 B2
Hinjosa del Valle E 50 B1
Hinojal E 49 B4
Hinojales E 55 B3
Hinojos E 55 B3
Hinojosa del Duque E 50 B2
Hinojosas de Calatrava E 51 B3
Hinterweidenthal D 13 B3
Hinwil CH 21 B3
Hirschhorn D 13 B4
Hirsingue F 20 B2
Hirson F 11 B4
Hittisau A 21 B4
Hobscheid L 12 B1
Hochdorf CH 20 B3
Hochfelden F 13 C3
Hochspeyer D 13 B3
Höchst im Odenwald D 13 B5
Hockenheim D 13 B4
Hoedekenskerke NL 7 A3
Hoegaarden B 7 B4
Hoek van Holland NL 7 A4
Hofheim D 13 A4
Hohenems A 21 B4
Hohentengen D 20 B3
Holguera E 49 B4
Homburg D 13 B3
Hondarribia E 38 A2
Hondón de los Frailes E 59 A4
Hondschoote F 6 B2
Honfleur F 9 A4
Honrubia E 52 B1
Hontalbilla E 45 A3
Hontheim D 12 A2
Hontoria de la Cantera E 37 B3
Hontoria del Pinar E 37 C3
Hontoria de Valdearados E 37 C3
Hoogerheide NL 7 A4
Hoogstraten B 7 A4
Horb am Neckar D 13 C4
Horcajada de la Torre E 52 A1
Horcajo de los Montes E 50 A3
Horcajo de Santiago E 45 C4
Horcajo-Medianero E 44 B2
Horche E 45 B4
Horgen CH 21 B3
Horna E 52 C2
Hornachos E 50 B1
Hornachuelos E 56 A2
Hornberg D 20 A3
Hornos E 58 A2
Hornoy-le-Bourg F 10 B1
Horta P 42 A2
Hortezuela E 45 A5
Hortiguela E 37 B3
Hösbach D 13 A5
Hosingen L 12 A2
Hospental CH 21 C3
Hossegor F 28 C1
Hostal de Ipiés E 39 B3
Hostalric E 41 C3
Hostens F 28 B2
Hotton B 7 B5
Houdain F 6 B2
Houdan F 10 C1
Houdelaincourt F 12 C1
Houeillès F 28 B3
Houffalize B 12 A1
Houlgate F 9 A3
Hourtin F 28 A1
Hourtin-Plage F 28 A1
Houthalen B 7 A5
Houyet B 7 B4
Hoya de Santa Maria E 55 B3
Hoya-Gonzalo E 52 C2
Hoyocasero E 44 B3
Hoyo de Manzanares E 45 B4
Hoyo de Pinares E 44 B3
Hoyos E 43 B3
Hoyos del Espino E 44 B2
Hucqueliers F 6 B1
Huélago E 57 A4
Huélamo E 46 B2
Huelgoat F 14 A2
Huelma E 57 A4
Huelva E 55 B3
Huéneja E 58 B2
Huércal de Almeria E 58 C2
Huércal-Overa E 58 B3
Huerta de Abajo E 37 B3
Huerta del Rey E 37 C3
Huerta de Valdecarabanos E 45 C4
Huertahernando E 46 B1
Huesa E 58 B1
Huesca E 39 B3
Huéscar E 58 B2
Huete E 45 B5
Huétor Tájar E 57 A3
Hüfingen D 20 B3
Hulst NL 7 A4
Humanes E 45 B4
Humilladero E 57 A3
Hürbel D 21 A4
Huttwil CH 20 B2
Huy B 7 B5
Hyères F 32 B2
Hyères Plage F 32 B2

## I

Ibahernando E 50 A2
Ibarranguelua E 37 A4
Ibeas de Juarros E 37 B3
Ibi E 53 C3
Ibiza = Eivissa E 60 C1
Ibros E 51 B4
Ichtegem B 6 A3
Idanha-a-Novo P 49 B3
Idar-Oberstein D 13 B3
Idiazábal E 38 B1
Ieper = Ypres B 6 B2
Igea E 38 B1
Iglesias E 37 B3
Igny-Comblizy F 11 B3
Igorre E 37 A4
Igries E 39 B3
Igualada E 41 C2
Igüeña E 35 B4
Iguerande F 25 A4
Ihringen D 20 A2
IJzendijke NL 7 A3
Ilanz CH 21 C4
Ilche E 39 C4
Ílhavo P 42 B1
Illana E 45 B5
Illano E 35 A4
Illar E 58 C2
Illas E 35 A5
Illats F 28 B2
Illescas E 45 B4
Ille-sur-Têt F 40 B3
Illfurth F 20 B2
Illiers-Combray F 9 B5
Illkirch-Graffenstaden F 13 C3
Íllora E 57 A4
Illueca E 46 A2
Immenstadt D 21 B5
Imon E 45 A5
Impéria I 33 B4
Imphy F 18 C2
Inca E 61 B2
Incinillas E 37 B3
Inerthal CH 21 B3
Infiesto E 36 A1
Ingelheim D 13 B4
Ingelmunster B 6 B3
Ingrandes
*Maine-et-Loire* F 15 B5
*Vienne* F 16 C2
Ingwiller F 13 C3
Iniesta E 52 B2
Innertkirchen CH 20 C3
Ins CH 20 B2
Interlaken CH 20 C2
Irrel D 12 B2
Iruela E 35 B4
Irún E 38 A2
Irurita E 38 A2
Irurzun E 38 B2
Isaba E 38 B3
Isabela E 51 B4
Iscar E 44 A3
Ischgl A 21 B5
Isdes F 17 B4
Iselle I 27 A5
Iseltwald CH 20 C2
Isigny-sur-Mer F 8 A2
Isla Canela E 55 B2
Isla Cristina E 55 B2
Islares E 37 A3
Isna P 48 B3
Isny D 21 B5
Isoba E 36 A1
Isola F 32 A3
Isola d'Asti I 27 C5
Isona E 41 B2
Ispagnac F 30 A2
Issigeac F 29 B3
Issogne I 27 B4
Issoire F 24 B3
Issoncourt F 11 C5
Issoudun F 17 C4
Is-sur-Tille F 19 B4
Issy-l'Evêque F 18 C2
Istán E 56 B3
Istres F 31 B3
Itoiz E 38 B2
Itrabo E 57 B4
Ivoz Ramet B 7 B5
Ivrea I 27 B4
Ivry-en-Montagne F 18 B3
Ivry-la-Bataille F 10 C1
Iwuy F 6 B3
Izarra E 37 B4
Izeda P 43 A3
Izegem B 6 B3
Izernore F 26 A2
Iznájar E 57 A3
Iznalloz E 57 A4
Iznatoraf E 58 A1

## J

Jabalquinto E 51 B4
Jabugo E 55 B3
Jaca E 39 B3
Jadraque E 45 B5
Jaén E 57 A4
Jalance E 53 B2
Jaligny-sur-Besbre F 25 A3
Jallais F 16 B1
Jalón E 53 C3
Jâlons F 11 C4
Jamilena E 57 A4
Jamoigne B 12 B1
Janville F 17 A3
Janzé F 15 B4
Jarafuel E 53 B2
Jaraicejo E 50 A2
Jaraíz de la Vera E 44 B2
Jarandilla de la Vera E 44 B2
Jaray E 46 A1
Jard-sur-Mer F 22 B2
Jargeau F 17 B4
Jarnac F 23 C3
Jarny F 12 B1
Jarzé F 16 B1
Jasseron F 26 A2
Játar E 57 B4
Jaun CH 20 C2
Jausiers F 32 A2
Jávea E 53 C4
Javerlhac F 23 C4
Javier E 38 B2
Javron F 9 B3
Jayena E 57 B4
Jegun F 29 C3
Jenaz CH 21 C4
Jeres del Marquesado E 58 B1
Jerez de la Frontera E 56 B1
Jerez de los Caballeros E 49 C4
Jerica E 53 B3
Jerte E 44 B2
Jeumont F 7 B4
Jijona E 53 C3
Jimena E 57 A4
Jimena de la Frontera E 56 B2
Jimera de Libar E 56 B2
João da Loura P 48 C2
Jódar E 57 A4
Jodoigne B 7 B4
Joeuf F 12 B1
Joigny F 18 B2
Joinville F 11 C5
Jonchery-sur-Vesle F 11 B3
Jonzac F 22 C3
Jorba E 41 C2
Jorquera E 52 B2
Josselin F 15 B3
Jou P 42 A2
Jouarre F 10 C3
Joué-lès-Tours F 16 B2
Joué-sur-Erdre F 15 B4
Joux-la-Ville F 18 B2
Jouy F 10 C1
Jouy-le-Châtel F 10 C3
Jouy-le-Potier F 17 B3
Joyeuse F 31 A3
Joze F 24 B3
Juan-les-Pins F 32 B3
Jubera E 38 B1
Jubrique E 56 B2
Jugon-les-Lacs F 15 A3
Juillac F 29 A4
Juillan F 39 A4
Jullouville F 8 B2
Jumeaux F 25 B3
Jumièges F 9 A4
Jumilhac-le-Grand F 23 C5
Jumilla E 53 C2
Juncosa E 47 A4
Juneda E 41 C1
Jungingen D 13 C5
Junglingster L 12 B2
Juniville F 11 B4
Junqueira P 43 A2
Juromenha P 49 C3
Jussac F 24 C2
Jussey F 19 B4
Jussy F 10 B3
Juvigny-le-Terte F 8 B2
Juvigny-sous-Andaine F 9 B3
Juzennecourt F 19 A3

## K

Kaatscheuvel NL 7 A5
Kahl D 13 A5
Kaiserslautern D 13 B3
Kalmthout B 7 A4
Kaltbrunn CH 21 B4
Kandel D 13 B4
Kandern D 20 B2
Kandersteg CH 20 C2
Kapellen B 7 A4
Kappel D 13 C3
Kappl A 21 B5
Karlsruhe D 13 B4
Kastellaun D 13 A3
Kasterlee B 7 A4
Kaub D 13 A3
Kaysersberg F 20 A2
Keerbergen B 7 A4
Kehl D 13 C3
Kell D 12 B2
Kelsterbach D 13 A4
Kempten D 21 B5
Kemptthal CH 21 B3
Kenzingen D 20 A2
Kérien F 14 A2
Kerlouan F 14 A1
Kernascléden F 14 A2
Kerns CH 20 C3
Kerzers CH 20 C2
Kimratshofen D 21 B5
Kirchberg
CH 20 B2
*Rheinland-Pfalz* D 13 B3
Kirchheimbolanden D 13 B4
Kirchzarten D 20 B2
Kirn D 13 B3
Kisslegg D 21 B4
Klingenberg D 13 B5
Klingenmunster D 13 B4
Kloosterzande NL 7 A4
Klösterle A 21 B5
Klosters CH 21 C4
Kloten CH 21 B3
Kluisbergen B 7 B3
Klundert NL 7 A4
Knesselare B 6 A3
Knokke-Heist B 6 A3
Koblenz CH 20 B3
Koekelare B 6 A2
Koksijde B 6 A2
Köniz CH 20 C2
Konstanz D 21 B4
Kontich B 7 A4
Konz D 12 B2
Kopstal L 12 B2
Kortrijk B 6 B3
Kressbronn D 21 B4
Kreuzlingen CH 21 B4
Kriegsfeld D 13 B3
Kriens CH 20 B3
Krimpen aan de IJssel NL 7 A4
Kruishoutem B 7 B3
Küblis CH 21 C4
Kuppenheim D 13 C4
Kusel D 13 B3
Küsnacht CH 20 B3
Küttingen CH 20 B3
Kyllburg D 12 A2

## L

La Adrada E 44 B3
La Alameda E 51 B4
La Alberca E 43 B3
La Alberca de Záncara E 52 B1
La Albergueria de Argañán E 43 B3
La Albuera E 49 C4
La Aldea del Portillo del Busto E 37 B3
La Algaba E 56 A1
La Aliseda de Tormes E 44 B2
La Almarcha E 52 B1
La Almolda E 47 A3
La Almunia de Doña Godina E 46 A2
La Antillas E 55 B2
La Arena E 35 A4
La Aulaga E 55 B3
La Balme-de-Sillingy F 26 B3
La Bañeza E 35 B5
La Barca de la Florida E 56 B2
La Barre-de-Monts F 22 B1
La Barre-en-Ouche F 9 B4
La Barrosa E 56 B1
La Barthe-de-Neste F 39 A4
La Bassée F 6 B2
La Bastide-de-Sèrou F 40 A2
La Bastide-des-Jourdans F 32 B1
Labastide-Murat F 29 B4
La Bastide-Puylaurent F 25 C3
Labastide-Rouairoux F 30 B1
Labastide-St Pierre F 29 C4
La Bathie F 26 B3
La Baule-Escoublac F 15 B3
La Bazoche-Gouet F 16 A2
La Bégude-de-Mazenc F 31 A3
Labenne F 28 C1
La Bernerie-en-Retz F 22 A1
La Bisbal d'Empordà E 41 C4
Lablachère F 31 A3
La Boissière F 9 A4
Labouheyre F 28 B2
La Bourboule F 24 B2
La Bóveda de Toro E 44 A2
La Brède F 28 B2
La Bresse F 20 A1
La Bridoire F 26 B2
La Brillanne F 32 B1
Labrit F 28 B2
Labros E 46 A2
La Bruffière F 22 A2
Labruguière F 30 B1
Labrujo P 42 A1
L'Absie F 22 B3
La Bussière F 17 B4
La Caillère F 22 B3
Lacalahorra E 58 B1
La Calmette F 31 B3
La Calzada de Oropesa E 44 C2
La Campana E 56 A2
La Cañada E 44 B3
Lacanau F 28 B1
Lacanau-Océan F 28 A1
Lacanche F 18 B3
La Canourgue F 30 A2
La Capelle F 11 B3
Lacapelle-Marival F 29 B4
La Cardanchosa E 50 B2
La Caridad E 35 A4
La Carlota E 56 A3
La Carolina E 51 B4
Lacaune F 30 B1
La Cava E 47 B4
La Cavalerie F 30 A2
La Celle-en-Moravan F 18 B3
La Celle-St Avant F 16 B2
La Cerca E 37 B3
La Chaise-Dieu F 25 B3
La Chaize-Giraud F 22 B2
La Chaize-le-Vicomte F 22 B2
La Chambre F 26 B3
La Chapelaude F 24 A2
La Chapelle-d'Angillon F 17 B4
La Chapelle-en-Aalgaudémar F 26 C3
La Chapelle-en-Vercors F 26 C2
La Chapelle-Glain F 15 B4
La Chapelle-la-Reine F 10 C2
La Chapelle-Laurent F 24 B3
La Chapelle-St Luc F 11 C4
La Chapelle-sur-Erdre F 15 B4
La Chapelle-Vicomtesse F 17 B3
La Charce F 32 A1
La Charité-sur-Loire F 18 B2
La Chartre-sur-le-Loir F 16 B2
La Châtaigneraie F 22 B3
La Châtre F 17 C3
La Chaussée-sur-Marne F 11 C4
La Chaux-de-Fonds CH 20 B1
Lachen CH 21 B3
La Cheppe F 11 B4
La Chèze F 15 A3
La Ciotat F 32 B1
La Clayette F 25 A4
La Clusaz F 26 B3
La Codosera E 49 B3
La Concha E 37 A3
La Condamine-Châtelard F 32 A2
La Contienda E 55 A3
La Coquille F 23 C4
La Coronada E 50 B2
La Côte-St André F 26 B2
La Cotinière F 22 C2
La Courtine F 24 B2
Lacq F 39 A3
La Crau F 32 B2
La Crèche F 23 B3
La Croix F 16 B2
Lacroix-Barrez F 24 C2
Lacroix-St Ouen F 10 B2
Lacroix-sur-Meuse F 12 C1
La Croix-Valmer F 32 B2
La Cumbre E 50 A2
Ladignac-le-Long F 23 C5
Ladoeiro P 49 B3
Ladon F 17 B4
La Douze F 29 A3
La Espina E 35 A4
La Estrella E 50 A2
La Farga de Moles E 40 B2
La Fatarella E 47 A4
La Felipa E 52 B2
La Fère F 10 B3
La Ferrière
*Indre-et-Loire* F 16 B2
*Vendée* F 22 B2
La Ferrière-en-Parthenay F 23 B3
La-Ferté-Alais F 10 C2
La Ferté-Bernard F 16 A2
La Ferté-Frênel F 9 B4
La Ferté-Gaucher F 10 C3
La Ferté-Imbault F 17 B3
La Ferté-Macé F 9 B3
La Ferté-Milon F 10 B3
La Ferté-sous-Jouarre F 10 C3
La Ferté-St-Aubin F 17 B3
La Ferté-St-Cyr F 17 B3
La Ferté-Vidame F 9 B4
La Ferté Villeneuil F 17 B3
La Feuillie F 10 B1
La Flèche F 16 B1
La Flotte F 22 B2
La Font de la Figuera E 53 C3
La Fouillade F 30 A1
Lafrançaise F 29 B4
La Fregeneda E 43 B3
La Fresneda E 47 B4
La Fuencubierta E 56 A3
La Fuente de San Esteban E 43 B3
La Fulioala E 41 C2
La Gacilly F 15 B3
La Galera E 47 B4
Lagarde F 40 A2
La Garde-Freinet F 32 B2
Lagares
*Coimbra* P 42 B2
*Porto* P 42 A1
La Garnache F 22 B2
La Garriga E 41 C3
La Garrovilla E 49 C4
Lagartera E 44 C2
La Gaubretière F 22 B2
La Gineta E 52 B1
Lagnieu F 26 B2
Lagny-sur-Marne F 10 C2
Lagôa P 54 B1
Lagoaça P 43 A3
Lagos P 54 B1
La Granadella
*Alicante* E 53 C4
*Lleida* E 47 A4
La Grand-Combe F 31 A3
La Grand-Croix F 25 B4
La Grande-Motte F 31 B3
La Granja d'Escarp E 47 A4
La Granjuela E 50 B2
Lagrasse F 40 A3
La Grave F 26 B3
La Gravelle F 15 A4
Laguardia E 37 B4

La Guardia E 45 C4
La Guardia de Jaén E 57 A4
Laguarres E 39 B4
Laguenne F 24 B1
Laguépie F 29 B4
La Guerche-de-Bretagne F 15 B4
La Guerche-sur-l'Aubois F 18 C1
La Guérinière F 22 B1
Laguiole F 24 C2
Laguna de Duera E 44 A3
Laguna del Marquesado E 46 B2
Laguna de Negrillos E 36 B1
Lagunilla E 43 B3
La Haba E 50 B2
Laharie F 28 B1
La Haye-du-Puits F 8 A2
La Haye-Pesnel F 8 B2
La Herlière F 6 B2
La Hermida E 36 A2
La Herrera E 52 C1
Laheycourt F 11 C5
La Higuera E 52 C2
La Hiniesta E 43 A4
La Horcajada E 44 B2
La Horra E 37 C3
Lahr D 13 C3
La Hulpe B 7 B4
La Hutte F 9 B4
L'Aigle F 9 B4
La Iglesuela E 44 B3
La Iglesuela del Cid E 47 B3
Laignes F 18 B3
Laiguéglia I 33 B4
L'Aiguillon-sur-Mer F 22 B2
Laina E 46 A1
La Iruela E 58 B2
Laissac F 30 A1
La Javie F 32 A2
La Jonchère-St Maurice F 24 A1
La Jonquera E 40 B3
La Lantejuela E 56 A2
L'Albagès E 47 A4
Lalbenque F 29 B4
L'Alcudia E 53 B3
L'Aldea E 47 B4
Lalín E 34 B2
Lalinde F 29 B3
La Línea de la Concepción E 56 B2
Lalizolle F 24 A3
La Llacuna E 41 C2
Lalley F 26 C2
La Londe-les-Maures F 32 B2
La Loupe F 9 B5
La Louvière B 7 B4
L'Alpe-d'Huez F 26 B3
La Luisiana E 56 A2
Laluque F 28 C1
La Machine F 18 C2
Lamadrid E 36 A2
Lamagistère F 29 B3
La Mailleraye-sur-Seine F 9 A4
La Malène F 30 A2
La Mamola E 57 B4
La Manresana dels Prats E 41 C2
Lamarche F 19 A4
Lamarche-sur-Saône F 19 B4
Lamargelle F 19 B3
Lamarosa P 48 B2
Lamarque F 28 A2
Lamas P 42 B1
La Masadera E 39 C3
Lamas de Moaro P 34 B2
Lamastre F 25 C4
La Mata E 44 C3
La Mata de Ledesma E 43 A4
La Mata de Monteagudo E 36 B1
Lamballe F 15 A3
Lambesc F 31 B4
Lamego P 42 A2
La Meilleraye-de-Bretagne F 15 B4
La Ménitré F 16 B1
L'Ametlla de Mar E 47 B4
La Mojonera E 58 C2
La Mole F 32 B2
La Molina E 41 B2
La Monnerie-le-Montel F 25 B3
La Morera E 49 C4
La Mothe-Achard F 22 B2
Lamothe-Cassel F 29 B4
Lamothe-Montravel F 28 B3
La Mothe-St Héray F 23 B3
Lamotte-Beuvron F 17 B4
La Motte-Chalançon F 31 A4
La Motte-du-Caire F 32 A2
La Motte-Servolex F 26 B2
Lampertheim D 13 B4
L'Ampolla E 47 B4
La Mudarra E 36 C2
La Muela E 46 A2
La Mure F 26 C2
Lamure-sur-Azergues F 25 A4
Lanaja E 39 C3
Lanarce F 25 C3
La Nava E 55 B3
La Nava de Ricomalillo E 50 A3
La Nava de Santiago E 49 B4
Lançon-Provence F 31 B4
Landau D 13 B4
Landen B 7 B5
Landerneau F 14 A1
Landete E 52 B2
Landévant F 14 B2
Landévennec F 14 A1
Landivisiau F 14 A1
Landivy F 8 B2
Landos F 25 C3
Landouzy-la-Ville F 11 B4
Landquart CH 21 C4
Landrecies F 11 A3
Landreville F 18 A3
Landscheid D 12 B2
Landstuhl D 13 B3
Lanester F 14 B2
Lanestosa E 37 A3
La Neuve-Lyre F 9 B4
La Neuveville CH 20 B2
Langa de Duero E 45 A4
Langeac F 25 B3
Langeais F 16 B2
Langemark-Poelkapelle B 6 B2
Langen D 13 B4
Langenbruck CH 20 B2
Langenlonsheim D 13 B3
Langenthal CH 20 B2
Langnau CH 20 C2
Langogne F 25 C3
Langon F 28 B2
Langreo E 36 A1
Langres F 19 B4
Langueux F 15 A3
Languidic F 14 B2
Langwies CH 21 C4
Lanheses P 42 A1
Lanildut F 14 A1
Lanjarón E 57 B4
Lanmeur F 14 A2
Lannéanou F 14 A2
Lannemezan F 39 A4
Lanneuville-sur-Meuse F 11 B5
Lannilis F 14 A1
Lannion F 14 A2
La Nocle-Maulaix F 18 C2
Lanouaille F 23 C5
Lanslebourg-Mont-Cenis F 27 B3
Lanta F 29 C4
Lantadilla E 36 B2
Lanton F 28 B1
Lantosque F 33 B3
La Nuez de Arriba E 37 B3
Lanvollon F 14 A3
Lanza E 34 A2
Lanzada E 34 B2
Lanzahita E 44 B3
Lanzo Torinese I 27 B4
Laon F 11 B3
Laons F 9 B5
La Paca E 58 B3
La Pacaudière F 25 A3
Lapalisse F 25 A3
La Palma d'Ebre E 47 A4
La Palma del Condado E 55 B3
La Palme F 40 B4
La Palmyre F 22 C2
La Parra E 49 C4
La Pedraja de Portillo E 44 A3
La Peraleja E 46 B1
La Petit-Pierre F 13 C3
Lapeyrade F 28 B2
Lapeyrouse F 24 A2
La Pinilla E 59 B3
La Plagne F 26 B3
La Plaza E 35 A4
Laplume F 29 B3
La Pobla de Lillet E 41 B2
La Pobla de Vallbona E 53 B3
La Pobla Llarga E 53 B3
La Pola de Gordón E 36 B1
la Porta F 62 A2
La Pouëze F 16 B1
Lapoutroie F 20 A2
La Póveda de Soria E 37 B4
La Preste F 40 B3
La Primaube F 30 A1
La Puebla de Almoradie E 51 A4
La Puebla de Cazalla E 56 A2
La Puebla de los Infantes E 56 A2
La Puebla del Río E 56 A1
La Puebla de Montalbán E 44 C3
La Puebla de Roda E 39 B4
La Puebla de Valdavia E 36 B2
La Puebla de Valverde E 46 B3
La Pueblanueva E 44 C3
La Puerta de Segura E 58 A2
La Punt CH 21 C4
La Quintana E 56 A3
La Quintera E 56 A2
La Rábita
*Granada* E 58 C1
*Jaén* E 57 A3
Laracha E 34 A2
Laragne-Montéglin F 32 A1
La Rambla E 57 A3
l'Arboç E 41 C2
L'Arbresle F 25 B4
Larceveau F 38 A2
Larche
*Alpes-de-Haute-Provence* F 32 A2
*Corrèze* F 29 A4
Lardosa P 49 B3
Laredo E 37 A3
La Redondela E 55 B2
La Réole F 28 B2
Largentière F 31 A3
L'Argentière-la-Bessée F 26 C3
La Riera E 35 A4
La Riera de Gaià E 41 C2
La Rinconada E 56 A1
Lariño E 34 B1
La Rivière-Thibouville F 9 A4
Larmor-Plage F 14 B2
La Robla E 36 B1
La Roca de la Sierra E 49 B4
La Roche CH 20 C2
La Rochebeaucourtet-Argentine F 23 C4
La Roche-Bernard F 15 B3
La Roche-Canillac F 24 B1
La Roche-Chalais F 28 A3
La Roche Derrien F 14 A2
La Roche-des-Arnauds F 32 A1
La Roche-en-Brénil F 18 B3
La Rochefoucauld F 23 C4
La Roche-Guyon F 10 B1
La Rochelle F 22 B2
La Roche-Posay F 23 B4
La Roche-sur-Foron F 26 A3
La Roche-sur-Yon F 22 B2
Larochette L 12 B2
La Rochette F 31 A4
La Roda
*Albacete* E 52 B1
*Oviedo* E 35 A4
La Roda de Andalucía E 56 A3
Laroquebrou F 24 C2
La Roquebrussanne F 32 B1
Laroque d'Olmes F 40 B2
La Roque-Gageac F 29 B4
La Roque-Ste Marguerite F 30 A2
Laroque-Timbaut F 29 B3
Larouco E 35 B3
Larraga E 38 B2
Larrau F 38 A3
Larrazet F 29 C4
La Rubia E 37 C4
Laruns F 39 A3
Larva E 58 B1
La Sagrada E 43 B3
La Salceda E 45 A4
Lasalle F 31 A2
La Salle F 26 C3
La Salvetat-Peyralés F 30 A1
La Salvetat-sur-Agout F 30 B1
Las Arenas E 36 A2
La Sarraz CH 19 C5
Lasarte E 38 A1
Las Cabezadas E 45 A4
Las Cabezas de San Juan E 56 B2
Las Correderas E 51 B4
Las Cuevas de Cañart E 47 B3
La Seca E 44 A3
La Selva del Camp E 41 C2
La Senia E 47 B4
La Serra E 41 C2
La Seu d'Urgell E 40 B2
La Seyne-sur-Mer F 32 B1
Las Gabias E 57 A4
Las Herencias E 44 C3
Las Herrerias E 55 B2
Las Labores E 51 A4
Las Mesas E 52 B1
Las Minas E 58 A3
Las Navas E 57 A3
Las Navas de la Concepción E 50 C2
Las Navas del Marqués E 44 B3
Las Navillas E 51 A3
Las Negras E 58 C3
La Solana E 51 B4
La Souterraine F 24 A1
Las Pajanosas E 55 B3
Laspaules E 39 B4
Las Pedroñas E 52 B1
Las Planes d'Hostoles E 41 B3
Laspuña E 39 B4
Las Rozas
*Cantabria* E 36 B2
*Madrid* E 44 B3
Lassay-les-Châteaux F 9 B3
Lasseube F 39 A3
Lassigny F 10 B2
Lastras de Cuéllar E 45 A3
Las Uces E 43 A3
La Suze-sur-Sarthe F 16 B2
Las Veguillas E 43 B4
Las Ventas con Peña Aguilera E 51 A3
Las Ventas de San Julián E 44 B2
Las Villes E 47 B4
Latasa E 38 B2
La Teste F 28 B1
La Thuile I 27 B3
La Toba E 46 B2
La Toledana E 51 A3
La Torre de Cabdella E 40 B1
La Torre de Esteban Hambrán E 45 B3
La Torre del l'Espanyol E 47 A4
La Torresaviñán E 46 B1
La Tour d'Aigues F 32 B1
La Tour de Peilz CH 20 C1
La Tour-du-Pin F 26 B2
La Tranche-sur-Mer F 22 B2
La Tremblade F 22 C2
La Trimouille F 23 B5
La Trinité F 14 B2
La Trinité-Porhoët F 15 A3
Latronquière F 24 C2
Latterbach CH 20 C2
La Turballe F 15 B3
Laubert F 25 C3
Laufen CH 20 B2
Lauffen D 13 B5
Laujar de Andarax E 58 C2
La Uña E 36 A1
La Unión E 59 B4
Launois-sur-Vence F 11 B4
Laurière F 24 A1
Lausanne CH 20 C1
Laussonne F 25 C4
Lauterach A 21 B4
Lauterbrunnen CH 20 C2
Lauterecken D 13 B3
Lautrec F 30 B1
Lauzerte F 29 B4
Lauzès F 29 B4
Lauzun F 29 B3
Laval F 16 A1
La Vall d'Uixó E 53 B3
Lavardac F 29 B3
Lavaris P 42 B1
Lavau F 18 B1
Lavaur F 29 C4
La Vecilla de Curueño E 36 B1
La Vega
*Asturias* E 35 A5
*Asturias* E 36 A1
*Cantabria* E 36 A2
Lavelanet F 40 B2
La Velilla E 45 A4
La Velles E 44 A2
La Ventosa E 46 B1
La Victoria E 56 A3
La Vid E 45 A4
La Vilavella E 53 B3
La Vilella Baixa E 41 C1
La Villa de Don Fadrique E 51 A4
Lavilledieu F 31 A3
La Villedieu F 23 B3
La Ville Dieu-du-Temple F 29 B4
Lavit F 29 C3
Lavoncourt F 19 B4
Lavos P 42 B1
La Voulte-sur-Rhône F 25 C4
Lavoûte-Chilhac F 25 B3
Lavradio P 48 C1
Lavre P 48 C2
La Wantzenau F 13 C3
Laxe E 34 A2
La Yesa E 53 B3
Laza E 35 B3
Lazkao E 38 A1
La Zubia E 57 A4
Lebach D 12 B2
Le Barcarès F 40 B4
Le Barp F 28 B2
Le Bar-sur-Loup F 32 B2
Le Béage F 25 C4
Le Beausset F 32 B1
Lebekke B 7 A4
Le Bessat F 25 B4
Le Blanc F 23 B5
Le Bleymard F 30 A2
Leboreiro E 34 B3
Le Boullay-Mivoye F 9 B5
Le Boulou F 40 B3
Le Bourg F 29 B4
Le Bourg-d'Oisans F 26 B3
Le Bourget-du-Lac F 26 B2
Le Bourgneuf-la-Forêt F 15 A5
Le Bousquet d'Orb F 30 B2
Le Brassus CH 19 C5
Le Breuil F 25 A3
Le Breuil-en-Auge F 9 A4
Lebrija E 56 B1
Le Brusquet F 32 A2
Le Bry CH 20 C2
Le Bugue F 29 B3
Le Buisson F 29 B3
Leca da Palmeira P 42 A1
Le Caloy F 28 C2
Le Cap d'Agde F 30 B2
Le Cateau Cambrésis F 11 A3
Le Caylar F 30 B2
Le Cayrol F 24 C2
Lécera E 47 A3
Lech A 21 B5
Le Chambon-Feugerolles F 25 B4
Le Chambon-sur-Lignon F 25 B4
Le Château d'Oléron F 22 C2
Le Châtelard F 26 B3
Le Châtelet F 17 C4
Le Chatelet-en-Brie F 10 C2
Le Chesne F 11 B4
Le Cheylard F 25 C4
Leciñena E 39 C3
Le Collet-de-Deze F 31 A2
Le Conquet F 14 A1
Le Creusot F 18 C3
Le Croisic F 15 B3
Le Crotoy F 6 B1
Lectoure F 29 C3
Ledaña E 52 B2
Lede B 7 B3
Le Deschaux F 19 C4
Ledesma E 43 A3
Lédignan F 31 B3
Lédigos E 36 B2
Le Donjon F 25 A3
Le Dorat F 23 B5
Leerdam NL 7 A5
Le Faou F 14 A1
Le Faoüet F 14 A2
Le Folgoet F 14 A1
Le Fossat F 40 A2
Le Fousseret F 40 A2
Le Fugeret F 32 A2
Leganés E 45 B4
Legau D 21 B5
Le Gault-Soigny F 11 C3
Legé F 22 B2
Lège-Cap-Ferret F 28 B1
Léglise B 12 B1
Le Grand-Bornand F 26 B3
Le-Grand-Bourg F 24 A1
Le-Grand-Lucé F 16 B2
Le Grand-Pressigny F 16 C2
Le Grand-Quevilly F 9 A5
Le Grau-du-Roi F 31 B3
Léguevin F 29 C4
Legutiano E 37 B4
Le Havre F 9 A4
Le Hohwald F 13 C3
Le Houga F 28 C2
Leignon B 7 B5
Leimen D 13 B4
Leiria P 48 B2
Leitza E 38 A2
Lekeitio E 37 A4
Lekunberri E 38 A2
Le Lardin-St Lazare F 29 A4
Le Lauzet-Ubaye F 32 A2
Le Lavandou F 32 B2
Le Lion-d'Angers F 16 B1
Le Locle CH 20 B1
Le Loroux-Bottereau F 15 B4
Le Louroux-Béconnais F 15 B5
Le Luc F 32 B2
Le Lude F 16 B2
Le Malzieu-Ville F 24 C3
Le Mans F 16 A2
Le Mas-d'Azil F 40 A2
Le Massegros F 30 A2
Le Mayet-de-Montagne F 25 A3
Le May-sur-Evre F 15 B5
Lembach F 13 B3
Lemberg F 13 B3
Lembèye F 39 A3
Le Mêle-sur-Sarthe F 9 B4
Le Ménil F 19 A5
Le Merlerault F 9 B4
Le Mesnil-sur-Oger F 11 C4
Le Miroir F 19 C4
Le Molay-Littry F 8 A3
Le Monastier-sur-Gazeille F 25 C3
Le Monêtier-les-Bains F 26 C3
Le Mont-Dore F 24 B2
Le Montet F 24 A3
Le Mont-St Michel F 8 B2
Lempdes F 24 B3
Le Muret F 28 B2
Le Muy F 32 B2
Lencloître F 16 C2
Le Neubourg F 9 A4
Lenk CH 20 C2
Le Nouvion-en-Thiérache F 11 A3
Lens
B 7 B3
F 6 B2
Lens Lestang F 25 B5
Lentellais E 35 B3
Lenzburg CH 20 B3
Lenzerheide CH 21 C4
León E 36 B1
Léon F 28 C1
Leonberg D 13 C5
Léoncel F 26 C2
Leopoldsburg B 7 A5
Le Palais F 14 B2
Le Parcq F 6 B2
Lepe E 55 B2
Le Péage-de-Roussillon F 25 B4
Le Pellerin F 15 B4
Le Perthus F 40 B3
Le Pertuis F 25 B4
Le Petit-Bornand F 26 B3
L'Epine F 32 A1
Le Poët F 32 A1
Le Poirè-sur-Vie F 22 B2
Le Pont CH 19 C5
Le Pont-de-Montvert F 30 A2
Le Porge F 28 B1
Le Porge-Océan F 28 B1
Le Portel F 6 B1
Le Pouldu F 14 B2
Le Pouliguen F 15 B3
Le Puy-en-Velay F 25 B3
Le Puy-Ste Réparade F 31 B4
Le Quesnoy F 7 B3
Le Rayol F 32 B2
Leré F 17 B4
Lerin E 38 B2
Lerma E 37 B3
Lerm-et-Musset F 28 B2
Le Roeulx B 7 B4
Le Rouget F 24 C2
Lérouville F 12 C1
Le Rozier F 30 A2
Le Russey F 20 B1
Lés E 39 B4
Les Abrets F 26 B2
Les Aix-d'Angillon F 17 B4
Lesaka E 38 A2
Les Ancizes-Comps F 24 B2
Les Andelys F 10 B1
Les Arcs
*Savoie* F 27 B3
*Var* F 32 B2
Les-Aubiers F 16 C1
Les Baux-de-Provence F 31 B3
Les Bézards F 17 B4
Les Bois CH 20 B1
Les Bordes F 17 B4
Les Borges Blanques E 41 C1
Les Borges del Camp E 41 C2
Les Brunettes F 18 C2
Les Cabannes F 40 B2
L'Escala E 41 B4
Lescar F 39 A3
L'Escarène F 33 B3
Lescheraines F 26 B3
Lesconil F 14 B1
Les Contamines-Montjoie F 26 B3
les Coves de Vinroma E 47 B4
Les Déserts F 26 B2
Les Deux-Alpes F 26 C3
Les Diablerets CH 27 A4
Lesdins F 10 B3
Les Echelles F 26 B2
Le Sel-de-Bretagne F 15 B4
Le Sentier CH 19 C5
Les Escaldes AND 40 B2
Les Essarts F 22 B2
Les Estables F 25 C4
Les Eyzies-de-Tayac F 29 B4
Les Gets F 26 A3
Les Grandes-Ventes F 9 A5
Les Haudères CH 27 A4
Les Herbiers F 22 B2
Les Hôpitaux-Neufs F 19 C5
Les Lucs-sur-Boulogne F 22 B2
Les Mages F 31 A3
Les Mazures F 11 B4
Les Mées F 32 A1
Lesmont F 11 C4
Les Mureaux F 10 C1
Lesneven F 14 A1
Les Omergues F 32 A1
Les Ormes-sur-Voulzie F 10 C3
Les Orres F 32 A2
Le Souquet F 28 C1
Lesparre-Médoc F 28 A2
l'Espérance F 11 B3
l'Esperou F 30 A2
Les Pieux F 8 A2
Lesponne F 39 A4
Les Ponts-de-Cé F 16 B1
Les Ponts-de-Martel CH 20 C1
Les Praz F 27 B3
L'Espunyola E 41 B2
Les Riceys F 18 B3
Les Roches F 25 B4
Les Rosaires F 15 A3
Les Rosiers F 16 B1
Les Rousses F 19 C5
Les Sables-d'Olonne F 22 B2
Lessay F 8 A2
Les Settons F 18 B3
Lessines B 7 B3
L'Estany E 41 C3
Les Ternes F 24 B2
Lesterps F 23 B4
Les Thilliers en-Vexin F 10 B1
Les Touches F 15 B4
Les Trois Moûtiers F 16 B2
Les Vans F 31 A3
Les Verrières CH 19 C5
Les Vignes F 30 A2
Le Teil F 31 A3
Le Teilleul F 8 B3
Le Temple-de-Bretagne F 15 B4
Le Theil F 9 B4
Le Thillot F 20 B1
Le Touquet-Paris-Plage F 6 B1
Le Touvet F 26 B2
Le Translay F 10 B1
Le Tréport F 10 A1
Letur E 58 A2
Letux E 47 A3
Leucate F 40 B4
Leuglay F 19 B3
Leuk CH 27 A4
Leukerbad CH 27 A4
Leutkirch D 21 B5
Leuven B 7 B4
Leuze-en-Hainaut B 7 B3
Le Val F 32 B2
Le Val-André F 15 A3
Le Val-d'Ajol F 19 B5
Levaré F 8 B3
Le Verdon-sur-Mer F 22 C2
Le Vernet F 32 A2
Levet F 17 C4
Levie F 62 B2
Levier F 19 C5
Le Vigan F 30 B2
Lévignen F 10 B2
Le Vivier-sur-Mer F 8 B2
Levroux F 17 C3
Leysin CH 27 A4
Lézardrieux F 14 A2
Lézat-sur-Léze F 40 A2
Lezay F 23 B3
Lézignan-Corbières F 30 B1
Lezignan-la-Cèbe F 30 B2
Lézinnes F 18 B3
Lezoux F 25 B3
Lezuza E 52 C1
Lherm F 40 A2
Lhommaizé F 23 B4
L'Hospitalet F 40 B2
L'Hospitalet de l'Infant E 41 D1
L'Hospitalet de Llobregat E 41 C3
L'Hospitalet-du-Larzac F 30 B2
Lhuître F 11 C4
Liancourt F 10 B2
Liart F 11 B4
Liber E 35 B3
Libourne F 28 B2
Libramont B 12 B1
Librilla E 59 B3
Libros E 46 B2
Liceros E 45 A4
Lichères-près-Aigremont F 18 B2
Lichtensteig CH 21 B4
Lichtervelde B 6 A3
Licques F 6 B1
Lier B 7 A4
Liernais F 18 B3
Liestal CH 20 B2
Liétor E 52 C2
Lieurac F 40 B2
Lieurey F 9 A4
Liévin F 6 B2
Liffol-le-Grand F 12 C1
Liffré F 15 A4
Ligardes F 29 B3
Ligne F 15 B4
Lignières F 17 C4
Ligny-en-Barrois F 12 C1
Ligny-le-Châtel F 18 B2
Ligueil F 16 B2
L'Île-Bouchard F 16 B2
l'Île-Rousse F 62 A1
Lille
B 7 A4
F 6 B3
Lillebonne F 9 A4
Lillers F 6 B2
Lillo E 51 A4
Limésy F 9 A4
Limoges F 23 C5
Limogne-en-Quercy F 29 B4
Limoise F 18 C2
Limone Piemonte I 33 A3
Limons F 25 B3
Limours F 10 C2
Limoux F 40 A3
Linares E 51 B4
Linares de Mora E 47 B3
Linares de Riofrio E 43 B4
Linas de Broto E 39 B3
Lindau D 21 B4
Lindenberg im Allgäu D 21 B4
Lindoso P 42 A1
Linkenheim D 13 B4
Linthal CH 21 C4
Linyola E 41 C1
Lion-sur-Mer F 9 A3
Liposthey F 28 B2
Liré F 15 B4
Lisboa = Lisbon P 48 C1
Lisbon = Lisboa P 48 C1
Lisieux F 9 A4
L'Isle CH 19 C5
L'Isle-Adam F 10 B2
L'Isle-de-Noé F 29 C3
L'Isle-en-Dodon F 39 A4
L'Isle-Jourdain
*Gers* F 29 C4
*Vienne* F 23 B4
L'Isle-sur-la-Sorgue F 31 B4
L'Isle-sur-le Doubs F 19 B5
L'Isle-sur-Serein F 18 B3
Lisle-sur-Tarn F 29 C4
Listrac-Médoc F 28 A2
Lit-et-Mixe F 28 B1
Livarot F 9 B4
Livernon F 29 B4
Livigno I 21 C5
Livorno Ferraris I 27 B5
Livron-sur-Drôme F 25 C4

Livry-Louvercy F 11 B4
Lixheim F 12 C3
Lizy-sur-Ourcq F 10 B3
Lladurs E 41 B2
Llafranc E 41 C4
Llagostera E 41 C3
Llançà E 40 B4
Llandudec F 14 A1
Llanes E 36 A2
Llanteno E 37 A3
Llavorsí E 40 B2
Lleida E 47 A4
Llera E 50 B1
Llerena E 50 B1
Lles E 40 B2
Llessui E 40 B2
Llinars E 41 B2
Lliria E 53 B3
Llivia E 40 B2
Llodio E 37 A4
Lloret de Mar E 41 C3
Llosa de Ranes E 53 B3
Lloseta E 61 B2
Llucena del Cid E 47 B3
Llucmajor E 61 B2
Llutxent E 53 C3
Loano I 33 A4
Loarre E 39 B3
Lobón E 49 C4
Locana I 27 B4
Lochau A 21 B4
Loches F 16 B2
Locmaria F 14 B2
Locmariaquer F 14 B3
Locminé F 14 B3
Locquirec F 14 A2
Locronan F 14 A1
Loctudy F 14 B1
Lodares de Osma E 45 A5
Lodève F 30 B2
Lodosa E 38 B1
Loeches E 45 B4
Logroño E 37 B4
Logrosán E 50 A2
Loivos P 42 A2
Loivos do Monte P 42 A2
Loja E 57 A3
Lokeren B 7 A3
L'Olleria E 53 C3
Lombez F 40 A1
Lommel B 7 A5
Londerzeel B 7 A4
Londinières F 9 A5
Longares E 46 A2
Longchamp-sur-Aujon F 19 A3
Longchaumois F 26 A2
Longeau F 19 B4
Longecourt-en-Plaine F 19 B4
Longeville-les-St Avold F 12 B2
Longeville-sur-Mer F 22 B2
Longny-au-Perche F 9 B4
Longré F 23 B3
Longroiva P 43 B2
Longueau F 10 B2
Longué-Jumelles F 16 B1
Longuyon F 12 B1
Longvic F 19 B4
Longvilly B 12 A1
Longwy F 12 B1
Lons-le-Saunier F 19 C4
Loone-Plage F 6 A2
Loon op Zand NL 7 A5
Lo Pagán E 59 B4
Lopera E 51 C3
Lopigna F 62 A1
Lor F 11 B4
Lora de Estepa E 56 A3
Lora del Río E 56 A2
Loranca del Campo E 45 B5
Lorbé E 34 A2
Lorca E 58 B3
Lorch D 13 A3
Lorgues F 32 B2
Lorient F 14 B2
Lorignac F 22 C3
Loriol-sur-Drôme F 25 C4
Lormes F 18 B2
Lorquí E 59 A3
Lörrach D 20 B2
Lorrez-le-Bocage F 17 A4
Lorris F 17 B4
Losacino E 43 A3
Los Alcázares E 59 B4
Los Arcos E 38 B1
Losar de la Vera E 44 B2
Los Barios de Luna E 35 B5
Los Barrios E 56 B2
Los Caños de Meca E 56 B1
Los Cerricos E 58 B2
Los Corrales E 56 A3
Los Corrales de Buelna E 36 A2
Los Dolores E 59 B3
Los Gallardos E 58 B3
Losheim D 12 B2
Los Hinojosos E 52 B1
Los Isidros E 53 B2
Los Molinos E 45 B3
Los Morales E 56 A2
Los Navalmorales E 50 A3
Los Navalucillos E 50 A3
Losne F 19 B4
Los Nietos E 59 B4
Los Palacios y Villafranca E 56 A2
Los Pozuelos de Calatrava E 51 B3
Los Rábanos E 37 C4
Los Santos E 43 B4
Los Santos de la Humosa E 45 B4
Los Santos de Maimona E 49 C4
Lossburg D 13 C4
Losse F 28 B2
Los Tijos E 36 A2
Los Villares E 57 A4
Los Yébenes E 51 A4
Louargat F 14 A2
Loudéac F 15 A3
Loudun F 16 B2
Loué F 16 B1
Louhans F 19 C4
Loulay F 22 B3
Loulé P 54 B1
Lourdes F 39 A3
Lourenzá E 35 A3
Loures P 48 C1
Loures-Barousse F 39 A4
Louriçal P 48 A2
Lourinhã P 48 B1
Lourmarin F 31 B4
Loury F 17 B4
Lousa
*Bragança* P 43 A2
*Castelo Branco* P 49 B3
Lousã P 42 B1
Lousa P 48 C1
Lousada
E 34 B3
P 42 A1
Louverné F 16 A1
Louvie-Juzon F 39 A3
Louviers F 9 A5
Louvigné-du-Désert F 8 B2
Louvois F 11 B4
Lozoya E 45 B4
Lozoyuela E 45 B4
Luanco E 35 A5
Luarca E 35 A4
Lubersac F 23 C5
Lubia E 46 A1
Lubian E 35 B4
Lubrin E 58 B2
Luc F 25 C3
Lucainena de las Torres E 58 B2
Lúcar E 58 B2
Luçay-le-Mâle F 17 B3
Lucciana F 62 A2
Lucé F 10 C1
Lucena
*Córdoba* E 57 A3
*Huelva* E 55 B3
Lucenay-les-Aix F 18 C2
Lucenay-l'Evéque F 18 B3
Luc-en-Diois F 26 C2
Luceni E 38 C2
Lucens CH 20 C1
Luceram F 33 B3
Luciana E 51 B3
Luçon F 22 B2
Luc-sur-Mer F 9 A3
Ludweiler Warndt D 12 B2
Ludwigshafen D 13 B4
Luesia E 38 B2
Lugny F 19 C3
Lugo E 34 A3
Lugones E 35 A5
Lugros E 57 A4
Luintra E 34 B3
Lújar E 57 B4
Lumbier E 38 B2
Lumbrales E 43 B3
Lumbreras E 37 B4
Lumbres F 6 B2
Lummen B 7 B5
Lumpiaque E 46 A2
Luna E 38 B3
Lunas F 30 B2
Lunel F 31 B3
Lunéville F 12 C2
Lungern CH 20 C3
Lupión E 51 B4
Luque E 57 A3
Lurcy-Lévis F 18 C1
Lure F 19 B5
Luri F 62 A2
Lury-sur-Arnon F 17 B4
Lusignan F 23 B4
Lusigny-sur-Barse F 18 A3
Luso P 42 B1
Lussac F 28 B2
Lussac-les-Châteaux F 23 B4
Lussac-les-Eglises F 23 B5
Lussan F 31 A3
Lustenau A 21 B4
Lutry CH 20 C1
Luxembourg L 12 B2
Luxeuil-les-Bains F 19 B5
Luxey F 28 B2
Luz
*Évora* P 49 C3
*Faro* P 54 B1
*Faro* P 54 B2
Luzarches F 10 B2
Luzech F 29 B4
Luzern CH 20 B3
Luz-St Sauveur F 39 B3
Luzy F 18 C2
Lyon F 25 B4
Lyons-la-Forêt F 10 B1
Lyss CH 20 B2

## M

Mably F 25 A4
Macael E 58 B2
Maçanet de Cabrenys E 40 B3
Mação P 48 B2
Macau F 28 A2
Maceda E 34 B3
Macedo de Cavaleiros P 43 A3
Maceira
*Guarda* P 42 B2
*Leiria* P 48 B2
Machault F 11 B4
Machecoul F 22 B2
Macieira P 42 A1
Macinaggio F 62 A2
Macon B 11 A4
Mâcon F 25 A4
Macotera E 44 B2
Macugnaga I 27 B4
Made NL 7 A4
Maderuelo E 45 A4
Madrid E 45 B4
Madridejos E 51 A4
Madrigal de las Altas Torres E 44 A2
Madrigal de la Vera E 44 B2
Madrigalejo E 50 A2
Madrigalejo de Monte E 37 B3
Madriguera E 45 A4
Madrigueras E 52 B2
Madroñera E 50 A2
Maël-Carhaix F 14 A2
Maella E 47 A4
Maello E 44 B3
Mafra P 48 C1
Magacela E 50 B2
Magallon E 38 C2
Magaluf E 60 B2
Magán E 45 C4
Magaña E 38 C1
Magaz E 36 C2
Magescq F 28 C1
Magioto P 48 C1
Magnac-Bourg F 23 C5
Magnac-Laval F 23 B5
Magnieres F 12 C2
Magny-Cours F 18 C2
Magny-en-Vexin F 10 B1
Maguilla E 50 B2
Mahide E 35 C4
Mahora E 52 B2
Maia
E 38 A2
P 42 A1
Maiaelrayo E 45 A4
Maials E 47 A4
Maîche F 20 B1
Maienfeld CH 21 B4
Maignelay Montigny F 10 B2
Maillezais F 22 B3
Mailly-le-Camp F 11 C4
Mailly-le-Château F 18 B2
Mainar E 46 A2
Maintenon F 10 C1
Mainvilliers F 10 C1
Mainz D 13 A4
Maiorca P 42 B1
Mairena de Aljarafe E 56 A1
Mairena del Alcor E 56 A2
Maison-Rouge F 10 C3
Maisse F 10 C2
Maizières-lès-Vic F 12 C2
Majadahonda E 45 B4
Majadas E 44 C2
Málaga E 57 B3
Malagón E 51 A4
Malaguilla E 45 B4
Malaucène F 31 A4
Malaunay F 9 A5
Malborn D 12 B2
Malbuisson F 19 C5
Malcocinado E 50 B2
Maldegem B 7 A3
Malemort F 29 A4
Malesherbes F 10 C2
Malestroit F 15 B3
Malgrat de Mar E 41 C3
Malhadas P 43 A3
Malicorne-sur-Sarthe F 16 B1
Malijai F 32 A2
Mallemort F 31 B4
Mallén E 38 C2
Malléon F 40 A2
Malpartida E 49 B4
Malpartida de la Serena E 50 B2
Malpartida de Plasencia E 44 C1
Malpas E 39 B4
Malpica P 49 B3
Malpica de Bergantiños E 34 A2
Malpica de Tajo E 44 C3
Malsch D 13 C4
Maltat F 18 C2
Malva E 36 C1
Malveira P 48 C1
Mamarrosa P 42 B1
Mamer L 12 B2
Mamers F 9 B4
Mamirolle F 19 B5
Manacor E 61 B3
Mancera de Abajo E 44 B2
Mancha Real E 57 A4
Manchita E 50 B1
Manciet F 28 C3
Mandayona E 45 B5
Mandelieu-la-Napoule F 32 B2
Mane
*Alpes-de-Haute-Provence* F 32 B1
*Haute-Garonne* F 39 A4
Mañeru E 38 B2
Manganeses de la Lampreana E 43 A4
Manganeses de la Polvorosa E 35 B5
Mangiennes F 12 B1
Mangualde P 42 B2
Manilva E 56 B2
Manises E 53 B3
Manlleu E 41 C3
Männedorf CH 21 B3
Mannheim D 13 B4
Manosque F 32 B1
Manresa E 41 C2
Mansilla de Burgos E 37 B3
Mansilla de las Mulas E 36 B1
Mansle F 23 C4
Manso F 62 A1
Manteigas P 42 B2
Mantes-la-Jolie F 10 C1
Mantes-la-Ville F 10 C1
Manthelan F 16 B2
Manuel E 53 B3
Manzanal de Arriba E 35 B4
Manzanares E 51 A4
Manzanares el Real E 45 B4
Manzaneda
*León* E 35 B4
*Orense* E 35 B3
Manzanedo E 37 B3
Manzaneque E 51 A4
Manzanera E 47 B3
Manzanilla E 55 B3
Manzat F 24 B2
Manziat F 25 A4
Maó E 61 B4
Maqueda E 44 B3
Mara E 46 A2
Maraña E 36 A1
Maranchón E 46 A1
Marans F 22 B2
Marateca P 48 C2
Marbach F 12 C2
Marbella E 56 B3
Marboz F 26 A2
Marcenat F 24 B2
Marchamalo E 45 B4
Marchaux F 19 B5
Marche-en-Famenne B 7 B5
Marchena E 56 A2
Marchenoir F 17 B3
Marcheprime F 28 B2
Marciac F 28 C3
Marcigny F 25 A4
Marcilla E 38 B2
Marcillac-la-Croisille F 24 B2
Marcillac-Vallon F 30 A1
Marcillat-en-Combraille F 24 A2
Marcille-sur-Seine F 11 C3
Marcilloles F 26 B2
Marcilly-le-Hayer F 11 C3
Marck F 6 B1
Marckolsheim F 20 A2
Marco de Canevezes P 42 A1
Marennes F 22 C2
Maresquel F 6 B1
Mareuil F 23 C4
Mareuil-en-Brie F 11 C3
Mareuil-sur-Arnon F 17 C4
Mareuil-sur-Lay F 22 B2
Mareuil-sur-Ourcq F 10 B3
Margaux F 28 A2
Margerie-Hancourt F 11 C4
Margès F 25 B5
Margone I 27 B4
Marguerittes F 31 B3
Margut F 11 B5
Maria E 58 B2
Mariana E 46 B1
Mariembourg B 11 A4
Marieux F 10 A2
Marignane F 31 B4
Marigny
*Jura* F 19 C4
*Manche* F 8 A2
Marigny-le-Châtel F 11 C3
Marín E 34 B2
Marinaleda E 56 A3
Marine de Sisco F 62 A2
Marines F 10 B1
Maringues F 24 B3
Marinha das Ondas P 48 A2
Marinha Grande P 48 B2
Marinhas P 42 A1
Marjaliza E 51 A4
Markdorf D 21 B4
Markgröningen D 13 C5
Markina-Xemein E 37 A4
Marle F 11 B3
Marlieux F 25 A5
Marmagne F 18 C3
Marmande F 28 B3
Marmelete P 54 B1
Marmolejo E 51 B3
Marmoutier F 13 C3
Marnay F 19 B4
Marnheim D 13 B4
Marolles-les-Braults F 9 B4
Maromme F 9 A5
Marquion F 6 B3
Marquise F 6 B1
Marratxi E 60 B2
Marrupe E 44 B3
Marsac F 29 C5
Marsac-en-Livradois F 25 B3
Marseillan F 30 B2
Marseille = Marseilles F 31 B4
Marseille en Beauvaisis F 10 B1
Marseilles = Marseille F 31 B4
Mars-la-Tours F 12 B1
Marson F 11 C4
Martel F 29 B4
Martelange B 12 B1
Marthon F 23 C4
Martiago E 43 B3
Martigné-Briand F 16 B1
Martigné-Ferchaud F 15 B4
Martigné-sur-Mayenne F 16 A1
Martigny CH 27 A4
Martigny-les-Bains F 19 A4
Martigues F 31 B4
Martim-Longo P 54 B2
Martinamor E 44 B2
Martin de la Jara E 56 A3
Martin Muñoz de las Posadas E 44 A3
Martinshöhe D 13 B3
Martinszell D 21 B5
Martorell E 41 C2
Martos E 57 A4
Martres Tolosane F 40 A1
Marugán E 44 B3
Marvão P 49 B3
Marvejols F 30 A2
Marville F 12 B1
Masa E 37 B3
Mas-Cabardès F 40 A3
Mascaraque E 51 A4
Mascarenhas P 43 A2
Mas de Barberáns E 47 B4
Mas de las Matas E 47 B3
Masegoso E 52 C1
Masegoso de Tajuña E 45 B5
Masera I 27 A5
Masevaux F 20 B1
Maside E 34 B2
Maslacq F 38 A3
Masone I 33 A4
Massamagrell E 53 B3
Massanassa E 53 B3
Massat F 40 B2
Massay F 17 B3
Masseret F 24 B1
Masseube F 39 A4
Massiac F 24 B3
Massignac F 23 C4
Masueco E 43 A3
Mata de Alcántara E 49 B4
Matalascañas E 55 B3
Matalebreras E 38 C1
Matallana de Torio E 36 B1
Matamala E 45 A5
Mataporquera E 36 B2
Matapozuelos E 44 A3
Mataró E 41 C3
Matet E 53 B3
Matha F 23 C3
Mathay F 20 B1
Matignon F 15 A3
Matilla de los Caños del Rio E 43 B4
Matosinhos P 42 A1
Matour F 25 A4
Mattos P 48 B2
Maubert-Fontaine F 11 B4
Maubeuge F 7 B3
Maubourguet F 39 A4
Mauguio F 31 B3
Maulbronn D 13 C4
Maule F 10 C1
Mauléon F 22 B3
Mauléon-Barousse F 39 B4
Mauléon-Licharre F 38 A3
Maulévrier F 22 A3
Maure-de-Bretagne F 15 B4
Maureilhan F 30 B2
Mauriac F 24 B2
Mauron F 15 A3
Maurs F 24 C2
Maury F 40 B3
Maussane-les-Alpilles F 31 B3
Mauvezin F 29 C3
Mauzé-sur-le-Mignon F 22 B3
Maxent F 15 B3
Maxey-sur-Vaise F 12 C1
Maxial P 48 B1
Maxieira P 48 B2
Mayalde E 43 A4
Mayenne F 8 B3
Mayet F 16 B2
Mayorga E 36 B1
Mayres F 25 C4
Mazagón E 55 B3
Mazaleón E 47 A4
Mazamet F 30 B1
Mazan F 31 A4
Mazarambroz E 51 A3
Mazarete E 46 B1
Mazaricos E 34 B2
Mazarrón E 59 B3
Mazères F 40 A2
Mazères-sur-Salat F 39 A4
Mazières-en-Gâtine F 23 B3
Mazuelo E 37 B3
Mealhada P 42 B1
Méan B 7 B5
Meaulne F 17 C4
Meaux F 10 C2
Mecerreyes E 37 B3
Mechelen B 7 A4
Mecina-Bombarón E 58 C1
Meckenbeuren D 21 B4
Meckenheim D 13 B4
Meckesheim D 13 B4
Meda P 43 B2
Medelim P 49 A3
Medinaceli E 46 A1
Medina de las Torres E 49 C4
Medina del Campo E 44 A3
Medina de Pomar E 37 B3
Medina de Rioseco E 36 C1
Medina Sidonia E 56 B2
Medinilla E 44 B2
Meerle B 7 A4
Meersburg D 21 B4
Meeuwen B 7 A5
Megève F 26 B3
Mehun-sur-Yèvre F 17 B4
Meilen CH 21 B3
Meilhan F 28 C2
Meimôa P 43 B2
Meina I 27 B5
Meira E 35 A3
Meiringen CH 20 C3
Meisenheim D 13 B3
Meix-devant-Virton B 12 B1
Melgaço P 34 B2
Melgar de Arriba E 36 B1
Melgar de Fernamental E 36 B2
Melgar de Yuso E 36 B2
Meliana E 53 B3
Melide E 34 B2
Melides P 54 A1
Melisey F 19 B5
Melle
B 7 A3
F 23 B3
Melón E 34 B2
Mels CH 21 B4
Melun F 10 C2
Membrilla E 51 B4
Membrio E 49 B3
Memer F 29 B4
Memmingen D 21 B5
Memoria P 48 B2
Menasalbas E 51 A3
Menat F 24 A2
Mendavia E 38 B1
Mendaza E 38 B1
Mende F 30 A2
Mendiga P 48 B2
Ménéac F 15 A3
Menen B 6 B3
Menetou-Salon F 17 B4
Mengamuñoz E 44 B3
Mengen D 21 A4
Mengibar E 51 C4
Menou F 18 B2
Mens F 26 C2
Menton F 33 B3
Méntrida E 45 B3
Méobecq F 23 B5
Méounes-les-Montrieux F 32 B1
Mequinenza E 47 A4
Mer F 17 B3
Mera
*Coruña* E 34 A2
*Coruña* E 34 A3
Mercadillo E 37 A3
Merchtem B 7 B4
Merdrignac F 15 A3
Meré E 36 A2
Meréville F 10 C2
Méribel F 26 B3
Méribel Motraret F 26 B3
Mérida E 49 C4
Mérignac F 28 B2
Merksplas B 7 A4
Merlimont Plage F 6 B1
Mersch L 12 B2
Mers-les-Bains F 10 A1
Mértola P 54 B2
Méru F 10 B2
Merufe P 34 B2
Mervans F 19 C4
Merville F 6 B2
Méry-sur-Seine F 11 C3
Merzig D 12 B2
Mesão Frio P 42 A2
Mesas de Ibor E 50 A2
Meschers-sur-Gironde F 22 C3
Meslay-du-Maine F 16 B1
Messac F 15 B4
Messancy B 12 B1
Messei F 8 B3
Messejana P 54 B1
Messkirch D 21 B4
Messtetten D 21 A3
Mestanza E 51 B3
Mesvres F 18 C3
Mettendorf D 12 B2
Mettet B 7 B4
Mettlach D 12 B2
Mettlen CH 20 C2
Metz F 12 B2
Metzervisse F 12 B2
Meulan F 10 B1
Meung-sur-Loire F 17 B3
Meuzac F 23 C5
Meximieux F 26 B2
Meylan F 26 B2
Meymac F 24 B2
Meyrargues F 32 B1
Meyrueis F 30 A2
Meyssac F 29 A4
Meysse F 25 C4
Meyzieu F 25 B4
Mèze F 30 B2
Mézériat F 25 A5
Mézidon-Canon F 9 A3
Mézières-en-Brenne F 23 B5
Mézières-sur-Issoire F 23 B4
Mézilhac F 25 C4
Mézilles F 18 B2
Mézin F 28 B3
Mézos F 28 B1
Mezquita de Jarque E 47 B3
Miajadas E 50 A2
Michelstadt D 13 B5
Middelburg NL 7 A3
Middelharnis NL 7 A4
Middelkerke B 6 A2
Miedes de Aragón E 46 A2
Miedes de Atienza E 45 A4
Miélan F 39 A4
Miengo E 37 A3
Mieres
*Asturias* E 35 A5
*Girona* E 41 B3
Miesau D 13 B3
Migennes F 18 B2
Migné F 23 B5
Miguel Esteban E 51 A4
Miguelturra E 51 B4
Mijares E 44 B3
Mijas E 57 B3
Milagro E 38 B2
Milhão P 43 A3
Millançay F 17 B3
Millares E 53 B3
Millas F 40 B3
Millau F 30 A2
Millesimo I 33 A4
Millevaches F 24 B2
Milly-la-Forêt F 10 C2
Milmarcos E 46 A2
Mimizan F 28 B1
Mimizan-Plage F 28 B1
Mina de Juliana P 54 B1
Mina de São Domingos P 54 B2
Minas de Riotinto E 55 B3
Minateda E 52 C2
Minaya E 52 B1
Minde P 48 B2
Minglanilla E 52 B2
Mingorria E 44 B3
Miño E 34 A2
Miño de San Esteban E 45 A4
Mios F 28 B2
Mira
E 52 B2
P 42 B1
Mirabel E 49 B4
Mirabel-aux-Baronnies F 31 A4
Miradoux F 29 B3
Miraflores de la Sierra E 45 B4
Miralrio E 45 B5
Miramar P 42 A1
Miramas F 31 B3
Mirambeau F 22 C3
Miramont-de-Guyenne F 29 B3
Miranda de Arga E 38 B2
Miranda de Ebro E 37 B4
Miranda do Corvo P 42 B1
Miranda do Douro P 43 A3
Mirande F 29 C3
Mirandela P 43 A2
Mirandilla E 49 C4
Miravet E 47 A4
Miré F 16 B1
Mirebeau F 16 C2
Mirebeau-sur-Bèze F 19 B4
Mirecourt F 19 A5
Mirepoix F 40 A2
Miribel F 25 B4
Missillac F 15 B3
Mittelberg A 21 B5
Mittersheim F 12 C2
Mitton F 28 B2
Moaña E 34 B2
Mocejón E 45 C4
Mochales E 46 A1
Moclin E 57 A4
Modane F 26 B3
Moëlan-sur-Mer F 14 B2
Moerbeke B 7 A3
Móes P 42 B2
Mogadouro P 43 A3
Mogor E 34 B2
Moguer E 55 B3
Mohedas E 43 B3
Mohedas de la Jara E 50 A2

Möhlin CH 20 B2
Moià E 41 C3
Moimenta da Beira P 42 B2
Moirans F 26 B2
Moirans-en-Montagne F 26 A2
Moisdon-la-Rivière F 15 B4
Moissac F 29 B4
Moita
Coimbra P 42 B1
Guarda P 43 B2
Santarém P 48 B2
Setúbal P 48 C1
Moita dos Ferreiros P 48 B1
Moixent E 53 C3
Mojacar E 58 B3
Mojados E 44 A3
Mol B 7 A5
Molare I 33 A4
Molaretto I 27 B4
Molas F 39 A4
Moledo do Minho P 42 A1
Molières F 29 B4
Molina de Aragón E 46 B2
Molina de Segura E 59 A3
Molinar E 37 A3
Molinaseca E 35 B4
Molinet F 18 C2
Molinicos E 52 C1
Molinos de Duero E 37 C4
Molins de Rei E 41 C3
Molledo E 36 A2
Mollerussa E 41 C1
Mollet de Perelada E 40 B3
Mollina E 57 A3
Molló E 40 B3
Molompize F 24 B3
Moloy F 19 B3
Molsheim F 13 C3
Molvizar E 57 B4
Mombeltrán E 44 B2
Mombris D 13 A5
Mombuey E 35 B4
Momo I 27 B5
Monasterio de Rodilla E 37 B3
Monbahus F 29 B3
Monbazillac F 29 B3
Moncada E 53 B3
Moncalieri I 27 B4
Moncalvo I 27 B5
Monção P 34 B2
Moncarapacho P 54 B2
Moncel-sur-Seille F 12 C2
Monchique P 54 B1
Monclar-de-Quercy F 29 C4
Moncofa E 53 B3
Moncontour F 15 A3
Moncoutant F 22 B3
Monda E 56 B3
Mondariz E 34 B2
Mondéjar E 45 B4
Mondim de Basto P 42 A2
Mondoñedo E 35 A3
Mondorf-les-Bains L 12 B2
Mondoubleau F 16 B2
Mondov ì I 33 A3
Mondragon F 31 A3
Monegrillo E 47 A3
Monein F 39 A3
Mónesi I 33 A3
Monesiglio I 33 A4
Monesterio E 55 A3
Monestier-de-Clermont F 26 C2
Monestiés F 30 A1
Monéteau F 18 B2
Monfero E 34 A2
Monflanquin F 29 B3
Monflorite E 39 B3
Monforte P 49 B3
Monforte da Beira
E 49 B3
P 49 B3
Monforte d'Alba I 33 A3
Monforte del Cid E 59 A4
Monforte de Lemos E 34 B3
Monforte de Moyuela E 46 A2
Monistrol-d'Allier F 25 C3
Monistrol de Montserrat
E 41 C2
Monistrol-sur-Loire F 25 B4
Monnaie F 16 B2
Monnerville F 10 C2
Monóvar E 53 C3
Monpazier F 29 B3
Monreal E 38 B2
Monreal del Campo E 46 B2
Monroy E 49 B4
Monroyo E 47 B3
Mons B 7 B3
Monsaraz P 49 C3
Monségur F 28 B3
Montafia I 27 C5
Montagnac F 30 B2
Montaigu F 22 B2
Montaigu-de-Quercy F 29 B4
Montaiguët-en-Forez F 25 A3
Montaigut F 24 A2
Montaigut-sur-Save F 29 C4
Montainville F 10 C1
Montalbán E 47 B3
Montalbán de Córdoba
E 57 A3
Montalbo E 52 B1
Montalegre P 42 A2
Montalieu-Vercieu F 26 B2
Montalivet-les-Bains F 22 C2
Montalvão P 49 B3
Montamarta E 43 A4
Montana-Vermala CH 27 A4
Montánchez E 50 A1
Montanejos E 47 B3
Montans F 29 C4
Montargil P 48 B2
Montargis F 17 B4
Montastruc-la-Conseillère
F 29 C4
Montauban F 29 B4
Montauban-de-Bretagne
F 15 A3
Montbard F 18 B3
Montbarrey F 19 B4
Montbazens F 30 A1
Montbazon F 16 B2
Montbéliard F 20 B1
Montbenoit F 19 C5
Montbeugny F 18 C2
Montblanc E 41 C2
Montbozon F 19 B5
Montbrison F 25 B4
Montbron F 23 C4
Montbrun-les-Bains F 31 A4
Montceau-les-Mines F 18 C3
Montcenis F 18 C3
Montchanin F 18 C3
Montcornet F 11 B4
Montcuq F 29 B4
Montdardier F 30 B2
Mont-de-Marsan F 28 C2
Montdidier F 10 B2
Monteagudo E 59 A3
Monteagudo de
las Vicarias E 46 A1
Montealegre E 36 C2
Montealegre
del Castillo E 53 C2
Montebourg F 8 A2
Monte-Carlo MC 33 B3
Montech F 29 C4
Montechiaro d'Asti I 27 B5
Monte Clara P 49 B3
Monte Clérigo P 54 B1
Monte da Pedra P 49 B3
Monte de Goula P 49 B3
Montederramo E 35 B3
Monte do Trigo P 49 C3
Montefrío E 57 A4
Monte Gordo P 54 B2
Montehermoso E 43 B3
Montejicar E 57 A4
Montejo de la Sierra E 45 A4
Montejo de Tiermes E 45 A4
Monte Juntos P 49 C3
Montel-de-Gelat F 24 B2
Montelier F 25 C5
Montélimar F 31 A3
Montella E 40 B2
Montellano E 56 A2
Montemagno I 27 C5
Montemayor E 57 A3
Montemayor
de Pinilla E 44 A3
Montemolin E 55 A3
Montemor-o-Novo P 48 C2
Montemor-o-Velho P 42 B1
Montendre F 28 A2
Montenegro
de Cameros E 37 B4
Monteneuf F 15 B3
Monte Real P 48 B2
Montereau-
Faut-Yonne F 10 C2
Monte Redondo P 48 B2
Monterosso Grana I 33 A3
Monterrey E 35 C3
Monterroso E 34 B3
Monterrubio de
la Serena E 50 B2
Montesa E 53 C3
Montesalgueiro E 34 A2
Montesclaros E 44 B3
Montesquieu-
Volvestre F 40 A2
Montesquiou F 29 C3
Montestruc-sur-Gers F 29 C3
Montes Velhos P 54 B1
Monte Vilar P 48 B1
Montfaucon F 15 B4
Montfaucon-
d'Argonne F 11 B5
Montfaucon-en-Velay F 25 B4
Montferrat
Isère F 26 B2
Var F 32 B2
Montfort-en-Chalosse F 28 C2
Montfort-l'Amaury F 10 C1
Montfort-le-Gesnois F 16 A2
Montfort-sur-Meu F 15 A4
Montfort-sur-Risle F 9 A4
Montgai E 41 C1
Montgaillard F 39 A4
Montgenèvre F 26 C3
Montgiscard F 40 A2
Montguyon F 28 A2
Monthermé F 11 B4
Monthey CH 27 A3
Monthois F 11 B4
Monthureux-
sur-Saône F 19 A4
Montiel E 52 C1
Montier-en-Der F 11 C4
Montiglio I 27 B5
Montignac F 29 A4
Montigny-le-Roi F 19 B4
Montigny-lès-Metz F 12 B2
Montigny-sur-Aube F 19 B3
Montijo
E 49 C4
P 48 C2
Montilla E 57 A3
Montillana E 57 A4
Montilly F 18 C2
Montivilliers F 9 A4
Montjaux F 30 A1
Montjean-sur-Loire F 16 B1
Montlhéry F 10 C2
Montlieu-la-Garde F 28 A2
Mont-Louis F 40 B3
Montlouis-sur-Loire F 16 B2
Montluçon F 24 A2
Montluel F 25 B5
Montmarault F 24 A2
Montmartin-sur-Mer F 8 B2
Montmédy F 12 B1
Montmélian F 26 B3
Montmeyan F 32 B2
Montmeyran F 25 C4
Montmirail
Marne F 11 C3
Sarthe F 16 A2
Montmiral F 26 B2
Montmirat F 31 B3
Montmirey-
le-Château F 19 B4
Montmoreau-
St Cybard F 23 C4
Montmorency F 10 C2
Montmorillon F 23 B4
Montmort-Lucy F 11 C3
Montoir-de-Bretagne F 15 B3
Montoire-sur-le-Loir F 16 B2
Montoito P 49 C3
Montolieu F 40 A3
Montoro E 51 B3
Montpellier F 31 B2
Montpezat-de-Quercy F 29 B4
Montpezat-sous-
Bouzon F 25 C4
Montpon-Ménestérol F 28 A3
Montpont-en-Bresse F 19 C4
Montréal
Aude F 40 A3
Gers F 28 C3
Montredon-Labessonnié
F 30 B1
Montréjeau F 39 A4
Montrésor F 17 B3
Montret F 19 C4
Montreuil
Pas de Calais F 6 B1
Seine St Denis F 10 C2
Montreuil-aux-Lions F 10 B3
Montreuil-Bellay F 16 B1
Montreux CH 20 C1
Montrevault F 15 B4
Montrevel-en-Bresse F 26 A2
Montrichard F 17 B3
Montricoux F 29 B4
Mont-roig del Camp E 41 C1
Montrond-les-Bains F 25 B4
Montroy E 53 B3
Montsalvy F 24 C2
Montsauche-
les-Settons F 18 B3
Montseny E 41 C3
Montsoreau F 16 B2
Mont-sous-Vaudrey F 19 C4
Monts-sur-Guesnes F 16 C2
Mont-St Aignan F 9 A5
Mont-St Vincent F 18 C3
Montsûrs F 16 A1
Montuenga E 44 A3
Montuïri E 61 B3
Monturque E 57 A3
Monzón E 39 C4
Monzón de Campos E 36 B2
Moorslede B 6 B3
Moos D 21 B3
Mora E 51 A4
Móra P 48 C2
Mòra d'Ebre E 47 A4
Mora de Rubielos E 47 B3
Moradillo de Roa E 45 A4
Moraime E 34 A1
Morais P 43 A3
Mòra la Nova E 47 A4
Moral de Calatrava E 51 B4
Moraleda de
Zafayona E 57 A4
Moraleja E 43 B3
Moraleja del Vino E 44 A2
Morales del Vino E 44 A2
Morales de Toro E 44 A2
Morales de Valverde E 35 C5
Moralina E 43 A3
Morasverdes E 43 B3
Morata de Jalón E 46 A2
Morata de Jiloca E 46 A2
Morata de Tajuña E 45 B4
Moratalla E 58 A3
Morbach D 12 B3
Morbier F 19 C5
Morcenx F 28 B2
Morcuera E 45 A4
Mordelles F 15 A4
Moréac F 14 B3
Moreda
Granada E 57 A4
Oviedo E 36 A1
Morée F 17 B3
Moreles de Rey E 35 B5
Morella E 47 B3
Moreruela de
los Infanzones E 43 A4
Morés E 46 A2
Morestel F 26 B2
Moret-sur-Loing F 10 C2
Moretta I 27 C4
Moreuil F 10 B2
Morez F 19 C5
Mörfelden D 13 B4
Morgat F 14 A1
Morges CH 19 C5
Morgex I 27 B4
Morhange F 12 C2
Morhet B 12 B1
Morialmé B 7 B4
Morianes P 54 B2
Moriani Plage F 62 A2
Moriles E 57 A3
Morille E 44 B2
Morlaàs F 39 A3
Morlaix F 14 A2
Morley F 11 C5
Mormant F 10 C2
Mornant F 25 B4
Mornay-Berry F 17 B4
Morón de Almazán E 46 A1
Morón de la Frontera E 56 A2
Morozzo I 33 A3
Mörsch D 13 C4
Mortagne-au-Perche F 9 B4
Mortagne-sur-
Gironde F 22 C3
Mortagne-sur-Sèvre F 22 B3
Mortágua P 42 B1
Mortain F 8 B3
Morteau F 19 B5
Mortemart F 23 B4
Mortrée F 9 B4
Mortsel B 7 A4
Morzine F 26 A3
Mosbach D 13 B5
Mosca P 43 A3
Moscavide P 48 C1
Mosqueruela E 47 B3
Mössingen D 13 C5
Móstoles E 45 B4
Mostuéjouls F 30 A2
Mota del Cuervo E 52 B1
Mota del Marqués E 44 A2
Motilla del Palancar E 52 B2
Motril E 57 B4
Mouchard F 19 C4
Moudon CH 20 C1
Mougins F 32 B2
Mouilleron-en-Pareds F 22 B3
Mouliherne F 16 B2
Moulinet F 33 B3
Moulins F 18 C2
Moulins-Engilbert F 18 C2
Moulins-la-Marche F 9 B4
Moulismes F 23 B4
Moult F 9 A3
Moura P 54 A2
Mourão P 49 C3
Mourenx F 39 A3
Mouriés F 31 B3
Mourmelon-le-Grand F 11 B4
Mouronho P 42 B1
Mouscron B 6 B3
Moussac F 31 B3
Moussey F 12 C2
Mousteru F 14 A2
Moustey F 28 B2
Moustiers-Ste Marie F 32 B2
Mouthe F 19 C5
Mouthier-Haute-Pierre F 19 B5
Mouthoumet F 40 B3
Moutier CH 20 B2
Moûtiers F 26 B3
Moutiers-les-
Mauxfaits F 22 B2
Mouy F 10 B2
Mouzon F 11 B5
Moyenmoutier F 12 C2
Moyenvic F 12 C2
Mózar E 35 C5
Mucientes E 36 C2
Muda P 54 B1
Mudau D 13 B5
Muel E 46 A2
Muelas del Pan E 43 A4
Mugardos E 34 A2
Muge P 48 B2
Mugron F 28 C2
Mugueimes E 34 C3
Mühlacker D 13 C4
Muhleberg CH 20 C2
Mühleim D 21 A3
Muirteira P 48 B1
Mula E 59 A3
Mulegns CH 21 C4
Mulhouse F 20 B2
Müllheim D 20 B2
Munana E 44 B2
Muñás E 35 A4
Mundaka E 37 A4
Munderkingen D 21 A4
Munera E 52 B1
Mungia E 37 A4
Muñico E 44 B2
Muniesa E 47 A3
Muñopepe E 44 B3
Muñotello E 44 B2
Münsingen CH 20 C2
Münster
CH 20 C3
Hessen D 13 B4
Munster F 20 A2
Muntibar E 37 A4
Muotathal CH 21 C3
Muras E 34 A3
Murat F 24 B2
Murato F 62 A2
Murat-sur-Vèbre F 30 B1
Murazzano I 33 A4
Murça P 42 A2
Murchante E 38 B2
Murcia E 59 B3
Mur-de-Barrez F 24 C2
Mur-de-Bretagne F 14 A2
Mur-de-Sologne F 17 B3
Muret F 40 A2
Murg CH 21 B4
Murguia E 37 B4
Muri CH 20 B3
Murias de Paredes E 35 B4
Muriedas E 37 A3
Muriel Viejo E 37 C4
Murillo de Rio Leza E 37 B4
Murillo el Fruto E 38 B2
Muro
E 61 B3
F 62 A1
Muro de Alcoy E 53 C3
Murol F 24 B2
Muron F 22 B3
Muros E 34 B1
Muros de Nalón E 35 A4
Mürren CH 20 C2
Murtas E 58 C1
Murten CH 20 C2
Murtosa P 42 B1
Murviel-lès-Béziers F 30 B2
Musculdy F 38 A3
Mussidan F 29 A3
Musson B 12 B1
Mussy-sur-Seine F 18 B3
Mutriku E 37 A4
Muxía E 34 A1
Muxilka-Ugarte E 37 A4
Muzillac F 15 B3
Myennes F 18 B1


## N


Naaldwijk NL 7 A4
Nabais P 42 B2
Näfels CH 21 B4
Nagold D 13 C4
Nagore E 38 B2
Naharros E 46 B1
Nailloux F 40 A2
Naintré F 23 B4
Najac F 29 B4
Nájera E 37 B4
Nalda E 37 B4
Nalliers F 22 B2
Nalzen F 40 B2
Namur B 7 B4
Nançay F 17 B4
Nanclares de la Oca E 37 B4
Nancy F 12 C2
Nangis F 10 C3
Nant F 30 A2
Nanterre F 10 C2
Nantes F 15 B4
Nanteuil-le-Haudouin F 10 B2
Nantiat F 23 B5
Nantua F 26 A2
Naraval E 35 A4
Narbonne F 30 B1
Narbonne-Plage F 30 B2
Narón E 34 A2
Narros del Castillo E 44 B2
Narzole I 33 A3
Nasbinals F 24 C3
Naters CH 27 A5
Naucelle F 30 A1
Nava E 36 A1
Navacerrada E 45 B3
Navaconcejo E 43 B4
Nava de Arévalo E 44 B3
Nava de la Asunción E 44 A3
Nava del Rey E 44 A2
Navafriá E 45 A4
Navahermosa E 51 A3
Naval E 39 B4
Navalacruz E 44 B3
Navalcán E 44 B2
Navalcarnero E 45 B3
Navaleno E 37 C3
Navalmanzano E 45 A3
Navalmoral E 44 B3
Navalmoral de
la Mata E 44 C2
Naválón E 53 C3
Navalonguilla E 44 B2
Navalperal de Pinares E 44 B3
Navalpino E 51 A3
Navaltalgordo E 44 B3
Navaltoril E 50 A3
Navaluenga E 44 B3
Navalvillar de Pela E 50 A2
Navaperal de Tormes E 44 B2
Navarclés E 41 C2
Navarredonda
de Gredos E 44 B2
Navarrenx F 38 A3
Navarrés E 53 B3
Navarrete E 37 B4
Navarrevisca E 44 B3
Navás E 41 C2
Navascués E 38 B2
Navas del Madroño E 49 B4
Navas del Rey E 45 B3
Navas del Sepillar E 57 A3
Navas de Oro E 44 A3
Navas de San Juan E 51 B4
Navasfrias E 43 B3
Nave de Haver P 43 B3
Navés E 41 C2
Navezuelas E 50 A2
Navia E 35 A4
Navia de Suarna E 35 B4
Navilly F 19 C4
Nay F 39 A3
Nazaré P 48 B1
Nebreda E 37 C3
Neckargemünd D 13 B4
Neda E 34 A2
Neerpelt B 7 A5
Negredo E 45 A5
Negreira E 34 B2
Nègrepelisse F 29 B4
Negueira de Muñiz E 35 A4
Neila E 37 B4
Néive I 27 C5
Nelas P 42 B2
Nemours F 17 A4
Nenzing A 21 B4
Nérac F 29 B3
Néré F 23 C3
Néris-les Bains F 24 A2
Nerja E 57 B4
Néronde F 25 B4
Nérondes F 17 C4
Nerpio E 58 A2
Nerva E 55 B3
Nesle F 10 B2
Nesslau CH 21 B4
Netstal CH 21 B4
Nettancourt F 11 C4
Neuchâtel CH 20 C1
Neudorf D 13 B4
Neuenbürg D 13 C4
Neuerburg D 12 A2
Neuf-Brisach F 20 A2
Neufchâteau
B 12 B1
F 12 C1
Neufchâtel-en-Bray F 10 B1
Neufchâtel-sur-Aisne F 11 B4
Neuflize F 11 B4
Neuhausen CH 21 B3
Neuhausen ob Eck D 21 B3
Neuillé-Pont-Pierre F 16 B2
Neuilly-en-Thelle F 10 B2
Neuilly-le-Réal F 18 C2
Neuilly-l'Évêque F 19 B4
Neuilly-St Front F 10 B3
Neu-Isenburg D 13 A4
Neulise F 25 B4
Neumagen D 12 B2
Neung-sur-Beuvron F 17 B3
Neunkirch
Luzern CH 20 B3
Schaffhausen CH 21 B3
Neunkirchen D 12 B3
Neuravensburg D 21 B4
Neureut D 13 B4
Neussargues-
Moissac F 24 B2
Neustadt D 13 B4
Neuves-Maisons F 12 C2
Neuvic
Corrèze F 24 B2
Dordogne F 29 A3
Neuville-aux-Bois F 17 A4
Neuville-de-Poitou F 23 B4
Neuville-les-Dames F 25 A5
Neuville-sur-Saône F 25 B4
Neuvy-le-Roi F 16 B2
Neuvy-Santour F 18 A2
Neuvy-St Sépulchre F 17 C3
Neuvy-sur-Barangeon F 17 B4
Névache F 26 B3
Nevers F 18 C2
Névez F 14 B2
Nexon F 23 C5
Nice F 33 B3
Niebla E 55 B3
Niederbipp CH 20 B2
Niederbronn-
les-Bains F 13 C3
Nieder-Olm D 13 B4
Niederurnen CH 21 B4
Nierstein D 13 B4
Nieul-le-Dolent F 22 B2
Nieul-sur-Mer F 22 B2
Nieuwerkerken B 7 B5
Nieuwpoort B 6 A2
Nigüelas E 57 B4
Níjar E 58 C2
Nijlen B 7 A4
Nîmes F 31 B3
Ninove B 7 B4
Niort F 22 B3
Nisa P 49 B3
Nissan-lez-Ensérune F 30 B2
Nitry F 18 B2
Nivelles B 7 B4
Nizza Monferrato I 27 C5
Noailles F 10 B2
Noain E 38 B2
Noalejo E 57 A4
Noblejas E 45 C4
Noceda E 35 B4
Nods F 19 B5
Noé F 40 A2
Noeux-les-Mines F 6 B2
Noez E 51 A3
Nogales E 49 C4
Nogarejas E 35 B4
Nogaro F 28 C2
Nogent F 19 A4
Nogent l'Artaud F 10 C3
Nogent-le-Roi F 10 C1
Nogent-le-Rotrou F 9 B4
Nogent-sur-Seine F 11 C3
Nogent-sur-Vernisson F 17 B4
Noguera E 46 B2
Noguerones E 57 A3
Nohfelden D 12 B3
Noia E 34 B2
Noirétable F 25 B3
Noirmoutier-en-l'Île F 22 A1
Noja E 37 A3
Nolay F 18 C3
Noli I 33 A4
Nombela E 44 B3
Nomeny F 12 C2
Nomexy F 12 C2
Nonancourt F 9 B5
Nonant-le-Pin F 9 B4
Nonaspe E 47 A4
None I 27 C4
Nontron F 23 C4
Nonza F 62 A2
Nordausques F 6 B2
Noreña E 36 A1
Norrent-Fontes F 6 B2
Nort-sur-Erdre F 15 B4
Nossa Senhora
do Cabo P 48 C1
Nouan-le-Fuzelier F 17 B4
Nouans-les-Fontaines F 17 B3
Nougaroulet F 29 C3
Nouvion F 6 B1
Nouzonville F 11 B4
Novalaise F 26 B2
Novales E 39 B3
Novelda E 59 A4
Novés E 45 B3
Noves F 31 B3
Novés de Segre E 41 B2
Noville B 12 A1
Novion-Porcien F 11 B4
Novy-Chevrières F 11 B4
Noyalo F 15 B3
Noyal-Pontivy F 14 A3
Noyant F 16 B2
Noyelles-sur-Mer F 6 B1
Noyen-sur-Sarthe F 16 B1
Noyers F 18 B2
Noyers-sur-Cher F 17 B3
Noyers-sur-Jabron F 32 A1
Noyon F 10 B2
Nozay F 15 B4
Nuaillé F 16 B1
Nuaillé-d'Aunis F 22 B3
Nuars F 18 B2
Nubledo E 35 A5
Nuéno E 39 B3
Nuestra Señora
Sa Verge des Pilar E 60 C1
Nueva E 36 A2
Nueva Carteya E 57 A3
Nuevalos E 46 A2
Nuits F 18 B3
Nuits-St Georges F 19 B3
Nules E 53 B3
Numansdorp NL 7 A4
Nuñomoral E 43 B3
Nus I 27 B4
Nusplingen D 21 A3
Nyon CH 26 A3
Nyons F 31 A4


## O


O Barco E 35 B4
Obejo E 50 B3
Oberbruck F 20 B1
Oberdiessbach CH 20 C2
Oberdorf CH 20 B2
Oberkirch D 13 C4
Obernai F 13 C3
Obernburg D 13 B5
Oberndorf D 13 C4
Oberriet CH 21 B4
Oberstaufen D 21 B5
Oberstdorf D 21 B5
Oberwesel D 13 A3
Óbidos P 48 B1
Objat F 29 A4
O Bolo E 35 B3
Obrigheim D 13 B5
Ocaña E 45 C4
O Carballiño E 34 B2
Occimiano I 27 B5
Ochagavía E 38 B2
Ochsenhausen D 21 A4
O Corgo E 35 B3
Octeville F 8 A2
Odeceixe P 54 B1
Odeleite P 54 B2
Odemira P 54 B1
Odiáxere P 54 B1
Odivelas P 54 A1
Odón E 46 B2

Offenburg D 13 C3
Offranville F 9 A5
Ofterschwang D 21 B5
Ogihares E 57 A4
Ohanes E 58 B2
Ohey B 7 B5
Oia E 34 B2
Oiã P 42 B1
Oiartzun E 38 A2
Oimbra E 42 A2
Oiselay-et-Grachoux F 19 B4
Oisemont F 10 B1
Oisterwijk NL 7 A5
Ojén E 56 B3
Ojuelos Altos E 50 B2
Olagüe E 38 B2
Olargues F 30 B1
Olazagutia E 38 B1
Olea E 36 B2
Oledo P 49 B3
Oleiros
*Coruña* E 34 A2
*Coruña* E 34 B1
P 48 B3
Olen B 7 A4
Olesa de Montserrat E 41 C2
Oletta F 62 A2
Olette F 40 B3
Olhão P 54 B2
Olhavo P 48 B1
Oliana E 41 B2
Olias del Rey E 45 C4
Oliete E 47 B3
Olite E 38 B2
Oliva E 53 C3
Oliva de la Frontera E 48 C3
Oliva de Mérida E 50 B1
Oliva de Plasencia E 43 B3
Olival P 48 B2
Olivar E 57 B4
Olivares E 55 B3
Olivares de Duero E 36 C2
Olivares de Júcar E 52 B1
Oliveira de Azeméis P 42 B1
Oliveira de Frades P 42 B1
Oliveira do Conde P 42 B2
Oliveira do Douro P 42 A1
Oliveira do Hospital P 42 B2
Olivenza E 49 C3
Olivet F 17 B3
Olivone CH 21 C3
Olliergues F 25 B3
Olmedilla de Alarcón E 52 B1
Olmedillo de Roa E 37 C3
Olmedo E 44 A3
Olmeto F 62 B1
Olmillos de Castro E 43 A3
Olmos de Ojeda E 36 B2
Olocau del Rey E 47 B3
Olonne-sur-Mer F 22 B2
Olonzac F 30 B1
Oloron-Ste Marie F 39 A3
Olost E 41 C3
Olot E 41 B3
Olsene B 7 B3
Olten CH 20 B2
Olula del Rio E 58 B2
Olvega E 38 C2
Olvera E 56 B2
Omegna I 27 B5
On B 7 B5
Oña E 37 B3
Oñati E 37 A4
Onda E 53 B3
Ondara E 53 C4
Ondarroa E 37 A4
Onesse-et-Laharie F 28 B1
Onhaye B 7 B4
Onil E 53 C3
Onis E 36 A2
Ontinyent E 53 C3
Ontur E 52 C2
Onzain F 17 B3
Onzonilla E 36 B1
Oostburg NL 7 A3
Oostende B 6 A2
Oosterhout NL 7 A4
Oosterzele B 7 B3
Oostkamp B 6 A3
Oostmalle B 7 A4
Oostvoorne NL 7 A4
O Páramo E 34 B3
O Pedrouzo E 34 B2
Oper Thalkirchdorf D 21 B5
O Pino E 34 B2
O Porriño E 34 B2
Oppenau D 13 C4
Oppenheim D 13 B4
Orada P 49 C3
Oradour-sur-Glane F 23 C5
Oradour-sur-Vayres F 23 C4
Oraison F 32 B1
Orange F 31 A3
Orba E 53 C3
Orbacém P 42 A1
Orbais F 11 C3
Orbassano I 27 B4
Orbe CH 19 C5
Orbec F 9 A4
Orbigny F 17 B3
Orce E 58 B2
Orcera E 58 A2
Orchamps-Vennes F 19 B5
Orches F 16 C2
Orchete E 53 C3
Orchies F 6 B3
Orcières F 26 C3
Ordes E 34 A2
Ordino AND 40 B2
Ordizia E 38 A1
Orduña E 37 B4
Orea E 46 B2
Orellana E 50 A2
Orellana de la Sierra E 50 A2
Organyà E 41 B2
Orgaz E 51 A4
Orgelet F 19 C4
Orgères-en-Beauce F 17 A3
Orgibet F 39 B4
Orgnac-l'Aven F 31 A3
Orgon F 31 B4
Oria E 58 B2
Origny-Ste Benoite F 11 B3
Orihuela E 59 A4
Orihuela del Tremedal
E 46 B2
Oriola P 48 C3
Orjiva E 57 B4
Orléans F 17 B3
Ormea I 33 A3
Ornans F 19 B5
Oron-la-Ville CH 20 C1
Oropa I 27 B4
Oropesa
*Castellón de la Plana*
E 47 B4
*Toledo* E 44 C2
O Rosal E 34 C2
Orozko E 37 A4
Orreaga-Roncesvalles
E 38 A2
Orsay F 10 C2
Orscholz D 12 B2
Orsennes F 17 C3
Orsières CH 27 A4
Orthez F 28 C2
Ortigueira E 34 A3
Ortilla E 39 B3
Orusco E 45 B4
Orvalho P 49 A3
Orvault F 15 B4
Osann-Monzel D 12 B2
Oseja de Sajambre E 36 A1
Osera de Ebro E 47 A3
Osorno E 36 B2
Os Peares E 34 B3
Ospedaletti I 33 B3
Ossa de Montiel E 52 C1
Ossun F 39 A3
Ostheim F 20 A2
Osthofen D 13 B4
Ostiz E 38 B2
Ostrach D 21 B4
Osuna E 56 A2
Oteiza E 38 B2
Oteo E 37 A3
Otero de Herreros E 45 B3
Otero de O Bodas E 35 C4
Ottenhöfen D 13 C4
Otterbach D 13 B3
Otterberg D 13 B3
Ottersweier D 13 C4
Ottignies B 7 B4
Ottmarsheim F 20 B2
Ottobeuren D 21 B5
Ottweiler D 12 B3
Ouanne F 18 B2
Ouarville F 10 C1
Oucques F 17 B3
Oud-Beijerland NL 7 A4
Ouddorp NL 7 A3
Oudenaarde B 7 B3
Oudenbosch NL 7 A4
Oudenburg B 6 A3
Oude-Tonge NL 7 A4
Oud Gastel NL 7 A4
Oudon F 15 B4
Ouguela P 49 B3
Ouistreham F 9 A3
Oulchy-le-Château F 11 B3
Oullins F 26 B1
Oulmes F 22 B3
Oulx I 27 B3
Ourém P 48 B2
Ourense E 34 B3
Ourique P 54 B1
Ourol E 34 A3
Ouroux-en-Morvan F 18 B2
Oust F 40 B2
Outeiro P 42 B1
Outeiro de Rei E 34 A3
Outes E 34 B2
Outreau F 6 B1
Ouzouer-le-Marché F 17 B3
Ouzouer-sur-Loire F 17 B4
Ovada I 33 A4
Ovar P 42 B1
Overijse B 7 B4
Overpelt B 7 A5
Oviedo E 35 A5
Oviglio I 27 C5
Oyonnax F 26 A2
Ozaeta E 37 B4
Ozzano Monferrato I 27 B5


## P


Paal B 7 A5
Paços de Ferreira P 42 A1
Pacy-sur-Eure F 9 A5
Paderne P 54 B1
Padornelo P 42 A1
Padrón E 34 B2
Padul E 57 A4
Paesana I 27 C4
Pagny-sur-Moselle F 12 C2
Pailhès F 40 A2
Paimboeuf F 15 B3
Paimpol F 14 A2
Paimpont F 15 A3
Pajares E 35 A5
Pajares de los Oteros E 36 B1
Palacios de la Sierra E 37 C3
Palaciòs de la
Valduerna E 35 B5
Palacios del Sil E 35 B4
Palacios de Sanabria E 35 B4
Palaciosrubios E 44 A2
Palafrugell E 41 C4
Palaiseau F 10 C2
Palamós E 41 C4
Palas de Rei E 34 B3
Palavas-les-Flots F 31 B2
Palazuelos de
la Sierra E 37 B3
Palencia E 36 B2
Palenciana E 57 A3
Palhaça P 42 B1
Palheiros da Tocha P 42 B1
Palheiros de Quiaios P 42 B1
Paliseul B 11 B5
Pallanza I 27 B5
Pallares E 55 A3
Pallaruelo de
Monegros E 47 A3
Pallerols E 40 B2
Palluau F 22 B2
Palma P 48 C2
Palma del Río E 56 A2
Palma de Mallorca E 60 B2
Palma Nova E 60 B2
Palmela P 48 C2
Palmerola E 41 B3
Palomares E 58 B3
Palomares del Campo E 52 B1
Palomas E 50 B1
Palos de la Frontera E 55 B3
Pals E 41 C4
Pamiers F 40 A2
Pampaneira E 57 B4
Pamparato I 33 A3
Pampilhosa
*Aveiro* P 42 B1
*Coimbra* P 42 B2
Pampliega E 37 B3
Pamplona E 38 B2
Pancalieri I 27 C4
Pancey F 11 C5
Pancorvo E 37 B3
Pancrudo E 46 B2
Panes E 36 A2
Panissières F 25 B4
Pannes F 17 A4
Pantano de Cíjara E 50 A3
Panticosa E 39 B3
Pantín E 34 A2
Pantoja E 45 B4
Pantón E 34 B3
Panxon E 34 B2
Parada
*Bragança* P 43 A3
*Viseu* P 42 B1
Paradas E 56 A2
Paradela E 34 B3
Parades de Rubiales E 44 A2
Paradinas de
San Juan E 44 B2
Paramé F 8 B2
Páramo E 35 A4
Páramo del Sil E 35 B4
Parandaça P 42 A2
Paravadella E 35 A3
Paray-le-Monial F 18 C3
Parceiros P 48 B2
Parcey F 19 B4
Pardilla E 45 A4
Paredes
E 45 B5
P 42 A1
Paredes de Coura P 34 C2
Paredes de Nava E 36 B2
Paredes de Siguenza E 45 A5
Pareja E 45 B5
Parennes F 16 A1
Parentis-en-Born F 28 B1
Pargny-sur-Saulx F 11 C4
Pari-Gagné F 25 A4
Parigné-l'Évêque F 16 B2
Paris F 10 C2
Parisot F 29 B4
Parla E 45 B4
Parlavá E 41 B4
Parolis E 58 A2
Parrillas E 44 B2
Parthenay F 16 C1
Passais F 8 B3
Passegueiro P 42 B1
Passy F 26 B3
Pastrana E 45 B5
Patay F 17 A3
Paterna E 53 B3
Paterna del Campo E 55 B3
Paterna del Madera E 52 C1
Paterna de Rivera E 56 B2
Patrimonio F 62 A2
Pau F 39 A3
Pauillac F 28 A2
Paulhaguet F 25 B3
Paulhan F 30 B2
Pavia P 48 C2
Pavias E 53 B3
Pavilly F 9 A4
Payerne CH 20 C1
Paymogo E 55 B2
Payrac F 29 B4
Paziols F 40 B3
Peal de Becerro E 58 B1
Pechao P 54 B2
Pedrafita E 35 B3
Pedrajas de
San Esteban E 44 A3
Pedralba E 53 B3
Pedralba de
la Praderia E 35 B4
Pedraza E 45 A4
Pedreguer E 53 C4
Pedrera E 56 A3
Pedro Abad E 51 C3
Pedro Bernardo E 44 B3
Pedroche E 50 B3
Pedrógão P 54 A2
Pedrógão P 43 B2
Pedrógão P 48 B2
Pedrógão Grande P 48 B2
Pedrola E 38 C2
Pedro-Martinez E 58 B1
Pedro Muñoz E 52 B1
Pedrosa del Rey E 44 A2
Pedrosa del Rio Urbel E 37 B3
Pedrosa de Tobalina E 37 B3
Pedrosillo de
los Aires E 44 B2
Pedrosillo el Ralo E 44 A2
Peer B 7 A5
Pega P 43 B2
Pegalajar E 57 A4
Pegli I 33 A4
Pego E 53 C3
Pegões-Estação P 48 C2
Pegões Velhos P 48 C2
Peguera E 60 B2
Peisey-Nancroix F 26 B3
Pelahustán E 44 B3
Pélissanne F 31 B4
Pellegrue F 28 B3
Pellevoisin F 17 C3
Peloche E 50 A2
Pelussin F 25 B4
Peñacerrada E 37 B4
Penacova P 42 B1
Peña de Cabra E 43 B4
Peñafiel E 45 A3
Penafiel P 42 A1
Peñaflor E 56 A2
Peñalba de Santiago E 35 B4
Peñalsordo E 50 B2
Penalva do Castelo P 42 B2
Penamacôr P 43 B2
Peñaparda E 43 B3
Peñaranda de
Bracamonte E 44 B2
Peñaranda de Duero E 37 C3
Peñarroya de
Tastavins E 47 B4
Peñarroya-
Pueblonuevo E 50 B2
Peñarrubla E 35 B3
Peñascosa E 52 C1
Peñas de San Pedro E 52 C2
Peñausende E 43 A4
Pendueles E 36 A2
Penedono P 42 B2
Penela P 48 A2
Pénestin F 15 B3
Penhas Juntas P 43 A2
Peniche P 48 B1
Penilhos P 54 B2
Peñíscola E 47 B4
Penmarch F 14 B1
Penne-d'Agenais F 29 B3
Pera Boa P 42 B2
Perafita P 42 A1
Peraleda de la Mata E 44 C2
Peraleda del Zaucejo E 50 B2
Peraleda de
San Román E 50 A2
Perales de Alfambra E 46 B2
Perales del Puerto E 43 B3
Perales de Tajuña E 45 B4
Peralta E 38 B2
Peralta de la Sal E 39 C4
Peralva P 54 B2
Peralveche E 46 B1
Percy F 8 B2
Perdiguera E 39 C3
Peredo P 43 A3
Pereiro
*Faro* P 54 B2
*Guarda* P 43 B2
*Santarém* P 48 B2
Pereiro de Aguiar E 34 B3
Perelada E 41 B4
Perelejos de
las Truchas E 46 B2
Pereña E 43 A3
Pereruela E 43 A4
Periana E 57 B3
Périers F 8 A2
Périgueux F 29 A3
Pernes P 48 B2
Pernes-les-Fontaines F 31 A4
Peroguarda P 54 A1
Pérols F 31 B2
Péronne F 10 B2
Péronnes B 7 B4
Pero Pinheiro P 48 C1
Perorrubio E 45 A4
Perosa Argentina I 27 C4
Perozinho P 42 A1
Perpignan F 40 B3
Perrecy-les-Forges F 18 C3
Perrero I 27 C4
Perrignier F 26 A3
Perros-Guirec F 14 A2
Persan F 10 B2
Pertuis F 31 B4
Péruwelz B 7 B3
Perwez B 7 B4
Pesadas de Burgos E 37 B3
Pesaguero E 36 A2
Pesmes F 19 B4
Peso da Régua P 42 A2
Pesquera de Duero E 36 C2
Pessac F 28 B2
Pétange L 12 B1
Petín E 35 B3
Petra E 61 B3
Petrer E 53 C3
Petreto-Bicchisano F 62 B1
Pétrola E 52 C2
Peuntenansa E 36 A2
Peveragno I 33 A3
Peyrat-le-Château F 24 B1
Peyrehorade F 28 C1
Peyriac-Minervois F 40 A3
Peyrins F 25 B5
Peyrissac F 24 B1
Peyrolles-en-
Provence F 32 B1
Peyruis F 32 A1
Pézarches F 10 C2
Pézenas F 30 B2
Pezuls F 29 B3
Pfaffenhoffen F 13 C3
Pfäffikon CH 21 B3
Pfetterhouse F 20 B2
Pforzheim D 13 C4
Pfullendorf D 21 B4
Pfungstadt D 13 B4
Pfyn CH 21 B3
Phalsbourg F 12 C3
Philippeville B 7 B4
Piana F 62 A1
Piana Crixia I 33 A4
Pias E 35 B4
Pias P 54 A2
Picassent E 53 B3
Picón E 51 A3
Picquigny F 10 B2
Piedicavallo I 27 B4
Piedicroce F 62 A2
Piedimulera I 27 A5
Piedrabuena E 51 A3
Piedraescrita E 50 A3
Piedrafita E 36 A1
Piedrahita E 44 B2
Piedralaves E 44 B3
Piedras Albas E 49 B4
Piedras Blancas E 35 A5
Piera E 41 C2
Pierre-Buffière F 23 C5
Pierrecourt F 19 B4
Pierre-de-Bresse F 19 C4
Pierrefeu-du-Var F 32 B2
Pierrefitte-Nestalas F 39 B3
Pierrefitte-sur-Aire F 12 C1
Pierrefonds F 10 B2
Pierrefontaine-
les-Varans F 19 B5
Pierrefort F 24 C2
Pierrelatte F 31 A3
Pierrepont
*Aisne* F 11 B3
Pierrepont *continued*
*Meurthe-et-Moselle* F 12 B1
Pietra Ligure I 33 A4
Pieve di Teco I 33 A3
Pigna I 33 B3
Pignan F 30 B2
Pilar de la Horadada E 59 B4
Pilas E 55 B3
Pina de Ebro E 47 A3
Piñar E 57 A4
Pinas F 39 A4
Pineda de la Sierra E 37 B3
Pineda de Mar E 41 C3
Pinerolo I 27 C4
Piney F 11 C4
Pinhal Novo P 48 C2
Pinhão P 42 A2
Pinheiro
*Aveiro* P 42 A1
*Aveiro* P 42 B1
Pinheiro Grande P 48 B2
Pinhel P 43 B2
Pinilla E 52 C2
Pinilla de Toro E 44 A2
Pino F 62 A2
Pino del Rio E 36 B2
Pino de Val E 34 B2
Pinofranqueado E 43 B3
Pinols F 25 B3
Piñor E 34 B2
Pinos del Valle E 57 B4
Pinoso E 53 C2
Pinos Puente E 57 A4
Pinto E 45 B4
Pinzio P 43 B2
Pionsat F 24 A2
Piornal E 44 B2
Pipriac F 15 B4
Piré-sur-Seiche F 15 A4
Piriac-sur-Mer F 15 B3
Pirmasens D 13 B3
Pisany F 22 C3
Pissos F 28 B2
Pithiviers F 17 A4
Pitres E 57 B4
Pizarra E 57 B3
Plabennec F 14 A1
Placencia E 37 A4
Plaffeien CH 20 C2
Plaisance
*Gers* F 28 C3
*Haute-Garonne* F 29 C4
*Tarn* F 30 B1
Plan E 39 B4
Planchez F 18 B3
Plancoët F 15 A3
Plancy-l'Abbaye F 11 C3
Plan-de-Baix F 26 C2
Plan-d'Orgon F 31 B3
Plasencia E 43 B3
Plasenzuela E 50 A1
Platja d'Aro E 41 C4
Pléaux F 24 B2
Pleine-Fougères F 8 B2
Plélan-le-Grand F 15 B3
Plémet F 15 A3
Pléneuf-Val-André F 15 A3
Plentzia E 37 A4
Plérin F 15 A3
Plessé F 15 B4
Plestin-les-Grèves F 14 A2
Pleubian F 14 A2
Pleumartin F 23 B4
Pleumeur-Bodou F 14 A2
Pleurs F 11 C3
Pleyben F 14 A2
Pleyber-Christ F 14 A2
Pliego E 59 B3
Ploemeur F 14 B2
Ploërmel F 15 B3
Ploeuc-sur-Lie F 15 A3
Plogastel St Germain F 14 B1
Plogoff F 14 A1
Plombières-les-Bains F 19 B5
Plonéour-Lanvern F 14 B1
Plouagat F 14 A2
Plouaret F 14 A2
Plouarzel F 14 A1
Plouay F 14 B2
Ploubalay F 15 A3
Ploubazlanec F 14 A2
Ploudalmézeau F 14 A1
Ploudiry F 14 A1
Plouescat F 14 A1
Plouézec F 14 A3
Plougasnou F 14 A2
Plougastel-Daoulas F 14 A1
Plougonven F 14 A2
Plougonver F 14 A2
Plougrescant F 14 A2
Plouguenast F 15 A3
Plouguerneau F 14 A1
Plouha F 14 A3
Plouhinec F 14 A1
Plouigneau F 14 A2
Ploumanach F 14 A2
Plounévez-Quintin F 14 A2
Plouray F 14 A2
Plouzévédé F 14 A1
Plozévet F 14 B1
Pluméliau F 14 B3
Pluvigner F 14 B3
Pobes E 37 B4
Pobla de Segur E 39 B4
Pobladura del Valle E 36 B1
Pobla-Tornesa E 47 B4
Pobra de Trives E 35 B3
Pobra do Brollón E 35 B3
Pobra do Caramiñal E 34 B2
Poceirão P 48 C2
Podence P 43 A3
Podensac F 28 B2
Pogny F 11 C4
Poiares P 42 B1
Poio E 34 B2
Poirino I 27 C4
Poisson F 25 A4
Poissons F 11 C5
Poissy F 10 C2
Poitiers F 23 B4
Poix-de-Picardie F 10 B1
Poix-Terron F 11 B4
Pol E 35 A3
Pola de Allande E 35 A4
Pola de Laviana E 36 A1
Pola de Lena E 35 A5
Pola de Siero E 36 A1
Pola de Somiedo E 35 A4
Polaincourt-et-
Clairefontaine F 19 B5
Polán E 45 C3
Poleñino E 39 C3
Poligny F 19 C4
Pollas E 44 A2
Pollença E 61 B3
Polminhac F 24 C2
Pomarez F 28 C2
Pombal P 48 B2
Pommard F 19 B3
Pompey F 12 C2
Poncin F 26 A2
Ponferrada E 35 B4
Pons F 22 C3
Pont I 27 B4
Pont-a-Celles B 7 B4
Pontacq F 39 A3
Pontailler-sur-Saône F 19 B4
Pont-a-Marcq F 6 B3
Pont-à-Mousson F 12 C2
Pontão P 48 B2
Pontarion F 24 B1
Pontarlier F 19 C5
Pontaubault F 8 B2
Pont-Audemer F 9 A4
Pontaumur F 24 B2
Pont-Aven F 14 B2
Pont Canavese I 27 B4
Pontcharra F 26 B3
Pontcharra-
sur-Turdine F 25 B4
Pontchâteau F 15 B3
Pont-Croix F 14 A1
Pont-d'Ain F 26 A2
Pont-de-Beauvoisin F 26 B2
Pont-de-Buis-
lès-Quimerch F 14 A1
Pont-de-Chéruy F 26 B2
Pont de Dore F 25 B3
Pont-de-Labeaume F 25 C4
Pont-de-l'Arche F 9 A5
Pont de Molins E 41 B3
Pont-de-Roide F 20 B1
Pont-de-Salars F 30 A1
Pont-d'Espagne F 39 B3
Pont de Suert E 39 B4
Pont-de-Vaux F 25 A4
Pont-de-Veyle F 25 A4
Pont d'Ouilly F 9 B3
Pont-du-Château F 24 B3
Pont-du-Navoy F 19 C4
Ponteareas E 34 B2
Ponte-Caldelas E 34 B2
Ponteceso E 34 A2
Pontecesures E 34 B2
Ponte da Barca P 42 A1
Pontedássio I 33 B4
Pontedécimo I 33 A4
Ponte de Lima P 42 A1
Ponte de Sor P 48 B2
Pontedeume E 34 A2
Ponte di Nava I 33 A3
Ponte-Leccia F 62 A2
Pont-en-Royans F 26 B2
Pontenx-les-Forges F 28 B1
Pontevedra E 34 B2
Pont Farcy F 8 B2
Pontfaverger-
Moronvillers F 11 B4
Pontgibaud F 24 B2
Pontigny F 18 B2
Pontijou F 17 B3
Pontinvrea I 33 A4
Pontivy F 14 A3
Pont-l'Abbé F 14 B1
Pont-l'Évêque F 9 A4
Pontlevoy F 17 B3
Pontoise F 10 B2
Pontones E 58 A2
Pontonx-sur-l'Abour F 28 C2
Pontorson F 8 B2
Pont-Remy F 10 A1
Pontresina CH 21 C4
Pontrieux F 14 A2
Ponts E 41 C2
Ponts-aux-Dames F 10 C2
Pont Scorff F 14 B2
Pont-Ste Maxence F 10 B2
Pont-St Esprit F 31 A3
Pont-St Mamet F 29 B3
Pont-St Martin
F 15 B4
I 27 B4
Pont-St Vincent F 12 C2
Pont-sur-Yonne F 18 A2
Pontvallain F 16 B2
Poo E 36 A2
Poperinge B 6 B2
Poppel B 7 A5
Pópulo P 42 A2
Porcuna E 57 A3
Pordic F 14 A3
Pornic F 15 B3
Pornichet F 15 B3
Porquerolles F 32 C2
Porrentruy CH 20 B2
Porreres E 61 B3
Porspoder F 14 A1
Port-a-Binson F 11 B3
Portaje E 49 B4
Portalegre P 49 B3
Portbail F 8 A2
Portbou E 40 B4
Port-Camargue F 31 B3
Port d'Andratx E 60 B2
Port-de-Bouc F 31 B3
Port-de-Lanne F 28 C1
Port de Pollença E 61 B3
Port-des-Barques F 22 C2
Port de Sóller E 60 B2
Portel P 49 C3
Portela P 42 B1
Portelo P 35 C4
Portemouro E 34 B2
Port-en-Bessin F 8 A3
Portes-lès-Valence F 25 C4
Portets F 28 B2
Portezuelo E 49 B4
Porticcio F 62 B1
Portilla de la Reina E 36 A2

Portillo E . . . 44 A3
Portimao P . . . 54 B1
Portinatx E . . . 60 B1
Portinho da Arrabida P . . 48 C1
Port-Joinville F . . . 22 B1
Port-la-Nouvelle F . . . 30 B2
Port Louis F . . . 14 B2
Portman E . . . 59 B4
Port Manech F . . . 14 B2
Port-Navalo F . . . 14 B3
Porto
F . . . 62 A1
P . . . 42 A1
Porto-Alto P . . . 48 C2
Porto Colom E . . . 61 B3
Porto Covo P . . . 54 B1
Porto Cristo E . . . 61 B3
Porto de Lagos P . . . 54 B1
Porto de Mos P . . . 48 B2
Porto de Rei P . . . 48 C2
Porto do Son E . . . 34 B2
Portomarin E . . . 34 B3
Portonovo E . . . 34 B2
Porto Petro E . . . 61 B3
Porto-Vecchio F . . . 62 B2
Portsall F . . . 14 A1
Port-Ste Marie F . . . 29 B3
Port-St-Louis-du-Rhône
F . . . 31 B3
Port-sur-Saône F . . . 19 B5
Portugalete E . . . 37 A4
Port-Vendres F . . . 40 B4
Porzuna E . . . 51 A3
Posada
*Oviedo* E . . . 35 A5
*Oviedo* E . . . 36 A2
Posada de Valdeón E . . . 36 A2
Posadas E . . . 56 A2
Possesse F . . . 11 C4
Potes E . . . 36 A2
Potigny F . . . 9 B3
Potries E . . . 53 C3
Pouancé F . . . 15 B4
Pougues-les-Eaux F . . . 18 B2
Pouilly-en-Auxois F . . . 18 B3
Pouilly-sous Charlieu F . 25 A4
Pouilly-sur-Loire F . . . 18 B1
Poujol-sur-Orb F . . . 30 B2
Poullaouen F . . . 14 A2
Pourcy F . . . 11 B3
Pourrain F . . . 18 B2
Pouyastruc F . . . 39 A4
Pouy-de-Touges F . . . 40 A2
Pouzauges F . . . 22 B3
Pova de Santa Iria P . . . 48 C1
Povedilla E . . . 52 C1
Póvoa
*Beja* P . . . 55 A2
*Santarém* P . . . 48 B2
Póvoa de Lanhoso P . . . 42 A1
Póvoa de Varzim P . . . 42 A1
Póvoa e Meadas P . . . 49 B3
Poyales del Hoyo E . . . 44 B2
Poza de la Sal E . . . 37 B3
Pozaldez E . . . 44 A3
Pozán de Vero E . . . 39 B4
Pozo Alcón E . . . 58 B2
Pozoantiguo E . . . 44 A2
Pozoblanco E . . . 50 B3
Pozo Cañada E . . . 52 C2
Pozo de Guadalajara E . 45 B4
Pozo de la Serna E . . . 51 B4
Pozohondo E . . . 52 C2
Pozondón E . . . 46 B2
Pozuel del Campo E . . . 46 B2
Pozuelo de Alarcón E . . 45 B4
Pozuelo de Calatrava E 51 B4
Pozuelo del Páramo E . . 36 B1
Pozuelo de Zarzón E . . . 43 B4
Prada E . . . 35 B3
Pradelle F . . . 26 C2
Pradelles F . . . 25 C3
Prades
E . . . 41 C1
F . . . 40 B3
Prado
E . . . 36 A1
P . . . 42 A1
Prado del Rey E . . . 56 B2
Pradoluengo E . . . 37 B3
Pragelato I . . . 27 B3
Prahecq F . . . 23 B3
Praia P . . . 48 B1
Praia da Rocha P . . . 54 B1
Praia da Viera P . . . 48 B2
Praia de Mira P . . . 42 B1
Pralognan-la-Vanoise F . 26 B3
Prat F . . . 40 A1
Prat de Compte E . . . 47 B4
Pratdip E . . . 41 C1
Prats-de-Mollo-la-Preste
F . . . 40 B3
Prauthoy F . . . 19 B4
Pravia E . . . 35 A4
Prayssac F . . . 29 B4
Prazzo I . . . 32 A3
Préchac F . . . 28 B2
Précy-sur-Thil F . . . 18 B3
Pré-en-Pail F . . . 9 B3
Préfailles F . . . 15 B3
Preignan F . . . 29 C3
Prémery F . . . 18 B2
Prémia I . . . 27 A5
Premiàde Mar E . . . 41 C3
Prémont F . . . 11 A3
Presencio E . . . 37 B3
Presly F . . . 17 B4
Pressac F . . . 23 B4
Preuilly-sur-Claise F . . . 23 B4
Prevenchères F . . . 31 A2
Préveranges F . . . 24 A2
Priaranza del Bierzo E . . 35 B4
Priay F . . . 26 A2
Priego E . . . 46 B1
Priego de Córdoba E . . . 57 A3
Primel-Trégastel F . . . 14 A2
Primstal D . . . 12 B2
Priorio E . . . 36 B2
Privas F . . . 25 C4
Proaza E . . . 35 A4
Proença-a-Nova P . . . 48 B3
Proença-a-Velha P . . . 49 A3
Profondeville B . . . 7 B4
Propriano F . . . 62 B1
Provins F . . . 10 C3
Pruna E . . . 56 B2
Prunelli-di-Fiumorbo F . 62 A2
Pruniers F . . . 17 C4
Puchevillers F . . . 10 A2
Puçol E . . . 53 B3
Puebla de Albortón E . . 47 A3
Puebla de Alcocer E . . . 50 B2
Puebla de Beleña E . . . 45 B4
Puebla de Don Fadrique
E . . . 58 B2
Puebla de Don Rodrigo
E . . . 50 A3
Puebla de Guzmán E . . . 55 B2
Puebla de la Calzada E . 49 C4
Puebla de la Reina E . . . 50 B1
Puebla de Lillo E . . . 36 A1
Puebla del Maestre E . . 55 A3
Puebla del Principe E . . 52 C1
Puebla de Obando E . . . 49 B4
Puebla de Sanabria E . . 35 B4
Puebla de Sancho Pérez
E . . . 49 C4
Puente Almuhey E . . . 36 B2
Puente de Domingo Flórez
E . . . 35 B4
Puente de Génave E . . . 58 A2
Puente del Congosto E . 44 B2
Puente de Montañana E 39 B4
Puente Duero E . . . 44 A3
Puente-Genil E . . . 56 A3
Puente la Reina E . . . 38 B2
Puente la Reina de Jaca
E . . . 38 B3
Puentelarra E . . . 37 B3
Puente Mayorga E . . . 56 B2
Puente Viesgo E . . . 37 A3
Puertas
*Asturias* E . . . 36 A2
*Salamanca* E . . . 43 A3
Puerto de Mazarrón E . . 59 B3
Puerto de Santa Cruz E . 50 A2
Puerto de San Vicente
E . . . 50 A2
Puerto-Lápice E . . . 51 A4
Puertollano E . . . 51 B3
Puerto Lumbreras E . . . 58 B3
Puerto Moral E . . . 55 B3
Puerto Real E . . . 56 B1
Puerto Rey E . . . 50 A2
Puerto Seguro E . . . 43 B3
Puerto Serrano E . . . 56 B2
Puget-Sur-Argens F . . . 32 B2
Puget-Théniers F . . . 32 B2
Puget-ville F . . . 32 B2
Puigcerdà E . . . 40 B2
Puigpunyent E . . . 60 B2
Puig Reig E . . . 41 C2
Puillon F . . . 28 C2
Puimichel F . . . 32 B2
Puimoisson F . . . 32 B2
Puiseaux F . . . 17 A4
Puisieux F . . . 10 A2
Puisserguier F . . . 30 B2
Puivert F . . . 40 B3
Pujols F . . . 28 B2
Pulgar E . . . 51 A3
Pulpí E . . . 58 B3
Punta Prima E . . . 61 B4
Puntas de Calnegre E . . 59 B3
Punta Umbria E . . . 55 B3
Purchena E . . . 58 B2
Purullena E . . . 58 B1
Putanges-Pont-
Ecrepin F . . . 9 B3
Putte B . . . 7 A4
Puttelange-aux-Lacs F . 12 B2
Püttlingen D . . . 12 B2
Puy-Guillaume F . . . 25 B3
Puylaroque F . . . 29 B4
Puylaurens F . . . 40 A3
Puy-l'Évêque F . . . 29 B4
Puymirol F . . . 29 B3
Puyôo F . . . 28 C2
Puyrolland F . . . 22 B3
Pyla-sur-Mer F . . . 28 B1


## Q


Quargnento I . . . 27 C5
Quarré-les-Tombes F . . . 18 B2
Quarteira P . . . 54 B1
Quatre-Champs F . . . 11 B4
Queige F . . . 26 B3
Queipo E . . . 55 B3
Queixans E . . . 40 B2
Quel E . . . 38 B1
Quelaines-St-Gault F . . . 16 B1
Queljada P . . . 42 A1
Quemada E . . . 37 C3
Queralbs E . . . 41 B3
Quérigut F . . . 40 B3
Quero E . . . 51 A4
Querqueville F . . . 8 A2
Quesada E . . . 58 B1
Questembert F . . . 15 B3
Quettehou F . . . 8 A2
Quevauvillers F . . . 10 B2
Quevy B . . . 7 B4
Quiaois P . . . 42 B1
Quiberon F . . . 14 B2
Quiberville F . . . 9 A4
Quiévrain B . . . 7 B3
Quillan F . . . 40 B3
Quillebeuf F . . . 9 A4
Quimper F . . . 14 A1
Quimperlé F . . . 14 B2
Quincampoix F . . . 9 A5
Quincoces de Yuso E . . . 37 B3
Quincy F . . . 17 B4
Quinéville F . . . 8 A2
Quingey F . . . 19 B4
Quinson F . . . 32 B2
Quinssaines F . . . 24 A2
Quinta-Grande P . . . 48 C2
Quintana de la Serena
E . . . 50 B2
Quintana del Castillo E . 35 B4
Quintana del Marco E . . 35 B5
Quintana del Puenta E . 36 B2
Quintana-Martin
Galindez E . . . 37 B3
Quintanaortuño E . . . 37 B3
Quintanapalla E . . . 37 B3
Quintanar de
la Orden E . . . 51 A4
Quintanar de la Sierra E 37 C3
Quintanar del Rey E . . . 52 B2
Quintanilla de la Mata E 37 C3
Quintanilla del Coco E . 37 C3
Quintanilla de Onésimo
E . . . 44 A3
Quintanilla de Somoza
E . . . 35 B4
Quintas de Valdelucio E 36 B2
Quintela P . . . 42 B2
Quintin F . . . 14 A3
Quinto E . . . 47 A3
Quiroga E . . . 35 B3
Quismondo E . . . 44 B3
Quissac F . . . 31 B2


## R


Raamsdonksveer NL . . . 7 A4
Rábade E . . . 34 A3
Rabanales E . . . 43 A3
Rabastens F . . . 29 C4
Rabastens-de-Bigorre F 39 A4
Racconigi I . . . 27 C4
Rachecourt-sur-Marne
F . . . 11 C5
Radolfzell D . . . 21 B3
Raigada E . . . 35 B3
Rairiz de Veiga E . . . 34 B3
Raiva
*Aveiro* P . . . 42 A1
*Coimbra* P . . . 42 B1
Ramacastañas E . . . 44 B2
Ramales de la Victoria
E . . . 37 A3
Rambervillers F . . . 12 C2
Rambouillet F . . . 10 C1
Rambucourt F . . . 12 C1
Ramerupt F . . . 11 C4
Ramirás E . . . 34 B2
Ramiswil CH . . . 20 B2
Ramonville-St Agne F . . 29 C4
Ramstein-
Meisenbach D . . . 13 B3
Rance B . . . 11 A4
Randan F . . . 25 A3
Randin E . . . 34 C3
Rânes F . . . 9 B3
Rankweil A . . . 21 B4
Ranvalhal P . . . 48 B1
Raon-l'Étape F . . . 12 C2
Raposa P . . . 48 B2
Rapperswil CH . . . 21 B3
Rasal E . . . 39 B3
Rascafria E . . . 45 B4
Rasines E . . . 37 A3
Rasquera E . . . 47 A4
Rastatt D . . . 13 C4
Rasueros E . . . 44 A2
Raucourt-et-Flaba F . . . 11 B4
Raulhac F . . . 24 C2
Rauville-la-Bigot F . . . 8 A2
Rauzan F . . . 28 B2
Ravels B . . . 7 A4
Ravensburg D . . . 21 B4
Razes F . . . 23 B5
Razo E . . . 34 A2
Réalmont F . . . 30 B1
Rebais F . . . 10 C3
Rebordelo P . . . 43 A2
Recas E . . . 45 B4
Recey-sur-Ource F . . . 19 B3
Recezinhos P . . . 42 A1
Recogne B . . . 12 B1
Recoules-
Prévinquières F . . . 30 A1
Redange L . . . 12 B1
Redon F . . . 15 B3
Redondela E . . . 34 B2
Redondo P . . . 49 C3
Régil E . . . 38 A1
Regniéville F . . . 12 C1
Regny F . . . 25 B4
Rego da Leirosa P . . . 48 A2
Regueiro E . . . 34 B2
Reguengo
*Portalegre* P . . . 49 B3
*Santarém* P . . . 48 B2
Reguengos de
Monsaraz P . . . 49 C3
Reichelsheim D . . . 13 B4
Reichshoffen F . . . 13 C3
Reiden CH . . . 20 B2
Reigada
E . . . 35 A4
P . . . 43 B3
Reillanne F . . . 32 B1
Reillo E . . . 52 B2
Reims F . . . 11 B4
Reinach CH . . . 20 B3
Reinheim D . . . 13 B4
Reinosa E . . . 36 A2
Relleu E . . . 53 C3
Rémalard F . . . 9 B4
Rembercourt-
aux-Pots F . . . 11 C5
Remedios P . . . 48 B1
Remich L . . . 12 B2
Rémilly F . . . 12 B2
Remiremont F . . . 19 A5
Remolinos E . . . 38 C2
Remoulins F . . . 31 B3
Rémuzat F . . . 31 A4
Renaison F . . . 25 A3
Renazé F . . . 15 B4
Renchen D . . . 13 C4
Rencurel F . . . 26 B2
Renedo E . . . 44 A3
Renens CH . . . 19 C5
Rennes F . . . 15 A4
Rennes-les-Bains F . . . 40 B3
Rentería E . . . 38 A2
Requena E . . . 53 B2
Réquista F . . . 30 A1
Resende P . . . 42 A2
Ressons-sur-Matz F . . . 10 B2
Restábal E . . . 57 B4
Retamal E . . . 49 C4
Rethel F . . . 11 B4
Retie B . . . 7 A5
Retiers F . . . 15 B4
Retortillo E . . . 43 B3
Retortillo de Soria E . . . 45 A4
Retournac F . . . 25 B4
Retuerta del Bullaque E 51 A3
Reuilly F . . . 17 B4
Reus E . . . 41 C2
Reusel NL . . . 7 A5
Revel F . . . 40 A2
Revello I . . . 27 C4
Revenga E . . . 45 B3
Revest-du-Bion F . . . 32 A1
Revigny-sur-Ornain F . . 11 C4
Revin F . . . 11 B4
Reyero E . . . 36 B1
Rezé F . . . 15 B4
Rhaunen D . . . 13 B3
Rheinau D . . . 13 C3
Rheinfelden D . . . 20 B2
Rhêmes-Notre-Dame I . . 27 B4
Rialé F . . . 15 B4
Riaño E . . . 36 B1
Rians F . . . 32 B1
Rianxo E . . . 34 B2
Riaza E . . . 45 A4
Riba E . . . 37 A3
Ribadavia E . . . 34 B2
Ribadeo E . . . 35 A3
Riba de Saelices E . . . 46 B1
Ribadesella E . . . 36 A1
Ribaflecha E . . . 37 B4
Ribaforada E . . . 38 C2
Riba-roja d'Ebre E . . . 47 A4
Riba-Roja de Turia E . . . 53 B3
Ribeauvillé F . . . 20 A2
Ribécourt-
Dreslincourt F . . . 10 B2
Ribeira da Pena P . . . 42 A2
Ribeira de Piquín E . . . 35 A3
Ribemont F . . . 11 B3
Ribérac F . . . 29 A3
Ribera de Cardós E . . . 40 B2
Ribera del Fresno E . . . 50 B1
Ribesalbes E . . . 53 A3
Ribes de Freser E . . . 41 B3
Ribiers F . . . 32 A1
Richebourg F . . . 19 A4
Richelieu F . . . 16 B2
Richisau CH . . . 21 B3
Richterswil CH . . . 21 B3
Ricla E . . . 46 A2
Ridderkerk NL . . . 7 A4
Riddes CH . . . 27 A4
Riec-sur-Bélon F . . . 14 B2
Riedlingen D . . . 21 A4
Riedstadt D . . . 13 B4
Riego de la Vega E . . . 35 B5
Riego del Camino E . . . 43 A4
Riello E . . . 35 B5
Rienne B . . . 11 B4
Riénsena E . . . 36 A2
Rieumes F . . . 40 A2
Rieupeyroux F . . . 30 A1
Rieux-Volvestre F . . . 40 A2
Riez F . . . 32 B2
Riggisberg CH . . . 20 C2
Rignac F . . . 30 A1
Rijen NL . . . 7 A4
Rijkevorsel B . . . 7 A4
Rillé F . . . 16 B2
Rillo de Gallo E . . . 46 B2
Rimogne F . . . 11 B4
Rincón de la Victoria E . 57 B3
Rincón de Soto E . . . 38 B2
Rinlo E . . . 35 A3
Rio E . . . 34 B3
Riobo E . . . 34 B2
Riodeva E . . . 46 B2
Rio do Coures P . . . 48 B2
Rio Douro P . . . 42 A2
Riofrio E . . . 44 B3
Rio Frio P . . . 48 C2
Riofrio de Aliste E . . . 43 A3
Rio frio de Riaza E . . . 45 A4
Riogordo E . . . 57 B3
Rioja E . . . 58 C2
Riolobos E . . . 49 B4
Riom F . . . 24 B3
Rio Maior P . . . 48 B2
Riom-ès-Montagnes F . . 24 B2
Rion-des-Landes F . . . 28 C2
Rionegro del Puente E . . 35 B4
Riopar E . . . 52 C1
Riós E . . . 35 C3
Rioseco E . . . 36 A1
Rioseco de Tapia E . . . 35 B5
Rio Tinto P . . . 42 A1
Riotord F . . . 25 B4
Riotorto E . . . 35 A3
Rioz F . . . 19 B5
Ripoll E . . . 41 B3
Riscle F . . . 28 C2
Riva Ligure I . . . 33 B3
Rivarolo Canavese I . . . 27 B4
Rive-de-Gier F . . . 25 B4
Rivedoux-Plage F . . . 22 B2
Rives F . . . 26 B2
Rivesaltes F . . . 40 B3
Rivoli I . . . 27 B4
Rixheim F . . . 20 B2
Roa E . . . 37 C3
Roanne F . . . 25 A4
Robleda E . . . 43 B3
Robledillo de Trujillo E . 50 A2
Robledo
*Albacete* E . . . 52 C1
*Orense* E . . . 35 B4
Robledo de Chavela E . . 45 B3
Robledo del Buey E . . . 50 A3
Robledo del Mazo E . . . 50 A3
Robledollano E . . . 50 A2
Robles de la Valcueva
E . . . 36 B1
Robliza de Cojos E . . . 43 B4
Robres E . . . 39 C3
Robres del Castillo E . . 38 B1
Rocafort de Queralt E . . 41 C2
Rocamadour F . . . 29 B4
Rochechouart F . . . 23 C4
Rochefort
B . . . 7 B5
F . . . 22 C3
Rochefort-en-Terre F . . 15 B3
Rochefort-Montagne F . 24 B2
Rochefort-sur-Nenon F . 19 B4
Roche-lez-Beaupré F . . 19 B5
Rochemaure F . . . 31 A3
Rocheservière F . . . 22 B2
Rociana del Condado E . 55 B3
Rockenhausen D . . . 13 B3
Rocroi F . . . 11 B4
Roda de Bara E . . . 41 C2
Roda de Ter E . . . 41 C3
Rodalben D . . . 13 B3
Rodeiro E . . . 34 B3
Ródenas E . . . 46 B2
Rödermark D . . . 13 B4
Rodez F . . . 30 A1
Rodoñá E . . . 41 C2
Roesbrugge B . . . 6 B2
Roeschwoog F . . . 13 C4
Roeselare B . . . 6 B3
Roffiac F . . . 24 B3
Rogliano F . . . 62 A2
Rognes F . . . 31 B4
Rogny-les-7-Ecluses F . 17 B4
Rohan F . . . 15 A3
Rohrbach-lès-Bitche F . 12 B3
Roisel F . . . 10 B3
Rojales E . . . 59 A4
Rolampont F . . . 19 B4
Rollán E . . . 43 B4
Rolle CH . . . 19 C5
Romagnano Sésia I . . . 27 B5
Romagné F . . . 8 B2
Romanèche-Thorins F . 25 A4
Romanshorn CH . . . 21 B4
Romans-sur-Isère F . . . 26 B2
Rombas F . . . 12 B2
Romeán E . . . 35 B3
Romenay F . . . 19 C4
Romeral E . . . 51 A4
Romilly-sur-Seine F . . . 11 C3
Romont CH . . . 20 C1
Romorantin-
Lanthenay F . . . 17 B3
Roncal E . . . 38 B3
Ronce-les-Bains F . . . 22 C2
Ronchamp F . . . 20 B1
Ronco Canavese I . . . 27 B4
Ronda E . . . 56 B2
Ronse B . . . 7 B3
Roosendaal NL . . . 7 A4
Ropuerelos del
Páramo E . . . 35 B5
Roquebilière F . . . 33 A3
Roquebrun F . . . 30 B2
Roquecourbe F . . . 30 B1
Roquefort F . . . 28 B2
Roquemaure F . . . 31 A3
Roquesteron F . . . 32 B3
Roquetas de Mar E . . . 58 C2
Roquetes E . . . 47 B4
Roquevaire F . . . 32 B1
Rorschach CH . . . 21 B4
Rosal de la Frontera E . 55 B2
Rosans F . . . 32 A1
Rosário P . . . 54 B1
Roscoff F . . . 14 A2
Rosel UK . . . 8 A1
Rosell E . . . 47 B4
Roselló E . . . 47 A4
Rosenfeld D . . . 13 C4
Roses E . . . 41 B4
Rosheim F . . . 13 C3
Rosières-en-Santerre F . 10 B2
Rosmaninhal P . . . 49 B3
Rosoy F . . . 18 A2
Rosporden F . . . 14 B2
Rosquete P . . . 48 B2
Rossas
*Aveiro* P . . . 42 B1
*Braga* P . . . 42 A1
Rossiglione I . . . 33 A4
Rossignol B . . . 12 B1
Rostrenen F . . . 14 A2
Rota E . . . 55 C3
Rothéneuf F . . . 8 B2
Rotova E . . . 53 C3
Rottenburg D . . . 13 C4
Rotterdam NL . . . 7 A4
Rottweil D . . . 21 A3
Roubaix F . . . 6 B3
Roudouallec F . . . 14 A2
Rouen F . . . 9 A5
Rouffach F . . . 20 B2
Rougé F . . . 15 B4
Rougemont F . . . 19 B5
Rougemont-le-
Château F . . . 20 B1
Rouillac F . . . 23 C3
Rouillé F . . . 23 B4
Roujan F . . . 30 B2
Roulans F . . . 19 B5
Roussac F . . . 23 B5
Roussennac F . . . 30 A1
Rousses F . . . 30 A2
Roussillon F . . . 25 B4
Rouvroy-sur-Audry F . . . 11 B4
Rouy F . . . 18 B2
Royan F . . . 22 C2
Royat F . . . 24 B3
Roybon F . . . 26 B2
Roye F . . . 10 B2
Royère-de-Vassivière F . 24 B1
Royos E . . . 58 B2
Rozadas E . . . 35 A4
Rozalén del Monte E . . . 45 C5
Rozay-en-Brie F . . . 10 C2
Rozoy-sur-Serre F . . . 11 B4
Ruanes E . . . 50 A2
Rubí E . . . 41 C3
Rubiá E . . . 35 B4
Rubiacedo de Abajo E . . 37 B3
Rubielos Bajos E . . . 52 B1
Rubielos de Mora E . . . 47 B3
Rucandio E . . . 37 B3
Ruddervorde B . . . 6 A3
Rüdesheim D . . . 13 B3
Rue F . . . 6 B1
Rueda E . . . 44 A3
Rueda de Jalón E . . . 46 A2
Ruelle-sur-Touvre F . . . 23 C4
Ruerrero E . . . 37 B3
Ruffec F . . . 23 B4
Rugles F . . . 9 B4
Ruidera E . . . 52 C1
Ruillé-sur-le-Loir F . . . 16 B2
Ruiselede B . . . 6 A3
Rulles B . . . 12 B1
Rülzheim D . . . 13 B4
Rumigny F . . . 11 B4
Rumilly F . . . 26 B2
Rumont F . . . 11 C5
Runa P . . . 48 B1
Ruoms F . . . 31 A3
Rupt-sur-Moselle F . . . 20 B1
Rus E . . . 51 B4
Rüsselsheim D . . . 13 B4
Rustrel F . . . 31 B4
Rute E . . . 57 A3
Rüti CH . . . 21 B3
Ruynes-en-Margeride F . 24 C3


## S


Saales F . . . 12 C3
Saanen CH . . . 20 C2
Saarbrücken D . . . 12 B2
Saarburg D . . . 12 B2
Saarlouis D . . . 12 B2
Saas-Fee CH . . . 27 A4
Sabadell E . . . 41 C3
Sabero E . . . 36 B1
Sabiñánigo E . . . 39 B3
Sabiote E . . . 51 B4
Sables-d'Or-les-Pins F . 15 A3
Sablé-sur-Sarthe F . . . 16 B1
Sabóia P . . . 54 B1
Sabres F . . . 28 B2
Sabrosa P . . . 42 A2
Sabugal P . . . 43 B2
Sacecorbo E . . . 46 B1
Saceda del Rio E . . . 45 B5
Sacedón E . . . 45 B5
Saceruela E . . . 50 B3
Sacramenia E . . . 45 A4
Sada E . . . 34 A2
Sádaba E . . . 38 B2
Sadernes E . . . 41 B3
Saelices E . . . 45 C5
Saelices de Mayorga E . . 36 B1
Saeul L . . . 12 B1
Safara P . . . 55 A2
S'Agaro E . . . 41 C4
Sagone F . . . 62 A1
Sagres P . . . 54 C1
Sagunt E . . . 53 B3
Sagy F . . . 19 C4
Sahagún E . . . 36 B1
Saignelégier CH . . . 20 B1
Saignes F . . . 24 B2
Saillagouse F . . . 40 B3
Saillans F . . . 26 C2
Sains Richaumont F . . . 11 B3
St Affrique F . . . 30 B1
St Agnan F . . . 18 C2
St Agnant F . . . 22 C3
St Agrève F . . . 25 B4
St Aignan F . . . 17 B3
St Aignan-sur-Roë F . . . 15 B4
St Alban-sur-
Limagnole F . . . 25 C3
St Amand-en-Puisaye F . 18 B2
St Amand-les-Eaux F . . . 7 B3
St Amand-Longpré F . . . 17 B3
St Amand-Montrond F . . 17 C4
St Amans F . . . 25 C3
St Amans-Soult F . . . 30 B1
St Amant-
Roche-Savine F . . . 25 B3
St Amarin F . . . 20 B1
St Ambroix F . . . 31 A3
St Amé F . . . 20 A1
St Amour F . . . 26 A2
St André-de-Corcy F . . . 25 B4
St André-de-Cubzac F . . 28 B2
St André-de-l'Eure F . . . 9 B5
St André-de-
Roquepertuis F . . . 31 A3
St André-de-
Sangonis F . . . 30 B2
St Andre-de-
Valborgne F . . . 30 A2
St André-les-Alpes F . . . 32 B2
St Angel F . . . 24 B2
St Anthème F . . . 25 B3
St Antoine F . . . 62 A2
St Antoine-de-Ficalba F . 29 B3
St Antönien CH . . . 21 C4
St Antonin-Noble-Val F . 29 B4
St Août F . . . 17 C3
St Armant-Tallende F . . 24 B3
St Arnoult F . . . 10 C1
St Astier F . . . 29 A3
St Auban F . . . 32 B2
St Aubin
CH . . . 20 C1
F . . . 19 B4
UK . . . 8 A1
St Aubin-d'Aubigne´ F . . 15 A4
St Aubin-du-Cormier F . . 15 A4
St Aubin-sur-Aire F . . . 12 C1
St Aubin-sur-Mer F . . . 9 A3
St Aulaye F . . . 28 A3
St Avit F . . . 24 B2
St Avold F . . . 12 B2
St Aygulf F . . . 32 B2
St Bauzille-de-Putois F . 30 B2
St Béat F . . . 39 B4
St Beauzély F . . . 30 A1
St Benim-d'Azy F . . . 18 C2
St Benoît-du-Sault F . . . 23 B5
St Benoit-en-Woëvre F . 12 C1
St Berthevin F . . . 16 A1
St Blaise-la-Roche F . . . 12 C3
St Blin F . . . 19 A4
St Bonnet F . . . 26 C3
St Bonnet Briance F . . . 23 C5
St Bonnet-de-Joux F . . . 18 C3
St Bonnet-le-Château F . 25 B4
St Bonnet-le-Froid F . . . 25 B4
St Brévin-les-Pins F . . . 15 B3
St Briac-sur-Mer F . . . 15 A3
St Brice-en-Coglès F . . . 8 B2
St Brieuc F . . . 15 A3
St Bris-le-Vineux F . . . 18 B2
St Broladre F . . . 8 B2
St Calais F . . . 16 B2
St Cannat F . . . 31 B4
St Cast-le-Guildo F . . . 15 A3
St Céré F . . . 29 B4
St Cergue CH . . . 26 A3
St Cergues F . . . 26 A3
St Cernin F . . . 24 B2
St Chamant F . . . 24 B1
St Chamas F . . . 31 B4
St Chamond F . . . 25 B4
St Chély-d'Apcher F . . . 24 C3
St Chély-d'Aubrac F . . . 24 C2

St Chinian F 30 B1
St Christol F 31 A4
St Christol-lès-Alès F 31 A3
St Christoly-Médoc F 22 C3
St Christophe-du-Ligneron F 22 B2
St Christophe-en-Brionnais F 25 A4
St Ciers-sur-Gironde F 28 A2
St Clair-sur-Epte F 10 B1
St Clar F 29 C3
St Claud F 23 C4
St Claude F 26 A2
St Come-d'Olt F 30 A1
St Cosme-en-Vairais F 9 B4
St Cyprien
*Dordogne* F 29 B4
*Pyrenées-Orientales* F 40 B4
St Cyr-sur-Loire F 16 B2
St Cyr-sur-Mer F 32 B1
St Cyr-sur-Methon F 25 A4
St Denis F 10 C2
St Denis-d'Oléron F 22 B2
St Denis d'Orques F 16 A1
St Didier F 25 A4
St Didier-en-Velay F 25 B4
St Dié F 12 C2
St Dier-d'Auvergne F 25 B3
St Dizier F 11 C4
St Dizier-Leyrenne F 24 A1
Ste Adresse F 9 A4
Ste Anne F 9 B4
Ste Anne-d'Auray F 14 B3
Ste Croix CH 19 C5
Ste Croix-Volvestre F 40 A2
Ste Engrâce F 38 A3
Ste Enimie F 30 A2
St Efflam F 14 A2
Ste Foy-de-Peyrolières F 40 A2
Ste Foy-la-Grande F 28 B3
Ste Foy l'Argentiere F 25 B4
Ste Gauburge-Ste Colombe F 9 B4
Ste Gemme la Plaine F 22 B2
Ste Geneviève F 10 B2
St Égrève F 26 B2
Ste Hélène F 28 B2
Ste Hélène-sur-Isère F 26 B3
Ste Hermine F 22 B2
Ste Jalle F 31 A4
Ste Livrade-sur-Lot F 29 B3
St Eloy-les-Mines F 24 A2
Ste Marie-aux-Mines F 20 A2
Ste Marie-du-Mont F 8 A2
Ste Maure-de-Touraine F 16 B2
Ste Maxime F 32 B2
Ste Ménéhould F 11 B4
Ste Mère-Église F 8 A2
St Emiland F 18 C3
St Émilion F 28 B2
Sainteny F 8 A2
Ste Ode B 12 A1
Saintes F 22 C3
Ste Savine F 11 C4
Ste Sévère-sur-Indre F 17 C4
Ste Sigolène F 25 B4
St Esteben F 38 A2
St Estèphe F 28 A2
Ste Suzanne F 16 A1
St Étienne F 25 B4
St Etienne-de-Baigorry F 38 A2
St Étienne-de-Cuines F 26 B3
St Etienne-de-Fursac F 24 A1
St Etienne-de-Montluc F 15 B4
St-Etienne-de-St-Geoirs F 26 B2
St Étienne-de-Tinée F 32 A2
St Étienne-du-Bois F 26 A2
St Étienne-du-Rouvray F 9 A5
St Etienne-les-Orgues F 32 A1
Ste Tulle F 32 B1
St Fargeau F 18 B2
St Félicien F 25 B4
St Felix-de-Sorgues F 30 B1
St Félix-Lauragais F 40 A2
St Firmin F 26 C3
St Florent F 62 A2
St Florentin F 18 B2
St Florent-le-Vieil F 15 B4
St Florent-sur-Cher F 17 C4
St Flour F 24 B3
St Flovier F 17 C3
St Fort-sur-le-Né F 23 C3
St Fulgent F 22 B2
St Galmier F 25 B4
St Gaudens F 39 A4
St Gaultier F 23 B5
St Gély-du-Fesc F 30 B2
St Genest-Malifaux F 25 B4
St Gengoux-le-National F 18 C3
St Geniez F 32 A2
St Geniez-d'Olt F 30 A1
St Genis-de-Saintonge F 22 C3
St Genis-Pouilly F 26 A3
St Genix-sur-Guiers F 26 B2
St Georges Buttavent F 8 B3
St Georges-d'Aurac F 25 B3
St Georges-de-Commiers F 26 B2
St Georges-de-Didonne F 22 C3
St Georges-de-Luzençon F 30 A1
St Georges-de Mons F 24 B2
St Georges-de-ReneinsF 25 A4
St Georges d'Oléron F 22 C2
St Georges-en-Couzan F 25 B3
St Georges-lès-BaillargeauxF 23 B4
St Georges-sur-Loire F 16 B1
St Georges-sur-Meuse B 7 B5
St Geours-de-Maremne F 28 C1
St Gérand-de-Vaux F 25 A3
St Gérand-le-Puy F 25 A3
St Germain F 19 B5
St Germain-Chassenay F 18 C2
St Germain-de-Calberte F 30 A2
St Germain-de-Confolens F 23 B4
St Germain-de-Joux F 26 A2
St Germain-des-Fossés F 25 A3
St Germain-du-Bois F 19 C4
St Germain-du-Plain F 19 C3
St Germain-du Puy F 17 B4
St Germain-en-Laye F 10 C2
St Germain-Laval F 25 B4
St Germain-Lembron F 24 B3
St Germain-les-Belles F 24 B1
St Germain-Lespinasse F 25 A3
St Germain-l'Herm F 25 B3
St Gervais-d'Auvergne F 24 A2
St Gervais-les-Bains F 26 B3
St Gervais-sur-Mare F 30 B2
St Gildas-de-Rhuys F 14 B3
St Gildas-des-Bois F 15 B3
St Gilles
*Gard* F 31 B3
*Ille-et-Vilaine* F 15 A4
St Gilles-Croix-de-Vie F 22 B2
St Gingolph F 27 A3
St Girons
*Ariège* F 40 B2
*Landes* F 28 C1
St Girons-Plage F 28 C1
St Gobain F 11 B3
St Gorgon-Main F 19 B5
St Guénolé F 14 B1
St Helier UK 8 A1
St Herblain F 15 B4
St Hilaire
*Allier* F 18 C2
*Aude* F 40 A3
St Hilaire-de-Riez F 22 B2
St Hilaire-des-Loges F 22 B3
St Hilaire-de-Villefranche F 22 C3
St Hilaire-du-Harcouët F 8 B2
St Hilaire-du-Rosier F 26 B2
St Hippolyte
*Aveyron* F 24 C2
*Doubs* F 20 B1
St Hippolyte-du-Fort F 30 B2
St Honoré-les-Bains F 18 C2
St Hubert B 12 A1
St Imier CH 20 B2
St Izaire F 30 B1
St Jacques-de-la-Lande F 15 A4
St Jacut-de-la-Mer F 15 A3
St James F 8 B2
St Jaume d'Enveja E 47 B4
St Jean-Brévelay F 15 B3
St Jean-d'Angély F 22 C3
St Jean-de-Belleville F 26 B3
St Jean-de-Bournay F 26 B2
St Jean-de-Braye F 17 B3
St Jean-de-Côle F 23 C4
St Jean-de-Daye F 8 A2
St Jean de Losne F 19 B4
St Jean-de-Luz F 38 A2
St Jean-de-Maurienne F 26 B3
St Jean-de-Monts F 22 B1
St Jean-d'Illac F 28 B2
St Jean-du-Bruel F 30 A2
St Jean-du-Gard F 31 A2
St Jean-en-Royans F 26 B2
St Jean-la-Riviere F 33 B3
St Jean-Pied-de-Port F 38 A2
St Jean-Poutge F 29 C3
St Jeoire F 26 A3
St Joachim F 15 B3
St Jorioz F 26 B3
St Joris Winge B 7 B4
St Jouin-de-Marnes F 16 C1
St Juéry F 30 B1
St Julien F 26 A2
St Julien-Chapteuil F 25 B4
St Julien-de-Vouvantes F 15 B4
St Julien-du-Sault F 18 A2
St Julien-du-Verdon F 32 B2
St Julien-en-Born F 28 B1
St Julien-en-Genevois F 26 A3
St Julien-l'Ars F 23 B4
St Julien la-Vêtre F 25 B3
St Julien-Mont-Denis F 26 B3
St Julien-sur-Reyssouze F 26 A2
St Junien F 23 C4
St Just F 31 A3
St Just-en-Chaussée F 10 B2
St Just-en-Chevalet F 25 B3
St Justin F 28 C2
St Just-St Rambert F 25 B4
St Lary-Soulan F 39 B4
St Laurent-d'Aigouze F 31 B3
St Laurent-de-Chamousset F 25 B4
St Laurent-de-Condel F 9 A3
St Laurent-de-la-Cabrerisse F 40 A3
St Laurent-de-la-Salanque F 40 B3
St Laurent-des-Autels F 15 B4
St Laurent-du-Pont F 26 B2
St Laurent-en-Caux F 9 A4
St Laurent-en-Grandvaux F 19 C4
St Laurent-Médoc F 28 A2
St Laurent-sur-Gorre F 23 C4
St Laurent-sur-Mer F 8 A3
St Laurent-sur-Sèvre F 22 B3
St Leger B 12 B1
St Léger-de-Vignes F 18 C2
St Léger-sous-Beuvray F 18 C3
St Léger-sur-Dheune F 18 C3
St Léonard-de-Noblat F 24 B1
St Lô F 8 A2
St Lon-les-Mines F 28 C1
St Louis F 20 B2
St Loup F 25 A3
St Loup-de-la-Salle F 19 C3
St Loup-sur-Semouse F 19 B5
St Lunaire F 15 A3
St Lupicin F 26 A2
St Lyphard F 15 B3
St Lys F 40 A2
St Macaire F 28 B2
St Maclou F 9 A4
St Maixent-l'École F 23 B3
St Malo F 8 B1
St Mamet-la-Salvetat F 24 C2
St Mandrier-sur-Mer F 32 B1
St Marcel
*Drôme* F 25 C4
*Saône-et-Loire* F 19 C3
St Marcellin F 26 B2
St Marcellin sur Loire F 25 B4
St Marcet F 39 A4
St Mards-en-Othe F 18 A2
St Mars-la-Jaille F 15 B4
St Martin-d'Ablois F 11 C3
St Martin-d'Auxigny F 17 B4
St Martin-de-Belleville F 26 B3
St Martin-de-Bossenay F 11 C3
St Martin-de-Crau F 31 B3
St Martin-de-Londres F 30 B2
St Martin-d'Entraunes F 32 A2
St Martin-de-Queyrières F 26 C3
St Martin-de-Ré F 22 B2
St Martin des Besaces F 8 A3
St Martin-d'Estreaux F 25 A3
St Martin-de-Valamas F 25 C4
St Martin-d'Hères F 26 B2
St Martin-du-Frêne F 26 A2
St Martin-en-Bresse F 19 C4
St Martin-en-Haut F 25 B4
St Martin-la-Méanne F 24 B1
St Martin-Osmonville F 10 B1
St Martin-sur-Ouanne F 18 B2
St Martin-Valmeroux F 24 B2
St Martin-Vésubie F 33 A3
St Martory F 39 A4
St Mathieu F 23 C4
St Mathieu-de-Tréviers F 31 B2
St Maurice CH 27 A3
St Maurice-Navacelles F 30 B2
St Maurice-sur-Moselle F 20 B1
St Maximin-la-Ste Baume F 32 B1
St Méard-de-Gurçon F 28 B3
St Médard-de-Guizières F 28 A2
St Médard-en-Jalles F 28 B2
St Méen-le-Grand F 15 A3
St Menges F 11 B4
St M'Hervé F 15 A4
St Michel
*Aisne* F 11 B4
*Gers* F 39 A4
St Michel-Chef-Chef F 15 B3
St Michel-de-Castelnau F 28 B2
St Michel-de-Maurienne F 26 B3
St Michel-en-Grève F 14 A2
St Michel-enl'Herm F 22 B2
St Michel-Mont-Mercure F 22 B3
St Mihiel F 12 C1
St Montant F 31 A3
St Moritz CH 21 C4
St Nazaire F 15 B3
St Nazaire-en-Royans F 26 B2
St Nazaire-le-Désert F 31 A4
St Nectaire F 24 B2
St Nicolas-de-Port F 12 C2
St Nicolas-de-Redon F 15 B3
St Nicolas-du-Pélem F 14 A2
St Niklaus B 7 A4
St Omer F 6 B2
St Pair-sur-Mer F 8 B2
St Palais F 38 A2
St Palais-sur-Mer F 22 C2
St Pardoux-la-Rivière F 23 C4
St Paul-Cap-de-Joux F 29 C4
St Paul-de-Fenouillet F 40 B3
St Paul-de-Varax F 26 A2
St Paulien F 25 B3
St Paul-le-Jeune F 31 A3
St Paul-lès-Dax F 28 C1
St Paul-Trois-Châteaux F 31 A3
St Pé-de-Bigorre F 39 A3
St Pée-sur-Nivelle F 38 A2
St Péravy-la-Colombe F 17 B3
St Péray F 25 C4
St Père-en-Retz F 15 B3
St Peter Port UK 8 A1
St Philbert-de-Grand-Lieu F 22 A2
St Pierre F 30 B1
St Pierre-d'Albigny F 26 B3
St Pierre-d'Allevard F 26 B3
St Pierre-de-Chartreuse F 26 B2
St Pierre-de-Chignac F 29 A3
St Pierre-de-la-Fage F 30 B2
St Pierre-d'Entremont F 26 B2
St Pierre-d'Oléron F 22 C2
St Pierre-Eglise F 8 A2
St Pierre-en-Port F 9 A4
St Pierre-le-Moûtier F 18 C2
St Pierre Montlimart F 15 B4
St Pierre-Quiberon F 14 B2
St Pierre-sur-Dives F 9 A3
St Pierreville F 25 C4
St Pieters-Leeuw B 7 B4
St Plancard F 39 A4
St Poix F 15 B4
St Pol-de-Léon F 14 A2
St Polgues F 25 B3
St Pol-sur-Ternoise F 6 B2
St Pons-de-Thomières F 30 B1
St Porchaire F 22 C3
St Pourçain-sur-Sioule F 24 A3
St Priest F 25 B4
St Privat F 24 B2
St Quay-Portrieux F 14 A3
St Quentin F 10 B3
St Quentin-la-Poterie F 31 A3
St Quentin-les-Anges F 16 B1
St Rambert-d'Albon F 25 B4
St Rambert-en-Bugey F 26 B2
St Raphaël F 32 B2
St Rémy-de-Provence F 31 B3
St Rémy-du-Val F 9 B4
St Remy-en-Bouzemont F 11 C4
St Renan F 14 A1
St Révérien F 18 B2
St Riquier F 10 A1
St Romain-de-Colbosc F 9 A4
St Rome-de-Cernon F 30 A1
St Rome-de-Tarn F 30 A1
St Sadurni-d'Anoia E 41 C2
St Saëns F 9 A5
St Sampson UK 8 A1
St Samson-la-Poterie F 10 B1
St Saturnin-de-Lenne F 30 A2
St Saturnin-lès-Apt F 31 B4
St Sauflieu F 10 B2
St Saulge F 18 B2
St Sauveur
*Finistère* F 14 A2
*Haute-Saône* F 19 B5
St Sauveur-de-Montagut F 25 C4
St Sauveur-en-Puisaye F 18 B2
St Sauveur-en-Rue F 25 B4
St Sauveur-Lendelin F 8 A2
St Sauveur-le-Vicomte F 8 A2
St Sauveur-sur-Tinée F 32 A3
St Savin
*Gironde* F 28 A2
*Vienne* F 23 B4
St Savinien F 22 C3
St Savournin F 31 B4
St Seine-l'Abbaye F 19 B3
St Sernin-sur-Rance F 30 B1
St Sevan-sur-Mer F 8 B1
St Sever F 28 C2
St Sever-Calvados F 8 B2
St Sorlin-d'Arves F 26 B3
St Soupplets F 10 B2
St Sulpice F 29 C4
St Sulpice-Laurière F 24 A1
St Sulpice-les-Feuilles F 23 B5
St Symphorien F 28 B2
St Symphoriende-Lay F 25 B4
St Symphorien d'Ozon F 25 B4
St Symphoriensur-Coise F 25 B4
St Thégonnec F 14 A2
St Thiébault F 19 A4
St Trivier-de-Courtes F 26 A2
St Trojan-les-Bains F 22 C2
St Tropez F 32 B2
St Truiden B 7 B5
St Vaast-la-Hougue F 8 A2
St Valérien F 18 A2
St Valery-en-Caux F 9 A4
St Valéry-sur-Somme F 6 B1
St Vallier
*Drôme* F 25 B4
*Saône-et-Loire* F 18 C3
St Vallier-de-Thiey F 32 B2
St Varent F 16 C1
St Vaury F 24 A1
St Venant F 6 B2
St Véran F 27 C3
St Vincent I 27 B4
St Vincent-de-Tyrosse F 28 C1
St Vit F 19 B4
St Vivien-de-Médoc F 22 C2
St Yan F 25 A4
St Ybars F 40 A2
St Yorre F 25 A3
St Yrieix-la-Perche F 23 C5
Saissac F 40 A3
Saja E 36 A2
Salamanca E 44 B2
Salar E 57 A3
Salardú E 39 B4
Salas E 35 A4
Salas de los Infantes E 37 B3
Salau F 40 B2
Salavaux CH 20 C2
Salbertrand I 27 B3
Salbris F 17 B4
Salce E 35 B4
Saldaña E 36 B2
Salem D 21 B4
Salernes F 32 B2
Salers F 24 B2
Salgueiro P 49 B3
Salientes E 35 B4
Salies-de-Béarn F 38 A3
Salies-du-Salat F 39 A4
Salignac-Eyvigues F 29 B4
Saligney-sur-Roudon F 18 C2
Salinas
*Alicante* E 53 C3
*Huesca* E 39 B4
Salinas de Medinaceli E 46 A1
Salinas de Pisuerga E 36 B2
Salindres F 31 A3
Salins-les-Bains F 19 C4
Salir P 54 B1
Sallanches F 26 B3
Sallent E 41 C2
Sallent de Gállego E 39 B3
Salles F 28 B2
Salles-Curan F 30 A1
Salles-sur-l'Hers F 40 A2
Salmerón E 46 B1
Salmiech F 30 A1
Salmoral E 44 B2
Salobreña E 57 B4
Salon-de-Provence F 31 B4
Salorino E 49 B3
Salornay-sur-Guye F 18 C3
Salou E 41 C2
Salses-le-Chateau F 40 B3
Salt E 41 C3
Salto P 42 A2
Salussola I 27 B5
Saluzzo I 27 C4
Salvacañete E 46 B2
Salvada P 54 B2
Salvagnac F 29 C4
Salvaleon E 49 C4
Salvaterra de Magos P 48 B2
Salvaterra do Extremo P 49 B4
Salvatierra
*Avila* E 37 B4
*Badajoz* E 49 C4
Salvatierra de Santiago E 50 A1
Salviac F 29 B4
Samadet F 28 C2
Samatan F 40 A1
Samedan CH 21 C4
Samer F 6 B1
Samnaun CH 21 C5
Samoëns F 26 A3
Samogneux F 12 B1
Samora Correia P 48 C2
Samos E 35 B3
Samper de Calanda E 47 A3
Sampéyre I 33 A3
Sampigny F 12 C1
San Adrián E 38 B2
San Agustín E 58 C2
San Agustín de Guadalix E 45 B4
San Amaro E 34 B2
San Andrês del Rabanedo E 36 B1
San Antolín de Ibias E 35 A4
Sanary-sur-Mer F 32 B1
San Asensio E 37 B4
San Bartoloméde las Abiertas E 44 C3
San Bartoloméde la Torre E 55 B2
San Bartoloméde Pinares E 44 B3
San Benito E 50 B3
San Benito de la Contienda E 49 C3
San Calixto E 50 C2
San Carlo CH 27 A5
San Carlos del Valle E 51 B4
San Cebrián de Castro E 43 A4
Sancergues F 18 B1
Sancerre F 17 B4
Sancey-le-Long F 19 B5
Sanchiorian E 44 B3
Sanchonuño E 45 A3
San Cibrao das Viñas E 34 B3
San Ciprián E 35 A3
San Clemente E 52 B1
San Clodio E 35 B3
Sancoins F 18 C1
San Crisóbal de Entreviñas E 36 B1
San Cristóbal de la Polantera E 35 B5
San Cristóbal de la Vega E 44 A3
San Cristovo E 35 C3
Sancti-Petri E 56 B1
Sancti-Spiritus E 43 B3
San Damiano d'Asti I 27 C5
San Damiano Macra I 33 A3
Sandillon F 17 B4
Sando E 43 B3
San Emiliano E 35 B5
San Enrique E 56 B2
San Esteban E 35 A4
San Esteban de Gormaz E 45 A4
San Esteban de la Sierra E 43 B4
San Esteban de Litera E 39 C4
San Esteban del Molar E 36 C1
San Esteban del Valle E 44 B3
San Esteban de Valdueza E 35 B4
San Felices E 37 B3
San Felices de los Gallégos E 43 B3
San Fernando E 56 B1
San Fernando de Henares E 45 B4
Sangatte F 6 B1
San Germano Vercellese I 27 B5
Sangonera la Verde E 59 B3
Sangüesa E 38 B2
Sanguinet F 28 B1
San Javier E 59 B4
San Jorge P 48 B2
San José E 58 C2
San Juan E 37 B3
San Juan de Alicante E 59 A4
San Juan de la Nava E 44 B3
San Justo de la Vega E 35 B4
Sankt Anton am Arlberg A 21 B5
Sankt Blasien D 20 B3
Sankt Gallen CH 21 B4
Sankt Gallenkirch A 21 B4
Sankt Georgen D 20 A3
Sankt Ingbert D 12 B3
Sankt Margrethen CH 21 B4
Sankt Niklaus CH 27 A4
Sankt Paul F 32 A2
Sankt Peter D 20 A3
Sankt Wendel D 12 B3
San Leonardo de Yagüe E 37 C3
San Lorenzo al Mare I 33 B3
San Lorenzo de Calatrava E 51 B4
San Lorenzo de El Escorial E 45 B3
San Lorenzo de la Parrilla E 52 B1
San Lourenco P 54 A1
Sanlúcar de Barrameda E 55 C3
Sanlúcar de Guadiana E 54 B2
Sanlúcar la Mayor E 55 B3
San Marcial E 43 A4
San Martin de Castañeda E 35 B4
San Martin de la Vega E 45 B4
San Martin de la Vega del Alberche E 44 B2
San Martin del Tesorillo E 56 B2
San Martin de Luiña E 35 A4
San Martin de Montalbán E 51 A3
San Martin de Oscos E 35 A4
San Martin de Pusa E 44 C3
San Martin de Unx E 38 B2
San Martín de Valdeiglesias E 44 B3
San-Martino-di-Lota F 62 A2
San Mateo de Gallego E 38 C3
San Michele Mondov i I 33 A3
San Miguel de Aguayo E 36 A2
San Miguel de Bernuy E 45 A4
San Miguel del Arroyo E 44 A3
San Miguel de Salinas E 59 B4
San Millán de la Cogolla E 37 B4
San Muñoz E 43 B3
San Nicolás del Puerto E 50 C2
San Pablo de los Montes E 51 A3
San Pedro
*Albacete* E 52 C1
*Oviedo* E 35 A4
San Pedro de Alcántara E 56 B3
San Pedro de Ceque E 35 B4
San Pedro del Arroyo E 44 B3
San Pedro de Latarce E 36 C1
San Pedro del Pinatar E 59 B4
San Pedro del Romeral E 37 A3
San Pedro de Merida E 50 B1
San Pedro de Valderaduey E 36 B2
San Pedro Manrique E 38 B1
San Rafael del Rio E 47 B4
San Remo I 33 B3
San Román de Cameros E 37 B4
San Roman de Hernija E 44 A2
San Román de la Cuba E 36 B2
San Roman de los Montes E 44 B3
San Romao P 49 C3
San Roque E 56 B2
San Roque de Riomera E 37 A3
San Sabastián de los Ballesteros E 56 A3
San Salvador de Cantamuda E 36 B2
San Sebastián de los Reyes E 45 B4
San Silvestre de Guzmán E 55 B2
Santa Agnès E 60 B1
Santa Amalia E 50 A1
Santa Ana
*Cáceres* E 50 A2
*Jaén* E 57 A4
Santa Ana de Pusa E 44 C3
Santa Barbara E 47 B4
Santa Bárbara P 54 B1
Santa Barbara de Casa E 55 B2
Santa Bárbara de Padrões P 54 B2
Santacara E 38 B2
Santa Catarina P 54 B2
Santa Clara-a-Nova P 54 B1
Santa Clara-a-Velha P 54 B1
Santa Clara de Louredo P 54 B2
Santa Coloma de Farners E 41 C3
Santa Coloma de Gramenet E 41 C3
Santa Coloma de Queralt E 41 C2
Santa Colomba de Curueño E 36 B1
Santa Colomba de Somoza E 35 B4
Santa Comba E 34 A2
Santa Comba Dáo P 42 B1
Santa Comba de Rossas P 43 A3
Santa Cristina de la Polvorosa E 35 B5
Santa Cruz
E 34 A2
P 48 B1
Santa Cruz de Alhama E 57 A4
Santa Cruz de Campezo E 37 B4
Santa Cruz de Grio E 46 A2
Santa Cruz de la Salceda E 45 A4
Santa Cruz de la Sierra E 50 A2
Santa Cruz de la Zarza E 45 C4
Santa Cruz del Retamar E 45 B3
Santa Cruz del Valle E 44 B2
Santa Cruz de Moya E 53 B2
Santa Cruz de Mudela E 51 B4
Santa Cruz de Paniagua E 43 B3
Santa Elena E 51 B4
Santa Elena de Jamuz E 35 B5
Santaella E 56 A3
Santa Eufemia E 50 B3
Santa Eulalia E 46 B2
Santa Eulália P 49 C3
Santa Eulalia de Oscos E 35 A3
Santa Eulàlia des Riu E 60 C1
Santa Fe E 57 A4
Sant Agust ide Lluçanès E 41 B3
Santa Iria P 54 B2
Santa Leocadia P 42 A1
Santa Lucia-de-Porto-Vecchio F 62 B2
Santa Luzia P 54 B1
Santa Magdalena de Polpis E 47 B4
Santa Margalida E 61 B3
Santa Margarida P 48 B2

Santa Margarida do Sado P 54 A1
Santa Margaridao de Montbui E 41 C2
Santa Maria E 38 B3
Santa Maria da Feira P 42 B1
Santa Maria de Cayón E 37 A3
Santa Maria de Corco E 41 B3
Santa Maria de Huerta E 46 A1
Santa Maria de la Alameda E 45 B3
Santa Maria de las Hoyas E 37 C3
Santa Maria del Camí E 61 B2
Santa Maria del Campo E 37 B3
Santa Maria del Campo Rus E 52 B1
Santa Maria del Páramo E 36 B1
Santa Maria de Mercadillo E 37 C3
Santa Maria de Nieva E 58 B3
Santa Maria de Trassierra E 50 C3
Santa Maria la Real de Nieva E 44 A3
Santa Maria Maggiore I 27 A5
Santa Maria Ribarredonda E 37 B3
Santa Marina del Rey E 35 B5
Santa Marta
*Albacete* E 52 B1
*Badajoz* E 49 C4
Santa Marta de Magasca E 50 A1
Santa Marta de Penaguião P 42 A2
Santa Marta de Tormes E 44 B2
Santana
*Évora* P 48 C2
*Setúbal* P 48 C1
Santana da Serra P 54 B1
Sant'Ana de Cambas P 54 B2
Santana do Mato P 48 C2
Santander E 37 A3
Sant Antoni de Calonge E 41 C4
Sant Antoni de Portmany E 60 C1
Santanyí E 61 B3
Santa Olalla
*Huelva* E 55 B3
*Toledo* E 44 B3
Santa Pau E 41 B3
Santa Pola E 59 A4
Santa Ponça E 60 B2
Santarém P 48 B2
Santa Severa F 62 A2
Santas Martas E 36 B1
Santa Susana P 48 C2
Santa Suzana P 49 C3
Santa Uxia E 34 B2
Sant Boi de Llobregat E 41 C3
Sant Carles de la Ràpita E 47 B4
Sant Carlos E 60 B1
Sant Celoni E 41 C3
Sant Climent E 61 B4
Santed E 46 A2
Santelices E 37 A3
San Telmo E 55 B3
Santervas de la Vega E 36 B2
Sant Feliu E 41 C3
Sant Feliu de Codines E 41 C3
Sant Feliu de Guíxols E 41 C4
Sant Feliu Sasserra E 41 C3
Sant Ferran E 60 C1
Sant Francesc de Formentera E 60 C1
Sant Francesc de ses Salines E 60 C1
Santhià I 27 B5
Sant Hilari Sacalm E 41 C3
Sant Hipòlit de Voltregà E 41 B3
Santiago de Alcántara E 49 B3
Santiago de Calatrava E 57 A3
Santiago de Compostela E 34 B2
Santiago de la Espade E 58 A2
Santiago de la Puebla E 44 B2
Santiago de la Ribera E 59 B4
Santiago del Campo E 49 B4
Santiago de Litem P 48 B2
Santiago do Cacém P 54 B1
Santiago do Escoural P 48 C2
Santiago Maior P 49 C3
Santibáñez de Béjar E 44 B2
Santibáñez de la Peña E 36 B2
Santibáñez de Murias E 36 A1
Santibáñez de Vidriales E 35 B4
Santibáñez el Alto E 43 B3
Santibáñez el Bajo E 43 B3
Santillana E 36 A2
Santiponce E 56 A1
San Tirso de Abres E 35 A3
Santisteban del Puerto E 51 B4
Santiuste de San Juan Bautiste E 44 A3
Santiz E 43 A4
Sant Jaume dels Domenys E 41 C2
Sant Joan Baptista E 60 B1
Sant Joan de les Abadesses E 41 B3
Sant Jordi E 47 B4
Sant Josep de sa Talaia E 60 C1
Sant Juliáde Loria AND 40 B2
Sant Llorençde Morunys E 41 B2
Sant Llorençdes Carctassar E 61 B3
Sant Llorenç Savall E 41 C3
Sant Luis E 61 B4
Sant Mart ide Llemaná E 41 B3
Sant Martí de Maldà E 41 C2
Sant Martí Sarroca E 41 C2
Sant Mateu E 47 B4
Sant Miquel E 60 B1
Santo Aleixo P 55 A2
Santo Amado P 55 A2
Santo Amaro P 49 C3
Santo André P 54 A1
Santo Domingo E 49 C3
Santo Domingo de la Calzada E 37 B4
Santo Domingo de Silos E 37 C3
Santo Estêvão
*Faro* P 54 B2
*Santarém* P 48 C2
Santomera E 59 A3
Santoña E 37 A3
Santo-Pietro-di-Tenda F 62 A2
Santo Tirso P 42 A1
Santotis E 36 A2
Santo Tomé E 58 A1
Santovenia
*Burgos* E 37 B3
*Zamora* E 36 C1
Sant Pau de Seguries E 41 B3
Santpedor E 41 C2
Sant Pere de Riudebitlles E 41 C2
Sant Pere Pescador E 41 B4
Sant Pere Sallavinera E 41 C2
Sant Quirze de Besora E 41 B3
Sant Rafel E 60 C1
Sant Ramon E 41 C2
Santutzi E 37 A3
Sant Vincençde Castellet E 41 C2
San Vicente de Alcántara E 49 B3
San Vicente de Arana E 38 B1
San Vicente de la Barquera E 36 A2
San Vicente de la Sonsierra E 37 B4
San Vicente de Toranzo E 37 A3
San Vietro E 43 A3
San Vincente del Raspeig E 59 A4
Sanxenxo E 34 B2
São Aleixo P 49 C3
São Barnabé P 54 B1
São Bartolomé da Serra P 54 A1
São Bartolomeu de Messines P 54 B1
São Bento P 34 C2
São Brás P 54 B2
São Brás de Alportel P 54 B2
São Braz do Reguedoura P 48 C2
São Cristóvão P 48 C2
São Domingos P 54 B1
São Geraldo P 48 C2
São Jacinto P 42 B1
São João da Madeira P 42 B1
São João da Pesqueira P 42 A2
São João da Ribeira P 48 B2
São João da Serra P 42 B1
São João da Venda P 54 B2
São João dos Caldeireiros P 54 B2
São Julião P 49 B3
São Leonardo P 49 C3
São Luis P 54 B1
São Manços P 49 C3
São Marcos da Ataboeira P 54 B2
Saõ Marcos da Serra P 54 B1
São Marcos de Campo P 49 C3
São Martinho da Cortiça P 42 B1
São Martinho das Amoreiras P 54 B1
São Martinho do Porto P 48 B1
São Matias
*Beja* P 54 A2
*Évora* P 48 C2
São Miguel d'Acha P 49 A3
São Miguel de Machede P 49 C3
São Pedro da Torre P 34 C2
São Pedro de Cadeira P 48 B1
São Pedro de Moel P 48 B1
São Pedro de Solis P 54 B2
São Pedro do Sul P 42 B1
Saorge F 33 B3
São Romão P 48 C2
São Sebastião dos Carros P 54 B2
São Teotónio P 54 B1
São Torcato P 42 A1
Sapataria P 48 C1
Sapiãos P 42 A2
Sa Pobla E 61 B3
Saramon F 29 C3
Sa Rapita E 61 B3
Sarcelles F 10 B2
Sardoal P 48 B2
Sardón de Duero E 44 A3
Sare F 38 A2
S'Arenal E 60 B2
Sargans CH 21 B4
Sari-d'Orcino F 62 A1
Sarilhos Grandes P 48 C2
Sariñena E 39 C3
Sarlat-la-Canéda F 29 B4
Sarliac-sur-l'Isle F 29 A3
Sarnadas P 49 B3
Sarnen CH 20 C3
Sarpoil F 25 B3
Sarracin E 37 B3
Sarral E 41 C2
Sarralbe F 12 B3
Sarrancolin F 39 B4
Sarras F 25 B4
Sarre I 27 B4
Sarreaus E 34 B3
Sarrebourg F 12 C3
Sarreguemines F 12 B3
Sarre-Union F 12 C3
Sarria E 35 B3
Sarriàde Ter E 41 B3
Sarrión E 47 B3
Sarroca de Lleida E 47 A4
Sarron F 28 C2
Sartène F 62 B1
Sartilly F 8 B2
Sarzeau F 15 B3
Sarzedas P 49 B3
Sasamón E 36 B2
Sa Savina E 60 C1
Sassello I 33 A4
Sástago E 47 A3
Sas van Gent NL 7 A3
Satão P 42 B2
Satillieu F 25 B4
Satteins A 21 B4
Saucats F 28 B2
Saucelle E 43 A3
Saugues F 25 C3
Saujon F 22 C3
Saulces Monclin F 11 B4
Saulgau D 21 A4
Saulieu F 18 B3
Saulnot F 20 B1
Sault F 31 A4
Sault-Brénaz F 26 B2
Sault-de-Navailles F 28 C2
Saulx F 19 B5
Saulxures-sur-Moselotte F 20 B1
Saulzais-le-Potier F 17 C4
Saumos F 28 B1
Saumur F 16 B1
Saurat F 40 B2
Sausset-les-Pins F 31 B4
Sauteyrargues F 31 B2
Sauvagnat F 24 B2
Sauve F 31 B2
Sauveterre-de-Béarn F 38 A3
Sauveterre-de-Guyenne F 28 B2
Sauviat-sur-Vige F 24 B1
Sauxillanges F 25 B3
Sauzet
*Drôme* F 25 C4
*Lot* F 29 B4
Sauzé-Vaussais F 23 B4
Sauzon F 14 B2
Savenay F 15 B4
Saverdun F 40 A2
Saverne F 13 C3
Savières F 11 C3
Savigliano I 27 C4
Savignac-les-Eglises F 29 A3
Savigny-sur-Braye F 16 B2
Saviñán E 46 A2
Savines-le-lac F 32 A2
Savognin CH 21 C4
Savona I 33 A4
Savournon F 32 A1
Sax E 53 C3
Sayalonga E 57 B3
Sayatón E 45 B5
Scaër F 14 A2
Scey-sur-Saône et St Albin F 19 B4
Schaffhausen CH 21 B3
Schangnau CH 20 C2
Schapbach D 13 C4
Scheidegg D 21 B4
Schiedam NL 7 A4
Schiers CH 21 C4
Schillingen D 12 B2
Schiltach D 13 C4
Schiltigheim F 13 C3
Schirmeck F 12 C3
Schliengen D 20 B2
Schluchsee D 20 B3
Schmelz D 12 B2
Schomberg D 21 A3
Schönau D 20 B2
Schoondijke NL 7 A3
Schoonhoven NL 7 A4
Schopfheim D 20 B2
Schramberg D 20 A3
Schröcken A 21 B5
Schruns A 21 B4
Schüpfheim CH 20 C3
Schwaigern D 13 B5
Schwanden CH 21 C4
Schwarzenburg CH 20 C2
Schweich D 12 B2
Schweighausen D 20 A2
Schwenningen D 21 A3
Schwetzingen D 13 B4
Schwyz CH 21 B3
Scionzier F 26 A3
Scopello I 27 B5
Scuol CH 21 C5
Sebazac-Concourès F 30 A1
Seborga I 33 B3
Séchault F 11 B4
Seclin F 6 B3
Secondigny F 22 B3
Seda P 49 B3
Sedan F 11 B4
Sedano E 37 B3
Sedella E 57 B3
Séderon F 31 A4
Seebach F 13 C3
Seeheim-Jugenheim D 13 B4
Seelbach D 13 C3
Sées F 9 B4
Segonzac F 23 C3
Segorbe E 53 B3
Segovia E 45 B3
Segré F 15 B5
Segura
E 38 B1
P 49 B3
Segura de León E 55 A3
Segura de los Baños E 46 B3
Ségur-les-Villas F 24 B2
Segurrilla E 44 B3
Seia P 42 B2
Seiches-sur-le-Loir F 16 B1
Seignelay F 18 B2
Seijo E 34 C2
Seilhac F 24 B1
Seilles B 7 B5
Seissan F 39 A4
Seixal P 48 C1
Sélestat F 20 A2
Selgua E 39 C4
Seligenstadt D 13 A4
Selles-St Denis F 17 B3
Selles-sur-Cher F 17 B3
Sellières F 19 C4
Selongey F 19 B4
Selonnet F 32 A2
Seltz F 13 C4
Selva E 61 B2
Semide
F 11 B4
P 42 B1
Semur-en-Auxois F 18 B3
Sena E 39 C3
Sena de Luna E 35 B5
Senarpont F 10 B1
Sénas F 31 B4
Sencelles E 61 B2
Sendim P 43 A3
Seneffe B 7 B4
Senés E 58 B2
Senez F 32 B2
Sengouagnet F 39 B4
Senlis F 10 B2
Sennecey-le-Grand F 19 C3
Sennwald CH 21 B4
Senonches F 9 B5
Senones F 12 C2
Sens F 18 A2
Sens-de-Bretagne F 15 A4
Senterada E 39 B4
Seoane E 35 B3
Seon CH 20 B3
Sépeaux F 18 B2
Sépey CH 27 A4
Seppois F 20 B2
Septeuil F 10 C1
Sepúlveda E 45 A4
Sequeros E 43 B3
Seraincourt F 11 B4
Sérent F 15 B3
Sérifontaine F 10 B1
Sérignan F 30 B2
Sermaises F 10 C2
Sermaize-les-Bains F 11 C4
Sernache de Bonjardim P 48 B2
Sernancelhe P 42 B2
Serón E 58 B2
Serón de Najima E 46 A1
Serooskerke NL 7 A3
Seròs E 47 A4
Serpa P 54 B2
Serrada E 44 A3
Serra de Outes E 34 B2
Serradilla E 49 B4
Serradilla del Arroyo E 43 B3
Serradilla del Llano E 43 B3
Serranillos E 44 B3
Serravalle I 27 B5
Serrejón E 44 C2
Serres F 32 A1
Serrières F 25 B4
Serrières-de-Briord F 26 B2
Sertã P 48 B2
Sertig Dörfli CH 21 C4
Servance F 20 B1
Serverette F 25 C3
Servian F 30 B2
Serviers F 31 A3
Serzedelo P 42 A1
Seseña Nuevo E 45 B4
Sesimbra P 48 C1
Sesma E 38 B1
Ses Salines E 61 B3
Sestao E 37 A4
Sestriere I 27 C3
Setcases E 40 B3
Sète F 30 B2
Setenil E 56 B2
Séttimo Torinese I 27 B4
Settimo Vittone I 27 B4
Setúbal P 48 C2
Seurre F 19 C4
Sévérac-le-Château F 30 A2
Sever do Vouga P 42 B1
Sévigny F 11 B4
Sevilla = Seville E 56 A2
Sevilla la Nueva E 45 B3
Seville = Sevilla E 56 A2
Sevilleja de la Jara E 50 A3
Sevrier F 26 B3
Seyches F 29 B3
Seyne F 32 A2
Seynes F 31 A3
Seyssel F 26 B2
Sézanne F 11 C3
Sezulfe P 43 A2
's-Gravendeel NL 7 A4
's-Gravenzande NL 7 A4
's-Hertogenbosch NL 7 A5
Siauges-St Romain F 25 B3
Sierck-les-Bains F 12 B2
Sierentz F 20 B2
Sierra de Fuentes E 49 B4
Sierra de Luna E 38 B3
Sierra de Yeguas E 56 A3
Sierre CH 27 A4
Sietamo E 39 B3
Sigean F 30 B1
Sigmaringen D 21 A4
Signes F 32 B1
Signy-l'Abbaye F 11 B4
Signy-le-Petit F 11 B4
Sigogne F 23 C3
Sigueiro E 34 B2
Sigüenza E 45 A5
Sigües E 38 B2
Siles E 58 A2
Silgueiros P 42 B2
Silla E 53 B3
Silleda E 34 B2
Sillé-le-Guillaume F 16 A1
Sils E 41 C3
Silvaplana CH 21 C4
Silvares P 42 B2
Silves P 54 B1
Simandre F 19 C3
Simard F 19 C4
Simat de Valldigna E 53 B3
Simmerberg D 21 B4
Simmern D 13 B3
Simplon CH 27 A5
Sinarcas E 53 B2
Sindelfingen D 13 C5
Sines P 54 B1
Sineu E 61 B3
Singen D 21 B3
Sinlabajos E 44 A3
Sins CH 20 B3
Sinsheim D 13 B4
Sint Annaland NL 7 A4
Sint Oedenrode NL 7 A5
Sintra P 48 C1
Sinzheim D 13 C4
Sion CH 27 A4
Siorac-en-Périgord F 29 B3
Siruela E 50 B2
Sisante E 52 B1
Sissach CH 20 B2
Sissonne F 11 B3
Sistelo P 34 C2
Sisteron F 32 A1
Sitges E 41 C2
Sixt-Fer-á-Cheval F 27 A3
Sizun F 14 A1
Sluis NL 6 A3
Sober E 34 B3
Sobernheim D 13 B3
Sobrado
*Coruña* E 34 A2
*Lugo* E 35 B3
Sobral da Adica P 55 A2
Sobral de Monte Agraço P 48 C1
Sobreira Formosa P 48 B3
Socovos E 58 A3
Socuéllamos E 52 B1
Sodupe E 37 A3
Soengas P 42 A1
Sohren D 13 B3
Soignies B 7 B4
Soissons F 10 B3
Solana de los Barros E 49 C4
Solana del Pino E 51 B3
Solares E 37 A3
Soleils F 32 B2
Solenzara F 62 B2
Solera E 57 A4
Solesmes F 7 B3
Solgne F 12 C2
Solignac F 23 C5
Solivella E 41 C2
Sollana E 53 B3
Sóller E 60 B2
Solliès-Pont F 32 B2
Solomiac F 29 C3
Solórzano E 37 A3
Solothurn CH 20 B2
Solre-le-Château F 7 B4
Solsona E 41 C2
Somain F 6 B3
Sombernon F 18 B3
Sombreffe B 7 B4
Sommariva del Bosco I 27 C4
Sommeilles F 11 C4
Sommepy-Tahure F 11 B4
Sommesous F 11 C4
Somme-Tourbe F 11 B4
Sommières F 31 B3
Sommières-du-Clain F 23 B4
Somo E 37 A3
Somontín E 58 B2
Somosiero E 45 A4
Sompuis F 11 C4
Son Bou E 61 B4
Sonceboz CH 20 B2
Soncillo E 37 B3
Soneja E 53 B3
Songeons F 10 B1
Sonseca E 51 A4
Son Servera E 61 B3
Sonthofen D 21 B5
Sopelana E 37 A4
Sorbas E 58 B2
Sore F 28 B2
Sörenberg CH 20 C3
Sorèze F 40 A3
Sorges F 23 C4
Sorgues F 31 A3
Soria E 37 C4
Sorihuela del Guadalimar E 58 A1
Sornac F 24 B2
Sort E 40 B2
Sos F 28 B3
Sos del Rey Católico E 38 B2
Sospel F 33 B3
Sotillo de Adrada E 44 B3
Sotillo de la Ribera E 37 C3
Sotobañado y Priorato E 36 B2
Soto de la Marina E 37 A3
Soto del Barco E 35 A4
Soto de los Infantes E 35 A4
Soto de Real E 45 B4
Soto de Ribera E 35 A5
Sotoserrano E 43 B3
Soto y Amío E 35 B5
Sotresgudo E 36 B2
Sotrondio E 36 A1
Sotta F 62 B2
Sotuélamos E 52 B1
Souain F 11 B4
Soual F 40 A3
Soucy F 18 A2
Soudron F 11 C4
Souesmes F 17 B4
Soufflenheim F 13 C3
Souillac F 29 B4
Souilly F 11 B5
Soulac-sur-Mer F 22 C2
Soulaines-Dhuys F 11 C4
Soulatgé F 40 B3
Soultz-Haut-Rhin F 20 B2
Soultz-sous-Forêts F 13 C3
Soumoulou F 39 A3
Souppes-sur-Loing F 17 A4
Souprosse F 28 C2
Sourdeval F 8 B3
Soure P 48 A2
Sournia F 40 B3
Souro Pires P 43 B2
Sours F 10 C1
Sousceyrac F 24 C2
Sousel P 49 C3
Soustons F 28 C1
Soutelo de Montes E 34 B2
Souto P 42 B2
Soutochao E 35 C3
Souto da Carpalhosa P 48 B2
Souvigny F 18 C2
Souzay-Champigny F 16 B1
Soyaux F 23 C4
Spaichingen D 21 A3
Speicher D 12 B2
Speyer D 13 B4
Spézet F 14 A2
Spiez CH 20 C2
Spigno Monferrato I 33 A4
Spijkenisse NL 7 A4
Spincourt F 12 B1
Splügen CH 21 C4
Spotorno I 33 A4
Stabroek B 7 A4
Staden B 6 B3
Stäfa CH 21 B3
Stainville F 11 C5
Stalden CH 27 A4
Stans CH 20 C3
Staufen D 20 B2
Stavenisse NL 7 A4
Stechelberg CH 20 C2
Steckborn CH 21 B3
Steeg A 21 B5
Steenbergen NL 7 A4
Steenvoorde F 6 B2
Steffisburg CH 20 C2
Steinach D 20 A3
Stein an Rhein CH 21 B3
Steinen D 20 B2
Steinheim D 21 A5
Stekene B 7 A4
Stellendam NL 7 A4
Stenay F 11 B5
Stes Maries-de-la-Mer F 31 B3
Stockach D 21 B4
Stöckalp CH 20 C3
Strasbourg F 13 C3
Stresa I 27 B5
Strijen NL 7 A4
Stromberg D 13 B3
Stroppiana I 27 B5
St-Trivier-sur-Moignans F 25 A4
Stuben A 21 B5
Suances E 36 A2
Sucina E 59 B4
Sueca E 53 B3
Sugères F 25 B3
Sugny B 11 B4
Suippes F 11 B4
Sulgen CH 21 B4
Sully-sur-Loire F 17 B4
Sülz D 13 C4
Sulzbach
*Bayern* D 13 B5
*Saarland* D 12 B3
Sumiswald CH 20 B2
Sunbilla E 38 A2
Super Sauze F 32 A2
Surgères F 22 B3
Sùria E 41 C2
Surin F 23 B4
Sursee CH 20 B3
Sury-le-Comtal F 25 B4
Susa I 27 B4
Susch CH 21 C5
Suze-la-Rousse F 31 A3


## T


Tabanera la Luenga E 45 A3
Tabaqueros E 52 B2
Tábara E 43 A4
Tabenera de Cerrato E 36 B2
Tabernas E 58 B2
Taboada E 34 B3
Taboadela E 34 B3
Tábua P 42 B1
Tabuaco P 42 A2
Tabuenca E 46 A2
Tabuyo del Monte E 35 B4
Tafalla E 38 B2
Taganheira P 54 B1
Tággia I 33 B3
Tagnon F 11 B4
Tahal E 58 B2
Tailfingen D 21 A4
Taillis F 15 A4
Tain-l'Hermitage F 25 B4
Taipadas P 48 C2
Tal E 34 B2
Talant F 19 B3
Talarrubias E 50 A2
Talaván E 49 B4
Talavera de la Reina E 44 C3
Talavera la Real E 49 C4
Talayuela E 44 C2
Talayuelas E 53 B2
Talhadas P 42 B1
Táliga E 49 C3
Talizat F 24 B3
Tallard F 32 A2
Talloires F 26 B3
Talmay F 19 B4
Talmont-St Hilaire F 22 B2
Talmont-sur-Gironde F 22 C3
Tamajón E 45 B4
Tamame E 43 A4
Tamames E 43 B3
Tamarit de Mar E 41 C2
Tamarite de Litera E 39 C4
Tamariu E 41 C4
Tameza E 35 A4
Tamurejo E 50 B3
Tañabueyes E 37 B3
Tancarville F 9 A4
Taninges F 26 A3
Tannay
*Ardennes* F 11 B4
*Nièvre* F 18 B2
Tanus F 30 A1
Tapia de Casariego E 35 A4
Tapio F 40 A2
Taradell E 41 C3
Taramundi E 35 A3
Tarancón E 45 B4
Tarare F 25 B4
Tarascon F 31 B3
Tarascon-sur-Ariège F 40 B2
Tarazona E 38 C2

Tarazona de la Mancha
E 52 B2
Tarbena E 53 C3
Tarbes F 39 A4
Tardajos E 37 B3
Tardelcuende E 45 A5
Tardets-Sorholus F 38 A3
Tardienta E 39 C3
Targon F 28 B2
Tarifa E 56 B2
Tariquejas E 55 B2
Tarnos F 28 C1
Tarouca P 42 A2
Tarragona E 41 C2
Tàrrega E 41 C2
Tartas F 28 C2
Täsch CH 27 A4
Taulé F 14 A2
Taulignan F 31 A3
Tauste E 38 C2
Tauves F 24 B2
Tavannes CH 20 B2
Tavaux F 19 B4
Tavernes de la Valldigna
E 53 B3
Taverny F 10 B2
Tavescan E 40 B2
Tavira P 54 B2
Tazones E 36 A1
Teba E 56 B3
Teillay F 15 B4
Teillet F 30 B1
Teixeiro E 34 A2
Tejada de Tiétar E 44 B2
Tejado E 46 A1
Tejares E 44 B2
Tembleque E 51 A4
Temiño E 37 B3
Temse B 7 A4
Tenay F 26 B2
Tence F 25 B4
Tende F 33 A3
Tenneville B 12 A1
Teo E 34 B2
Tera E 37 C4
Terena P 49 C3
Teresa de Cofrentes E 53 B2
Tergnier F 10 B3
Termas de
Monfortinho P 49 A4
Terme di Valdieri I 33 A3
Termens E 39 C4
Termes F 24 C3
Terneuzen NL 7 A3
Terras do Bouro P 42 A1
Terrassa E 41 C3
Terrasson-Lavilledieu F 29 A4
Terrazos E 37 B3
Terriente E 46 B2
Terrugem P 49 C3
Teruel E 46 B2
Tervuren B 7 B4
Terzaga E 46 B2
Tessy-sur-Vire F 8 B2
Teterchen F 12 B2
Tettnang D 21 B4
Teulada E 53 C4
Thalfang D 12 B2
Thalkirch CH 21 C4
Thalwil CH 21 B3
Thann F 20 B2
Thaon-les-Vosges F 19 A5
Tharsis E 55 B2
Thayngen CH 21 B3
Thénezay F 16 C1
Thenon F 29 A4
Therouanne F 6 B2
Thézar-les-Corbières F 40 A3
Thèze F 39 A3
Thiberville F 9 A4
Thibie F 11 C4
Thiéblemont-
Farémont F 11 C4
Thierrens CH 20 C1
Thiers F 25 B3
Thiezac F 24 B2
Thionville F 12 B2
Thiron-Gardais F 9 B4
Thivars F 10 C1
Thiviers F 23 C4
Thizy F 25 A4
Tholen NL 7 A4
Tholey D 12 B3
Thônes F 26 B3
Thonnance-
les-Joinville F 11 C5
Thonon-les-Bains F 26 A3
Thorame-Basse F 32 A2
Thorame-Haute F 32 A2
Thorens-Glières F 26 A3
Thorigny-sur-Oreuse F 11 C3
Thouarcé F 16 B1
Thouars F 16 C1
Thueyts F 25 C4
Thuin B 7 B4
Thuir F 40 B3
Thun CH 20 C2
Thuret F 24 B3
Thurey F 19 C4
Thüringen A 21 B4
Thurins F 25 B4
Thury-Harcourt F 9 B3
Thusis CH 21 C4
Tibi E 53 C3
Tiedra E 44 A2
Tiefencastel CH 21 C4
Tiel NL 7 A5
Tielmes E 45 B4
Tielt B 6 A3
Tienen B 7 B4
Tiengen D 20 B3
Tiercé F 16 B1
Tierga E 46 A2
Tiermas E 38 B2
Tierrantona E 39 B4
Tignes F 27 B3
Tigy F 17 B4
Tijola E 58 B2
Tilburg NL 7 A5
Til Châtel F 19 B4
Tilh F 28 C2
Tillac F 39 A4
Tille F 10 B2
Tilloy Bellay F 11 B4
Tilly F 23 B5
Tilly-sur-Seulles F 8 A3
Tinajas E 46 B1
Tinalhas P 49 B3
Tinchebray F 8 B3
Tincques F 6 B2
Tineo E 35 A4
Tinlot B 7 B5
Tinténiac F 15 A4
Tintigny B 12 B1
Tiriez E 52 C1
Tirig E 47 B4
Tirteafuera E 51 B3
Titaguas E 53 B2
Titisee-Neustadt D 20 B3
Tivisa E 47 A4
Tobarra E 52 C2
Tocane-St Apre F 29 A3
Tocha P 42 B1
Tocina E 56 A2
Tocón E 57 A4
Todtmoos D 20 B3
Todtnau D 20 B2
Toén E 34 B3
Toledo E 45 C3
Tolosa
E 38 A1
P 49 B3
Tolox E 56 B3
Tolva E 39 B4
Tomar P 48 B2
Tombeboeuf F 29 B3
Tomellosa E 45 B5
Tomelloso E 51 A4
Tomiño E 34 C2
Tona E 41 C3
Tondela P 42 B1
Tongeren B 7 B5
Tonnay-Boutonne F 22 C3
Tonnay-Charente F 22 C3
Tonneins F 29 B3
Tonnerre F 18 B2
Topares E 58 B2
Topas E 44 A2
Toques E 34 B3
Torà E 41 C2
Toral de
los Guzmanes E 36 B1
Toral de los Vados E 35 B4
Torcy-le-Petit F 9 A5
Tordehumos E 36 C1
Tordera E 41 C3
Tordesillas E 44 A2
Tordesilos E 46 B2
Torellò E 41 B3
Toreno E 35 B4
Torfou F 22 A2
Torgueda P 42 A2
Torhout B 6 A3
Torigni-sur-Vire F 8 A3
Torija E 45 B4
Toril E 46 B2
Torino = Turin I 27 B4
Torla E 39 B3
Tornada P 48 B1
Tornavacas E 44 B2
Tornos E 46 B2
Toro E 44 A2
Torquemada E 36 B2
Torralba de Burgo E 45 A5
Torralba de Calatrava E 51 A4
Torrão P 48 C2
Torreblacos E 37 C4
Torreblanca E 47 B4
Torreblascopedro E 51 B4
Torrecaballeros E 45 A3
Torrecampo E 50 B3
Torre Cardela E 57 A4
Torrecilla E 46 B1
Torrecilla de la Jara E 50 A3
Torrecilla de la Orden E 44 A2
Torrecilla del Pinar E 45 A3
Torrecilla en Cameros
E 37 B4
Torrecillas de la Tiesa E 50 A2
Torre das Vargens P 48 B3
Torre de Coelheiros P 48 C3
Torre de Dom Chama P 43 A2
Torre de Juan Abad E 51 B4
Torre del Bierzo E 35 B4
Torre del Burgo E 45 B4
Torre del Campo E 57 A4
Torre del Mar E 57 B3
Torredembarra E 41 C2
Torre de
Miguel Sesmero E 49 C4
Torre de Moncorvo P 43 A2
Torre de Santa Maria E 50 A1
Torredonjimeno E 57 A4
Torre do Terranho P 42 B2
Torregrosa E 41 C1
Torreira P 42 B1
Torrejoncillo E 49 B4
Torrejón de Ardoz E 45 B4
Torrejón de la Calzada
E 45 B4
Torrejón del Rey E 45 B4
Torrejon el Rubio E 50 A1
Torrelaguna E 45 B4
Torrelapaja E 46 A2
Torre la Ribera E 39 B4
Torrelavega E 36 A2
Torrelobatón E 44 A2
Torrelodones E 45 B4
Torre los Negros E 46 B2
Torremanzanas E 53 C3
Torremayor E 49 C4
Torremocha E 50 A1
Torremolinos E 57 B3
Torrenostra E 47 B4
Torrent E 53 B3
Torrente de Cinca E 47 A4
Torrenueva
*Ciudad Real* E 51 B4
*Granada* E 57 B4
Torreorgaz E 49 B4
Torre-Pacheco E 59 B4
Torre Péllice I 27 C4
Torreperogil E 51 B4
Torres E 57 A4
Torresandino E 37 C3
Torres-Cabrera E 57 A3
Torres de la Alameda E 45 B4
Torres Novas P 48 B2
Torres Vedras P 48 B1
Torrevieja E 59 B4
Torrijos E 45 C3
Torroal P 48 C2
Torroella de Montgrì E 41 B4
Torrox E 57 B4
Tórtoles E 44 B2
Tórtoles de Esgueva E 36 C2
Tortosa E 47 B4
Tortosendo P 48 A3
Tortuera E 46 B2
Tortuero E 45 B4
Torviscón E 57 B4
Tossa de Mar E 41 C3
Tosse F 28 C1
Totana E 59 B3
Tôtes F 9 A5
Touça P 43 A2
Toucy F 18 B2
Toul F 12 C1
Toulon F 32 B1
Toulon-sur-Allier F 18 C2
Toulon-sur-Arroux F 18 C3
Toulouse F 29 C4
Tourcoing F 6 B3
Tour de la Parata F 62 B1
Tourlaville F 8 A2
Tournai B 6 B3
Tournan-en-Brie F 10 C2
Tournay F 39 A4
Tournon-d'Agenais F 29 B3
Tournon-St Martin F 23 B4
Tournon-sur-Rhône F 25 B4
Tournus F 19 C3
Touro
E 34 B2
P 42 B2
Tourouvre F 9 B4
Tourriers F 23 C4
Tours F 16 B2
Tourteron F 11 B4
Tourves F 32 B1
Toury F 17 A3
Touvedo P 42 A1
Touvois F 22 B2
Trabada E 35 A3
Trabadelo E 35 B4
Trabanca E 43 A3
Trabazos E 43 A3
Traben-Trarbach D 12 B3
Trafaria P 48 C1
Tragacete E 46 B2
Traiguera E 47 B4
Trainel F 11 C3
Tramacastilla de Tena E 39 B3
Tramagal P 48 B2
Tramelan CH 20 B2
Trampot F 12 C1
Trana I 27 B4
Trancoso P 42 B2
Trans-en-Provence F 32 B2
Trappes F 10 C2
Trasierra E 50 B1
Trasmiras E 34 B3
Traspinedo E 44 A3
Travo F 62 B2
Treban F 24 A3
Trébeurden F 14 A2
Trebujena E 55 C3
Treffort F 26 A2
Trégastel-Plage F 14 A2
Tréguier F 14 A2
Trégunc F 14 B2
Treignac F 24 B1
Treignat F 24 A2
Treignes B 11 A4
Trélazé F 16 B1
Trélissac F 29 A3
Trélon F 11 A4
Trélou-sur-Marne F 11 B3
Tremblay-le-Vicomte F 9 B5
Tremés P 48 B2
Tremp E 39 B4
Trensacq F 28 B2
Trept F 26 B2
Trespaderne E 37 B3
Trets F 32 B1
Trevelez E 57 B4
Treviana E 37 B3
Trévoux F 25 B4
Trézelles F 25 A3
Triacastela E 35 B3
Triaize F 22 B2
Triaucourt-en-
Argonne F 11 C5
Triberg D 20 A3
Trier D 12 B2
Trie-sur-Baïse F 39 A4
Trignac F 15 B3
Trigueros E 55 B3
Trigueros del Valle E 36 C2
Trillo E 46 B1
Trilport F 10 C2
Trindade
*Beja* P 54 B2
*Bragança* P 43 A2
Trino I 27 B5
Trinta P 42 B2
Triora I 33 B3
Triste E 38 B3
Trivero I 27 B5
Troarn F 9 A3
Trofa P 42 A1
Troia P 48 C2
Troisvierges L 12 A2
Tronget F 24 A3
Tronzano-Vercellese I 27 B5
Trôo F 16 B2
Trosly-Breuil F 10 B3
Trossingen D 21 A3
Trouville-sur-Mer F 9 A4
Troyes F 18 A3
Trubia E 35 A5
Truchas E 35 B4
Trujillanos E 49 C4
Trujillo E 50 A2
Trun
CH 21 C3
F 9 B4
Tschagguns A 21 B4
Tua P 42 A2
Tubilla del Lago E 37 C3
Tübingen D 13 C5
Tubize B 7 B4
Tuchan F 40 B3
Tudela E 38 B2
Tudela de Duero E 44 A3
Tuejar E 53 B2
Tuffé F 16 A2
Tui E 34 B2
Tulette F 31 A3
Tulle F 24 B1
Tullins F 26 B2
Tunes P 54 B1
Turbenthal CH 21 B3
Turcia E 35 B5
Turcifal P 48 B1
Turckheim F 20 A2
Turégano E 45 A4
Turin = Torino I 27 B4
Turis E 53 B3
Turleque E 51 A4
Turnhout B 7 A4
Turón E 58 C1
Turquel P 48 B1
Turries F 32 A2
Turtmann CH 27 A4
Tuttlingen D 21 B3

## U

Úbeda E 51 B4
Überlingen D 21 B4
Ubidea E 37 A4
Ubrique E 56 B2
Ucero E 37 C3
Uchaud F 31 B3
Uclés E 45 C5
Uetendorf CH 20 C2
Ugarana E 37 A4
Ugíjar E 58 C1
Ugine F 26 B3
Ujué E 38 B2
Uleila del Campo E 58 B2
Ulldecona E 47 B4
Ulldemolins E 41 C1
Ulme P 48 B2
Uncastillo E 38 B2
Unhais da Serra P 42 B2
Unquera E 36 A2
Unterägeri CH 21 B3
Unteriberg CH 21 B3
Unterschächen CH 21 C3
Ur F 40 B2
Urçay F 17 C4
Urda E 51 A4
Urdax E 38 A2
Urdilde E 34 B2
Urdos F 39 B3
Urnäsch CH 21 B4
Urracal E 58 B2
Urries E 38 B2
Urroz E 38 B2
Ury F 10 C2
Usagre E 50 B1
Useldange L 12 B1
Ussé F 16 B2
Usséglio I 27 B4
Ussel
*Cantal* F 24 B2
*Corrèze* F 24 B2
Usson-du-Poitou F 23 B4
Usson-en-Forez F 25 B3
Usson-les-Bains F 40 B3
Ustaritz F 38 A2
Uster CH 21 B3
Utebo E 46 A3
Utiel E 53 B2
Utrera E 56 A2
Utrillas E 47 B3
Uttenweiler D 21 A4
Uza F 28 B1
Uzein F 39 A3
Uzel F 14 A3
Uzerche F 24 B1
Uzès F 31 A3
Uznach CH 21 B3

## V

Vaas F 16 B2
Vabre F 30 B1
Vacqueyras F 31 A3
Vadillo de la Sierra E 44 B2
Vadillos E 46 B1
Vado Ligure I 33 A4
Vaduz FL 21 B4
Vagney F 20 A1
Vagos P 42 B1
Vaiges F 16 A1
Vaihingen D 13 C4
Vaillant F 19 B4
Vailly-sur-Aisne F 11 B3
Vailly-sur Sauldre F 17 B4
Vaison-la-Romaine F 31 A4
Vaite F 19 B4
Valada P 48 B2
Valadares P 42 A1
Valado P 48 B1
Valberg F 32 A2
Valbom P 42 A1
Valbonnais F 26 C2
Valbuena de Duero E 36 C2
Valdahon F 19 B5
Valdaracete E 45 B4
Valdealgorfa E 47 B3
Valdecaballeros E 50 A2
Valdecabras E 46 B1
Valdecarros E 44 B2
Valdeconcha E 45 B5
Valdeflores E 55 B3
Valdefresno E 36 B1
Valdeganga E 52 B2
Valdelacasa E 44 B2
Valdelacasa de Tajo E 50 A2
Valdelarco E 55 B3
Valdelosa E 43 A4
Valdeltormo E 47 B4
Valdelugeros E 36 B1
Valdemanco
de Esteras E 50 B3
Valdemorillo E 45 B3
Valdemoro E 45 B4
Valdemoro Sierra E 46 B2
Valdenoceda E 37 B3
Valdeobispo E 43 B3
Valdeolivas E 46 B1
Valdepeñas E 51 B4
Valdepeñas de Jaén E 57 A4
Valdepiélago E 36 B1
Valdepolo E 36 B1
Valderas E 36 B1
Valderrobres E 47 B4
Valderrueda E 36 B2
Val de San Lorenzo E 35 B4
Val de
Santo Domingo E 44 B3
Val d'Esquières F 32 B2
Valdestillas E 44 A3
Valdetorres E 50 B1
Valdetorres
de Jarama E 45 B4
Valdeverdeja E 44 C2
Valdevimbre E 36 B1
Valdieri I 33 A3
Valdilecha E 45 B4
Val-d'Isère F 27 B3
Valdocondes E 37 C3
Valdoviño E 34 A2
Vale de Açor
*Beja* P 54 B2
*Portalegre* P 48 B3
Vale de Agua P 54 B1
Vale de Cambra P 42 B1
Vale de Lobo P 54 B1
Vale de Prazeres P 42 B2
Vale de Reis P 48 C2
Vale de Rosa P 54 B2
Vale de Santarém P 48 B2
Vale de Vargo P 54 B2
Vale do Peso P 49 B3
Valega P 42 B1
Valeiro P 48 C2
Valença P 34 B2
Valençay F 17 B3
Valence
*Charente* F 23 C4
*Drôme* F 25 C4
Valence d'Agen F 29 B3
Valence d'Albigeois F 30 A1
Valence-sur-Baise F 29 C3
Valencia E 53 B3
Valencia de Alcántara
E 49 B3
Valencia de Don Juan E 36 B1
Valencia de las Torres
E 50 B1
Valencia del Ventoso E 55 A3
Valencia de Mombuey E 55 A2
Valenciennes F 7 B3
Valensole F 32 B1
Valentigney F 20 B1
Valentine F 39 A4
Valenzuela E 57 A3
Valenzuela
de Calatrava E 51 B4
Valera de Abajo E 52 B1
Valeria E 52 B1
Valflaunes F 31 B2
Valgorge F 31 A3
Valgrisenche I 27 B4
Valhelhas P 42 B2
Valkenswaard NL 7 A5
Vallada E 53 C3
Vallado E 35 A4
Valladolid E 44 A3
Vall d'Alba E 47 B3
Valldemossa E 60 B2
Valle de Abdalajís E 57 B3
Valle de Cabuérniga E 36 A2
Valle de la Serena E 50 B2
Valle de Matamoros E 49 C4
Valle de Santa Ana E 49 C4
Vallelado E 44 A3
Valle Mosso I 27 B5
Valleraugue F 30 A2
Vallet F 15 B4
Vallfogona
de Riucorb E 41 C2
Valloire F 26 B3
Vallon-Pont-d'Arc F 31 A3
Vallorbe CH 19 C5
Vallouise F 26 C3
Valls E 41 C2
Valmadrid E 47 A3
Valmojado E 45 B3
Valmont F 9 A4
Valognes F 8 A2
Valonga P 42 B1
Valongo P 42 A1
Válor E 58 C1
Valoria la Buena E 36 C2
Valpaços P 42 A2
Valpelline I 27 B4
Valras-Plage F 30 B2
Valréas F 31 A3
Vals CH 21 C4
Valsavarenche I 27 B4
Valsequillo E 50 B2
Vals-les-Bains F 25 C4
Valsonne F 25 B4
Val-Suzon F 19 B3
Valtablado del Rio E 46 B1
Val Thorens F 26 B3
Valtiendas E 45 A4
Valtierra E 38 B2
Valtournenche I 27 B4
Valverde E 38 C2
Valverde de Burguillos
E 49 C4
Valverde de Júcar E 52 B1
Valverde de la Vera E 44 B2
Valverde de la Virgen E 36 B1
Valverde del Camino E 55 B3
Valverde del Fresno E 43 B3
Valverde de Llerena E 50 B2
Valverde de Mérida E 50 B1
Vanault-les-Dames F 11 C4
Vandenesse F 18 C2
Vandenesse-en-Auxois
F 18 B3
Vannes F 15 B3
Vaour F 29 B4
Vaqueiros P 54 B2
Varacieux F 26 B2
Varades F 15 B4
Varages F 32 B1
Varallo I 27 B5
Varazze I 33 A4
Varengeville-sur-Mer F 9 A4
Varennes-en-Argonne F 11 B5
Varennes-le-Grand F 19 C3
Varennes-St Sauveur F 19 C4
Varennes-sur-Allier F 25 A3
Varennes-sur-Amance
F 19 B4
Vargas
E 37 A3
P 48 B2
Varilhes F 40 A2
Váriz P 43 A3
Varreddes F 10 C2
Vars F 26 C3
Varzjelas P 42 B1
Varzo I 27 A5
Varzy F 18 B2
Vassieux-en-Vercors F 26 C2
Vassy F 8 B3
Vatan F 17 B3
Vatry F 11 C4
Vättis CH 21 C4
Vauchamps F 11 C3
Vauchassis F 18 A2
Vaucouleurs F 12 C1
Vaudoy-en-Brie F 10 C3
Vaulruz CH 20 C1
Vaulx Vraucourt F 10 A2
Vaumas F 18 C2
Vausseroux F 23 B3
Vauvenargues F 32 B1
Vauvert F 31 B3
Vauvillers F 19 B5
Vaux-sur-Sure B 12 B1
Vayrac F 29 B4
Vecinos E 43 B4
Vedra E 34 B2
Vega E 36 A1
Vega de Espinareda E 35 B4
Vega de Infanzones E 36 B1
Vegadeo E 35 A3
Vega de Pas E 37 A3
Vega de Valcarce E 35 B4
Vega de Valdetronco E 44 A2
Vegas de Coria E 43 B3
Vegas del Condado E 36 B1
Veguillas E 45 B4
Vejer de la Frontera E 56 B2
Velada E 44 B3
Velayos E 44 B3
Velefique E 58 B2
Velez Blanco E 58 B2
Vélez de Benaudalla E 57 B4
Vélez-Málaga E 57 B3
Vélez Rubio E 58 B2
Velilla del Río Carrió E 36 B2
Velilla de San Antonio
E 45 B4
Velles F 17 C3
Vellisca E 45 B5
Velliza E 44 A3
Venaco F 62 A2
Venarey-les-Laumes F 18 B3
Venaria I 27 B4
Venasca I 33 A3
Vence F 32 B3
Venda Nova
*Coimbra* P 48 A2
*Leiria* P 48 B2
Vendas Novas P 48 C2
Vendays-Montalivet F 22 C2
Vendeuil F 11 B3
Vendeuvre-sur-Barse F 18 A3
Vendoeuvres F 23 B5
Vendôme F 17 B3
Venelles F 31 B4
Venialbo E 44 A2
Vénissieux F 25 B4
Vennezey F 12 C2
Venta de Baños E 36 C2
Venta del Moro E 52 B2
Venta de los Santos E 51 B4
Venta las Ranas E 36 A1
Ventanueva E 35 A4
Ventas de Huelma E 57 A4
Ventas de Zafarraya E 57 B3
Ventavon F 32 A1
Ventimiglia I 33 B3
Ventosa de la Sierra E 37 C4
Ventosilla E 37 C4
Venzolasca F 62 A2
Vera E 58 B3
Vera Cruz P 54 A2
Vera de Bidasoa E 38 A2
Vera de Moncayo E 38 C2
Verbánia I 27 B5
Verberie F 10 B2
Verbier CH 27 A4
Vercelli I 27 B5
Vercel-Villedieu-
le-Camp F 19 B5
Vercheny F 26 C2
Verclause F 31 A4
Verdille F 23 C3
Verdú E 41 C2
Verdun F 12 B1
Verdun-sur-Garonne F 29 C4
Verdun-sur-le-Doubs F 19 C4
Verfeil F 29 C4
Vergel E 53 C4
Verges E 41 B4
Vergt F 29 A3
Verin E 35 C3
Veringenstadt D 21 A4
Vermand F 10 B3
Vermelha P 48 B1
Vermenton F 18 B2
Vernante I 33 A3
Vernantes F 16 B2
Vernayaz CH 27 A4
Vern-d'Anjou F 16 B1
Vernet F 40 A2
Vernet-les-Bains F 40 B3
Verneuil F 11 B3
Verneuil-sur-Avre F 9 B4
Vernier CH 26 A3
Vernon F 10 B1
Vernoux-en-Vivarais F 25 C4
Verrès I 27 B4
Verrey-sous-Salmaise F 18 B3
Verrières F 23 B4
Versailles F 10 C2
Versam CH 21 C4
Versoix CH 26 A3
Verteillac F 23 C4
Vertou F 15 B4
Vertus F 11 C3
Vervins F 11 B3
Verzuolo I 33 A3
Verzy F 11 B4
Vescovato F 62 A2
Vésime I 27 C5
Vesoul F 19 B5
Vétroz CH 27 A4

Veules-les-Roses F 9 A4
Veulettes-sur-Mer F 9 A4
Veurne B 6 A2
Vevey CH 20 C1
Vex CH 27 A4
Veynes F 32 A1
Veyre-Monton F 24 B3
Veyrier F 26 B3
Vézelay F 18 B2
Vézelise F 12 C2
Vézenobres F 31 A3
Vezins F 16 B1
Vézins-de-Lévézou F 30 A1
Vezzani F 62 A2
Via Gloria P 54 B2
Viana E 37 B4
Viana do Alentejo P 48 C2
Viana do Bolo E 35 B3
Viana do Castelo P 42 A1
Vianden L 12 B2
Viator E 58 C2
Vibraye F 16 A2
Vic E 41 C3
Vícar E 58 C2
Vicdesses F 40 B2
Vic-en-Bigorre F 39 A4
Vic-Fézensac F 29 C3
Vichy F 25 A3
Vic-le-Comte F 24 B3
Vico F 62 A1
Vic-sur-Aisne F 10 B3
Vic-sur-Cère F 24 C2
Vidago P 42 A2
Vidauban F 32 B2
Vide P 42 B2
Vidigueira P 54 A2
Vieille-Brioude F 25 B3
Vieira P 48 B2
Vieira do Minho P 42 A1
Vieiros P 49 C3
Vielha E 39 B4
Vielle-Aure F 39 B4
Viellespesse F 24 B3
Viellevigne F 22 B2
Vielmur-sur-Agout F 30 B1
Viels Maison F 11 C3
Vienne F 25 B4
Viernheim D 13 B4
Vierville-sur-Mer F 8 A3
Vierzon F 17 B4
Vieteren B 6 B2
Vieux-Boucau-les-Bains F 28 C1
Vif F 26 B2
Vigeois F 24 B1
Vignale I 27 B5
Vigneulles-lès-Hattonchâtel F 12 C1
Vignevieille F 40 B3
Vignory F 19 A4
Vignoux-sur-Barangeon F 17 B4
Vigo E 34 B2
Vigone I 27 C4
Vihiers F 16 B1
Vila Boim P 49 C3
Vila Chãde Ourique P 48 B2
Viladamat E 41 B4
Vila de Cruces E 34 B2
Vila de Rei P 48 B2
Vila do Bispo P 54 B1
Vila do Conde P 42 A1
Viladrau E 41 C3
Vila Flor P 43 A2
Vila Franca das Navas P 43 B2
Vilafranca del Maestrat E 47 B3
Vilafranca del Penedès E 41 C2
Vila Franca de Xira P 48 C1
Vila Fresca P 48 C1
Vilagarcía de Arousa E 34 B2
Vilajuiga E 41 B4
Vilamarin E 34 B3
Vilamartín de Valdeorras E 35 B3
Vila Nogueira P 48 C1
Vila Nova da Baronia P 48 C2
Vilanova de Castelló E 53 B3
Vila Nova de Cerveira P 34 C2
Vila Nova de Famalicão P 42 A1
Vila Nova de Foz Côa P 43 A2
Vila Nova de Gaia P 42 A1
Vila Nova de Milfontes P 54 B1
Vila Nova de Paiva P 42 B2
Vila Nova de São Bento P 55 B2
Vilanova de Sau E 41 C3
Vilanova i la Geltrú E 41 C2
Vilapedre E 34 A3
Vila Pouca de Aguiar P 42 A2
Vila Praja de Ancora P 42 A1
Vilarandelo P 42 A2
Vilar de Santos E 34 B3
Vilardevós E 35 C3
Vila Real P 42 A2
Vila-real de los Infantes E 53 B3
Vila Real de Santo António P 54 B2
Vilar Formosa P 43 B3
Vila-Rodona E 41 C2
Vila Ruiva P 54 A2
Vilasantar E 34 A2
Vilaseca E 41 C2
Vila Seca P 42 B1
Vilassar de Mar E 41 C3
Vila Velha de Ródão P 49 B3
Vila Verde
*Braga* P 42 A1
*Lisboa* P 48 B1
Vila Verde de Filcalho P 55 B2
Vila Viçosa P 49 C3
Vilches E 51 B4
Villabáñez E 44 A3
Villablanca E 55 B2
Villablino E 35 B4
Villabona E 38 A1
Villabragima E 36 C1
Villabuena del Puente E 44 A2
Villacadima E 45 A4
Villacañas E 51 A4
Villacarriedo E 37 A3
Villacarrillo E 58 A1
Villacastín E 44 B3
Villaconejos E 45 B4
Villaconejos de Trabaque E 46 B1
Villa Cova de Lixa P 42 A1
Villada E 36 B2
Villadangos del Páramo E 35 B5
Villadecanes E 35 B4
Villa del Prado E 44 B3
Villa del Rio E 51 C3
Villadepera E 43 A3
Villa de Peralonso E 43 A3
Villadiego E 36 B2
Villadompardo E 57 A3
Villadóssola I 27 A5
Villaeles de Valdavia E 36 B2
Villaescusa de Haro E 52 B1
Villafáfila E 36 C1
Villafeliche E 46 A2
Villaflores E 44 A2
Villafrades de Campos E 36 B2
Villafranca
*Avila* E 44 B2
*Navarra* E 38 B2
Villafranca de Córdoba E 51 C3
Villafranca del Bierzo E 35 B4
Villafranca de los Barros E 49 C4
Villafranca de los Caballeros E 51 A4
Villafranca-Montes de Oca E 37 B3
Villafranco del Campo E 46 B2
Villafranco del Guadalquivir E 55 B3
Villafrechós E 36 C1
Villafruela E 37 C3
Villagarcia de las Torres E 50 B1
Villagonzalo E 50 B1
Villagotón E 35 B4
Villagrains F 28 B2
Villaharta E 50 B3
Villahermosa E 52 C1
Villaherreros E 36 B2
Villahoz E 37 B3
Villaines-la-Juhel F 9 B3
Villajoyosa E 53 C3
Villalba E 34 A3
Villalba de Calatrava E 51 B4
Villalba de Guardo E 36 B2
Villalba del Alcor E 55 B3
Villalba de la Sierra E 46 B1
Villalba de los Alcores E 36 C2
Villalba de los Barros E 49 C4
Villalba del Rey E 45 B5
Villalcampo E 43 A3
Villalcázar de Sirga E 36 B2
Villalengua E 46 A2
Villalgordo del Júcar E 52 B1
Villalgordo del Marquesado E 52 B1
Villalmóndar E 37 B3
Villalón de Campos E 36 B1
Villalonga E 53 C3
Villalonso E 44 A2
Villalpando E 36 C1
Villaluenga E 45 B4
Villalumbroso E 36 B2
Villálvaro E 37 C3
Villamalea E 52 B2
Villamanán E 36 B1
Villamanín E 36 B1
Villamanrique E 51 B5
Villamanrique de la Condesa E 55 B3
Villamanta E 45 B3
Villamantilla E 45 B3
Villamartín E 56 B2
Villamartin de Campos E 36 B2
Villamartin de Don Sancho E 36 B1
Villamayor E 36 A1
Villamayor de Calatrava E 51 B3
Villamayor de Campos E 36 C1
Villamayor de Santiago E 51 A5
Villamblard F 29 A3
Villamejil E 35 B4
Villamesias E 50 A2
Villaminaya E 51 A4
Villamor de los Escuderos E 44 A2
Villamoronta E 36 B2
Villamuelas E 45 C4
Villamuriel de Cerrato E 36 C2
Villandraut F 28 B2
Villanova d'Asti I 27 C4
Villanova Mondovì I 33 A3
Villante E 37 B3
Villanubla E 36 C2
Villanueva de Alcardete E 51 A4
Villanueva de Alcorón E 46 B1
Villanueva de Algaidas E 57 A3
Villanueva de Argaña E 37 B3
Villanueva de Bogas E 51 A4
Villanueva de Córdoba E 50 B3
Villanueva de Gállego E 38 C3
Villanueva del Aceral E 44 A3
Villanueva de la Concepcion E 57 B3
Villanueva de la Fuente E 52 C1
Villanueva de la Jara E 52 B2
Villanueva de la Reina E 51 B4
Villanueva del Arzobispo E 58 A2
Villanueva de la Serena E 50 B2
Villanueva de la Sierra E 43 B3
Villanueva de las Manzanas E 36 B1
Villanueva de las Peras E 35 C5
Villanueva de las Torres E 58 B1
Villanueva de la Vera E 44 B2
Villanueva del Campo E 36 C1
Villanueva del Duque E 50 B3
Villanueva del Fresno E 49 C3
Villanueva del Huerva E 46 A2
Villanueva de los Castillejos E 55 B2
Villanueva de los Infantes E 51 B5
Villanueva del Rey E 50 B2
Villanueva del Rio E 56 A2
Villanueva del Rio y Minas E 56 A2
Villanueva del Rosario E 57 B3
Villanueva del Trabuco E 57 A3
Villanueva de Mesia E 57 A4
Villanueva de Nía E 36 B2
Villanueva de Oscos E 35 A4
Villanueva de San Carlos E 51 B4
Villanueva de San Juan E 56 A2
Villanueva de Tapia E 57 A3
Villanueva de Valdegovia E 37 B3
Villaquejida E 36 B1
Villaquilambre E 36 B1
Villaquiran de los Infantes E 36 B2
Villaralto E 50 B3
Villarcayo E 37 B3
Villard-de-Lans F 26 B2
Villar de Barrio E 34 B3
Villar de Cañas E 52 B1
Villar de Chinchilla E 52 C2
Villar de Ciervo E 43 B3
Villardeciervos E 35 C4
Villar de Domingo Garcia E 46 B1
Villardefrades E 36 C1
Villar del Arzobispo E 53 B3
Villar del Buey E 43 A3
Villar del Cobo E 46 B2
Villar del Humo E 52 B2
Villar de los Navarros E 46 A2
Villar del Pedroso E 50 A2
Villar del Rey E 49 B4
Villar del Rio E 37 B4
Villar del Saz de Navalón E 46 B1
Villar de Rena E 50 A2
Villarejo E 45 A4
Villarejo de Fuentes E 52 B1
Villarejo de Orbigo E 35 B5
Villarejo de Salvanes E 45 B4
Villarejo-Periesteban E 52 B1
Villares del Saz E 52 B1
Villaretto I 27 B4
Villargordo del Cabriel E 52 B2
Villarino E 43 A3
Villarino de Conso E 35 B3
Villarluengo E 47 B3
Villarobe E 37 B3
Villar Perosa I 27 C4
Villarramiel E 36 B2
Villarrasa E 55 B3
Villarreal de San Carlos E 44 C1
Villarrin de Campos E 36 C1
Villarrobledo E 52 B1
Villarroya de la Sierra E 46 A2
Villarroya de los Pinares E 47 B3
Villarrubia de los Ojos E 51 A4
Villarrubia de Santiago E 45 C4
Villarrubio E 45 C5
Villars-les-Dombes F 25 A5
Villarta E 52 B2
Villarta de los Montes E 50 A3
Villarta de San Juan E 51 A4
Villasana de Mena E 37 A3
Villasandino E 36 B2
Villasante E 37 A3
Villasarracino E 36 B2
Villasayas E 45 A5
Villasdardo E 43 A3
Villaseca de Henares E 45 B5
Villaseca de Laciana E 35 B4
Villaseca de la Sagra E 45 C4
Villaseco de los Gamitos E 43 A3
Villaseco de los Reyes E 43 A3
Villasequilla de Yepes E 45 C4
Villastar E 46 B2
Villastellone I 27 C4
Villatobas E 45 C4
Villatorp E 44 B2
Villatoya E 52 B2
Villavaliente E 52 B2
Villavelayo E 37 B4
Villavella E 35 B3
Villaver de Guadalimar E 52 C1
Villaverde del Rio E 56 A2
Villaviciosa E 36 A1
Villaviciosa de Córdoba E 50 B3
Villaviciosa de Odón E 45 B4
Villavieja de Yeltes E 43 B3
Villayón E 35 A4
Villé F 13 C3
Villebois-Lavalette F 23 C4
Villecerf F 10 C2
Villecomtal F 30 A1
Villedieu-les-Poêles F 8 B2
Villedieu-sur-Indre F 17 C3
Ville-di-Pietrabugno F 62 A2
Villedômain F 17 B3
Villefagnan F 23 B4
Villefontaine F 26 B2
Villefort F 31 A2
Villefranche-d'Albigeois F 30 B1
Villefranche-d'Allier F 24 A2
Villefranche-de-Lauragais F 40 A2
Villefranche-de-Lonchat F 28 B3
Villefranche-de-Panat F 30 A1
Villefranche-de-Rouergue F 30 A1
Villefranche-du-Périgord F 29 B4
Villefranche-sur-Cher F 17 B3
Villefranche-sur-Mer F 33 B3
Villefranche-sur-Saône F 25 A4
Villegenon F 17 B4
Villel E 46 B2
Villemaur-sur-Vanne F 18 A2
Villemontais F 25 B3
Villemur-sur-Tarn F 29 C4
Villena E 53 C3
Villenauxe-la-Grande F 11 C3
Villenave-d'Ornon F 28 B2
Villeneuve
CH 27 A3
F 29 B5
Villeneuve-d'Ascq F 6 B3
Villeneuve-de-Berg F 31 A3
Villeneuve-de-Marsan F 28 C2
Villeneuve-de-Rivière F 39 A4
Villeneuve-la-Guyard F 10 C3
Villeneuve-l'Archevêque F 18 A2
Villeneuve-le-Comte F 10 C2
Villeneuve-lès-Avignon F 31 B3
Villeneuve-les-Corbières F 40 B3
Villeneuve-St Georges F 10 C2
Villeneuve-sur-Allier F 18 C2
Villeneuve-sur-Lot F 29 B3
Villeneuve-sur-Yonne F 18 A2
Villeréal F 29 B3
Villerias E 36 C2
Villeromain F 17 B3
Villers-Bocage
*Calvados* F 8 A3
*Somme* F 10 B2
Villers-Bretonneux F 10 B2
Villers-Carbonnel F 10 B2
Villers-Cotterêts F 10 B3
Villersexel F 19 B5
Villers-Farlay F 19 C4
Villers-le-Gambon B 7 B4
Villers-le-Lac F 20 B1
Villers-sur-Mer F 9 A3
Villerupt F 12 B1
Villerville F 9 A4
Villeseneux F 11 C4
Ville-sous-la-Ferté F 19 A3
Ville-sur-Illon F 19 A5
Ville-sur-Tourbe F 11 B4
Villetrun F 17 B3
Villeurbanne F 25 B4
Villeveyrac F 30 B2
Villevocance F 25 B4
Villiers-St-Benoit F 18 B2
Villiers-St-Georges F 11 C3
Villingen D 20 A3
Villoldo E 36 B2
Villon F 18 B3
Villoria E 44 B2
Vilvestre E 43 A3
Vilvoorde B 7 B4
Vimeiro P 48 B1
Vimianzo E 34 A1
Vimieiro P 48 C3
Vimioso P 43 A3
Vimoutiers F 9 B4
Vimy F 6 B2
Vinadio I 33 A3
Vinaixa E 41 C1
Vinarós E 47 B4
Vinay F 26 B2
Vinca F 40 B3
Vinets F 11 C4
Vineuil F 17 B3
Vingrau F 40 B3
Vinhais P 43 A3
Viniegra de Arriba E 37 B4
Vinon F 17 B4
Vinon-sur-Verdon F 32 B1
Viñuela E 57 B3
Viñuela de Sayago E 43 A4
Viñuelas E 45 B4
Vinuesa E 37 C4
Viola I 33 A3
Violay F 25 B4
Vire F 8 B3
Vireux F 11 A4
Virgen de la Cabeza E 51 B3
Virieu F 26 B2
Virieu-le-Grand F 26 B2
Virton B 12 B1
Viry F 26 A3
Viseu P 42 B2
Visiedo E 46 B2
Viso del Marqués E 51 B4
Visone I 27 C5
Visp CH 27 A4
Vistabella del Maestrat E 47 B3
Vitigudino E 43 A3
Vitoria-Gasteiz E 37 B4
Vitré F 15 A4
Vitrey-sur-Mance F 19 B4
Vitry-en-Artois F 6 B2
Vitry-le-François F 11 C4
Vitry-sur-Seine F 10 C2
Vitteaux F 18 B3
Vittel F 19 A4
Viù I 27 B4
Vivario F 62 A2
Viveiro E 34 A3
Vivel del Rio Martin E 46 B3
Viver E 53 B3
Viverols F 25 B3
Viveros E 52 C1
Viviers F 31 A3
Vivonne F 23 B4
Vivy F 16 B1
Vizille F 26 B2
Vizzavona F 62 A2
Vlissingen NL 7 A3
Vogogna I 27 A5
Vogüé F 31 A3
Vöhrenbach D 20 A3
Void-Vacon F 12 C1
Voiron F 26 B2
Voise F 10 C1
Voisey F 19 B4
Voiteur F 19 C4
Völklingen D 12 B2
Vollore-Montagne F 25 B3
Voltri I 33 A4
Volvic F 24 B3
Volx F 32 B1
Voreppe F 26 B2
Vorey F 25 B3
Voué F 11 C4
Vouillé F 23 B4
Voulx F 10 C2
Voussac F 24 A3
Vouvray F 16 B2
Vouvry CH 27 A3
Vouzela P 42 B1
Vouziers F 11 B4
Voves F 17 A3
Vrigne-aux-Bois F 11 B4
Vron F 6 B1
Vught NL 7 A5
Vuillafans F 19 B5
Vy-lès Lure F 19 B5


## W


Waalwijk NL 7 A5
Waarschoot B 7 A3
Wädenswil CH 21 B3
Wadern D 12 B2
Waghäusel D 13 B4
Wald CH 21 B3
Waldböckelheim D 13 B3
Waldfischbach-Burgalben D 13 B3
Waldkirch D 20 A2
Wald-Michelbach D 13 B4
Waldmohr D 13 B3
Waldshut D 20 B3
Waldstatt CH 21 B4
Waldwisse F 12 B2
Walenstadt CH 21 B4
Walincourt F 10 A3
Wallers F 6 B3
Walshoutem B 7 B5
Waltenhofen D 21 B5
Wamba E 36 C2
Wangen im Allgäu D 21 B4
Wängi CH 21 B3
Waregem B 7 B3
Waremme B 7 B5
Warth A 21 B5
Wasselonne F 13 C3
Wassen CH 21 C3
Wasserauen CH 21 B4
Wassy F 11 C4
Waterloo B 7 B4
Watten F 6 B2
Wattwil CH 21 B4
Wavignies F 10 B2
Wavre B 7 B4
Weggis CH 20 B3
Wehr D 20 B2
Weierbach D 13 B3
Weil am Rhein D 20 B2
Weil der Stadt D 13 C4
Weinfelden CH 21 B4
Weingarten
*Baden-Württemberg* D 13 B4
*Baden-Württemberg* D 21 B4
Weinheim D 13 B4
Weisstannen CH 21 C4
Weitnau D 21 B5
Wellin B 11 A5
Welschenrohr CH 20 B2
Wengen CH 20 C2
Werkendam NL 7 A4
Westerlo B 7 A4
Westkapelle
B 6 A3
NL 7 A3
Wetteren B 7 A3
Wetzikon CH 21 B3
Weyersheim F 13 C3
Wiesbaden D 13 A4
Wiesen CH 21 C4
Wiesloch D 13 B4
Wiggen CH 20 C2
Wil CH 21 B4
Wildbad D 13 C4
Wildberg D 13 C4
Wildegg CH 20 B3
Wilhelmsdorf D 21 B4
Willebroek B 7 A4
Willgottheim F 13 C3
Willisau CH 20 B3
Wiltz L 12 B1
Wimereux F 6 B1
Wimmenau F 13 C3
Wimmis CH 20 C2
Wingene B 6 A3
Winnweiler D 13 B3
Winterthur CH 21 B3
Wintzenheim F 20 A2
Wissant F 6 B1
Wissembourg F 13 B3
Witry-les-Reims F 11 B4
Wittelsheim F 20 B2
Wittenheim F 20 B2
Wittlich D 12 B2
Woerth F 13 C3
Wohlen CH 20 B3
Woippy F 12 B2
Wolfach D 13 C4
Wolfegg D 21 B4
Wolfstein D 13 B3
Wolfurt A 21 B4
Wolhusen CH 20 B3
Worb CH 20 C2
Wormhout F 6 B2
Worms D 13 B4
Wörrstadt D 13 B4
Wörth
*Bayern* D 13 B5
*Rheinland-Pfalz* D 13 B4
Woumen B 6 A2
Wuustwezel B 7 A4


## X


Xátiva E 53 C3
Xeraco E 53 B3
Xert E 47 B4
Xerta E 47 B4
Xertigny F 19 A5
Xinzo de Limia E 34 B3
Xixón = Gijón E 36 A1
Xove E 34 A3
Xubia E 34 A2
Xunqueira de Ambia E 34 B3
Xunqueira de Espadañedo E 34 B3


## Y


Ydes F 24 B2
Yebra de Basa E 39 B3
Yecla E 53 C2
Yecla de Yeltes E 43 B3
Yenne F 26 B2
Yepes E 45 C4
Yerseke NL 7 A4
Yerville F 9 A4
Yeste E 58 A2
Ygos-St-Saturnin F 28 C2
Ygrande F 18 C1
Ymonville F 17 A3
Yport F 9 A4
Ypres = Ieper B 6 B2
Yssingeaux F 25 B4
Yuncos E 45 B4
Yunquera E 56 B3
Yunquera de Henares E 45 B4
Yverdon-les-Bains CH 20 C1
Yvetot F 9 A4
Yvignac F 15 A3
Yvoir B 7 B4
Yvonand CH 20 C1
Yzeure F 18 C2


## Z


Zaamslag NL 7 A3
Zafarraya E 57 B3
Zafra E 49 C4
Zagrilla E 57 A3
Zahara E 56 B2
Zahara de los Atunes E 56 B2
Zahinos E 49 C4
Zaidin E 47 A4
Zalamea de la Serena E 50 B2
Zalamea la Real E 55 B3
Zaldibar E 37 A4
Zalla E 37 A3
Zaltbommel NL 7 A5
Zambra E 57 A3
Zambugueira do Mar P 54 B1
Zamora E 43 A4
Zandhoven B 7 A4
Zaorejas E 46 B1
Zaragoza E 47 A3
Zarautz E 38 A1
Zarcilla de Ramos E 58 B3
Zarren B 6 A2
Zarza Capilla E 50 B2
Zarza de Alange E 50 B1
Zarza de Granadilla E 43 B3
Zarza de Tajo E 45 B4
Zarzadilla de Totana E 58 B3
Zarza la Mayor E 49 B4
Zarzuela del Monte E 44 B3
Zarzuela del Pinar E 45 A3
Zas E 34 A2
Zeberio E 37 A4
Zebreira P 49 B3
Zeebrugge B 6 A3
Zele B 7 A4
Zell
CH 20 B2
*Baden-Württemberg* D 13 C4
*Baden-Württemberg* D 20 B2
*Rheinland-Pfalz* D 12 A3
Zelzate B 7 A3
Zemst B 7 B4
Zerf D 12 B2
Zermatt CH 27 A4
Zernez CH 21 C5
Zestoa E 38 A1
Zevenbergen NL 7 A4
Zicavo F 62 B2
Zierikzee NL 7 A3
Zinal CH 27 A4
Zofingen CH 20 B2
Zomergem B 7 A3
Zoñán E 35 A3
Zonhoven B 7 B5
Zonza F 62 B2
Zorita E 50 A2
Zottegem B 7 B3
Zubieta E 38 A2
Zubiri E 38 B2
Zucaina E 47 B3
Zuera E 38 C3
Zufre E 55 B3
Zug CH 21 B3
Zuheros E 57 A3
Zújar E 58 B2
Zumaia E 38 A1
Zumárraga E 37 A4
Zundert NL 7 A4
Zurgena E 58 B2
Zürich CH 21 B3
Zurzach CH 20 B3
Zweibrücken D 13 B3
Zweisimmen CH 20 C2
Zwiefalten D 21 A4